Critical Essays on Homer

Critical Essays on
World Literature

Robert Lecker, General Editor
McGill University

Critical Essays on Homer

Kenneth Atchity

with Ron Hogart and Doug Price

G. K. Hall & Co. • Boston, Massachusetts

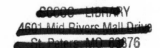

Library of Congress Cataloging in Publication Data

Critical essays on Homer.

  (Critical essays on world literature)
  Bibliography
  Includes index.
  1. Homer—Criticism and interpretation. I. Atchity, Kenneth
John. II. Hogart, Ron Charles, 1958-   III. Price, Doug. IV.
Series.
PA4037.C67 1986   883'.01   86-22726

ISBN 0-8161-8832-7 (alk. paper)

This publication is printed on permanent/durable acid-free paper
MANUFACTURED IN THE UNITED STATES OF AMERICA

To the memory of these Homeridae:

E. A. S. Butterworth,
Robert Fitzgerald, John Gardner,
Cedric Whitman, Eric Voegelin

CONTENTS

INTRODUCTION   1
        Kenneth Atchity

The Maker   13
        Jorge Luis Borges

On Homer

Greek Princes and Aegean Princesses:
        The Role of Women in the Homeric Poems   15
        Kenneth Atchity and E. J. W. Barber

[On Translating Homer]   37
        Robert Fitzgerald

Rose-Fingered Dawn and the Idea of Time   51
        Paolo Vivante

[Order and Disorder]   62
        Eric Voegelin

Image, Symbol, and Formula   83
        Cedric H. Whitman

[Review of *The Making of Homeric Verse:
The Collected Papers of Milman Parry,*
        Edited by Adam Parry]   106
        George E. Dimock, Jr.

On the Iliad

The Shield of Achilles   111
        W. H. Auden

Imitation   113
        James M. Redfield

Hector   127
        Rachel Bespaloff

Some Possible Indo-European Themes in the *Iliad*   132
        C. Scott Littleton

King Eëtion and Thebe as Symbols in the *Iliad*   146
    John W. Zarker

The *Iliad* or the Poem of Force   152
    Simone Weil

Andromache's Headdress   159
    Kenneth Atchity

On the Odyssey

A Valediction: Forbidding Mourning   167
    John Donne

The World as Meditation   168
    Wallace Stevens

Archery at the Dark of the Moon   169
    Norman Austin

[The Tales Odysseus Told Alkinoos, and
    an Akkadian Seal]   181
    E. A. S. Butterworth

The *Odyssey* and Primitive Religion   187
    Richard J. Sommer

The Renaming of Odysseus   211
    Alice Mariani

Ithaka   223
    C. P. Cavafy

SELECTED BIBLIOGRAPHY   225

INDEX   243

INTRODUCTION

Sacred, sonorous, is heard the long-muted speech of the Hellenes;
Shaken, my soul knows thee near, shade of the mighty old man.
— Alexander Pushkin, 1830*

Western literature without the Homeric epics is unimaginable, a mighty fortress without foundation. The influence of the *Iliad* and the *Odyssey* is pervasive and all-challenging. After two and a half millennia they remain unsurpassed in power and unsurpassed, except perhaps by Dante's *Divine Comedy*, in clarity of vision. Homer's imagination is vast and vital, electrifying and all-encompassing. The poems are no less moving today than they were for the ancient Greeks whose culture they express — the *Iliad*, that culture's glorious and heroic past; the *Odyssey*, its more morally sophisticated, semantically subtle, and philosophically "relative" future as the Athenians had envisioned, planned, and created it for themselves.

The Homeric poems are documents constructed at the end of a mythic culture by the first proponents of a logical culture, in testimony to their roots — to the strength of the founding myth. They are, therefore, organized mythic material: not in the original chaotic form by which an oral tradition is passed along more or less accurately (by literate standards), but oral memory managed by cultural intention. They represent the marriage of myth and logic, the systematization of a mythic vision. This central paradox greatly accounts for the power of Homeric poetry. The tension creates brilliance in expression and intensity in the audience's response.

The poems are the distillation of tradition, capturing the vision of the past favored by the distillers and at the same time conveying the distillers' determination of the present's values and the future's shape. What the original Homer, who may have lived in Ionia around 1200 B.C., weaves in the first great epic songs is memory and imagination. What his editors

---

*From "On the Translation of the *Iliad*," trans. Babette Deutsch, in *The Works of Alexander Pushkin*, ed. Avraham Yarmolinsky. © 1936 and renewed 1964 by Random House, Inc. Reprinted by permission of the publisher.

1

weave in Homer's name, creating the intentionally archaic literary version of the poems that have shaped Western culture since the fifth century B.C., is memory, imagination, and a full-bodied philosophy. They saw their redaction of the Homeric tradition as the fashioning of a shield by which their society would press its way into the future.

This volume represents the diversity of Homeric scholarship in the twentieth century as it has exploded and moved away from the philological obsession that dominated it from Milman Parry's death in 1935 to the late 1960s, when the jihad of "Parryism" began relinquishing its excesses. The history of Homeric scholarship and its relationship to Milman Parry's studies of the oral tradition is summarized fairly and fully in Adam Parry's introduction to *The Making of Homeric Verse* (see bibliography). "The Homeric Question" — really a series of interrelated and unanswerable questions including was there a Homer? when did he live? did he compose orally or in writing, or both?, etc. — need no longer be the end point for appreciation of Homer.

Instead the contemporary student may approach the *Iliad* and the *Odyssey* with an awareness of their oral origins but with the certain knowledge that they are literary and highly sophisticated and powerful texts. The *Iliad* collects the great epics of Troy into a single consistent and brilliantly focused narrative whose austerity and grandeur make it incontestably the greater of the two poems (although philosophically and intellectually it is the simpler). The *Iliad* is the artistic design of history: Helen weaving the stories of Achaians and Trojans fighting for her sake, and Hephaistos recording his vision of universal order on Achilles' great shield. In the *Odyssey* the Homeric "poet," fulfilling the instinct that created the shield of Achilles, recognizes and celebrates the power of words as a means of describing, creating, and replacing reality. In the heart of the *Odyssey* (book 13), a goddess and a mortal sit beneath the tree of wisdom and plot together the mortal's restoration of the tree of life, artistically designing action in advance. For the first time in Western culture, we are to understand that life can be designed as though it were a work of art — that the future, as well as the past, is subject to our shaping.

The *Odyssey* poetically equates Odysseus's thinking with Penelope's weaving, implying a new concept of human action and history in which humans take godlike responsibility for their fate: a conscious artistic attitude toward the premeditation of action so that it will be aesthetically memorable, rather than artistry that merely records completed action as in the *Iliad*. Weaving is the prototypical technique by which humans shape reality to their own images. Odysseus tells stories over and over again, each the same in semantic structure but different on the verbal surface; Penelope weaves and unweaves in order to hold together her options for the future — to hold the suitors in place should Odysseus not return, to hold them in abeyance should he come back.

Athene's relationship with Odysseus portrays the weaning of humankind from the gods, a mythic representation of the transference of moral authority from the gods to mortals. As a consequence, truth becomes relative and individual choice becomes pivotal to moral perspective. Her love for him is, in the heroic tradition, extraordinary; it is not physical but intellectual, not sexual but symbolic. The *Odyssey* carries on the *Iliad*'s investigation of the source of moral responsibility, displacing the archaic pantheon in favor of those gods who would have humankind grow up into their own image and likeness, influenced but not controlled by immortals. A host of peripheral and half-forgotten deities populate the *Odyssey* only in order to be dismissed. By the time Odysseus is back on Ithaka, none are important but Zeus and Athene; and the stage has been set for classical Athens. Ithaka becomes a metaphor for Athens, as the house of Atreus becomes a metaphor for Athens in Aeschylus's *Oresteia*.

Where the *Iliad* emphasizes the single-minded force of words, equating them with deeds, the *Odyssey* recognizes the many faces of truth the hero must learn to penetrate with his protean mind if he's to control his destiny and social environment. Odysseus's lies are like the feelers of a crustacean as it crosses an uncertain ocean bottom — just as Penelope's lies to Odysseus, who is himself disguised, have the effect of ascertaining his true identity before their remarriage can take place. When it occurs under the auspices of Athene but designed by Penelope and Odysseus, that remarriage celebrates the coming together of two "modern" individuals able to cope with the multiplicity of life through their own artful contrivances. The *Odyssey* changes the emphasis from the past glories of one's ancestors to the individual's actions in the present and their implications for the future.

Without discounting contributions from students of the Homeric Question, the richness and diversity of the essays and artistic responses collected here are offered as a foundation for an introductory reading of Homer. When the anonymous Athenian committee (their anonymity reflecting Homer's legendary blindness) sat down around 450 B.C. to provide the "authorized texts" of the Homeric poems, they were not primarily interested in providing evidence for later scholars that a formulaic oral tradition was the mode by which the original *Iliad* and *Odyssey* reached their workbench — although they were surely aware of the issues. Charged by a tyrant whose view of their city's cultural preeminence they no doubt heartily endorsed, these Athenians used what they found of the ancient tradition to be effective — and rewrote the rest, without worrying about anything other than the beauty of form and integrity of message found in our *Iliad* and *Odyssey*. What we read, twenty-five-hundred years later, is what they wrote for us, in books neatly divided along alphabetical lines.

Their principles of editorial composition were clear: Stylistically, they were to reproduce faithfully the hexameter of the oral tradition, which their generation had been the last to be nurtured on now that writing had taken the fore as the primary method of cultured communication. Their thematic aims were the glorification of Zeus, and his agent in the polis Athene, and emphasis on the governing principle of the Olympian pair — hierarchical orderliness, with "the best" at the top of the great chain of being. Both epics they edited and preserved serve that governing principle, and the essays in this collection offer a wide perspective indicating how richly open to diverse interpretation and manifold layers of meaning a unified text can nevertheless be. In the words of José Ortega y Gasset, "So many things fail to interest us, simply because they don't find enough surfaces on which to live, and what we have to do is increase the number of planes in our mind, so that a much larger number of themes can find a plane in it at the same time."[1]

There are increasing indications that the post–Persian War generation of Athenians was much concerned with national identity and ethnic roots — their Indo-European heritage. Dean Miller has found the tripartite Indo-European ideology in Sophocles' *Oedipus at Colonus,* and Udo Strutynski as well as George Devereux have long suspected that it permeates Greek drama in general. If the Indo-European resurgence is classical, it would lend strong argument to the revision of the recension date upward to the fifth century. The Indo-European structuring of the Shield of Achilles, that structurally integral "set-piece" that organizes the *Iliad*'s symbolism, would then be the natural first cousin of Sophocles' and Euripides' preoccupation with the same view of order.

Jorge Luis Borges's personal experience of blindness led him to poignant insight into what the Greek tradition considered the explanation of that brilliant Homeric clarity. Only the blind, as Oedipus learns from Teiresias, can see, without the confusion of the senses, the true form of things human and divine. Therefore the truest philosopher is he who sees only the unseen shape of things, the clearest poet he who sees as a philosopher. "The Maker," translated by Mildred Boyer and Harold Morland, allows a glimpse into the imagined Homer's mind so that we understand his traditional anonymity, his deification by the classical Greeks, why Aristotle argued that Homer's greatness was that in his works he himself is nowhere and his characters everywhere.

The first seven essays deal with general issues of Homeric study. "Greek Princes and Aegean Princesses: The Role of Women in the Homeric Poems" combines Elizabeth Barber's studies of ancient textiles and of Greek matrilineal structure (originally presented as a paper at an international conference in Dubrovnik in 1979) with my own study of the Homeric imagination, themes of order, and social hierarchy and myth. The essay explains the contradictory role of women in the Homeric canon and the later Greek political structure by arguing that the poems were written in a patrilineal society that worshiped Zeus and his motherless daughter Athene, and that they reflect and "conform" an earlier era of myth in which matrilineal forces dominated. Against this mythically archaic background, the Homeric poems express a classically Athenian vision of acceptable social order. Yet, once we recognize what they're about, we can read in them an eye-opening record of the very different social order that preceded the classical. In this earlier order, the questions of right of property and right of inheritance were answered along lines that fit the central economic role of the queen as the householder who literally wove her realm together while her men were out trading and protecting the fruits of her technical labors.

Robert Fitzgerald, whose beautiful poetic interpretations of the *Iliad* and the *Odyssey* continue to introduce students to Homer's vision, offers insight into the difficulties of both language and scholarship he encountered in creating his graceful translations. Fitzgerald discusses the essential, though undoubtedly subtle, role music played in the oral creation of Homer's epics in "On Translating Homer," which praises Homeric poetry as it bewails the impossibility of translation. Although the virtue and beauty of Homer's verse, his wit, and his art are apparent in translation, "as an aesthetic object," the work "is to be appreciated only in Greek." Fitzgerald imagines what the recitation of an oral epic was probably like in the phonetically musical Greek, before the advent of an alphabet. Fitzgerald's essay illustrates several examples of difficulty in translation — all of which primarily stem from an incomplete understanding of the culture and of the vocabulary. These difficulties highlight both modern scholarship's ultimate inability to accurately interpret a work of art created in an entirely different culture and time in the distant past, and the never-fading beauty of the work in its original language.

Paolo Vivante's poetic and perceptive writings have been a breath of clear and invigorating Homeric air amid the turbulent scholarly atmosphere of the past thirty years. The essay that represents him here, "Rose-Fingered Dawn and the Idea of Time," is a concise example of Vivante's approach, which combines precise observation of the text with an intuition of its formal sensibilities. Technique, compositional device, style are but the outcome of a way in which things are visualized and expressed. The phrase must thus be explained on the strength of a deeper poetic reason; it must be appreciated both in intrinsic value and in its relation to the context. Vivante lets us look at its occurrences, and then at what these occurrences imply as regards the conception of the poem as a whole. The result is to enhance our reading of an otherwise "dead epithet" so that we recognize, on the particular level, what we see of the whole: that Homer's vision of order encompasses the minutiae as well as the grandeur of his bright universe.

Eric Voegelin's brilliant two-volume study of sociology and the history of civilization, *Order and History*, has been neglected by the Homeric community. With the exception of Cyrus Gordon's erratic *Homer and the Bible*, no work had undertaken a serious study of the substantial parallels between the Hebrew Bible and the Homeric opus. Voegelin argues that the similarity between the two traditions extends to the intention of the redactors operating at the point in which the oral tradition in each culture converged with the written tradition. In both cases, the exploration of morality and human responsibility results in a reinterpretation of the past. Themes of order and disorder expressed in Homer and the Hebrew scriptures indicate that both traditions experienced definitive recensions at approximately the same time, a time in which humanity began looking inward—instead of toward the divine—for the source of moral responsibility. The comparisons argued by Voegelin are worthy of our closest attention. His work is a monument to the study of comparative culture.

The dean and provost of intelligent Homeric studies during the era of Parryism was Cedric Whitman. Whitman managed to comprehend the implications of oral theory within his aesthetic of Homeric literature without losing sight of the unified impact of the poetry and traditional insistence on the structural cohesion of both poems. His *Homer and the Heroic Tradition* is a masterpiece of critical interpretation, methodology, and insight. From it "Image, Symbol, and Formula" is reprinted here because of its general usefulness as an introduction to Homeric poetics—so different from that of modern European literature yet at the same time, because of the influence of one on the other, so familiar. Whitman explains the familiarity with a freshness and commonsensical level-headedness that make us eager to take up the text he illuminates.

The general section on Homer closes with George Dimock's succinct but comprehensive review of Adam Parry's edition of his father's life work, *The Making of Homeric Verse*. Adam Parry's excellent introduction to the Milman Parry collection summarizes the history of Homeric scholarship so clearly that it stands self-sufficient and must be recommended to anyone interested in the subject. Dimock's review puts the contribution of both Parrys and of Parryism into brief and wholesome perspective: "The oral technique of epic verse-making, whose mechanics [Milman] Parry was the first to describe, is simply a language some of whose rules are metrical." The student, from reading Dimock's review, will glimpse the general outlines of the twentieth-century controversy concerning the Homeric Question.

The section devoted to the *Iliad* begins with W. H. Auden's "The Shield of Achilles." Despite its presence in other anthologies, Auden's poem is an essential Homeric artifact, one on the level of Keats's "On First Looking into Chapman's Homer" in its evidence of the power of art to generate art, of vision to give issue to vision—and, in so doing, to maintain the underlying myth in all its metamorphoses. Though the scene depicted by the twentieth-century poet is familiar, the mood of bleakness, harshness, and terror contemporary with the atrocities of Auden's time reminds us of Homer's immediate subject without the redemptive and balancing effect of the Homeric simile and its constant consciousness of the orderly role played even by terrible war in the great drama of human history.

From James M. Redfield's *Nature and Culture in the Iliad: The Tragedy of Hektor*, one of the most cogent and incisive books on the *Iliad*, I have excerpted and abridged chapter 1, "Imitation," Redfield's discussion of Aristotelean poetics as they were derived from, and throw light on, Homer. Aristotle's *Poetics* began the quest to come to terms with artistic imagination. The *Poetics* suggest that the artists we exalt the most teach us the most about ourselves.

In Aristotle's time, it had become apparent that heroic stories derived from epic did not need to be historically true. Audiences did not have to believe that the story was true either. Instead, the audience must only believe that the events and sequence of the poet's story could happen. As Aristotle put it, the story must be "likely to happen in accordance with probability or necessity." "Probability" and "necessity" define the internal logic that links together the chain of events we call "plot." Homer's wisdom lay not in the retelling of heroic tales that everyone had heard, but in his creation of a plot by selecting the popular tales that revealed the inner logic he had discovered about those heroes.

Aristotle's view of fiction is tied to his view of ethics. Ethics and fiction have a common subject — human action. Ethics never allows us to comprehend our own actions because it orients us toward the result of our actions. "Since every result leads to a further result," we can never be sure that we are perceiving the final consequence of any action. Ethical action becomes a perpetual interplay between virtue and the circumstances we live in. And the happiness we're supposed to get from being virtuous in life becomes unintelligible — we'll never know if virtue will make us happy by examining the cause and effect of our experiences. Where "fiction enables us to recognize patterns of probability and necessity, [it] gives fiction an ethical standing." Unlike ethics, fiction illustrates "happiness and unhappiness in such a way that we can see the causal relations between the actor, his situation, and the event. Storytelling thus meets our need for ethical intelligibility" and gives us the opportunity to gain control of our experience. Redfield illustrates, then, the superiority of fiction to mere scientific observation, showing that the latter can give us only data while the former can reveal patterns within the data of experience. The epic poet's ability to create probable situations allows him to illustrate a universal truth about a human virtue or human nature. Thus, though the literal story of the epic may not be true, the universal story — the poet's insight into human virtue or human nature — must be true.

Rachel Bespaloff's moving celebration of Hektor (included from her book *On the Iliad*) was written, like Auden's poem, under the conscious influence of contemporary conflagration. Her essay explores the death of Hektor (the resistance hero) and of Achilles (the revenge hero). Both are related to the dynamics of force and the illusion of omniscience, and both to the Homeric awareness of the glory that comes only with memory—a glory bitterly futile for Hektor, though inspiring to those who hear of his honorable deeds.

In "Some Possible Indo-European Themes in the *Iliad*," C. Scott Littleton discusses the *Iliad* in terms of the "tripartite ideology" commonly found in Indo-European mythology—commonly found, that is, everywhere except in Greek tradition, perhaps due to what Georges Dumézil terms the "Greek miracle." Littleton agrees with Yoshida (see bibliography), who points out that elements of this "tripartite" tradition are, in fact, found in the *Iliad*, and particularly in Homer's description of the shield of Achilles. The three "functions" of the Indo-European ideology; "juridical sovereignty," "war activity," and the "provision of nourishment" are all closely paralleled in the three-way division of Achilles' shield. Furthermore, leading characters in the *Iliad*, and the very nature of the conflict between the Achaeans (representing the juridical and the warlike) and the Trojans (representing concern with physical well-being, via the "Judgment of Paris") are in line, although subtly, with the Indo-European tradition. Littleton concludes that Homer probably inherited this Indo-European "tripartite ideology" through the oral tradition, although his own society had already undergone the post-Mycenaean deviation called the "Greek miracle."

In "King Eëtion and Thebes as Symbols in the *Iliad*," John Zarker suggests that Homer programs his auditors to think along certain lines and to experience certain emotions when either the king or his city are mentioned—and that he tells the story of Thebes, throughout the *Iliad*, without contradiction. As image after image accumulate into a consistent and recurring pattern, the symbol of Thebes becomes a microcosm of, and counterpoint to, the *Iliad*'s largest concerns about the horrors of expatriatism and hierarchical breakdown—afflicting the innocent wife and child of Hektor as well as the heroes themselves. Zarker's detailed focus illustrates the consistent interconnectedness of the poem and is eloquent testimony to the *Iliad*'s aesthetic integrity and consciousness of itself as a "strictly true" narrative quite distinct from the *Odyssey*'s many-layered ironic narrative.

Simone Weil's "The *Iliad* or the Poem of Force" is a poetic essay that haunts and incites the imagination as it strips away surface textures of name and setting to reveal the bare forms of beauty and horror that underlie the *Iliad*. The main character of the epic, Weil argues, is Force— and the poem has no other hero. The epic's inhuman vision is both a dismal monument to the failed human past and a strident, poignant warning that we continue to live as though we served that alien, faceless god. Weil's pessimistic view of Homeric poetry, like that of Thomas Greene's brilliant *The Descent from Heaven: A Study in Epic Continuity* (see bibliography), may surprise those who do not share the darkening vision of human experience; but both are powerful reminders that the personality of the seer and the character of the object seen are, of all mergers, the most difficult to separate.

The *Iliad* section concludes with a subchapter from my book, *Homer's Iliad: The Shield of Memory*. A close analysis of a single artifact — the headdress of Andromache, which she dashes to the ground the moment she learns of Hektor's death — allows us to study precisely how one image is related mnemonically with another in the mighty symbolism of the *Iliad*. The narrative "excursion" to define the headdress at the very moment the artifact plays its role in the drama recalls to mind a similar imagistic role played by a very different headdress — Hektor's war helmet — much earlier in the long epic. Through the effective focusing of the image, whose detailed history has the impact of telescoping it into a symbol, the two scenes (one of a family intact but threatened, the other of that family's integrity destroyed) are overlaid one on the other in the reader's memory. The resulting simultaneity of vision allows the audience's imagination to grasp the epic's theme on both an emotional and a cognitive level at the same time.

Consideration of the *Odyssey* begins with two poems that provide responsive starting points for exploring the mythic understructure of Homer's great second epic. John Donne's "A Valediction: Forbidding Mourning" provides a paradigm for understanding the relationship between the "many-turning" Odysseus, who lies his way back to Ithaka, and "circumspect Penelope," who weaves as she waits for him — her stationary turning in perfect synchronization with his own circumventing return. Wallace Stevens's "The World as Meditation" is perhaps the most subtle and beautiful of all poetic responses to the *Odyssey*'s theory of imagination. As with Glaukos and Diomedes in *Iliad* 6 ("Why ask me of my generation?"), the apparent powerlessness of words is often deceiving. Penelope effectively tricks Odysseus with words, undoing with her woven stratagem twenty years of his own verbal trickery and returning him to his original emotional state — the state, as in Wallace Stevens's poem, she dreamed of. Her weaving is a double-edged metaphor, holding Ithaka together, constantly re-creating the returning image of her husband the king. Stevens's insight into Homer's mastery is profound: recognizing the strength of character required by Penelope, whose dramatic presence in the poem, while actually intermittent, is nonetheless symbolically as constant as her dreams, as her own imagination, or as Donne's "fix'd foot." Penelope, as Stevens sees her, equates the protean force of Odysseus's wide-ranging intelligence with the orderly power of fully focused meditation.

The extract from Norman Austin's *Archery at the Dark of the Moon* offers a consideration of the "ceremonies of the heavens in which Homer's courtly hexameters rest, the phases of the sun and moon." Austin argues that "In weaving and unweaving [Odysseus's burial] shroud Penelope lays her husband in his grave by day and raises him, Lazarus-like, from the dead by night. She too performs her daily ceremony of opposition and conjunction." The primary action in the *Odyssey* is, according to Austin, in the nature of an "eleventh-hour crisis." When things finally get rolling to end Odysseus's seven-year rest on Calypso's island, they do so at the very last possible moment. In fact, Odysseus is caught in the first winter storm on his way home. The last-minute nature of these proceedings, including as well the activity in Ithaka involving Telemachos's sudden journey and the stubborn persistence of the suitors, is, from a human point of view, frenzied. For Athene, however, "her orchestration of time and persons" is simply a pleasure.

This difference in outlook descriptively enhances the opposition of immortals and mortals. Austin points out that Odysseus's return to Ithaka comes with the waning of the old moon and of winter, and the waxing of a new moon and the beginning of spring. And so, "conjunction and opposition in a ceaseless cycle" emerges as "the visible pattern of order in the universe." However, although it is ceaseless for the immortal, opposition must ultimately mean death for humans. Having been offered the immortal, Odysseus chooses mortality and the wife he has left behind. Because the gods must "sooner or later destroy" what Odysseus builds, it is only in song that Odysseus may achieve "anything beyond a momentary affirmation of his frail existence." Austin believes that only in song can humans be immortal — and then only for the duration of humankind — and so "of the gifts that the gods give, the greatest . . . is song."

One of the most provocative and wide-ranging mythographies, E. A. S. Butterworth's *The Tree at the Navel of the Earth*, is the source of "The Tales Odysseus Told Alkinoos, and an Akkadian Seal." Butterworth's controversial and iconoclastic study contends that the Homeric *Odyssey*, as an expression of the master myth of the world tree, states "the Greek Western preference for individuality and self-assertive nomenclature as opposed to Eastern philosophy having individualness merge with nature and reality. Odysseus's mastery of the tree leads him to put out the magic single eye of the Cyclops whom he proceeds to further destroy with language tricks. . . ."

Richard J. Sommer, in an extract from *The Odyssey and Primitive Religion*, expands Butterworth's thinking even further into the mythic substructure of the Odyssean vision. Sommer studies the inherent misogynism of the *Odyssey* as well as the Assyrian-Babylonian *Gilgamesh*, focusing on analogies and dissimilarities between Odysseus and Agamemnon. The *Odyssey*, he argues, dramatizes "the marks of the critical juncture of a ritual cycle, a rite of passage; . . . a possibility of death and a consequent rebirth; that Odysseus's commendable aim is to enjoy the revivifying effects of each episode without suffering the concomitant crudities; and that, in each case but one, the thematic connection of these adventures with Odysseus's final trial against the suitors for re-marriage to Penelope is strengthened by the appearance of a threatening female figure strongly associated with the more obviously ritualistic elements in the story." Sommer pursues the investigation by noting the recurrence of cave, tree, and gate as interwoven motifs relating one female figure with another and with the story of Odysseus and Penelope. His essay is a widely provocative example of comparative literature and mythography.

Alice Mariani, in "The Renaming of Odysseus," discusses the recognition episode with Eurycleia in terms of the name of Odysseus and the boar scar he bears on his leg. Countering Eric Auerbach's seminal but wrong-headed essay "Odysseus's Scar" (Mimesis, see bibliography), Mariani demonstrates that the "digression" in which the story of the scar is told is, in fact, a significant facet of Eurycleia's recognition and "renaming" of Odysseus. This "digression" contains the story of both how Odysseus received his name, and how he received his scar. Mariani agrees with George Dimock that "Trouble" is "perhaps as good a translation of Odysseus's name as any." Trouble, however, not only for others, but for himself as well. This episode with Eurycleia, occurring relatively late in the story, is significant because it highlights the underlying theme of mortality inherent in Odysseus's adventures. Ultimately a large part of Odysseus's experience is "to suffer and to make others do so"; and after all, that, in a broad sense, is the experience of humankind. This point is driven home when the boar-hunt is recounted, in which Odysseus "wounds" and "is wounded" by the beast.

Mariani discusses Odysseus's infliction of pain on others, and his own experience of pain, as resulting finally in the "recognition and the sense of one's own existence." Eurycleia's recognition of the boar scar, a remnant of a childhood exchange of pain, emphasizes that this "trouble" is indeed fundamental to Odysseus's entire life experience. Additionally, Homer's reference to the scar at this stage in the poem stresses Odysseus's status as a mortal. Just as Odysseus opts for mortality and leaves Calypso's island, Odysseus's scar is both "a token of triumphant heroic achievement and a mark of the hero's mortality." Odysseus, then, after spending a series of adventures coming to grips with his mortality and his sense of identity, is finally triumphant when he is recognized for what he is by Eurycleia, who then "renames" him.

The Odyssey section closes with Konstantin Cavafy's "Ithaka," a recasting of the Odyssey's ironic symbolism — one in which irony turns to a strangely haunting ambivalence and the protean is transformed to the shape of sheer multiplicity. Ithaka becomes a symbol of life, of death, and of voyage itself — and of the principle of purpose and its narrative, a principle the latter-day Homeric narrator urges his own audience to address.

Finally comes a selected bibliography of Homeric scholarship to offer direction for further information and insight. Although it cannot hope to be complete, the bibliography attempts to be interdisciplinary and open-minded, giving many avenues for fruitful exploration to adventures setting out to enhance their appreciation of "the *Odysseys* and *Iliads* . . . echoing concavely in the memory of man."

I wish to thank my son Vincent Atchity, who assisted with bibliographical research in the Library of Congress, editing, and indexing; and E. J. Barber, Scott Littleton, and Gerrit Schroder for general discussions on a number of facets entering into the preparation of this volume. I am also grateful to Occidental College for providing grant assistance, and to Amy Miller for assistance with the manuscript.

KENNETH ATCHITY

Occidental College

Notes

1. José Ortega y Gasset, *Meditations on Quixote* (1961; reprint, New York: W. W. Norton, 1963), 35.

The Maker

Jorge Luis Borges[*]

He had never dwelled on memory's delights. Impressions slid over him, vivid but ephemeral. A potter's vermilion; the heavens laden with stars that were also gods; the moon, from which a lion had fallen; the slick feel of marble beneath slow sensitive fingertips; the taste of wild boar meat, eagerly torn by his white teeth; a Phoenician word; the black shadow a lance casts on yellow sand; the nearness of the sea or of a woman; a heavy wine, its roughness cut by honey — these could fill his soul completely. He knew what terror was, but he also knew anger and rage, and once he had been the first to scale an enemy wall. Eager, curious, casual, with no other law than fulfillment and the immediate indifference that ensues, he walked the varied earth and saw, on one seashore or another, the cities of men and their palaces. In crowded marketplaces or at the foot of a mountain whose uncertain peak might be inhabited by satyrs, he had listened to complicated tales which he accepted, as he accepted reality, without asking whether they were true or false.

Gradually now the beautiful universe was slipping away from him. A stubborn mist erased the outline of his hand, the night was no longer peopled by stars, the earth beneath his feet was unsure. Everything was growing distant and blurred. When he knew he was going blind he cried out; stoic modesty had not yet been invented and Hector could flee with impunity. I will not see again, he felt, either the sky filled with mythical dread, or this face that the years will transform. Over this desperation of his flesh passed days and nights. But one morning he awoke; he looked, no longer alarmed, at the dim things that surrounded him; and inexplicably he sensed, as one recognizes a tune or a voice, that now it was over and that he had faced it, with fear but also with joy, hope, and curiosity. Then he descended into his memory, which seemed to him endless, and up from that vertigo he succeeded in bringing forth a forgotten recollection that shone like a coin under the rain, perhaps because he had never looked at it, unless in a dream.

[*]Reprinted from *Dreamtigers* (Austin and London: University of Texas Press, 1964), 22–23, by permission of the publisher. Translated by Mildred Boyer and Harold Morland.

The recollection was like this. Another boy had insulted him and he had run to his father and told him about it. His father let him talk as if he were not listening or did not understand; and he took down from the wall a bronze dagger, beautiful and charged with power, which the boy had secretly coveted. Now he had it in his hands and the surprise of possession obliterated the affront he had suffered. But his father's voice was saying, "Let someone know you are a man," and there was a command in his voice. The night blotted out the paths; clutching the dagger, in which he felt the foreboding of a magic power, he descended the rough hillside that surrounded the house and ran to the seashore, dreaming he was Ajax and Perseus and peopling the salty darkness with battles and wounds. The exact taste of that moment was what he was seeking now; the rest did not matter: the insults of the duel, the rude combat, the return home with the bloody blade.

Another memory, in which there was also a night and an imminence of adventure, sprang out of that one. A woman, the first the gods set aside for him, had waited for him in the shadow of a hypogeum, and he had searched for her through corridors that were like stone nets, along slopes that sank into the shadow. Why did those memories come back to him, and why did they come without bitterness, as a mere foreshadowing of the present?

In grave amazement he understood. In this night too, in this night of his mortal eyes into which he was now descending, love and danger were again waiting. Ares and Aphrodite, for already he divined (already it encircled him) a murmur of glory and hexameters, a murmur of men defending a temple the gods will not save, and of black vessels searching the sea for a beloved isle, the murmur of the Odysseys and Iliads it was his destiny to sing and leave echoing concavely in the memory of man. These things we know, but not those that he felt when he descended into the last shade of all.

On Homer

Greek Princes and Aegean Princesses: The Role of Women in the Homeric Poems

Kenneth Atchity and E. J. W. Barber*

One of the greatest internal paradoxes in Greek myths is the place of women. Fifth-century Greek women in most of Greece were constrained to stay at home, allowed out only for certain festivals and funerals, and certainly given no political power (for a candid picture, see, for example, Lysias's oration "On the Murder of Eratosthenes"). Yet fully half the extant fifth-century plays have women as the title characters. Helen, Antigone, Elektra, Iphigeneia, while living in haremlike seclusion, we are told, nonetheless succeeded in causing international scandals. Klytaimestra even succeeded in running her country for ten years, and Penelope hers for twenty.

Such a notable anomaly can be explained simply and easily, however, by assuming that the role of women in society had changed rather drastically between the time when the myths were generated and when they were written down. The earlier states of affairs are most readily visible in parts of the Homeric poems, which were, however, themselves written down by a post-Homeric society bent on emphasizing its own social value system. As such they reflect the blending of pre-Indo-European or Aegean values, apparently quite strong in Mycenaean times, with the Indo-European system again dominant in Attic society. The archaeological and other records available to us support such an assumption.

FROM MATRILINY TO PATRILINY

We know—indeed it is an axiom of Indo-European (IE) scholarship—that the IE's tended to be heavily patriarchal and patrilineal; and we know from ethnographic studies (e.g., Murdock 1967; van den Berghe 1979) what such systems tend to be like, and what traits they apparently never possess. For example, patrilineal systems are almost always virilocal; that is, newlyweds live at the husband's family's residence. Of Murdock's

*This essay was written specifically for this volume and is published here for the first time by permission of the authors.

sample of 399 patrilineal societies around the globe, 96.2% are virilocal, the tiny remainder being divided among bilocal, neolocal, and duolocal, but in no case uxorilocal (newlyweds live at the wife's family's residence) (van den Berghe 1979, p. 111). Uxorilocality seems invariably to be associated either with matriliny, which correlates with uxorilocality two thirds of the time (and virilocality only 15% of the time), or with bilaterality (where it accounts for 22% of that sample).

Such central stories in Greek mythology as that of Helen of Troy, however, show us uxorilocality — a social system unacceptable to the society responsible for putting together the authorized version of the epics that have come down to us. The unacceptability and perhaps even incomprehensibility of the previous historical tradition led to a number of adjustments in the story in order to avoid suggesting "the wrong behavior" as an ideal.

Helen was raised in Sparta, child of Leda and (ostensibly) Tyndareus, along with a sister and two brothers. The weak Tyndareus, Helen's father in the older myth, is somehow replaced in the patrilineal Indo-European tradition with Zeus, whether as a justification of the rest of Helen's story or as a polite cover-up for otherwise unacceptable promiscuity on the part of Leda. With the patrilineal chief god as her father, Helen has thus become the earthly counterpart of Athene. This revision of her origins has the effect of making Helen a "heroine" — half divine, half human — and therefore an anomaly. Her anomalous status enables the patrilineal mythographers to swallow her un-patrilineal-like exploits — and the poets to glorify it.

Menelaos moved in with Helen upon marrying her and became king of her land, Sparta. This is strange to patriliny on a second count, since she had two perfectly good brothers, Kastor and Polydeukes, who should unquestionably have inherited the throne by patrilineal standards. Yet they go off and find brides elsewhere without, apparently, any fuss or feeling of having been cheated of their birthright. Klytaimestra, too — perhaps she marries "away" because her sister Helen has the right to family lands even though Klytaimestra marries first (Rose 1959, p. 231) — settles down to establish her own characteristic matriliny: Her several daughters stay with her, but her one son, Orestes, she sends away the minute her husband leaves. No wonder her patrilineal Greek "in-laws" are so offended by her conduct! But her motives are easily justified from a matrilineal viewpoint: Agamemnon has committed the ultimate sin by slaying the queen's daughter Iphigeneia, the matrilineal heiress-apparent. It makes sense, then, that Klytaimestra, on her side, has little sentiment left for her royal husband.

When Agamemnon returns to Mycenae from Troy, assuming the integrity of the patrilineal household he thought he had left behind, he finds, instead, a complete reversion to matriliny (including his wife's having taken on a weak husband, Aegisthus, as his replacement) — and becomes the victim of that reversion, held up, in the *Odyssey*, as an example of the worst that can happen to a Greek.

Back in Sparta, the important child in the next generation is Hermione, Helen's daughter (and Menelaos's? — his fatherhood is not established in Homer), herself barren according to post-Homeric myth. Homer calls Helen's having only this one child a curse from the gods (*Odyssey* 4.14), brought on by her adultery with "a man of another folk" (23.219) — understandably a crime against the patriarchy. Homer's "curse" also emphasizes the lack of a male heir in the one kingdom that remained aloof from the patriliny that was gradually winning out elsewhere. Also in keeping with the strong matriliny at Sparta, we scarcely hear of Menelaos's two sons, but are told only that Megapenthes was the son of a slave woman (*Odyssey* 4.14).

Nor is this the only royal family with strong uxorilocal traditions. For example, Amphitryon goes to marry and live with Alkmene at her home, Mycenae, where the two of them reign despite the fact that Alcmene has a brother, Likymnios (Rose 1959, p. 206). Over and over among the legends, particularly those associated with southern Greece and Crete, we hear of influential daughters, daughters who inherit thrones, and sons who go away or are barely mentioned: in short, it seems, uxorilocal matriliny.[1]

Matriliny would also explain those large numbers of important progeny born of a human princess and fathered by a god. Now, *we* know that those children must have had human fathers. But how does a wife, raised in a society which condones and perhaps even encourages extramarital sex among its women, explain a child obviously conceived out of wedlock to a husband who feels that assurance of his paternity is essential because he grew up in a patrilineal society? She tactfully blames it on someone more awesome than he is. If Leda has a child by someone other than Tyndareus, she can keep the peace by blaming it on Zeus!

Matriliny does not exist in a vacuum, however, but is generally the result of a pattern of subsistence that fosters or even requires it. Brown (1970) has shown that the division of labor by sex is largely dictated by what jobs the women can and can't do while tending children at the same time. As a rule, whatever women can do while caretaking is considered by that society to be work either for women alone or for both sexes, and what they can't do is considered work either for men or for men and unmarried girls. Some of the main constraints are that the job can be neither dangerous to the children under foot nor of a sort that requires extended journeys from home, and that the job must be easily interruptable and easily resumed (Brown 1970, pp. 1075–76). Thus, horticultural societies, where the ground nearby is tilled by hand, not by large and potentially dangerous draft-animals, are among those most frequently matrilineal (van den Berghe 1979, p. 102). The men are thus freed to go off on long expeditions for meat and other needed resources: hunting, fishing, herding, perhaps even mining or trading.

We could not ask for a better fit to the local Aegean economy. The standard archaeological picture of Minoan Crete is of a "thalassocracy," which presumably arose from fishing expeditions and developed into a booming Bronze Age trade all over the Mediterranean. Journeys to Egypt and the Levant must have kept the menfolk away from home for long periods of time; trips about the Aegean would be shorter but still lengthy. But somehow the women at home had to eat, and otherwise get on with life. A good deal of evidence (Barber, forthcoming) suggests that the women at home were also busy manufacturing a major item for the men's export trade: textiles. Certainly weaving is just such an occupation as fits Brown's list of requisites for what one can do while tending children. And the herding of the large numbers of sheep for which we have evidence would have required still other men (young girls? — seemingly not) to range far from home.

A not unsimilar life-style seems to have been pursued by many Mycenaean Greeks, in that men were often away, raiding and trading, although they seem to have taken part, too, in the increasingly complex agriculture. In the purely Indo-European pattern, the nomadic outriders took their women with them; vestiges of this pattern may explain the Greeks' fierce attachment to their "shield-wives" in the *Iliad* — when they were away, they "reverted" to behavior typical of the pre-blended period. What must have happened, then, was an Indo-European patrilineal "overlay" on the preexisting Aegean matriliny. The incoming IE's married the resident non-IE's and created "the best" of both worlds: strong Aegean female householders, and strong IE male outriders to bring back the spoils of war and of trade (trading the arts created in the household). The most direct archaeological evidence of the Aegean-male-outrider paradigm seems to be the Egyptian frescoes of Aegean traders (who are consistently male).

Virtually every detail of the pre-IE Aegean matrilineal system we have reconstructed is present in Homer's picture of the Phaiakians (*Odyssey* 6 and 7), as though that fairy-island were a folk memory of an earlier phase of life. Nausikaa, the daughter of the royal household, tells the man from outside, Odysseus (who she wishes would settle there and marry her), to ignore the king but supplicate the queen — since the queen, not the king, makes decision about strangers in the homeland and, like Athene later, is the arbiter of quarrels. Moreover, Arete clearly assumes that Nausikaa's interest in Odysseus implies the necessity of careful consideration; she asks the nobles what they think of his appearance, stature, and intelligence (11. 336–37): He is likely to be their king. Odysseus, of course, turns down the matrilineal offer — as he does in the cases of Circe and Kalypso.[2]

The most essential features of Phaiakian life, as we encounter them, consist of (a) the outlying pastures, (b) the palace with its exotic goods, especially those of metal (necessarily imported, if this is the Aegean area), (c) the elaborate palace gardens, yielding all manner of horticultural produce, (d) the women weaving textiles in the palace, (e) the association of the palace with other arts such as dancing, singing, and athletics, and (f) the men congregating at the harbor among the fishing and trading vessels—their extraordinary excellence in navigation a gift of Poseidon. One very much gets the impression that the men run life at the harbor and on the sea, while the women expect to take care of most of the town and household life.

In sum, we can see not only a pattern of marriage and inheritance suggesting the presence of matriliny in the Aegean, but also patterns in the two-sided economy, making its existence highly probable. If we suppose then, that women were pivotal in the indigenous marriage, inheritance, and subsistence systems when the Greeks began to infiltrate from the north, we get a picture not inconsistent with the content of many of our myths and explanatory of many of their strange details, a picture of the patrilineal Greek "nobles" and chieftains attempting to intermarry with the matrilineal Aegean princesses—presumably as a bid to get control of their lands.

We may also note that the IE's tended to build their culture on social relationships, i.e., people, rather than on physical ties, e.g., land. For example, one of the greatest punishments among Greeks, Germanic peoples, and other Indo-Europeans was to be banished from the company and protection of one's kin. But if your kin went with you, moving wasn't so bad. Rulership consisted in particular of the power over a certain hierarchy of people (centrally the unilateral, patrilineal kin-group). Greek newcomers, like Penelope, inserted these kin-groups increasingly into the southern Aegean scene, attaching to the local royal households like a leech, in the person of the ruling prince of the Greek clan.

On the other hand, the "autochthonous" population, like many other cultures, seems to have identified strongly with local monuments and places, and rulership for them may well have meant power over certain areas. To a man raised in a patrilineal, kin-oriented culture, then, it would seem that all one had to do to acquire the land—after all, land was necessary for subsistence even if not ideologically important—was to acquire as wife the woman who held it. But Aegean princesses were not about to see themselves so easily disenfranchised, as is obvious from the resulting history of marital, political, and theological spats which comprise so much of our corpus of Greek mythology and which dominate the consciousness of the Homeric poems.

These tales of domestic strife were in turn handed down to another wave of incoming—and still heavily patrilineal and patriarchal—Greeks, the Dorians. And they in turn, mixed together with the now thoroughly diluted remnants of the earlier age in Attica and Ionia, had to revise the myths somewhat to make them more plausible—since either they could not understand how these women could have had so much power and made so many things happen; or, they understood all too well, at first, and made sure their children would receive an acceptably slanted version of the myth. In either case, formalizing the matrilineal myths came to have another important function, that of clarifying the threat in order to prevent its recurrence.[3]

Sequence of Events
Stages of Development

Society	Type	Basis	Years
Stage 1:			
Aegean or Autocthonous	Matrilineal (Pre-IE)	Land inheritance	pre-3000 to 1250
Stage 2:			
Mycenaean or Heroic	Patrilineal (IE)	Blood ties	1650 to 1100
Stage 3:			
Dorian or Classical	Patriarchal (post-IE)	Law	1200 to 550

In this sequence of events, the overlapping social structures provided the grounds for the paradoxes or the myth.

If a classical Greek king's wife had run off as Helen did, the king would probably have thought too little of her to think her worth chasing very far; and if he had got her back, he would have put her to death instantly—in fact, Strutynski (1970) cites just such a story of the Iron Age Corinthian tyrant Periander. Some legends even have Menelaos considering doing just that. But in Homer Menelaos gets all of Greece to help him fetch his wife back, at the cost of a ten-year war; and the next thing we know he is living amiably at home with her (*Odyssey* 4)—rewarded for the damage to his maleness by immortality (which may be the patrilineal mythographers' attempt to put him on a par with his heroine-wife). Meanwhile, Helen regales the guests with stories of her escapades at Troy! If indeed Helen carried the bloodline of the Lakedaimonian throne, as her line of succession implies, she would have had to be gotten back alive if Menelaos were to remain king of that region. And Homer says as much in the *Iliad*. Helen had eloped clandestinely with Paris, utterly abandoning everything and everyone she had at Sparta. Yet in book 3 (11.69–70), Paris and Menelaos agree to fight in single combat, the winner to take "Helen and all her possessions." What possessions? The passage makes real sense only if she is the inalienable heiress of Sparta, where the bereft Menelaos has been facing a challenge to his exercise of authority from the old palace guard loyal to the rights held by his purloined wife.

The legend that her daughter Hermione is barren is the IE attempt to insure that the matriliny will not be perpetuated in Sparta — although Spartan history evolved in what must have been a disappointing way for the original Dorians.

Penelope was a key figure for similar reasons. The *Odyssey*, in fact, records the near-reversion, on Ithaka, to a fully matrilineal system. When Odysseus leaves for Troy, he leaves a father who is opposed to the matrilineal inclinations of the local populace and a son too young to retain effective patrilineal control over the island. It seems probable that the throne of Ithaka had been matrilineal before the coming of Laertes to the court of Antikleia. The marriage, apparently, was without female issue — which tipped the scales in favor of the patriliny. Odysseus, son of the matriarch, would become the next king. When Penelope (daughter of the Argive Ikarios and a nameless mother) and Odysseus were betrothed, Penelope must have agreed to allow the patrilineal system of Odysseus's family to replace the matriliny still dominating the behavior of her cousins, Helen and Klytaimestra. Laertes, we deduce, never was king of Ithaka, but only the consort of the old queen and respected father of the new patriarchal king. This explains the otherwise rather un-Greek retirement of Laertes to the vineyard. Penelope, then, became the first patrilineal queen of a formerly matrilineal domain — her father, Ikarios, being Greek, and brother of Tyndareos. That Penelope's mother's name is not preserved suggests that the patriliny's dominance began at the point of Ikarios's marriage.

Conveniently for the patriarchy, Penelope and Odysseus also had no daughter. But because Telemachos was too young when Odysseus went off to war, the succession of Odysseus had not yet been established firmly enough to prevent others from seeing Penelope as the key to the wealth and power of Ithaka. Into the void, therefore, rush suitors willing to play the suicidal role of matrilineal king-designate, pressuring Penelope to choose one of them to displace Odysseus and the patriarchy. She, however, behaving as a good patrilineal wife (who nonetheless, by Odysseus's absence, has been handed all the trappings of matrilineal householder power), stands against them, wavering, and waits for the return of the husband she loves.

Three cousins — Klytaimestra, Penelope, and Helen — provide the full spectrum of female types in Homer: the faithless queen (matrilineal), the faithful queen (patrilineal), and the anomalous heroine (*hors de classe*; *Odyssey* 11. 395ff). At Odysseus's return Penelope is on the verge of giving up and reverting. She performs the royal function of opening the long-closed treasure chamber (*Odyssey* 21), and tells the suitors that the one who can pierce the holes in the ancient axes with an arrow will be (i.e., will become) her husband. When that one turns out to be (i.e., already be) her husband Odysseus — and it's very nearly Telemachos! (*Odyssey* 21.128) — the patriliny of Odysseus, Athene's charge, is safe after all. Penelope is given credit for having preserved it with her patience and her craft in weaving—both literally and metaphorically binding the Ithakan household together.

We can see from all of this that Bronze Age Aegean societies were very differently organized in terms of men's and women's roles than classical society; and it is also clear that classical Greeks, our main source of literary information, did not fully understand the tradition they were trying to transmit—or were intentionally garbling the transmission to justify their own view of the way things should be. Once we understand the source of their misunderstanding or intentional misdirection, however, we can begin to make sense out of what they gave us.

THE TWO TRADITIONS

We can learn more about the two societies and what must have been blended by looking at the core religions of each. In order to understand how they were synthesized, we must learn to separate out the two components. Let us begin with the IE input, since the extensive comparative work of Dumézil and others has given us an independent basis from which to work.

Taken from this analytical point of view, Greek mythology is by no means so barren of evidence of the tripartite functions postulated by Dumézil for PIE society and ideology as Dumézil and others appear to feel (Littleton 1970, reprinted in this volume).[4] The problem is largely in the avenue of attack. Although the ideology as Dumézil reconstructs it from other cultures is in fact very much present in the Greek legacy, there is much less of a tendency among the Greeks to personify the basic concepts in the mythology than there is among the Indo-Iranians and the Romans, who have been used as the basis for so much of Dumézil's work. Thus someone attuned only to looking through a list of gods and heroes, or even reading the straight myths, will be much less aware of the presence of this system that has been presented as idiosyncratically IE than someone who is steeped in the entire culture, via archaeology, art history, literature, and history, as well as via mythology and philology.

For example, one of the important details which Dumézil puts forward as being distinctively IE is the separate-but-equal status of "church" and "state"—that is, the division of the first function into two aspects, magico-religious (man's relation to the divine) and social (man's relation to other men). One does not have to look very far into Greek literature, especially Homer, to see that although Zeus is the sole ruler of the Olympian pantheon, two of his most important epithetical descriptions are: (a) such things as cloud-gatherer and thunder-wielder, the thunderbolt being the Greek symbol *par excellence* of his divine, even magical control over the entire universe;[5] and (b) "*xenios*": patron of the ultimate social contract in Greek society, "*xenia*," the host-guest relationship. In short, although Zeus is conceived of as a single deity, he is the embodiment of two quite separate ideas, the ultimate in divinity and the ultimate in social contract – not unlike Jupiter.

As if this weren't enough, there is a still more direct and thorough-going reflex of the dichotomy-within-unity of the first function in Greek culture. Throughout the history of Greek society, there is an antithesis of two kinds of law, *themis* and *nomos*. Roughly, both terms mean "law,"[6] but their real meanings can only be talked around in English, not translated. As a first approximation, let us characterize *themis* as divine law – better yet: as the kinds of rules which are so basic that even the gods "can't" break them. Socrates debates whether Apollo's oracle might have told a fib; but he concludes that Apollo cannot have his oracle lie, because it is not *themis* for Apollo to lie (*Apology* 21b – although another god could: Hera does, for example, in *Iliad* 14.197 ff.). We could interpret that to mean that it is against divine law; or that it is not part of the nature of which Apollo is the embodiment; or that it is against the natural laws of the universe (i.e., a contradiction in terms). And probably all of these notions are wrapped up together in the connotation of *themis*. But at any rate it has to do with facts and processes that mortals have no control over, analogous to the Homeric concept of "fate," and which therefore rank (within that culture) as divine creations, facts, and / or rules.[7] *Themis* is The Way Things Are.

Nomos, on the other hand, is human law – whether uncodified "common law," which in Greek terms would be the sum total of time-honored human customs; or "codified" law, that is, specific social contracts entered into explicitly by given social parties. Thus *nomos* can be changed, if the contracting parties agree to the changes, but *themis* is not within the power of mortals to change. Together *themis* and *nomos* were conceived of as ruling Greek society. If we now read Littleton's summary description of the two halves of the first function, reconstructed from four other IE cultures, there is no doubt as to what cultural complex we're in: "Like Varuna, Jupiter, and Othinn, Asa (the Zoroastrian spirit of "order") is concerned with the maintenance of religious order, and his domain includes the far reaches of the cosmos. Vohu Manah (the Zoroastrian spirit of "good thought") . . . corresponds to Mitra and represents the Zoroas-trian version of the juridical and contractual aspect of the first function. Like his Vedic counterpart, Vohu Manah is much closer to the world of men and presides over the moral relationships between members of the society" (Littleton 1982). The only difference is that *themis* and *nomos* are not normally deities – although *Themis* gets personified, in a broadly allegorical way, here and there among the Greek poets (e.g., *Odyssey* 2.68).

The two halves of the first function were evidently both embodied within the single person of Zeus, although clearly distinguished conceptu-ally as *themis* and *nomos*. But again in the social system which we see in Homer, the human embodiment of these concerns was as separate, as equal, and as "first" as Dumézil could wish. Oedipus and Agamemnon can bluster at their respective seers, Teiresias and Calchas, and even threaten them with bodily harm (Sophocles, *Oedipus the King* 339–462; *Iliad* 1.68–120); but the onlookers are horrified at what is evidently a considerable breach of etiquette (*nomos*), while the seers talk back with an obvious sense of their own right to contradict the worldly sovereign (Sophocles even has Teiresias retort that he owes higher allegiance to Apollo, i.e., Truth, than to the king of his earthly abode); and the king himself in each case is forced to back down. The feelings we get from these and other similar scenes is that prophet and king are considered very nearly equal in power and prestige, although in different domains, one social and earthly, the other divine and magical. In short, the IE ideology is strongly present in the Greek world, if we know where to look for it.

But what about the Aegean component? Having identified and set aside the IE part, can we see a useful pattern emerging from the residue for interpreting the local Old European culture? In the *Iliad* as a whole and in the shield of Achilles in particular, there are not one but two "war gods" — Athene and Ares, one for each side of the fray (e.g., 20.47–53). Now Ares would seem to correspond fairly closely, in gender, etc., to the war gods of other IE's; so who is Athene?

No matter which way you look at her — from literary remains or archaeological ones — Athene basically fits the role of an Aegean deity who has been grafted onto the Greek pantheon (cf. Nilsson, 1952, p. 26). That she may have been grafted in by being merged with some minor figure already in the pantheon is entirely possible; in which case we might legitimately try to chase down the function of her predecessor. Dumézil's reconstructed IE notion of a virgin helper of the king, who "conserves in herself, unutilized but not destroyed, . . . the creative power that is hers by nature" thereby symbolically stores up all the "various powers needed by society" (Dumézil, 1973, p. 123), looks, in fact, suspiciously like the grafting point.

But Athene, taken on her own terms, simply does not fit into the Dumézilian mold — and her failure to do so is as much a demonstration of the idiosyncratic and cultural nature of the tripartite scheme as the fact that the Greek separation of *themis* and *nomos* does fit it. To label her "transfunctionally" IE is to miss her central nature altogether, a typically Aegean nature.[8]

Athene is goddess of war (*Iliad* 6.384 ff., 18.516–19), goddess of weaving and other handicrafts (*Iliad* 6.86 ff.; 9.390; *Odyssey* 13.386; further illustrated by such myths as that of Arachne; the rituals of Athene Polias; etc.), goddess of agricultural fertility (cult of Athene Polias), sovereign and protectress of Athens, protectress of the household (cf. her position with respect to Athens, and her sacred snakes), arbiter of quarrels (e.g., in Aeschylus' *Eumenides*; cf. the remarkably similar set of attributes of the matrilineal Queen Arete, *Odyssey* 7.66–74, 108–111), and so forth. In tripartite IE terms, she has not only covered but hogged all three functions — all the more since she is set up[9] as the favorite child of Zeus, sprung from him alone without a mother, and the only deity in the pantheon who can wield at will his thunderbolts or wear the *aegis*, the cosmic and magical badges of his office as the king of gods. In fact, in this capacity it might appear that she all but supplants Zeus. But we must realize what's going on: the Greek Athene is the classical solution to the power of the matriliny. In her person, the culture can recognize the power of the female principle without endangering, and in fact while still serving, the male. As the favorite — and motherless — daughter of Zeus, she could stay at the head of the Aegean pantheon in all-but-top position; and the acknowledgement of her position could keep those royal family spats from getting out of hand in Mycenaean times. The Indo-Europeans always *were* rather good at adapting to their co-habitants' culture — to the extent that archaeologists are generally hard put to demonstrate the exact time and place of IE arrival in each area, when linguistic evidence is lacking.

If, then, Athene was an important local Aegean deity, what was her function in that society? What essential force did she represent? For her to be so important, it must have been a very powerful force in the lives of those people. The common thread in all her attributes is that aspect of her which the later Greeks still saw as central (although the Romans got it slightly garbled): She is goddess of *tekhne* — technology, or better yet, know-how: all those pursuits which humans learn to do by skill. Weaving, handcrafts, the skills of building a human house and home, the human practice of agriculture and animal-husbandry, the arts of communal warfare and of ship-building, the art of crafty speaking and persuasion, the administration of justice — all of these are human activities, requiring the acquisition of a skill practiced only by humans and (presumably) gods. (Except for the spider, who weaves a web. And she, we are told, learned her skill as a mortal of long ago — and was turned into an insect for daring to challenge Athene's ability to weave.)

If Athene is an original goddess of human skill, surely clever Odysseus is her natural devotee — or mortal counterpart (*Odyssey* 13.295–99).

Since contrastive features tend to be the easiest to reconstruct, not just in linguistic but also in other cultural systems, it is instructive to look more closely at Athene's most persistent adversary, Poseidon. They oppose each other, for example, over Odysseus's homecoming: Athene and her *tekhne* protect thoughtful Odysseus against the wrath of Poseidon, and against his uncivilized and unsociable offspring the Cyclops. Here we have, it seems, the deity or power of human skill pitted against a divinity or force of that which is untamed and chaotic. Then again Athene and Poseidon contest over who will possess the land which became Athens, Poseidon cracking the hillside to produce a salt spring, but Athene creating an olive tree, one of the most important domestic plants in the Aegean area. Athene is judged to have won, by producing something of great usefulness to the incipient community. (In the *Odyssey*, it is the olive tree over and over again which provides Odysseus with technical material for his homecoming: from the rudder he fashions for his raft to the stake he uses to put out the Cyclops' eye to the tree ["of wisdom"?] under which he and Athene weave a design [*metin hyphenon*] to thwart the suitors, to the tree of life itself—the marvelous bed he has fashioned for Penelope in the royal palace.) Athene's victory over Poseidon metaphorically pushes back the wild with the domestic. Poseidon fills out our picture of him as the essence of the untamed and not entirely tamable forces of nature by his next chaotic move: a poor loser, he sends a huge tidal flood in revenge.

Much has been written, of course, about Poseidon's relation to the IE water deity (Littleton, 1973b)—and it seems clear that, in the classical pantheon, Poseidon fills an originally IE slot as one of the three major male deities, sky, earth, and water. But Poseidon's main attributes in the early literature—earth-shaker, and keeper of bulls as well as horses[10]— make him appear far closer to what we can deduce of an Aegean earthquake deity, whose association with *tsunamis*, the most powerful water-phenomenon in the ancient Aegean, provided a convenient grafting-point for this terrifying divinity of natural forces into the place of the IE water god, whose mighty steppeland rivers had been left far behind and were no longer of importance. It is the heavy syncretism in the backgrounds of both Poseidon and Athene that has tended to confuse people.

We find such echoes of the old dichotomy between Athene and Poseidon throughout Homer. But now Athene's side is bolstered by her new daddy, Zeus. For starters, Athene and Poseidon spend the whole *Odyssey* scrapping over Odysseus's homecoming. And Poseidon is still a poor loser: he would destroy the Phaiakians entirely for helping Odysseus were it not for Zeus's diplomatic persuasiveness.[11] In the *Iliad* Athene's *aegis* gives Achilles the status to destroy the disorderly Trojans (Poseidon's friends; and disorderly because wife-stealing is taboo in the patriliny as well as in the matriliny—where the queen must remain at home at all costs—and Troy should not have retained Helen).

But both epics are hymns to Zeus / Athene and represent the classicization of the former gods—so much so that even Poseidon calls his brother, "Father Zeus" (*Odyssey* 13.128). It is at Zeus's behest, after all, that Hephaistos has built separate domiciles for the various gods on Olympos— but not, apparently, for his brothers, Hades and Poseidon, who are given more or less equal but quite separate realms as is typical in a patrilineal brotherhood.

Twice in the story of Poseidon's revenge, and certainly throughout the *Odyssey* (the story of how Odysseus, with Athene's spirit beside and inside him, overcame the wrath of Poseidon), we also find Poseidon specifically associated with water. Equally strongly in both stories he is connected with seismic action: splitting hills, tidal waves, and the heaving of huge rocks and mountains (e.g., the Cyclops, and the Phaiakians).

Teiresias's prophecy about the mission Odysseus is to undertake after he has reestablished order on Ithaka underlines the process by which the old god is displaced by the new Zeus / Athene pantheon (11.119–37). Odysseus is to find a spot so far inland that a passerby, seeing the oar on his shoulder, mistakes it for a winnowing fan. There he is to kneel and make sacrifice (bull, ram, and hog—the animals of Poseidon, his son the Cyclops, and of Circe!) and then to make his way home again and sacrifice to "the gods who hold the wide heaven, all of them in order." The peculiar gesture of implanting the oar returns the matrilineal society's god to his origins, safely distant from the newly-formed society of Zeus / Athene—due honor to the troublesome brother, but nonetheless effective exile.

We have tried to show on the one hand that Zeus and some other parts of the Greek myths are idiosyncratically IE; and on the other that Athene and the matrilineal system do not fit the IE mold but take their amalgamated characteristics from an equally idiosyncratic and quite different preexisting world view. From the strength of the two systems, after much confusion, arose the brilliant order of classical Athens.

By classical times, as well as in the *Iliad* and the *Odyssey*, it becomes clear that Zeus's motherless daughter Athene is the perfect mythographic solution to the fusion of the two cultures—the chief female deity of classical Greece is not matrilineal because she has only a male parent; but as a female she can retain those matrilineal values considered useful by the IE's. Moreover she acquires her power over Athens by jurisprudentially displacing Poseidon, a deity originally related to the matriliny and opposed to Zeus (*Odyssey* 13 shows Zeus using diplomacy to get Poseidon to agree to abandoning his direct supervision of human affairs); and later, as Littleton suggests, syncretically related to a secondary IE "source of waters" god.

The patriliny has finessed the matriliny by incorporating its goddess responsible for the technique needed to hold the house together; as a patrilineal chief god, Athene maintains her technique but now in service of the patriliny: compare, for example, the close of the *Odyssey* and of the *Oresteia* where Athene ends the matrilineal practice of vendetta through the evolved patrilineal process of judicial and diplomatic arbitration. For the Furies, she builds a temple on the Acropolis to placate them, just as she builds the temple to Poseidon at Sounion to placate that old god. In both cases, she effectively terminates the earlier divinity's hegemony in favor of her father Zeus's more civilized dispensation.

The Weaving Metphor

It is an axiom of anthropology that the structure of a society's pantheon reflects its social ideals. Athene is clearly one of the pivotal deities of classical and Homeric society, and we are gradually sorting out how and why she reached that position. As we have said, her particular domain is that of know-how, or craft; and foremost among her crafts is weaving. If we investigate this specifically female craft, we find that the technology of weaving in Mycenaean and archaic Greek society and the theme of weaving in Homer bring confirming perspective to the foregoing analysis.

We know from the evidence of archaeology and frescoes that the Mycenaeans, like the Minoans before them, were busy carrying on a massive textile trade in the Mediterranean. In the last month or so alone before the destruction of the palace of Knossos and its Linear B archive, we find tens of thousands of sheep recorded in the palace flocks (see Killen 1964 for a fairly thorough analysis of the Aegean wool industry). Aegean visitors to the Egyptian court are regularly shown wearing ornately patterned textiles and bringing bolts of cloth for trade, along with the more widely studied metal goods. Frescoes and Linear B archives together demonstrate a wide knowledge of dyestuffs, the use of which dates back deep into the Neolithic. As for skill in patterned weaving, the little studied south Europeans had been putting the famous Egyptians to shame for millennia: We have elaborately patterned "brocades" (weft-float designs) from Stone Age central Europe, at a time when the Egyptians hadn't gotten past plain white plain-weave, and the Aegean people may well have learned tapestry technique from Syria before the end of the Bronze Age (Barber, 1982, and forthcoming). So, contrary to the belief of most classicists, all the techniques, skills, and materials for elaborate patterned weaving were present in Mycenaean and classical Greece, and most of them had been there for thousands of years. The evidence of the visual arts (frescoes, vase paintings, etc.) must therefore be taken seriously, and not lightly dismissed as "artistic license."

What were Mycenaean women weaving? The slave women and small householders were apparently weaving the ordinary sheets and blankets, shirts and cloaks, intended for everyday use; and the making of these objects was clearly regarded as a time-consuming and tiring chore. Indeed, until the Industrial Revolution, that was the case in every household in Europe. But if spinning and weaving were such dreadful labor—labor for which one filled a palace with slaves—why is each and every queen shown weaving, too? Why is she who commands not exempt from this wearying task?

The evidence suggests that society accorded her the task of doing a spinning and weaving of a different kind: the weaving of special cloth. Helen is not spinning ordinary wool on her golden spindle in the *Odyssey*, but purple wool—wool dyed with the most expensive dye known to the ancient world. Both she and Andromache are explicitly stated to be weaving special patterns into their textiles, in the *Iliad*. Helen is weaving "the numerous struggles of Trojans . . . and bronze-armored Achaians" into a great colored robe (*Iliad* 3.126–27), while Andromache is weaving *thronoi*, or roses (Bolling 1958, p. 281), which throughout European folklore, all the way down to Faust, protect the possessor against evil by the sympathetic magic of the accompanying thorns.

And Penelope? What is Penelope weaving that it takes three years before the suitors even begin to suspect that something is wrong? A mere "shroud" of plain cloth (as the translators would have it) takes a couple of weeks to weave. Clearly our traditional assumption about the meaning of *tapheion pharos* (literally, "funerary-square-of-heavy-cloth") cannot work, and is predicated on our own burial customs. What, then, is the meaning?

In 1875, at Kertch in the Crimea, Russian antiquarians dug into the burial mound of a Greek colonist of the early fourth century B.C. Draped over the wooden sarcophagus, like a flag over the coffin of a veteran, were the remains of a huge piece of cloth that carried on it frieze after frieze of mythological and pseudo-historical scenes. Done in black, red, and white, it resembled nothing so closely as the friezes on Attic pottery — particularly those of the archaic period, such as the famous François Vase, or the masterpieces by Sophilos. In fact, if we look at these vases we find that queens and goddesses are regularly shown wearing garments that themselves are made of such friezed cloth. All the way back to the beginnings of Attic vase painting, with the great Dipylon funerary pots, we find everything coming at us in friezes of this sort. And Athens, least damaged of the Mycenaean strongholds from the turmoil at the end of the Bronze Age, was in the best condition to continue Mycenaean arts and crafts. Can we indeed be looking here at the remains of a Mycenaean textile tradition?

All available evidence suggests that the answer is yes. The last thing we see of Mycenaean art before it dives into the Dark Age is already of this same friezed form: the famous Warrior Vase, from Mycenae, and a remarkably similar funeral stele, which was made from a shaft grave stele plastered over and painted with friezes of warriors and animals. During the Dark Age, with the exception of the so-called "chariot craters" off in the easternmost reaches of the Greek world, pots don't look like this. They're lucky to be graced with a squiggly line or a few circles. So why is it that when vase painting gets back on its feet in the Geometric period, we have what is clearly a debased form of the same style? Where has it been hiding all those centuries? Most probably on a medium that hasn't survived down to our day — a medium that is itself built in long, frieze-shaped strips, unlike pots: namely textiles.

Euripides's *Ion* gives us a glimpse of what must have been happening. The play's hero was a temple foundling, and is now earning his keep as a temple servant. When asked by the Pythian priestess to set up a festive pavilion for some wealthy customers, Ion goes to the temple storerooms, the repositories of generations of expensive votive gifts, and picks out a number of tapestries with which to hang the pavilion walls (1140–64). We may smile at the artistic license with which Euripides has Ion choose a tapestry of the sun and starry constellations for the pavilion roof, and scenes of hunting, sailing, warfare, and religion for the sides. But we had best not dismiss the gist of the scene: that such tapestries existed in the temples, much as they lie about in today's museums—heirlooms from previous ages for all to admire (Homer's term: *thauma idesthai*, "a wonder to behold"). Indeed, the plot of the *Ion* hinges on the "beginner's" tapestry of a Gorgon which Ion's mother wove as a girl and laid with him in his basket when she abandoned him in a sacred cave (1417–25). As often happens in Homer (e.g., with Glaukos and Diomedes in *Iliad* 6.212ff), art, associated with memory, serves identity and life itself.

The *peplos* which the Athenians presented to Athene at the Panathenaic Festival brings more detailed enlightenment. We learn, for example, that it took two or more priestesses most of a year to weave the garment, although it could not have been significantly larger than any ordinary *peplos*, since the statue—that of Athene Polias, in the Erechtheum—was life-size (small enough, in fact, that it was easily snatched up and carried off to Salamis in the hasty retreat before the Persians in 480 B.C. [Herington 1955]). What took so long was that it was traditionally and invariably ornamented with the depiction of "The Battle of the Gods and the Giants," a victory in which Athene was said to have taken a leading part (see Pfuhl 1900, pp. 11–13, for complete sources). Now, if it takes two women a year to make such a tapestry, how long will it take one woman to make it?

Two years.

And when it gets well into three, her suitors finally start to suspect something!

Between the evidence of the *peplos* of Athene, the Kertch sarcophagus cover, and numerous other tinier clues, such as the Vari model of a funeral cart draped with a friezed "cloth" of clay, and the opinion of the scholiast of Venice that Homer took his history of the Trojan war from the scenes depicted on Helen's web (Perry, 1898), we conclude that Penelope was obliged, by her loyalty to the patriliny, to weave a major tapestry for Laertes's funeral—one which presumably depicted relevant clan history or mytho-history, as did the *peplos* of Athene, the Kertch cloth, Ion's tapestries, and the clay vases and statuettes of the archaic period.

When we look at the Homeric passages describing princesses weaving, all becomes clear. Consider the primary text, *Iliad* 3, where Helen is shown being interrupted at her work: "Now to Helen of the white arms came a messenger, Iris . . . / She came on Helen in the chamber; she was weaving a great web, / a red folding robe, and working into it the numerous struggles / of Trojans, breakers of horses, and bronze-armoured Achaians, / struggles that they endured for her sake at the hands of the war god" (*Iliad* 3.121, 125–28; trans. Lattimore). The interruption comes at the precise moment when what Helen weaves is no longer historically accurate. Battles are no longer being fought for her sake on the plain, because the truce is established. Therefore Helen must go to the Wall to look around in order to insure that her recording will retain its accuracy. The suitors interrupting Penelope's Athene-inspired weaving (*Odyssey* 2.94–116) is a marvelous variation on the motif: They object to the weaving's function, which is holding the succession in suspense awaiting Odysseus. Penelope is weaving a version of history they object to *because it does not include them.*

Andromache is pathetically depicted as weaving the protective rose talismans into a garment for her beloved Hektor. When the terrible news comes that he has already been killed (*Iliad* 22.437–38), she drops the shuttle in futility and despair.

Slaves wove to keep people warm and comfortable with clothes and blankets. But why do powerful women like Kalypso and Arete, Helen and Penelope, weave their way through the Homeric poems? Queens weave to say something important, to weave blessings and curses — and when we associate weaving with speaking, an even more spectacular pattern suggests itself: *The primary cultural function of the Queen's weaving is historical — to preserve the record of the household's achievements and relationships. Weaving insures the continuance of the noble tradition.*

Just as the gods spin out destiny for mortals (e.g., *Odyssey* 3.208) women — like the bards who report to them — weave their history — as shown on the much later parallel, the Bayeux tapestry. Homer doesn't show us what Penelope has woven into her loom — as he does in the cases of Helen and Andromache in the *Iliad* — because Penelope's history is not determined until Odysseus returns. The subject-matter of her weaving is historically indefinite, where the impetus of Homeric poetry is toward precise definition. In *Iliad* 1, when Agamemnon declares he prefers to have Chryseis at his loom to Klytaimestra, the blasphemous insult to his royal wife is complete. He prefers the slave-girl as historian to Klytaimestra, thereby justifying Klytaimestra's radical revision of Mycenae's history (the plot she is weaving for him with Aegisthus, that culminates in her throwing a woven net over the king before she kills him. It's to avoid being snared by such a net that Odysseus, throughout his homecoming, weaves a web of deceitful words. When Odysseus, with Circe's help, descends into Hades, he goes there to learn ancient history from the women — and recent news from men. Having learned both, he is now prepared to restore order in Ithaka by designing the present to join his version of the past with his vision of the future[12]).

The metaphor then goes back the other way: Those who say something important are metaphorically "weaving." The technical image is woven into the Homeric poems from one end to the other. The bard in particular is seen as a weaver, weaving his frieze-like song from memory prompted, may we suggest, by the woven textiles on the walls of the banquet hall — those he is seeing and has seen, remembering old songs as well as new ones in other courts. When his memory dims, the tapestries remind him of the story's structure; just as when it comes time to reweave the faded tapestry, the Queen undertakes the reweaving accompanied by the best bard available. Oral poetry and textiles may have survived the Dark Age together, both issuing in the sculpture and ceramics of the geometric period.

The Fates are depicted as spinners; the Muses are women who weave memory and song, as daughters of Zeus (the principle of order) and Memory (and the story of Arachne and Athene is a perfect structural parallel to that of Thamyris and the Muses); Hekabe's offering gift to Athene of a stolen *peplos* (robe) turns the goddess's head against Troy; and Priam gives the same Sidonian robes back to Achillas in *Iliad* 24 (see discussion in Atchity, 1978, pp. 47–49); Ariadne led Theseus out of the Cretan labyrinth with her golden thread; Dawn, each morning, weaves the world with her rosy fingers — an anagoge of the spinning Aphrodite; and *Odyssey* 13.107–12 may even imply that the sea is woven by the Nymphs, as a vestige of the widespread creation-through-weaving myth. The myth of Pandora's creation recorded in Hesiod is the patriliny's reaction to all this female power — and a parallel to Agamemnon's bitter remarks in Hades (*Odyssey* 11.436–39): Woman is the source of all confusion![13]

We could perhaps push this interpretation further into metaphor. In the *Odyssey*, Helen appears with her spindle but is not shown actually weaving. Instead, she gives Telemachos a robe she herself has woven. Her own identity is complete (already woven) but can now serve as a warning to Telemachos, and is the perfect gift to his patrilineal marriage (*Odyssey* 15.125ff) — warning his bride-of-the-future not to run away from her husband (and the robe to be kept for that occasion by his mother, who deserves the patrilineal trust). At the opening of the *Odyssey*, Telemachos declares that no one knows his own father (1.216) — by patrilineal standards, a most disturbing situation. At poem's end, Telemachos and Odysseus are recognized and established as father and son (along with Laertes, representing the previous generation). The identification of Telemachos-Odysseus begins when, at Athene's behest, Telemachos undertakes his own odyssey to Nestor and Menelaos — and Helen recognizes him as his father's son (*Odyssey* 4.143); one who, as he nearly strings his father's bow, clearly has the power to become king in his time.

Helen doesn't actually weave in the world of the *Odyssey* because her historical identity, unlike Penelope's at the start of the poem, is now permanently determined. Homer tells us that she and Menelaos will have no more children (*Odyssey* 4.12–13), so she can give the fruit of her weaving away. On the other hand, Penelope's weaving is vitally important to the history the poem records. Her subterfuge suggests a correspondence between her three-year weaving and Odysseus's weaving of words.[14] Penelope works on her web through the day, weaving her hoped-for future; she unravels it at night because events have not justified her hopes and she must begin with a clean slate in the morning (or face the reality of the suitors). Finally the suitors surprise Penelope at her wishful weaving and force her to stop weaving and face reality just as she herself, with her verbal trickery (*Odyssey* 23.175ff), forces Odysseus to stop weaving his web of lies. Finally Penelope's weaving is transformed into the weaving-together of her body with Odysseus's in the woven bed—as the continuance of the patriliny eclipses the matrilineal power represented by her former weaving.

Why are the Homeric poems so rich with details about the techniques of craft—not only weaving, but also bow-making, ship-building, divine shield-making, and singing itself? Because artistic craft is important to the record they transmit, and to the meaning of that record. The crafts record events and confirm values, and stir individuals to concern about those values. Before Agamemnon can be betrayed by his wife, the court poet has to be gotten out of the house. At Odysseus's house, on the other hand, the poet is still at work, keeping at least some people from forgetting. Demodokos's song at the court of Arete moves Odysseus into revealing his hitherto-concealed relationship to historical memory.

From all these investigations—of matriliny, of Athene, and of weaving—we see that the women of whom Homer speaks lived in a very different world than the women of classical Athens. Some of these "heroines" had political, inheritance, and reproductive rights unimaginable to the women—or the poets—of the age when our texts were recorded, and unpalatable to the older poets in the line of transmission. Between the revisionism and the misunderstandings, we have inherited a literature which requires a good deal of sorting out. But if, like Helen on the wall of Troy, we take a good hard look at what is really going on, we can learn how to weave our scholarly tapestry more accurately.

Notes

1. Bilateral descent, the minor possibility for uxorilocality, is generally a concomitant of very simple (e.g., hunting and gathering—e.g., the Eskimo) or very complex (e.g., modern industrial) societies (van den Berghe, 1967, 94–5). Given the level of technology and organization indicated by archaeological as well as mythological evidence, we are rather safe in discarding this other possibility. For an interesting discussion that parallels our conclusions, see Thornton (especially chapter two, "The Wanderings of Odysseus," pp. 16–37); and a book we discovered as this essay went to press: Sarah Pomeroy, *Goddesses, Whores, Wives, and Slaves: Women in Classical Antiquity* (New York, 1975).

2. His refusal is the beginning of the end for Arete's way of life, and seems to be an example of the patrilineal scribes showing how the agent of Athene, Odysseus, got the better of the matrilineal domain of Poseidon. When Odysseus hears that Poseidon is the Phaiakians' chief god, and that it has been prophesied that their civilization will be destroyed for helping strangers, Athene beautifies him for the games. Her act is the first step in the process by which he seduces, through his technical mastery of acrobatics and also of story-telling, the scions of Poseidon into aiding, suicidally, the patriliny.

3. The special personal relationship of Achilles and Patroklos in the *Iliad* — based on "adopted kinship" rather than blood kinship (Atchity, 1978, esp. pp. 294–98) — may even reflect the Dorians' contribution to the amalgamating value-system: Achilles's loyalty to his friend-sworn-to-brotherhood becomes the primary motivation, and finally leads to his recommitment to his warrior function that brings him to combat with Hektor. Book 23 of the *Iliad* — like the civic scenes emblazoned on the shield of Achilles by Zeus's court craftsman Hephaistos (in *Iliad* 18, see Atchity, 1978, pp. 158–88) — presents a society organized on civic and civil principles similar to those of classical Athens, where equitable arbitration is more important than relationships among families and even more important than an individual's relationship to a god.

4. Georges Dumézil postulates throughout his works that IE society is ideologically divided into three (or, in a sense, four) different functions: (1a.) magico-religious sovereignty; (1b.) social / juridical sovereignty; (2) warrior; and (3) herdsman / craftsman / cultivator. See Scott Littleton's article, "Some Possible Indo-European Themes in the *Iliad*," reprinted in this volume.

5. The thunderbolt is not normally a war device in Greek mythology, whatever it might be in other cultures. Occasionally Zeus, or even Athene, uses it to destroy someone — but only as an imperious last resort. In general, Zeus employs his thunderbolt as a prophetic warning to mortals (e.g., *Iliad* 15.377–78, 17.593–96), and Athene uses it at the close of the *Odyssey* (24.538ff) to announce an end to war. Ares, the god of war, is never allowed so much as to touch the thunderbolts.

6. These terms have been discussed in various contexts, for example, by Benveniste (1973; 69–70, 397ff). The characterizations given here are not particularly new, but are needed to clarify the discussion.

7. For its tripartite iconography, cf. Littleton, 1970, pp. 320–21, and Yoshida, 1964.

8. It is a well-known axiom in both linguistics and rhetoric that the wider the scope of reference a term has, the less "meaning" — that is, differential power — it has. "Transfunctionality" is interesting: Irish, Indic, and other IE cultures also have female deities which cross the functional lines. But to stop there, especially with Athene, leaves us with a largely meaningless term. If the functions of the IE male social world do not fit a goddess, what functions do fit, and why?

9. At least in Attica and Ionia, where her cult is strongest and where Mycenaean carryovers are strongest.

10. That he should have two animals may yet be another vestige of his double origin. Bulls are strongly associated with the Minoan earthquake god, persisting in such stories as the bull of Poseidon sending the tidal wave that destroys Hippolytus. (Compare the Atlantis legend, too, for a deity connected with bulls and earthquakes.) On the other hand, horses are mentioned, e.g., *Iliad* 21.130–32, as the special sacrifice, by drowning, to a river god (along with the more normal and general sacrifice of bulls) — a custom that presumably came into the Aegean with the people who had the horses, the IE's. — cf., the Rhodian horse sacrifice, in which they were driven off a cliff.

11. In *Odyssey* (13.125–87) Zeus convinces Poseidon to cease from his direct interventions in mortal affairs and accept his own "symbolic" mode of influence — Poseidon agrees to set their ship in stone as a symbol rather than striking their city with the flat of his hand. Note the similarity between this and the situation of Genesis, when Yahweh promises Noah, with the rainbow as symbol of the promise, that he will no longer utterly destroy all creation. In both stories, a new covenant has been made. (Atchity and Hogart, forthcoming.)

12. We were led to this observation by Gerrit Schroder's speculation that the function of Hades in the *Odyssey* is analogous to Memory. The narrative of book 11 is Odysseus's (as he tells about his descent into the Phaiakians). He knows before he begins that Arete holds the power he requires for his purpose (his return to Ithaka) and he structures his story to accomplish his end. All kinds of dead souls gather around him (11.36–41); but after dealing

with the soul of his perished companion Elpenor and then receiving Teiresias's prophecy (an accurate summary of books 13–24), Odysseus stays to question the other souls – to learn more than other heroes might consider necessary to know. First his mother Antikleia answers his questions and instructs him on the ways of the world and of the underworld, ending by identifying her son's shamanic-historian role: "remember these things for your wife, so you may tell her hereafter" (11.223–24, trans. Lattimore). Odysseus is to return to *tell his court historian the truth*. He shows himself next as the arranger of chronicles, one who collects the stories he needs *in the order he chooses* (11.228–34).

His instructors, as he retells their stories for Arete and Alkinoos – are the wives and daughters of princes (11.227): Tyro, Antiope, Alkmene, Epikaste, Chloris, Leda, Iphimedeia, Phaidra, Prokris, Ariadne, Maira, and Klymene. These venerable ladies are the weavers of what might be called the "back-story" of the *Odyssey*, the ancient history upon which the poem's present is founded (also a convenient way of summarizing this history for Homer's audience). He stops with the example of Eriphyle, "who accepted precious gold for the life of her own dear husband" (11.327). The Phaiakians are struck silent.

Arete is the first to respond: "what do you think now of this man before you / for beauty and stature, and for the mind well balanced within him?" (11.336–37). She claims him as her special guest and orders them to honor him and serve his needs – because she recognizes Odysseus as the singular man who can learn the lesson of history from the women who keep it. Her executive action links the deep-memory Odysseus has assimilated in Hades with the future he desires – a future of conjugal harmony, which allows Arete to forgive his rejection of Nausikaa.

After that is accomplished, Alkinoos asks for man's news (11.370ff) – the stuff of *recent* memory, which occupies the remainder of Book 11 and includes misogynism as a recurring theme. The heroes Odysseus encountered, as he shows them to us now, are all asking us for news (like Alkinoos) – where the women *told* history. Odysseus serves the heroes as successfully as a powerful chronicler (11.517ff) as he had served the women as a careful listener and recorder. The Homeric narrative, dividing book 11 this way, brilliantly connects past, present, and future for its audience.

13. But Agamemnon fell into *his* fate because he didn't study history, as Odysseus does in book 11.85–332.

14. An argument can be made (see Atchity, forthcoming) that in the Homeric poems, the equation is weaving = thinking = speaking = acting = doing, finally equating deeds and words in the artistic fashioning of history. For Odysseus, history is "woven" by words, song, and textiles. This hero weaves his own plot before it happens, as when he and Athene sit beneath the tree to weave the downfall of the suitors; here is an advance over the *Iliad*'s world, where Helen's weaving serves to record history after it happens – or, at best, as it is happening. The *Odyssey* in this respect signals the birth of artistic introspection and foresight, under the patronage of foresightful Athene, whose craft is reflected in the words and technical versatility of Odysseus, and the technical loomcraft and words of Penelope – as well as in the poem itself, where the Homeric narrator weaves himself into the character of the hero so that, in book 9.10ff, hero and poet become effectively indistinguishable.

The parallel function of weaving, poetry, and sex is another matter: All are ways in which the individual expresses daemonic power to perpetuate himself and his culture. Considered in this light, Penelope's web becomes a kind of womb which she holds in preparation for Odysseus's return; and the way in which he describes his weaving of their marriage bed from the living olive tree underlines the mythic association of weaving with creation.

Works Cited

The authors are grateful to C. Scott Littleton and Udo Strutynski for their comments on this article, and have also drawn on the following:

Barber, E. J. W. "New Kingdom Egyptian Textiles: Embroidery vs Weaving." *American Journal of Archaeology* 86 (1982): 442–5.

Bolling, George Melville. "*Poikilos* and *Throna.*" *American Journal of Philology* (1958):275–82.

Brown, J. K. "A Note on the Division of Labor by Sex." *American Anthropologist* 72 (1970):1073–78.

Chiñas, B. L. *The Isthmus Zapotecs: Women's Roles in Cultural Context.* New York: Holt, Rinehart, and Winston, 1973.

Evans, David. Review of *Myth and Law Among the Indo-Europeans* (Jean Puhvel, ed.). In *American Journal of Sociology* 77 (1972):804–6.

Herington, C. J. *Athene Parthenos and Athene Polias.* Manchester, England: Manchester University Press, 1955.

Killen, J. T. "The Wool Industry of Crete in the Late Bronze Age." *Annual of the British School at Athens* 59 (1964):1–15.

Littleton, C. Scott. "Some Possible Indo-European Themes in the *Iliad.*" Originally in *Myth and Law Among the Indo-Europeans*, ed. Jean Puhvel. Berkeley and Los Angeles: University of California Press, 1970. Reprinted in this volume.

_____. *The New Comparative Mythology.* 3rd ed. Berkeley and Los Angeles: University of California Press, 1982.

_____. (1973b) "Poseidon as a Reflex of the Indo-European 'Source of Waters' God." *Journal of Indo-European Studies* 1 (1973):423–40.

Murdock, George P. *Ethnographic Atlas.* Pittsburg: University of Pittsburg Press, 1967.

Nilsson, Martin P. *History of Greek Religion.* Oxford: Oxford University Press, 1952.

Perry, Walter Copland. *The Women of Homer.* New York, 1898.

Pfuhl, E. *De Atheniensium Pompis Sacris.* Berlin: Weidmann, 1900.

Rose, H. J. *A Handbook of Greek Mythology.* New York: Dutton, 1959.

Schlegel, A. *Male Dominance and Female Autonomy.* Human Relations Area Files Press, 1972.

Strutynski, Udo. "The Three Functions of the Indo-European Tradition in the *Eumenides* of Aeschylus." In *Myth and Law Among the Indo-Europeans*, ed. Jean Puhvel, 211–18. Berkeley and Los Angeles: University of California Press, 1972.

Thornton, Agathe. *People and Themes in Homer's Odyssey.* London: Metheun, 1970.

van den Berghe, Pierre L. *Human Family Systems: An Evolutionary View.* New York: Elsevier, 1979.

Yoshida, Atsuhiko. "La Structure de l'Illustration du Bouclier d'Achille." *Revue Belge de Philologie et d'Histoire* 42 (1964):5–15.

[On Translating Homer]   Robert Fitzgerald*

I

A living voice in firelight or in the open air, a living presence bringing into life his great company of imagined persons, a master performer at his ease, touching the strings, disposing of many voices, many tones and tempos, tragedy, comedy, and glory, holding his auditors in the palm of his hand: was Homer all of this? We can only suppose that he was. If what we imagine is true, Homer must himself have been his poems, in a physical sense unequalled in the case of any poet since. Imagine *Henry IV* and *The Tempest* composed not for production by a company of actors but as solo performances by Shakespeare himself. Or imagine it in the case of either, not both. The notion is still astonishing, and it is difficult to believe it.

I learn from W. S. Merwin, in the introduction to his translations of *Spanish Ballads* (Anchor, 1961), that the wandering *juglares* of medieval Spain, who sang and recited the epic *cantares*, "might be accompanied in their performance by mimes, known as *remendadores*, and *cazarros* — a name which included clowns and most varieties of stunt man." Well, stunt men, or tumblers, are mentioned as performing along with a poet or singer at Meneláos' court in Book IV of *The Odyssey*. But no mimes assist any [*àoidós*] in the Homeric poems. This of itself would not prove that Homer did his own impersonations. The [*àoidós*] as Homer presented him was a figure of the heroic age, four or five centuries before his time. But so far as I know there is no evidence whatever that Homer himself, or the [*àoidós*] in his immediate tradition, or their successors, the rhapsodes, were accompanied by mimes or actors.

We have no perfect word for [*àoidós*], for the kind of artist Homer was. "Bard" was fairly exact but has become a joke. "Skald" takes us too far into druidical regions. "Minstrel" is better but still too slight, too trammeled with doublet and hose, and faintly raffish after Gilbert & Sullivan. The Italian compound word *cantastorie* is at least neutral and is a definition of sorts. Lord did well to adopt the English equivalent, "singer of tales." But I am not satisfied. The term does not do justice to the creative and inventive power of the [*àoidós*]. It does not suggest his mimetic art. And there is a difficulty about "singer" as a term for the poet and performer of these things.

That the telling of a story, and the incidental acting of roles, should be called "singing" — this will strike us at first as affected or strange. We

*Abridgment of "Postscript" by Robert Fitzgerald, © 1962 by the Comparative Literature Committee of Indiana University and © 1963 by Robert Fitzgerald. Reprinted from *Homer: The Odyssey*, translated by Robert Fitzgerald. By permission of Doubleday & Company, Inc.

may indeed think of opera, disciplined and expressive opera like the *Orfeo* of Gluck, true lyric theatre as the Italians call it; but the orchestra and the stage, the whole convention, are alien to Homer. Perhaps it is enough to recall certain fine acting voices. As a child I sat aloft in the second balcony of an old theatre in Illinois while a traveling company played *Sancho Panza*, and I remember the beautiful voice of the late Otis Skinner rising effortless, malleable and pure, or falling to a crystalline whisper, far off there below, in unhurried declamation, while the whole theatre sat spellbound by that human instrument alone. There is no doubt that the master [*aoidós*] had a gift like that, a trained voice of great expressive and melodic range.

By all accounts, too, the Homeric performer used a second instrument and depended on it: the [*kítharis*], an affair of a few gut strings with some kind of resonator, possibly a tortoise shell, like the later lyre. It would be anachronistic to think of it as a guitar or lute, so I call it a "gittern harp" and sometimes refer to the performer as a harper. Homer describes him more than once as plucking or strumming an overture to a given tale or song, and he must have used the instrument not only for accompaniment but for pitch, and to fill pauses while he took thought for the next turn. No doubt the instrument marked rhythm, too.

We need not delude ourselves as to how far these generalities really take us. How in particular the voice, the metered verse, and the stringed instrument were related in these performances, and in the recital of poetry throughout antiquity, I do not well understand, and I do not think anyone does perfectly. In our own tradition the "music of verse" is one thing and "music" proper is another. A song is a song, not necessarily a poem. *The Peaceful Western Wind* and *Mistress Mine* indeed happen to be both, and I have heard Christopher Casson lean to a small Irish harp and sing *Oft in the Stilly Night* so attentively that it seemed twice the poem I had known before. But this is exceptional. Who would set to music the great lyrics of Yeats? Who could improve on Lear by scoring it? Here all is in the shape and movement of metered language. But we find the verse of Homer — and this is my point — as beautiful in itself as the verse of Yeats or Shakespeare. What we call a "musical arrangement" would disperse or confuse the effect of it. We can be sure, I think, that harp or [*kítharis*] played a very subdued part, however essential, in the original Homeric performance.

II

One of our first discoveries in reading Homer will be that he was a poet in our sense of the word, a man gifted at making verse. All the learning that we may later assemble, all we can know or guess of the artist as an improviser and entertainer, even our fugitive sense of him as the demiurge of a world transfigured, all this cannot supersede — indeed it is founded on — our pleasure in him line by line, the way we hear or read him. I will never forget how unexpectedly moved I was years ago when for the first time I heard Telémakhos in Book I speak of his father as [*anéros, oû dé pou leúk' ostéa púthetai ómbrōi*]. Looking up, I said to myself, in effect, "Why, this really is poetry!" and I meant poetry as good as "Call for the robin redbreast and the wren." Many times afterward, in reading or translating Homer, I have again paused over a line or a pair of lines in recognition and homage.

Parry thought this incomparable medium, the formulaic hexameter, had been shaped through centuries of trial and error, a testing and refining process conducted on many occasions before generations of auditors, so that in the end only the fittest language survived and the virtuoso had at his command the best words in the best order for anything he cared to relate or invent. I used at first to feel that the recurrent epithets and formula lines were a mere convention and a bore. In time I realized that they were musical phrases, brief incantations, of which the miserable renderings gave little or no idea. These formulas entered the repertory not only because they were useful but because they were memorable, I mean because nobody who had once heard them could easily forget them; and that is true to this day.

[Émos d' érigéneia phánē hrododáktulos éōs]

It is possible that by Homer's time even he could not have said precisely what the two epithets in this line meant—and there are a number of others of which the same is true—but the line had been kept for its fragrance, a fragrance of Dawn, inimitable and unsurpassable, no more boring in its recurrence than Dawn itself. Because there are hundreds of lines like this and more hundreds of half lines and phrases, the very medium of Homer is pervaded by lyric quality. The simplest phrases have it. Hear Hektor saying (*Iliad* VI, 264), "Don't offer me any sweet wine, dear Mother":

[mḗ moi oînon áeire melíphrona, pótnia mḗter]

How could you render that? Consider the voweling, and consider how the first epithet, after the ghost of a pause, hovers between "wine" and "mother." There is, besides, a peculiar cleanliness and lightness of movement, as often in Homer, and there is something else that I call the cut or sculpture of words. It is easiest to be aware of this in the last two feet of certain hexameters: [*noston hetaírōn* and *'éndon eóntōn*]. These are rounded shapes.

I am not being what Professor Irving Babbitt used to call "fanciful." If you will make the effort to imagine this Greek as still virgin of any visual signs at all, associated with no letters, no Greek characters, no script, no print—as purely and simply expressive sound, you will be able to perceive it in the air, its true medium, and to hear how it shapes and tempers the air by virtue of stops and tones. I will quote two more lines, one for consonants, and one for vowels. The first is Aphroditê saying in *Iliad* V, 359,

[*phíle kasígnēte, kómisaí té me dòs dé moi híppous*]

in which we hear the light tongue of the goddess of love herself in three coquettish particles, [*te . . . te . . . de . . .*]. My second example is the first line sung by those temptresses of the sea, known to Homer as Seirênês, and it is a typical triumph of formulary art since it is a modified version of a line that occurs in *The Iliad* in quite a different context, and in the mouth of quite a different personage. Here it is, XII 184:

[*Deûr' ắg' iồn, polúain' 'Oduseû, méga kūdos 'Achaiồn*]

There is a rhythm of anapests, and intricate rhyming: [*Deu*] and [*seu*] on the beat, [*iú*] on the offbeat and [*ku*] on the beat, [*ain*] and [*ai*] on the beat, [*ōn*] on the beat and [*ōn*] on the offbeat, and [*ag*] turned round widdershins on [*méga*]: this is a conjuring kind of echolalia. But more: the crooning vowels are for low seductive voices, rising in mid-line with [*ain*] and then rising and opening with a savage shout in [*Achaiồn*] at the end.

You might call this sort of thing "phonetic wit" — though it may have come to the artist without calculation. Along with it, in Homer, there is a lot of verbal wit enjoyed for its own sake and also syntactical wit, a quality of style that Chapman and Pope could appreciate. Chiastic order is a favorite form, and *The Iliad* especially teems with it.

[*lígxe biós, neurề dè még' iácken, ằlto d' ỏistos*]

I could go on indefinitely, but I should cut this short and say that we are not meant very often to stop and consider so curiously. The narrative pace does not encourage it. You can be a connoisseur of the single line if you like, but this is only the beginning of appreciation. Homer is lyric but rarely indulges the lyric, he keeps his surface alive but keeps it moving; the line is only the medium, as I began by calling it, and as such it is subordinate to practically everything else. It is subordinate in the first place to the passage, to the effect created by the placement of lines in succession. Continuous prose cannot achieve the switches and surprises that you get by playing on a regular meter, a measured base. Of these effects Homer, formulas and all, was a master. We have often heard how the movement of the hexameter line itself could be varied by pauses, lightened by dactyls, retarded by spondees; but we have heard less of what could happen in the movement from line to line and in the course of action or speeches. A change of pace, a change of mood, an ironic aside, a quick look into the past or into the distance — we find all these between one line and the next.

Homer's humor, too, in *The Iliad* rather grim or slapstick, in *The Odyssey* more subtly comic, often dawns on us at the unexpected swerve of a new line. In *Iliad* VIII there is a crash of lightning against the Akhaians and the best charioteers give way: Idómeneus retreats, Agamémnon retreats, big Aias and little Aias retreat, but Nestor? Nestor alone stood fast, we hear, and just as we begin to admire the veteran the next line says (81),

[oŭ ti ʿekōn, àll' híppos ʿeteíreto]

"Not that he wanted to in the least, but one of his horses was disabled," In *Odyssey* IV, after Helen's story of how virtuously she kept Odysseus' secret when she had recognized him spying in Troy, Meneláos cannot refrain from a pointed story to keep the record straight. There is a march of hexameters extolling Odysseus' courage when he and the Akhaian captains were waiting in the wooden horse to bring death upon the Trojans. Then abruptly, in 274, [êlthes ʿepeita sù keîse]. The words make a trochee and two amphibrachs: "Who should come by there but *you* then" — and he goes on to tell of the peril she put them all in by mimicking the voices of their wives. You can see this trick of the sudden change of movement and tone played by Eurýmakhos in *Odyssey* I, 405, when after several lines of hearty assurance to Telémakhos he looks at him harder, [àll' ʿethélō se, phériste, perì xeínoio ʿerésthai] and the sneer becomes, yes, audible.

Another thing, more highly dramatic, is of course the calculated and gradated heightening of tone or energy throughout a longer passage. For a crescendo of passion, I suppose Akhilleus' great tirade in *Iliad* IX, 307 sqq., cannot be matched, but Odysseus, among his other gifts of gab, has a way of beginning mild and ending deadly. In XVIII there are two examples, a relatively brief one in his reply to Iros, 15 sqq., and a longer one to Eurýmakhos, 366 sqq.

Now all these that I have mentioned are tiny applications of a principle everywhere at work over the expanse of both poems. Narrative art lives as a river lives, first by grace of tributaries — in Homer by the continual refreshment of invention and unlooked-for turns — and second by the direction of flow. If in the line and passage the poems are interesting, as they are, heaven knows they are even more interesting, in the ways they take as their currents widen. Not that Homer is free of *longueurs:* Phoinix' tale of Meleagros in *Iliad* IX strikes me as windy, and in the slow movement of *The Odyssey* at least one of the digressions and retards — the pedigree of Theoklýmenos — was too much even for this virtuoso to bring off. He nods, and we nod with him. But almost always the attention of the audience is courted and held. The earliest critics noticed how Homer varied his effects: for an offhand example, Telémakhos arrives off Pylos by sea at dawn, arrives at Sparta by land at nightfall. The battle scenes in *The Iliad* are sometimes thought monotonous; in fact they are prodigiously inventive and differ one from another not only in general shape but in detail: time after time, it is true, a man falls and his armor clangs upon him, but either he or the man next to him has just been killed in an entirely new way. The formulas give the narrative musical consistency; the innovations keep it alive. The more it is the same, the more it changes. In the very use of the formulas themselves, remarkable effects are got by slight additions or modifications. Penélopê's visits to the banquet hall in *The Odyssey* are formulary: she appears with her maids, she draws her veil down and across her face, she speaks, she retires, weeps, and goes to sleep. The first time (I, 365) after she is gone the suitors make a din, they all swear they will have her; the second time (XVI, 413) she appears and retires as before but there is no din, no swearing; the third time (XVIII, 212) there is no din, but on her appearance (not on her withdrawal) a new line is added to the formula, telling us that the suitors knees were weakened with lust for her; then comes the swearing line from Book I. Someone has called this trick of style "incremental repetition." It can be, as it is in this case, very powerful.

III

These notes may suggest some of the pleasures and complexities of going to see for yourself. I am forever grateful for my days on Ithaka as I am for other days, few but moving, in Athens and elsewhere in Greece. A rendering for the opening of Book III,

[*Ēélios d' anórouse, lipòn perikalléa límnēn*]

came into my head in the Saronic Gulf, and a week later at sunrise in Heraklion I found words for the next phrase, [*ouranòn es polúchalkon*]. By these and other keepsakes I am reminded that if I had never listened to the cicadas and drunk the resined wine I would have done the job differently, if I had done it at all. But most of it was what all writing is, a sedentary labor, or joy, sustained at a worktable. At one elbow, in this case, there were always those lines and parts of lines that have been pored over by so many for centuries. Of the puzzling ones I will give a few more examples, two at least of them notorious, with some account of the elucidation I think they demand. Multiply these cases by a thousand, and you will see what the preliminary or incidental work was like. As befits a dramatic poem, the first case is a tiny detail of action.

In Book XI, Odysseus hears the shade of Agamémnon tell how Aigísthos and Klytaimnestra murdered him on his return from Troy, and with him his companions. They were all butchered, he says bitterly, like swine. I take it that he means what he says. The way you butcher a pig is by piercing or cutting his throat, and it does not seem unreasonable to imagine here, and to bear in mind elsewhere, that this is what happened to Agamémnon. He describes the banquet scene, the laden tables, and the floor fuming with blood where the victims lay. Then, in line 421, he says he heard a most piteous cry from his royal slave and mistress, Kassandra,

. . . [*tèn kteíne Klytaiméstrē dolómētis
amph' emoí, autàr egò potì gaíēi cheíras aéirōn
bállon apothnéskōn perì phasgánōi*]

and great difficulty has been found in grasping precisely what action this passage was meant to convey. Klytaimnestra was in the act of killing Kassandra, so much is clear, and Kassandra was close beside the fallen Agamémnon. But what does he say he himself was doing? Consider it word for word in the order in which it appears: "but I upon (or against) the ground lifting my hands / was throwing [them] while dying around the swordblade." Half the problem is to divide or punctuate this.

On one prevailing interpretation we should divide or punctuate after [bállon] and must therefore take [apothnéskōn perì phasgánoi] to mean "dying around the swordblade," that is, with a blade left in his body. This is contrary to slaughtering procedure, but Professor W. B. Stanford in his annotated edition of *The Odyssey* tells us that there are many precedents for taking it so. He refers to four passages in *The Iliad* and to one in Sophocles' *Ajax*. With all respect I must say that none of these makes a good precedent for Stanford's reading, because in none of them does anyone die "around a swordblade" left in him by anyone else. Ajax has, of course, impaled himself on his own sword. Of the cases cited in *The Iliad*, one is concerned with an arrow and two with spears, weapons often left sticking in tenacious parts of the foe. It is otherwise with a sword; a sword in these poems was something a killer held onto if he could. The fourth case in *The Iliad* might be a better precedent, not for Stanford's notion of Agamémnon's wound but for mine (since it is an allusion to slaughtering), if the preposition used were not [perì] instead of [àmphi]. In short, the evidence is inconclusive.

Moreover, if you adopt this awkward reading, you are left with a clause that represents Agamémnon as lifting his hands and throwing them. With what purpose? Or perhaps I should ask, with what aim? Victor Bérard imagined that he meant to shield Kassandra. A. T. Murray, the Loeb translator, thought he tried to hit Klytaimnestra. Butcher and Lang, W. H. D. Rouse, and T. E. Lawrence accepted "let fall" as a translation of [bállon:] he lifted his hands and helplessly let them fall. Others, including Stanford, take [potì gaíē] as "against the ground" with [bállon] and suggest that he beat his hands against the ground to invoke vengeance from infernal powers.

I cannot myself hear the shade of the hero saying any of these things, except possibly what Murray has him say. But it is quite possible to punctuate the lines in another way, like this: "But I upon the ground, lifting my hands, was thowing them — while dying — around the swordblade." Or to put it in English, "As I lay on the ground I heaved up my hands and flung them with a dying effort around the swordblade." There is a scholion in which the lines are so understood, but the scholiast adds [pròs ekspásai tò xíphos] "to pull out the sword" — no doubt in order to die more quickly. G. H. Palmer, one of the few translators to follow the scholiast, settled for "clutched" as a rendering for [bállon]. This was logical, since Palmer, like the Alexandrian and like Stanford, conceived the blade as embedded in Agamémnon. A man with a blade in his midriff would not "fling" his hands around it when all he had to do was, precisely, to clutch it. But [*bállon*] is stronger than "clutch," and the sword was not in Agamémnon, in any case. He would have had to heave up and fling his hands around the blade if the blade were a short distance away, within reach but still requiring an effort. This is where the sword of Klytaimnestra must have been while she slashed or poked at Kassandra. Therefore I prefer to think that as Klytaimnestra used the sword, Agamémnon, reckless of his hands, tried to get it away from her. Alone among modern translators, so far as I can discover, E. V. Rieu adopted this reading. It not only satisfies all the conditions, syntactical and verbal, but it makes all possible dramatic sense of the line.

IV

If you think of the poem as a play or a cinema — inevitable if not irresistible thoughts — you will find many problems for the set designer and the property man. There are two fine ones in the big closing scenes. How precisely are we to visualize the contest with Odysseus' hunting bow, announced by Penélopê in Book XIX and carried out in Book XXI? And in Book XXII what precisely is the layout of the great hall and adjoining passage by which the suitors, for the moment out of sight of Odysseus, are given throwing spears at a crucial point in the fight? The Greek is ambiguous or sketchy.

In XIX Penélopê tells her interesting new confidant of a sudden decision: next day her suitors will be challenged to perform an old feat of her husband's, and she will be the prize. It is a feat (line 573) with [*pelékeas,*] axes,

> [*toùs pelékeas, toùs keînos enì megároisin eoîsin*
> *hístasch' hexeíes, druóchous ós, dṓdeka pántas.*
> *stàs d'hó ge pollòn áneuthe diarríptasken öïstón.*]

"those axes that he used to set up in his hall all twelve in line like a ship's ribs (or props), then he would take his stand far off and shoot an arrow through." The prize will go to that suitor who most easily strings her husband's bow and "shoots through all twelve axes." To this Odysseus replies in effect that tomorrow is not too soon; her husband will be there before any of the younger men can string the bow [*dioïsteusái te sidéron*] "and shoot through the iron." It need not escape us that this phrase is rather an addition. We might imagine shooting through twelve axes if they were arranged in a line slightly staggered, leaving an interval of an inch or so for the arrow to pass. The alternative is to image apertures in the axeheads, and the phrase of Odysseus, repeated by Telémakhos in Book XXI, inclines us to that. He speaks with familiarity, not to mention his remarkable confidence. It is not the speech of a man still interested in concealing from his wife how well he knows her husband.

If the arrow is to pass "through the iron" and we interpret this to mean through apertures in the axeheads, then what apertures are meant? D. B. Monro in his edition of *The Odyssey*, Books XIII–XXIV, printed drawings of two perforated ancient axeheads, one from a Mycenean excavation, another from an early classical metope, and a third drawing of the very late classical *bipennis*, a double axe whose crescent blades form by their inner edges two circular openings, the one above the haft open and unobstructed. An arrow could pass through any one of these types of axeheads. With archaeological backing, then, we may imagine twelve pervious axes in alignment for the contest. Penélopê's phrase, "like a ship's ribs (or props)," in fact makes us see twelve axes stuck in the ground by their helves.

Oddly enough, there are quite serious objections to this reading. When we say "axe" we mean axehead and helve together. But it seems more likely that the word [*pélekus*] to Penélopê meant "axehead" alone. In Book V when Kalypso gives Odysseus a [*pélekus*] for cutting timber, she must complete the gift with a [*steileión*], or helve of olive wood (line 236). In all the references to the gauntlet Odysseus' arrow had to run, there is no allusion to a [*steileión*], though a closely related word appears. On the contrary, when Penélopê brings the bow back from the storeroom in XXI, her maids bring along a basket full of iron and bronze "accessories of the contest," certainly axeheads without helves. Any normal axehead, then as now, had an aperture: it had the socket hole where a helve could be fitted. Is there positive evidence that this was the aperture in question? There is indeed.

When Odysseus finally makes his prize-winning shot in 21.420 sqq., we hear that

[*pelékeōn d'ouk ēmbrote pántōn*
prótēs steileiēs, dià d' amperès ēlthe thúraxe]

"he didn't miss the [*prótēs steileiēs*] of all the axeheads, and the arrow went clean through and out." Confusion about the word [*steileiē*] appears to be ancient and inexhaustible; it was taken very early to mean "helve" or "haft" — that is, to be a synonym for [*steileión*] — and translators in torment have tried to make sense of a shot that did not miss the first axe helve. But if Homer had meant that, if he had meant [*prótou steileioû*], he could have said it. It is metrically equivalent and phonetically a little better. Professor Stanford thinks, and with excellent reason, that the difference in gender may be significant. He agrees with the twelfth century Archbishop of Thessalonica, Eusthathius, that the feminine form, [*steileiē*], meant "socket" as [*steileión*] meant "helve." What Homer intended to say was very simple: that Odysseus didn't miss his bull's eye, the first socket hole in the line of twelve.

It is a perfect conclusion, but it lets us in for other difficulties. If the axeheads were without helves, if each was turned so that its socket hole faced the archer, how were they set up and supported? In what respect was the line of axeheads comparable to "a ship's ribs (or props)"? The second question is easier to answer: the point of similarity could have been merely that in both cases there were equal intervals between one and another. As to the way of setting up the axeheads, all we have to go on are two lines and a half, XXI sqq., in which Telémakhos prepares the contest:

> [prōtonmen pelékeas stēsen, dià táphron òrúxas
> pâsi mían makrḗn, kai èpì státhmēn ȉthunen,
> àmphì dè gaîan ḕnaxe.]

Literally, "first he set up the axeheads, after digging a trench through for all, a single trench, a long one, and he trued [it or them] to the line, and he pressed earth on both sides." It is pertinent to remember that in Homer's "additive" style items are not always given in any particular order. That is, the pressing of the earth could have preceded or accompanied the truing, and we may understand that he trued the axeheads, not the trench. If we held the theory that axeheads fitted on helves were being set up, a trench would bed the helves, around which earth could then be pressed to hold them upright. I have given the evidence against that. On the other and better theory that axeheads alone were used, is there anything in the context to suggest how they were held up?

Well, a byproduct of a trench is a long pile of loose earth. If the loose earth beside the trench were "pressed" up in a narrow ridge, with peaks at equal distances, the axeheads could be stuck in these, one blade in the earth and one out, since the [pélekus] was double-bladed. The verb [nássō] that appears here in the aorist active, [ḕnaxe], "pressed," had the sense "be piled" in the passive in later Greek. The very point of digging a trench could have been to supply enough earth for this purpose; if it had been a matter of embedding axe helves, they could have been planted in a line of holes like fence posts or fruit trees. It is a good deal to read into these lines, but I am willing to risk it because I see nothing else for it. Telémakhos made a bedding of earth for the axeblades and trued them [èpí státhmēn], to the line," by the wall builder's immemorial technique, a stretched cord. One more question: if set up in this way, could the axeheads have been high enough for the bowshot from the door? Odysseus made the bowshot while seated on his stool. He held the bow horizontally in the usual ancient style. If he shot from the hip just above knee level in a flat trajectory, the axeheads as I see them could have been at the right height.

V

Details like these may turn out to be self-consistent, but what of the poem as a whole? Does it hang together? Did a single composer hold it all in his mind? Whatever opinion we may hold on the famous Question, we may accept at least one modest principle: when proof to the contrary is lacking, any given passage should be interpreted in consonance with the rest. Take the eagles.

During the assembly scene in Book II, Zeus launches two eagles from a ridge, either [*tôi d'*] / [*tó d'*] according to the alternative readings. The Oxford editor, T. W. Allen, reasonably chose the first, meaning "for him," that is, for the last speaker, Telémakhos. The eagles are to be an omen for him. When in their gliding flight they reach a point over the center of the agora they wheel and beat their wings, and then we have two more alternative readings, [*es d' idétēn pántōn kephalás*] or [*es d' hikétēn pántōn kephalas*], that is, either the pair "looked at the heads of all [below]" or they "came down on" all the heads. Again Allen chose the reading more charged with life and sense: "came down on." In the next clause, [*óssonto d' óléthron,*] the verb has changed from the dual form, used when the pair of birds was the subject, to a plural form. Does this mean a change of subject? Not necessarily; Homer often uses plural verb forms for dual subjects; indeed he has already done so once in this passage, though not in this sentence. If it does mean a change of subject, then the "heads," or men in the crowd, are said to behold death or doom in the diving eagles; if it does not mean a change of subject, the diving eagles are said to make doom visible to the men, or in a word to menace them with doom. "Death was in their glare," as Murray ingeniously puts it, making perhaps the best of both alternatives. Perhaps, but wait. The next line presents us again with a dual form, this time in a middle participle. It goes:

[*drupsaménō d' ónúchessi pareiàs, amphí te deiràs.*]

"tearing, this pair, with talons, cheeks, and all around necks (or throats)."

Now, the received interpretation of this, cited by Liddell & Scott and followed by Murray and practically everyone, takes the middle voice of the verb as reflexive here, meaning they tore *each other's* cheeks and throats. But first let me observe that the middle may or may not have this shade of meaning. It is the voice you would use in Greek if you wanted to say, "We cut ourselves a slice," and you would not be referring to a knife fight. Second, if the two eagles are a sign, what after all do they signify? What future event do they portend? The old augur Halithersês has no doubt, and neither have we: they stand for the return of Odysseus and the doom of the suitors. Why two eagles? In order that the sign, a sign for Telémakhos, may give him, or at any rate ourselves, to understand that he and Odysseus together will attack the suitors. The two eagles correspond to the two royal assailants. Why then should they assail one another? What would any intelligent augur make of that? No, no, surely; they assail the suitors, who have been arraigned by Telémakhos in the assembly, and if this were not the case there would be no point in their having "come down on the heads of all," for an eagle fight would have been as well, or better conducted high in the air. A scholiast says, [*tò dè katadrúpsai tàs pareiàs tòn tōn mnēstérōn esémane phónon*], and *he* does not use the middle but the active voice: "that business of tearing the [suitors'] cheeks signified the suitors' violent death." We are to see the eagles' portent not merely "in their glare" but in their ripping talons.

Between Book II and Book XV no eagles fly, or at any rate no significant ones, but in Book XV, 160, as Telémakhos is taking leave of Menelaos and Helen, just as he is saying how fine it would be to meet his father on Ithaka so that he could tell him of their hospitality, [*epéptato dexiòs órnis, aietòs argēn chēna phérōn*] "a bird, an eagle, flew up on the right, lugging a white goose." This portent is quickly interpreted by Helen. It means, she says, that just as the eagle flew from the wild mountain of his birth to pounce on the domestic bird, so Odysseus will appear out of the rough world of his wanderings to avenge the wrongs done him at home. Near the end of the same Book (525 sqq.) the motif is repeated. Again the omen appears as if in comment on a speech by Telémakhos, who has just been wondering aloud whether anything will prevent his mother's marriage to Eurýmakhos. This time the portentous bird is not an eagle, [*aietós*], but a hawk, [*kírkos*], carrying a captured dove. And this time the interpretation is not given immediately; it is given to Penélopê in Book XVII (152 sqq.) by the diviner, Theoklýmenos, who tells her it meant that Odysseus had already landed on Ithaka. Again there is an interval of two Books, and in XIX (535 sqq.) the motif comes to a kind of flowering when Penélopê recounts her "dream" to the beggar, who is Odysseus. This time there is a more exact correspondence between the terms of the equation; Penélopê was in a position to be exact. Upon the geese feeding at her house

[*elthòn d'ex óreos mégas aietòs agkulocheíles*
pâsi kat' auchénas éxe kai éktanen]

"coming from the mountain a great eagle with crooked beak broke their necks and killed them all."

Thus in four passages the descent of Odysseus on the suitors has been foreboded or foreseen in strikes made by birds of prey. In three cases the attacking birds are eagles; once it is a hawk. The appearance of the motif twice in Book XVII and once again in Book XIX harks back to its introduction in Book II. It also anticipates the climax of the fight in Odysseus' hall in Book XXII. At that point Athena unfurls her storm cloud, the aegis, overhead, and the surviving suitors break and run like cattle stung by gadflies. Now (302) comes the simile:

[*hoi d'hōs t' aigypioí gampsónuches angkulocheîlai*
ex oréōn elthóntes ep' orníthessi thórōsi, ktl]

"But the pursuers, like [*aigypioí*] with hooked talons and crooked beak issuing from the mountains to dive on flights of birds, etc." We had expected eagles, [*aietoí*], or hawks, [*kírkoi*], but the word is [*aigypioí*], and I am distressed to say that the usual translation of it is "vultures."

Liddell & Scott give "vulture" for [*aigypiós*]. But let us consider the case patiently. We have not met the word before in *The Odyssey*. Liddell & Scott and the Homeric lexicographer, Autenrieth, cite three occurrences in *The Iliad*. In Book VII, 59, when Athena and Apollo are represented as taking their seats on the oak of Zeus as Hektor challenges the Akhaians,

[*hetzésthēn ŏrnisin eoikótes aigypioîsi*]

"They perched like birds, like [*aigypioí*]." In Book XVII, 460, Automedon making chariot forays among the Trojans is likened to an [*aigypioís*] among geese. Most interesting of all is the case in Book XVI, 428, when Patroklos and Sarpedon clash in battle — for here the first line of the simile is the very same line that we find repeated in *The Odyssey*:

[*hoi d'hŏs t' aigypioì gampsónuches ankulocheîlai
pétrē eph' hupsēle megála klátzonte máchōntai*

"like [*aigypioí*] with hooked talons and crooked beak / on a high rock, crying loud, they fought."

Now, it seems to me that on the Homeric evidence there is something wrong with translating this word as "vulture." A vulture as we understand the term is a carrion bird rather than a hunting bird, and in every context of both *Iliad* and *Odyssey* where a vulture in our sense is clearly indicated Homer uses the word [*gýps*]. In no instance, as we have seen, is [*aigypiós*] used of a carrion bird; on the contrary, in two cases, one in *The Iliad* and one on our climactic simile in *The Odyssey*, it is used of a hunting bird, and in one of the two remaining cases it supplies a simile for two gods at rest on a bough. If Homer had meant [*gýps*] he could have used [*gýps*], a handy word and one he used often enough elsewhere. But he used another word, and used it because he unquestionably meant another thing. He meant a bird like a hawk or an eagle, a killer, a threat to geese, a hunter of small birds in general. He did not mean the stinking buzzard that feeds on corpses left by others.

In the first edition of my *Odyssey* I translated [*aigypioí*] in Book XXII as "eagles" to go with the eagle passages that lead up to it. I went too far. If the poet had wished to say "eagles" he could have used the word for eagles, [*aietòi*]. Instead, he lifted a line from *The Iliad*, as he often did, presumably because it would suit his purpose here. How, then, should [*aigypioí*] be rendered? Well, I see that John Moore, in his recent excellent vision of Sophocles' *Ajax*, (The Complete Greek Tragedies, ed. Lattimore & Grene, Chicago), encountering this problem in line 169,

[*mégan aigypiòn d' hupodeísantes, ktl*]

translates

But fear of the huge falcon, etc.

possibly in view of considerations like those I have been expounding. In revising I have followed his example. I hope Homer would be better pleased. No doubt the four attackers in Book XII are more justly likened to falcons than to eagles if, as I suspect, falcons more often hunt in company; the wild eagle, unless paired by Zeus, I imagine hunts alone.

VI

A word about "translation." *The Odyssey*, considered strictly as an aesthetic object, is to be appreciated only in Greek. It can no more be translated into English than rhododendron can be translated into dogwood. You must learn Greek if you want to experience Homer, just as you must go to the Acropolis and look at it if you want to experience the Parthenon. There is a sense, however, in which the Greek poem was itself a translation. It was a translation into Homer's metered language, into his narrative and dramatic style, of an action invented and elaborated in the imagination. This action and the personages involved in it were what mattered most to poet and audience.

It might be possible to translate, or retranslate, this action into our language. We may assume that Homer used all the Greek he knew, all the resources of the language available to him and amenable to his meter. Three or more Greek dialects and perhaps half a millennium of Greek hexameter poetry contributed to Homer's language; so did a wide spectrum of idiom from the hieratic to the colloquial. Anglo-Irish-American provides comparable linguistic and poetic resources, a spectrum of idiom comparably wide. If you can grasp the situation and action rendered by the Greek poem, every line of it, and by the living performer that it demands, and if you will not betray Homer with prose or poor verse, you may hope to make an equivalent that he himself would not disavow.

Why care about an old work in a dead language that no one reads, or at least no one of those who, glancing at their Rolex watches, guide us into the future? Well, I love the future myself and expect everything of it: better artists than Homer, better works of art than *The Odyssey*. The prospect of looking back at our planet from the moon seems to me to promise a marvelous enlargement of our views. But let us hold fast to what is good, hoping that if we do anything any good those who come after us will pay us the same compliment. If the world was given to us to explore and master, here is a tale, a play, a song about that endeavor long ago, by no means neglecting self-mastery, which in a sense is the whole point. Electronic brains may help us to use our heads but will not excuse us from that duty, and as to our hearts — cardiograms cannot diagnose what may be most ill about them, or confirm what may be best. The faithful woman and the versatile brave man, the wakeful intelligence open to inspiration or grace — these are still exemplary for our kind, as they always were and always will be. Nor do I suppose that the pleasure of hearing a story in words has quite gone out. Even movies and TV make use of words. *The Odyssey* at all events was made for your pleasure, in Homer's words and in mine.

Rose-Fingered Dawn and the Idea of Time

Paolo Vivante*

1

A common view among scholars is that Homer's verse, "When the early-born (*ērigeneia*), rose-fingered (*rhododaktylos*) dawn appeared," is a conventional standard phrase used by Homer to say "when the day broke out." In this they of course follow Milman Parry who illustrated with this very phrase his famous definition of formula.[1]

This implies that we have here a mere piece of compositional technique. The poetic value of the phrase is either disregarded or taken for granted.[2] It is seen, at best, as a good instance of artistic craft — as one of those countless formulas which make up Homeric verse.

It is my contention that the phrase reflects a mode of perception and thought. Technique, compositional device, style are but the outcome of a way in which things are visualized and expressed. The phrase must thus be explained on the strength of a deeper poetic reason, it must be appreciated both in its intrinsic value and in its relation to the context. In order to do this, let us look at its occurrences, and then at what these occurrences imply as regards the conception of the poems as a whole.

2

Take a characteristic instance of the phrase — in *Il.*1.477f.: "When the early-born, rose-fingered dawn appeared, / Then they set sail toward the great camp of the Achaeans." This passage is typical. The rise of day is juxtaposed as an independent happening to the inception of a human task. So, most often in the *Odyssey*, it is so expressed as it coincides with the rising from bed, with the moment of departure, etc. (2.1, 3.491, etc.).

We have here an obvious human significance. To the inhabitants of earth dawn *touches*[3] the landscape into sudden radiance with the sun's slanting rays: houses, hills seem literally set aglow by the contact. And, as a counterpoint to the spectacle, the lives of people are touched into activity.

The phrase's function in so connecting sunrise with earth-bound mortals will be made more evident by the way in which Homer renders sunrise in connection with gods. We have in *Il.*8.1 (*cf.* 19.1, 24.695): "The saffron-robed (*krokopeplas*) dawn was spreading all over the earth, / And Zeus-delighting-in-thunder gathered the gods . . ." It is surely no coincidence that "rose-fingered" is never used in connection with gods, and "saffron-robed' never in connection with men. Seen from the heavenly

*Reprinted from *Ramus* 2 (1979):125–36, by permission of the author.

abodes, dawn appears as a generalized splendour extending over the world; and "saffron-robed" fits the picture. Compare also *Il*.23.226f., where the Morning-star is mentioned "after which the saffron-robed dawn spreads over the sea": we have a parenthetic sentence and, again, the phenomenon is abstracted from human activities. Another instance of dawn among gods is *Il*.11.1f., *Od*.5.1f., which presents dawn as the goddess wife of Tithonus. It is, again, noticeable that such a representation never occurs in a human context. *Il*.2.48, "Dawn the goddess arrived to lofty Olympus," is exceptional in connection with Agamemnon. Why do we not have the human earth-bound phrase? It is that the situation itself is exceptional, bringing Zeus directly into the picture. The Zeus-sent dream rouses Agamemnon, who forthwith gets up in the night; dawn follows. The divine presence alters the regular order and relation; the phrase is altered likewise. A foil to "rose-fingered dawn" is also *Od*.3.1f.: "The sun arose leaving the lovely waters. . . ." Daybreak is here out at sea, before Telemachus lands in Pylos; and it is the sea which prompted the expression: on the sea's surface there could be no room for what characterizes "rose-fingered dawn" — *viz*. the touch upon distinctive objects along with the parallelism between sunrise and human activities.

3

Let us now confine ourselves to dawn among people on earth. The parallelism underlined by the verse, "When early born rose-fingered dawn appeared," implies full juxtaposition between the natural phenomenon and the human condition. This means that the two juxtaposed things are on the same level of vision, without any undue subordination of the one to the other. What prevails is a purely representa*tional moment. The narrative does not condition the day or the human act to a straining or encroaching sequence.

It is therefore a further characteristic of the phrase to convey a regularity of rhythm. The regular recurrence of the phenomenon is bound up with the regular renewal of daily human tasks. Hence the verse in question is far more frequent in the *Odyssey* where convivial life is presented in its constant rhythm. In the *Iliad* it only recurs twice (1.475, 24.788). There is in the *Iliad* the great long day of books 11–18; elsewhere a restless wakefulness invades the boundaries of day and night, whence the phrase appears altered, broken.

This will be made clearer by comparing instances in which the advent of the new day is marked by a shortened, abrupt phrase and not by the full verse, "When the early-born, rose-fingered dawn appeared." In such cases there is perturbation, disquiet. Consider the following: (a) "So she said; at once came golden-throned (*chrysothronos*) dawn" (*Od*.20.91). The shorter phrase here presents dawn that comes and interrupts Penelope's night-long brooding; day breaks in upon a state that is running its indefinite course. The same phrase occurs with a similar effect in *Od.*10. 541, 12.142, 15.56: (b) "At once came lovely-throned (*euthronos*) dawn, which awakened / Fair-robed Nausicaa . . ." (*Od.*6.48f.). Again the phrase is abrupt: day-break cuts short Nausicaa's engrossing dream. Cf. *Od.*15.495, 14.502: similarly short phrases in unusual sequences: (c) "The rose-fingered dawn appeared on them mourning / Round the piteous corpse; but powerful Agamemnon . . ." (*Il.*23.108f.). The full phrase would not have been possible here. Its implication of harmony between man and nature would have jarred with the scene of mourning, although from a compositional point of view it would surely have been possible to say, "When the early-born, rose-fingered dawn appeared," followed by a suitable phrase in the first half of the next verse. As it is, the shortened phrase makes it possible to compress into the same verse both the sun and the group of mourning men. The focus shifts beautifully to the human moment.

Compare *Il.*24.12f.: "Nor unseen by him the dawn appeared on the sea and the beaches." Dawn is so presented to Achilles who wanders restlessly in the night after Patroclus' funeral. Again the presentation fits the passage. Dawn, without epithets, sinks into the background, a mere foil to Achilles' anguish which persists irrespective of the time. Hence a break in the regular succession of rest and wakefulness, of night and day. Almost imperceptibly the verbs take an iterative form.

4

The fullness of expression which we find in the verse, "When the early-born, rose-fingered dawn appeared," thus rests on a full contiguity with the human action. Such a fullness is proportionate to an expansive, unobstructed vision. We have seen how it yields, how it shrinks at any touch which affects the outright exposure.

Therefore no trace of this fullness will be found where the appearance of dawn is treated as a mere circumstance of what happens. Consider the following: (a) "With the appearing dawn we shall consider . . ." (*Il.*9.618). Cf. *Il.*9.682, 24.600, *Od.*4.407, 6.31, 7.222, 12.24, 15.396, 16.270. In these instances the phrase "together with the appearing dawn" points to the morrow in speeches of command, exhortation, promise, threat.[4] Resolution excludes any lingering touch on the moment of dawn. This is also true of hastening narrative. We find the same phrase, "with the appearing dawn," in compendious narrative lying outside the mainstream of the action: *Od.*14.266, 17.435, *Il.*11.685. In *Od.*16.2 *ham' ēoi*, "with dawn," takes up the narrative from 15.495. In *Od.*12.429 Odysseus says, "With the rising sun I came," summing up his ordeal's last dawn. Compare the way in which *ēōthen* comes to mean "on the morrow": *Il.*7.372,

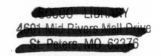

Od.1.153, etc: (b) (*Il*.8.530, 18.277, 303): "Dawn-encompassed (*prōi d'hypēoioi*) . . . let us fight." The moment of dawn is presented as a person's predicate — in a way which is difficult to translate in English. The idea "when day breaks out" is expressed as all one with the action. Resolution (as elsewhere compendious narrative) cuts expression short: (c) "Unquenchable at dawn rose the outcry" (*Il*.11.50; cf. *Od*.5.469). The outcry of men (or wind in the example of the *Odyssey*) merges with the vision of dawn; the notion of time gives way to that of space: "at dawn," "in front of dawn." Cf. *Il*.3.3: *ouranothi pro*, "in face of heaven."

5

If we survey these instances as a whole, one main distinction emerges which is founded on the logic of the situation: in dialogue dawn is mentioned, if at all, most briefly, whereas its expression is more or less full in the poet's direct representation.

It is as we should expect in dialogue: the speaker's purpose drives him to pass over the actual contours of things. We find few exceptions. Only the following occur to me. In *Il*.9.707, "But when the beauteous (*kalē*), rose-fingered (*rhododaktylos*) dawn appears" is spoken by Diomedes, in resignation after the failure of the embassy to Achilles: "Rest now," he says, "and eat and drink; but when the beauteous, rose-fingered dawn appears, gather the host. . . ." In *Il*.24.417 "when divine (*dia*) dawn appears" is said by Hermes, explaining to Priam how Hector's corpse is each morning restored to freshness by the will of the gods — a unique phrase for a unique occasion. In *Od*.22.197f. *ērigeneia* . . . *chrysothronos*, "the early-born . . . the golden-throned one," is a gruesome jest spoken by Eumaeus to tortured Melanthius.

The occurrence of the fuller phrases, on the other hand, is likewise what we should expect in the poet's direct representation (or in those passages which, though spoken by a character, are self-contained accounts of a certain event). It should be noted that in presenting the advent of a new day in the main action the poet never merely says "on the morrow" or "the day after." This with one exception which is itself significant. In *Iliad* 7 the Trojans decide in the night to ask for a truce; and in the early morning Idaeus goes to the camp of the Achaeans — *Il*.7.381: "On the morrow (*eōthen*) Idaeus went to the hollow ships." The narrative sequence is here very strong, with stress on cause and effect: a council, a decision, an order for the next morning and the order carried out. But even here the new day must be taken into full acount. The truce is brought into effect, and at 421 we find: "The sun was freshly striking the fields, / From the gentle deep streams of Oceanus / Rising up to the sky; and they met." It is as if the poet felt a need to make up for that perfunctory "on the morrow" mentioned a few lines before. The expression is again full-blown; but it is a singular one, justified by the singular sequence.

6

Look now quite generally at the variation of expression. What stands out is the concrete rendering. This is to say that the variation is never prompted by the intention to convey a certain mood, a certain atmosphere, a certain effect. It would thus be quite unlike Homer to convey that sense of morning wakefulness and alertness which we find, for instance, in Sophocles' *El.*17f.: "Already to use the bright light of day / Stirs into clearness the dawn-songs of birds." Even more unlike Homer would be such dismal grandeur as we find in Shakespeare's *Henry IV*, part I, 5.1.1ff.: "How bloodily the sun begins to peer / Above yon busky hill! The day looks pale / At his distemp'rature."

But how are we to understand this Homeric concreteness in a more positive sense? In what sense are these variations "concrete?" If they do not convey changing impressions of dawn directly affecting the mind, what is the tangible reason of the variation itself?

These variations are concrete in that they convey the existential, and not the purely human, occasion. What matters is not so much a character's mood as the way in which the character is physically juxtaposed or brought into contact with the break of day. It is a question of position, relation, balance, juncture.

Take, for instance, *Od.*6.48f., "At once came lovely-throned dawn, that awoke / Fair-robed Nausicaa," and 2.1f., "When the early-born, rose-fingered dawn appeared / The son of Odysseus arose. . . ." Dawn *comes* to Nausicaa, while it simply *appears* in the case of Telemachus and coincides with his getting up. There is incidence in the former instance, coincidence in the latter. It is the Nausicaa passage which diverges from the norm. Hence that "at once," *autika*, which (as in other similar instances) is sharp, sudden, curt. Nausicaa is here dreaming, dawn intrudes on her dream; she wakes and wonders. It is not the character's mood which primarily affects the different representation of dawn, it is the actual concrete occasion.

Or my argument could be put in grammatical terms. I could say that the expressions of dawn are different because the syntax is different: in the Nausicaa passage a principal clause coming in by itself, in the Telemachus passage a temporal one introduced by "when. . . ." But the different syntax reflects different forms of existential relation, and the difference of relation requires a difference in the wording. Homer would neither say "came rose-fingered dawn that awoke . . ." nor "when the lovely-throned dawn appeared, then. . . ."[5]

The remarkable thing is that Homer's expression changes according to such a sense of relation or position. A value of perception is implied. For what ultimately determines these basic variations is an inborn, keen realization of how such an event as day-break is actually seen in its happening — of how it affects a man or woman in the most concrete physical sense. The occurrence of day-break, in other words, is not abstracted from its actuality. It is not something to be designated one way or another for other reasons than those prompted by the event itself. The felicity of expression thus consists in congruity with reality. Such a style is neither the result of arbitrary choice nor a superimposed phraseology. It keeps its freshness by focussing on the truth of the moment.

Hence also, but indirectly and implicitly, the human significance of these expressions in their pertinent variations. When the existential situation is so naturally taken into account and in such a way that it must naturally be transcribed in the very syntax of the sentences and in their diction, it follows that a sense of the human condition is therein implied and that it must come to the surface. We may therefore find a spacious airy sense in the parallelism which is intimated by "when early-born, rose-fingered dawn appeared"; a constraint in "at once came golden-throned dawn"; imminence, crisis in "together with the appearing dawn."

7

Let us now turn, quite generally, to the expression of day-break, considering the persistence of form rather than the variations. For we see that the variations themselves take certain typical moulds.

Why this Homeric stress on dawn, in phrases which so often repeat the same form? It may be granted that it is a characteristic of all poetry to dwell on so striking a moment as dawn; but why is it that, whereas elsewhere the representation of dawn is infinitely varied, we find in Homer such a persistent regularity of form? Are not the Parryists right after all in positing their sets of formulas? Do we not have here a conventional stylistic feature?

If we wish to look seriously into the matter, we must try to explain this regularity of form by seeking in the form itself some intrinsic value of expression which is such as to justify this regularity. Our reasons must be internal to the issue. We must as far as possible refrain from appealing to such secondary motives as expedience, economy, traditional usage, facility of versification. This would be tantamount to confusing the conditions or external features of a phenomenon with the phenomenon itself — as if, say, we attributed the rise of literature to the invention of the alphabet or of writing materials. Even if we grant in all its fullness the traditional poetic language posited by the Parryists, the problem arises of why it ever came about, of why the expressions used are thought to be excellent, of why they proved so adequate to express a certain meaning. To allege the metrical requirements is to beg the question. The so-called formulas must have, after all, an expressive function which is one and all with their poetic value. We thus return to a problem of values.

Why then this regularity in the expressions of dawn?

I see the reason, again, in Homer's concreteness. There is an intimate connection between the regularity of these phrases and Homer's concrete conception of time whereby the action of the poems is presented within a series of days and not through an indefinite period.

Let us consider more closely the logic of these connections.

The expressions are concrete in that they portray the day's emergence unaltered by any subjective bias. For the same reason they have regularity of form: each successive day is seen as it comes in its existential condition, and no sense of any particular worth or import highlights any single day-break above the others.

This relation between concreteness and the sense of a certain day is a natural one. We may realize it in our own experience. Think of any event, summon it up in the actuality of its taking place; and you cannot help conceiving it in a certain moment. A day or night, however imaginary, must be associated with it; we do not abstract it, we do not separate it from its actual occasion, as when we describe a person's usual behaviour or make a historical survey. The same process is realized in Homer on a vast scale. The mythical or historical material is humanized, dramatized, and thus summoned up into a specious present. We are put in the *presence* of whatever happens. Hence what John Finley calls a day-lit frontality.[6]

Granted now that Homer's concreteness calls for the summoning up of a particular day; it yet remains to be seen how we may relate to it more closely the regularity of phrase. For, obviously, we might have renderings of day-break which are no less vivid or concrete for being varied. The answer lies in Homer's characteristic kind of concreteness. I understand it as a realization of things, acts, events in their basic consistency, and not as a realistic and digressive description of details. Hence day-break in its typical impact. The succession of its instances is what strikes the poet's imagination, or one great phenomenon characterized for what it is by any number of occasions. Varied description would lead us into abstraction of detail by removing certain features from the vital event in which they occur. We would lose the large Homeric outline. We would have landscape rather than nature, weather rather than natural time.

But now see how this concrete sense of time relates to the composition of the poems.

Homeric poetry is as abhorrent from any epitomizing as it is from any descriptive digression which would equally lead us into a conglomeration of static facts unpropelled by any forward movement. The focus is on the single acts closely following one another. Since each act is conceived as actually taking place before our eyes, it must take its allotted moment of time and fill a parcel of the day. And since act thus follows upon act in a visual or tangible realization, we have concrete sequences whose only possible point of reference in the world of existence is a certain day or order of days. Such being the case, the distinction of successive days is indispensable to Homer's composition. The compact action which we find in the poems could not possibly hang in mid-air. It must find its breathing space in the encompassing day. Without a sense of the day or the hour, we should have an intolerable accretion of events. As it is, the days give the action its necessary span; and this function is all the more evident where, as in Homer, the sense of reality is so strong and yet historical frames of reference so removed.

Thus the distribution of the action into successive days is not a convenient arrangement or a mere method of composition or a superimposed feature. If we had anything like days introducing chapters, we might indeed expect each new opening variously rendered to suit the occasion. But no. Since the action is rectilinear and uninterrupted, since what drives it on is a constant sense of time, it follows that the intervals of day and night are given to mark this progression, not to embellish the occasion or to enlarge descriptively upon it. Day-break is a necessary point of focus. Poetry lingers upon it for a moment, and passes on. An existential condition is inevitably accounted for, a regular cadence arrested in regularity of expression.

It would thus be absurd to require in the poems varied expressions of day-break producing some particular effect.

We find such variations in narrative which covers long stretches of time, whole lives or cycles of myth and history. Here the days cannot obviously be numbered; the continuity of time is naturally ignored; only single particular occasions are singled out, and then day-break or nightfall may be high-lighted to match a salient moment. In such cases abstraction sets in. There is a split between the time of nature and that of human experience. The focus shifts to the latter. Only a poignant day is remembered, the others forgotten; and the plenitude of time shrinks to make room for an ideal perspective or a deliberate point.

Take, for instance, the fourth book of the *Aeneid*. Aeneas' stay at Carthage covers an indefinite lapse of time, allowing for the stages of Dido's love, complications, denouement. Thus ll.6–8 provide a grand opening to Dido's confession of love:

> postera Phoebea lustrabat lampade terras
> umentemque Aurora polo dimoverat umbram,
> cum sic unanimam adloquitur male sana sororem.

> The next day's dawn was moving over the earth
>   with Phoebus' lamp
> And had scattered from the sky the damp
>   shadows,
> When, barely sane, she speaks to her loving sister.

At 129 a shorter rendering introduces the hunting expedition which is going to prove a momentous occasion:

> Oceanum interea surgens Aurora reliquit.

> Meanwhile dawn rising left the ocean.

Then again at ll.584–587 the rendering is ample, solemn in marking Aeneas' departure and Dido's vision of the sun-lit ships sailing away:

> et iam prima novo spargebat lumine terras
> Tithoni croceum linquens Aurora cubile.
> regina e speculis ut primam albescere lucem vidit. . .

> And now first dawn was sprinkling the earth with new light
> Leaving behind Tithonus' saffron bed.
> The queen, as soon as she saw from her watch-tower
>   the light whiten . . .

Why do these expressions of day-break vary in a way which is quite unlike Homer? One important reason is that in Virgil the action is not continuous, not realized from day to day. Virgil's focus is on a synthesis, a survey, a drama to be grasped in its totality and outcome. He has no eye for the single occasion, for the single moment as it takes place in the natural order of things. Where he singles out the break of day, we are made to pause and expect a crucial development before moving on. Hence the phrase expands more or less according to the burden of the occasion.

Note also, in Virgil, the connecting particles *iam* ("now"), *interea* ("meanwhile"), so different in purport from the Homeric ones. For they do not simply juxtapose, they do not simply relate the break of day to an existential condition. They fit it, rather, to the narrative or dramatic requirement. That *interea* makes us ready for the fatal nuptials decided upon by the gods in the preceding lines; that *iam* has a tragic ring which is like a prelude to Dido's death.

Such a style could find no place in Homer. It presupposes quite a different sort of vision: dark intervals coming to a breaking-point, climax and anticlimax arched over the immediate moments. This would do away with Homer's representation of single acts coextensive with daylight and with the rendering of dawn as a constant time-keeper.

8

"But how so?" we may be asked. "Are not these recurring phrases of day-break to be seen in the same light as all other recurring phrases in Homer? How do you account for this formulaic character?"

Let us look at the problem in this larger configuration, trying to find an answer outside the sterile concept of traditional diction. Whence this persistency of form? W. Arend saw an answer in the Greek love of the typical at the expense of the particular.[7] But why, again, this love of the typical? Is it not quite inadequate to look at it as a hall mark of what is Greek and thus take it for granted? Should we not try to see how it came about, how it arose as a principle of art in the actuality of the representation itself?

We may again find a reason in Homer's sense of time — in the way the factual matter is reduced into concrete moments, into pure outlines of rest or movement. We have instances rather than facts. Take such ordinary recurring expressions as "upon the laid-out victuals they put forth their hands," or "they drew down the ships to the sea divine," or "he bound the beautiful sandals under the glistening feet." The moment is isolated and thus made typical by being keenly perceived. Time is the quickening element. It permeates the short sentences. It draws into its rhythm the noun-epithet phrases. What stands out is incidence, cadence. We have sequences and not informative details. It is as if the touch of time penetrated each thing, relieving it of its static objectivity. Hands and victuals, sea and ship, sandals and feet are all one with the vivid occasion: they are hardly necessary to the narrative, they fill our sense of the instant by drawing momentary relevance from the human act and conferring to it, in their turn, an existential concreteness. All this would not have been possible, if the facts had been accounted for in a general way (by saying, e.g., "they ate and drank"), or if they had been described in detail (by giving us, e.g., an account of the victuals). Both general narrative and minute description would have been fatal to the momentary impact. But, as it is, we have time-filled instances, moments that come and go; we have rhythms and not a factual account.

Consider now this rendering of things on the voluminous Homeric scale, and see how it furthers a sense of what is typical. The recurring phrases compose the existential texture of the action. They attach any episode to its indispensable phases, to its vantage-points of duration. The recurrence of phrase thus reflects the recurrence of acts which mark basic points of succession. On the other hand, these recurrences naturally take a typical form. Hence a sense of what is typical springing from the perception of life. Hence a stylization which is continually sustained by a sense of developing outlines in the actuality of events. There is hardly any matter in the poems that seems exempt from this treatment. Like day-break and night-fall, human activities have their rising and setting.

Homer's way of perceiving things as they occur at a certain spot and a certain moment on so large a scale could hardly have manifested itself otherwise than by focussing on these typical recurrences. There is a logical reason in this. Any broad vision, in so far as it is concretely pursued, cannot but lead to a sense of what is vitally typical. Look at a general scenery, and it necessarily falls into prevailing outlines; try to divine a forest from one tree, and you necessarily imagine the tree in a myriad instances. The same happens with respect to time. Try to visualize a complex enduring event, and you can only see it in a series of instances which typify it. Hence in the *Iliad* the fighting scenes which rehearse the same event time after time. Homer carries out this process on a vast poetic level. His practice is to visualize rather than describe, summarize, idealize, dream, glorify, moralize.

And the plot, the story? How is the need of a narrative purpose compatible with this view of time which subjects the material to a series of recurrences? We may answer that the plot or story grows out of the existential matter distributed in successive points of time. We thus see, for instance (*Od.*2.1–39), the break of day, Telemachus rising from bed, donning his clothes, issuing out, calling the assembly, making his way, finally addressing the people and thus introducing a turning-point. His final dramatic step does not come in a temporal vacuum. It crowns a natural sequence of acts, each of them given in so far as it occupies a parcel of the day and thus presented in a sort of hieratic composure. It is not so much a lonely dramatic decision which occasions the action as the initial rise of day marking a starting point. Hence any living moment must be given its due irrespective of its narrative importance, and yet the sequence is so produced as to bear out its burden. The premonition of a crisis looms beyond each phrase. The salient moment comes where the existential rhythm quickens, thickens, breaks — even as a storm breaks out from the regular interplay of the elements. It is this persisting respect of continuous time which gives life to the encompassing stylization by imparting rhythm into any happening, so that even the most tragic event takes the form of a natural phenomenon. The recurring phrases are like key-notes to this treatment.

Notes

1. *The Making of Homeric Verse* (Oxford, 1971), 13f., *cf.* 76.

2. For an appreciation to the contrary, see Norman Austin, *Archery at the Dark of the Moon, Poetic Problems in Homer's Odyssey* (Berkeley, 1975), 67.

3. I give the sense of *touch* to "finger" in the epithet *rhododaktylos*. Compare *Iris aellopos*, "storm-footed Iris." Just as in *rhododaktylos* the finger conveys touch, in *aellopos* the foot conveys movements. The noun's meaning does not simply denote an objective feature; it also implies action. The names of parts of the body are good instances, thus, in Greek poetry, "foot" can by itself have the meaning of "motion," "journey" (e.g. *Il.*9.523, Aesch. *Septem* 374).

Hence *rhododaktylos* gives us a palpable sense of the natural phenomenon through human connotations. See M. Leumann, *Homerische Wörter* (Basel, 1950), 18.

For the sense of touch, compare *Il.*7.421: "The sun was freshly striking (*proseballen*) the fields." In *Hamlet*, 4.1.29f.: "The sun no sooner shall the mountains touch / but we will ship him hence."

4. *Cf.* N. Austin (n. 2 above), 67.

5. We could not find anything like, e.g., "at once (*autika*) early-born, rose-fingered (*rhododaktylos*) dawn appeared," or "when dawn came rising up lovely-throned (*euthronos*)." This would produce an intolerable use of words displaced from their pertinent contexts — removed, that is to say, from the existential relation which they underline. So, for instance, *rhododaktylos* ("rose-fingered") may never be interchanged with *chrysothronos* ("golden-throned") in spite of metrical equivalence.

6. J. H. Finley, Jr., *Homer's Odyssey* (Cambridge, Mass., and London, 1978), 15.

7. W. Arend, *Die typischen Scenen bei Homer* (Berlin, 1933), 25–27.

[Order and Disorder]   Eric Voegelin*

The primitive, Greek-speaking invaders of 1950 B.C. had become, through cultural syncretism and amalgamation with the indigenous population, the Achaeans of 1600. They had then through Minoization as well as through contacts with Egypt and Syria, gained their civilizational momentum. And after the demise of Cretan society in 1400, the Mycenaean had become the dominant civilization of the Aegean area. The area as a whole, thus, had been civilizationally penetrated for more than eight hundred years, before substantial parts of the Achaeans moved eastward under the pressure of the Doric migration.

The depth and strength of this past must not be forgotten in any consideration of the problems of order during the dark age that extends from c.1100 to the emergence of the Homeric epic in the eighth century B.C. However severe the loss of power and wealth, the fact of the Achaean mass migration as well as the foundation of new towns on the coast of Anatolia and the islands, proves that neither the cohesion of the society nor its spirits were broken; however straitened and precarious the material circumstances of the reorganized communities, the Achaeans were still the carriers of Mycenaean order. The Doric migration had displaced, not a primitive tribe, but the active center of civilization that once before had moved from Crete to Mycenae. From its new geopolitical and reduced material position, the Achaean nobility could recapture its past, if it had the stamina and ability. It could engage in its *recherche du temps perdu* and make the glory of its past the guide for its present and future; and it could even impose its own past as *their* history on the primitive ethnic relatives who now were sitting in Mycenae, Tiryns, and Crete, if a convincing form was found. An Aegean-wide society, in continuity with the earlier civilizational societies, could be formed in spite of the discouraging circumstances of the moment, if the consciousness of a common Aegean order in terms of the Minoan-Mycenaean past was awakened. This feat was indeed performed through the creation of the Homeric epic. . . .

In a study on order and history the enigma, for which the name of Homer stands, is not the authorship of a work of literature, but the creation of a symbolism which expresses a new experience of human existence under the gods, of the nature of order and the causes of disorder, and of the historical decline and fall of a society. Who was the man, if it was only one man, who broke with the cosmological myth and created a non-cosmological form of social order? The problem is adumbrated in a passage of Herodotus (II, 53): "Whence came into being each of the gods, or whether they had all for ever existed, and what forms they had, the Hellenes did not know until the other day, so to speak. For the age of

*Reprinted with permission of Louisiana State University Press from *The World of the Polis* (*Order and History*, Volume II), 82–110. © 1957.

Hesiod and Homer was not more than four hundred years before my own, I believe. And they were the first to compose theogonies for the Hellenes, to give the gods their epithets, to allot them their ranks and functions, and to describe their forms." From this text two pieces of information can be extracted. In the first place, the Hellenes knew that the order of their gods was of recent origin and could not be traced beyond the age of the epics. The time span surmised by Herodotus places the event, at the earliest, in the ninth century B.C. And second, they were convinced that the myth had not grown anonymously over a long period of time, but had been created by definite persons, the poets. These facts, to be sure, do not illuminate the darkness in which the historical Homer is shrouded, but they come close enough to the enigma to allow its circumscription through the definite questions: What is a poet? What is the source of his knowledge? And by what authority does he create a new symbolism of divine and human order?

The sources that will supply the answers to these questions are surprisingly scarce. Still, they are sufficient to make recognizable a relation between the poet and a divine source of revelation that resembles the relation between the Israelite prophet and the word of Yahweh. The *Iliad* opens with the verse: "The wrath do thou sing, O goddess, of the Pelide Achilles"; and the *Odyssey* with "Tell me, O Muse, of the man of many devices." As in the prophetic texts of the Bible Yahweh and his prophet are interchangeable as the speakers of the word, the *dabar*, so in the epic the Muse and the singer are interchangeable as the speakers of the poem. For the rest, the *Iliad* is uninformative since it invokes the goddess only by the standard formula: "Tell me now, O Muses, housed on Olympus . . .", as an authenticating opening line for a new section of the story. In the *Odyssey*, however, we find an interesting passage. Demodocus is introduced (VIII, 63–64) as "the singer [*aoidos*] whom the Muse loved greatly, and gave him both good and evil; of his sight she deprived him, and gave him sweet song." The passage suggests a connection between blindness to the world and song, since both are given by the Muse. And the theme is resumed in a paean of Pindar (VII, b) where the poet prays for inventive skill to Mnemosyne and her daughters, the Muses. "For the minds of men are blind"; they need help who, without the Muses, "seek the steep path of them that walked it by their wisdom [*sophia*]"; to the poet, Pindar, the Muses have charged this "immortal labor." The terseness of the verses, as well as their fragmentary character, make it impossible to decide whether the immortal labor means Pindar's walking of the "way of wisdom" for himself, or as the helper to his blind fellow men, but the latter seems to be the more probable meaning. The Homeric and Pindaric passages together formulate the great theme of blindness and seeing that recurs in Aeschylus and Plato: Who sees the world is blind and needs the help of the Muses to gain the true sight of wisdom; and who is blind to the world, is seeing in the wisdom of sweet song. The Muses, and through them the poets, are the helpers of man who seeks to ascend from his darkness to light.

The Hellenes had no Message and Covenant from Sinai to create them a Chosen People in historical form. They had no Moses to lead them from the bondage of Pharaoh to the freedom of God. But they had the prophetic singers who experienced man in his immediacy under the gods; who articulated the gulf between the misery of the mortal condition and the glory of memorable deeds, between human blindness and divine wisdom; and who created the paradigms of noble action as guides for men who desired to live in Memory. That was less than the Mosaic insight which placed the people in the present under God; but it was more in as much as the singers appealed to the psyche of every man singly. From its very beginning the appeal went to the divine essence of order in the soul, to the immortal core. The experience of immortality, to be sure, was still bound by the cosmos as were the gods. Man could not yet, through the sanctification of life and divine grace in death, move toward the beatific vision; but he could place himself before the gods forever by action that entered the stream of Memory through the song of their prophets.[1]

We still know nothing about the historical Homer. But we know that the Hellenes believed him to be the man who first transfigured their past into song.

When the memorable events are transfigured by song, they become the past of the society for which the poet sings. But the events transformed into past by the Homeric epic belong to the Achaean society with its power seat in Mycenae, while the poem is sung for the inchoate Hellenic society with its active center on the Anatolian coast. And the two are separated by the disasters of the Achaean and Ionic migrations. Hence, the question must be asked: What interest could the descendants of the refugees in Ionia have in the exploits of a society which, if the middle of the eighth century be accepted as the date of the epics, had been defunct for more than two hundred years? The answer to this question must be sought in the act of transfiguration which links the two societies into one.

As the subject matter of the *Iliad*, Homer did not choose a splendid enterprise, but an episode of disorder which presaged the catastrophe that was to overcome Mycenaean civilization. In an earlier context we have suggested the internal exhaustion of civilizational societies in the area of town culture by the twelfth century B.C. The *Iliad*, now, furnishes a paradigmatic study of the causes of decline in the Aegean-wide Mycenaean order. For Homer's Achaeans are not Hellenes, and his Trojans are not barbarians; they both belong to the same society and their strife is a civil war. The one Olympian order extends over them all: the Zeus who endows Agamemnon with his royal authority is also the protector of Troy against Hera who sides with the Achaeans. But the gods are divided. The rift among men is a disturbance in the Olympian order of the world; and the division among the gods is a disturbance of human order. While the war is conducted, on the pragmatic level, as a sanction against a Trojan violation of law, the human disorder reaches into the divine sphere. Something more is at stake than a breach of order that could be repaired by due compensation or by an Achaean victory. For the war itself, destructive for Troy and exhaustive for the Achaeans, is a wanton indulgence; it reveals a universal order — embracing both gods and men, both Trojans and Achaeans — in decline and judgment. The misery of the vanquished will fall back on the victors.

In the fall of Achaean society the poet found more than a political catastrophe. In the action and passion of the heroes he discovered the touch of divinity ordained fate, the element of tragedy which lets the events ascend to the realm of Mnemosyne. From the disaster he wrested his insight into the order of gods and men, from the suffering grew wisdom when the fall became song. In this act of transfiguration the poet transcended Achaean society and created the Hellenic symbolic form. We can speak of it as the style of self-transcendence, corresponding to the Israelite style of exodus from civilization and ultimately from itself. For with its past the new society had acquired its future. The Hellenic society did not have to die as did the Babylonian or Egyptian, the Cretan or Achaean. Hellas could transcend itself into Hellenism; and it could transcend the symbolic form of the Olympian myth, in which it had constituted itself, into philosophy as the symbolic form of mankind.

.   .   .

THE WRATH OF ACHILLES

The epics are not concerned with causes and effects on the level of pragmatic history but with the phenomenon of decline itself. The Homeric society is disordered in as much as on decisive occasions the conduct of its members is guided by passion rather than by reason and the common good. The blinding through passion, the *ate*, is not the cause of disorder, it is the disorder itself. Something is badly wrong with the leading Homeric characters; and under one aspect, therefore, the *Iliad* is a study in the pathology of heroes. The retracing of Homer's analysis will appropriately begin with his deliberate parallel construction of the wrath of Achilles with the war against Troy. The great war is caused by the abduction of Helen by Paris; the Trojan prince has violated the rule that a guest should not start an affair with the wife of his host, and the violation of this basic rule of civilized societies requires counter-measures. The wrath of Achilles is caused by Agamemnon's taking of Briseis; that is an insult to the honor of a king, and it also requires some counteraction on the part of Achilles. The parallel construction offers Homer the opportunity to analyze the cases of both Achilles and Helen. . . .

The wrath of Achilles is extraordinary in the literal sense. It is something outside human order. It is a gap in the order that binds men together, and through the gap is pouring an uncontrollable darkness from beyond. In order to describe this intangible, negative phenomenon Homer uses the device of confronting Achilles with the certain knowledge of his death in battle. The hero is a demi-god; and from his divine mother Thetis he has learned of the alternative fate that is in store for him: if he stays with the army at Troy he will not return home, he will perish in battle and thereby earn imperishable fame; if he boards his ship and returns home, an inglorious but long and happy life will be his lot (*Il.* I, 352, 414ff.; IX, 412f.). Homer explores the wrath of Achilles, first, by means of the divine revelation of the alternative and, second, by means of the various moods, situations, reasonings and decisions induced by the dilemma.

At this point of the analysis a source of rather common misunderstandings of the *Iliad* must be eliminated. The alternative fate of Achilles is not extraordinary by virtue of its content, but by virtue of its revelation. Homer's problem is not the fate of Achilles but the tension between a rather common fate and the uncommon reactions of the hero. The construction of the *Iliad* depends on this tension. Hence, the common character of the fate must be ascertained with some care. The dilemma of the fate, as hinted, is not particularly exciting in the situation of a war. Even without divine information one may reasonably assume, on the one hand, that a healthy specimen like Achilles will have a long and agreeable life if he succeeds to the throne of a prosperous kingdom in a remote region and does not deliberately look for trouble; and on the other hand, that he runs the risk of getting killed sooner or later, if he engages continuously in battle with such intensity that his fame will be imperishable. Moreover, the dilemma faces most of the princes in the army. As long as the war continues they run the risk of death in battle; if they would return home and conduct themselves with some circumspection, their life expectancy would rise. And finally, it should be realized that the alternative does not imply a genuine choice. The whole army would prefer to go home; but they stay because the war is a federal political action with the purpose of punishing a violation of public order. The dilemma of Achilles, thus, is a more or less common lot. The prediction of his fate is not introduced for the purpose of creating a romantic hero who makes a free choice for early death and eternal fame. Only if the dilemma is understood as a common lot will the response of Achilles reveal its uncommon character. The tension is used by Homer with artistic circumspection for the two purposes of, first, isolating the precise nature of the Achillean wrath and, second, contrasting the wrath with the attitude of the other heroes to substantially the same fate.

The dilemma itself, thus, is not out of the ordinary. The extraordinary character of the Achillean fate begins with the fact of its divine revelation in so far as the prediction raises the probability of death to certainty. In the case of Achilles the warrior's fate of a life in the shadow of death becomes, psychologically speaking, an obsession with death that isolates him from the common life of humanity. War is for him not hardship and danger to be undergone as a public duty with the purpose of restoring order, but the fated essence of his existence. He never has experienced order as a man, for he went to war "a mere child" (*Il.* IX, 439f.). And he will not return as a man to the order for which the war is fought, since his existence will end in the death which through nine years the adolescent has dealt to others. The tension of his existence between death inflicted and death suffered is not a biographical accident but (and this is one of the points illuminated by the prediction) truly its essence.

The revelation of the fate is not an event outside the personality of Achilles; to have such a revelation is part of his character. The interpretation of the prediction as an obsession with death is not perhaps an anachronistic "psychologization" but the very meaning intended by Homer. The prediction is known not to Achilles alone but to everybody in the army. If it were considered by the Homeric characters as a piece of reliable information, from a divine source, on the impending death of Achilles before Troy, it not only would affect the Pelide but also the conduct of his friends. But his friends and comrades act as if the prediction did not exist. They seriously offer him wealth, a family alliance with Agamemnon, and an expansion of his realm, though they ought to know that such splendid prospects can hold no appeal for a man who will die and not return home. And when he reminds the embassy of the reason why their offer can hardly interest him (IX, 412f.), they continue their argument as if he had not spoken. Achilles with his revelation lives in a private world; or rather, he lives in a private world in so far as he is preoccupied with this isolating revelation. The action of the *Iliad* becomes incomprehensible unless the prediction is understood as an obsession which a hero, in so far as he is a public character, is not supposed to have. Some light will be shed on this Homeric problem by the earlier discussed dream of Agamemnon. The courteous answer of Nestor, in that instance, barely veiled the warning that kings are not supposed to have such dreams; that they come from the gods is no excuse; a man's divine revelations are his personal affairs and do not create an obligation for others; if, in Agamemnon's case, the elders obeyed orders they did not trust the dream but respected the authority of the king. The position of Achilles, however, is not that of the commander-in-chief; in his case no such respect is due. The injection of his predicted fate as an argument in the debate is a display of poor taste which the other lords are well-bred enough quietly to ignore.

. . .

It will have become clear by now that in Homeric society a lordly wrath is not a private state of emotions. A *cholos*, a wrath, is a legal institution comparable to a Roman *inimicitia* or a medieval feud. If *ate* induces a man to violate another man's sphere of possessions and honor, the victim of the transgression will react with *cholos*, that is, with an upheaval of emotion, tending to inflict damage on the transgressor, with the ultimate purpose of compelling formal compensation and recognition of the rightful relation between them. Hence, in the compact Homeric *cholos* one must distinguish between the emotional, wrathful reaction against damage inflicted on a man's status and the customs that regulate the course of the emotion. The peculiar nature and problem of the *cholos* will be understood more clearly if we remember the differentiation of its components into Plato's virtues of *andreia* and *sophia*. *Andreia*, courage, is the habit of the soul to be moved emotionally to counteraction in the face of unjust action; and *sophia*, wisdom, is required for guiding and restraining courage, since emotion, however justly aroused, may overstep the measure. The Homeric *cholos* contains these components embedded in the compact medium of *themis* (right order, custom). Functioning within an established order, the *cholos*, as an emotion, will supply the force that will resist injustice and restore just order; and it will even discourage violations of order in so far as *cholos* can be expected as an expensive consequence of unjust action. The proper functioning of *cholos*, thus, is essential for the maintenance of order. If the *cholos* is not forthcoming, transgression will be encouraged; if it is unbridled, order cannot be restored. As an instrument of order *cholos* must be duly worked up and called off as required by custom.

Measured by these criteria the *cholos* of Achilles has a highly improper complexion. To be sure, it breaks out properly on occasion of the insult. But the outbreak is sensed by the others as something more than a fitting reaction to the situation; its roots seem to reach deeper into a disorderly disposition of Achilles. The proper *cholos* should be a sensitive reaction of the emotions against a threat to the customary status of a person; for if the first attack is not checked immediately, the threat may grow into a formidable danger that can no longer be met with success at a later stage. The *cholos* of Achilles, however, is not a finite reaction against a finite threat, with the purpose of repairing the momentary breach of order; it is rather an outburst of the deep-seated anxiety that has grown in him through preoccupation with his fate; it is caused by an emotional short-circuit between the diminution of his honor and the anticipation of his death. This outburst rightly causes uneasiness in the others because it is sensed as an absolute threat to the meaning of order. For the game of order, with its partial diminutions and restitutions, can be played only as long as life is accepted with a will to act it out regardless of the mystery of death. If death is not accepted as a mystery in life, as part of the mystery of life itself; if the attempt is made to transform the mystery through reflection into an experience of something, of a reality; then the reality of death will become the nothingness which destroys the reality of life. When a walking ghost like Achilles appears on the scene, the pallor of death falls over the game of order; it can no longer be taken seriously and the drama sputters out in futility and disorder. The other lords sense rightly the threat of deadly destruction in the conduct of Achilles; this particular *cholos* cannot be closed by customary compensation and reconciliation. But how, then, can it be closed at all?

The answer to this question is the content of the *Iliad*. The wrath of Achilles has an inner development, an action; and the inner drama of the wrath determines the external action of the *Iliad*. To the episode of the wrath corresponds militarily the great battle in which the Trojans throw the Achaeans back to their camp and set fire to the first ship. This terrible defeat of the Achaeans, approaching their destruction, is pragmatically caused by the abstention of Achilles from battle; but in the drama of Achilles it is a disaster that he inflicts on them by his active wish. When the hero receives the insult from Agamemnon he appeals to his divine mother: Thetis should move Zeus to bring the Achaeans to the brink of disaster so that they could see how they had profited by their great king and the king would learn what it meant to insult the best of his lords (I, 407–12). The good mother, deeply distressed that the short life of her son should be darkened by such ignoble treatment, fulfills his wish. The motivation of the wish is transparent. As Agamemnon rightly suspects, Achilles wants to triumph over the king; his overbearing conduct betrays a boundless desire to dominate. A triumph, however, would be impossible if the Achaeans were really destroyed and none were left to bear witness to the hero's exaltation; or if Achilles had returned home and could not witness the defeat. The wish, therefore, is carefully tailored to requirements: It must be a near defeat, Achilles must be on hand to witness it, and he must be able to appear as the savior at the last moment. Moreover, the wish betrays the nihilism of the Pelide's dreaming. Achilles wants a moment of triumph in which everybody recognizes his superiority; but he does not want to continue that moment into a permanent order by replacing Agamemnon as king of the Achaeans. The wish for that moment is not nurtured by political ambition; it is a subtle attempt to cheat his fate by converting the imperishable fame after death into a triumph in life. In order to achieve the fleeting moment he is quite willing to let his comrades perish in battle until his intervention is the last and uncontested means for turning defeat to victory.

Achilles carries the program out by sustaining his wrath against all reasonable attempts at reconciliation. But when the great moment approaches the chain of events slips from his hands. The Achaeans are pressed hard near the trenches of their camp and fire has touched the first ship. At last, while still not joining battle himself, he allows his friend Patroclus and the Myrmidones to intervene, so that the danger of fire will be averted. In this sortie Patroclus is killed by Hector. Achilles has cut the moment too fine and caused the death of his *alter ego*. That is the end of the murderous dream; the great moment of triumph has become a personal disaster.

The drama of the *cholos* hinges on the death of Patroclus. With the death of his friend the obsession of Achilles falls apart; and the reality of life and order is restored. The fifty verses in which Homer describes this process may justly be considered the psychological masterpiece of the *Iliad* (XVIII, 78–126). With groans the son confesses to his mother that his wishes have been granted; "but what joy [*edos*] do I have therein" now that Patroclus is dead whom he cherished like his own self (*kephale*). Patroclus is close enough to his self to let him experience death at last as the common lot; he is no longer an exception among men just because he must die. He returns to the reality of life in community; and the decisive symptom of this return is the readiness to shoulder its obligations even at the risk of death; for death has lost its horror when life again has become so supremely real that it is not worth living except at its own conditions. The first of these obligations is the revenge for his friend, even though the death of Hector, according to his predicted fate, will soon be followed by his own. He was sitting by the ships in his wrath, "a useless burden on the earth," making himself guilty by his inaction of the slaying of Patroclus and the other Achaeans, though his prowess in battle was the one gift of the gods by which he could make himself useful to others. He curses the strife (*eris*) and wrath (*cholos*) that disrupts the game of order and has burdened him with his guilt; remanding Agamemnon's insult to the past he is now ready to curb his indulgence. His fate he now accepts as do the others; and he will lie down to die like Heracles when Moira has so decided. And finally, perhaps the most subtle trait, he is now even willing to acquire imperishable renown by his deeds in the common run of his obligations as an Achaean warrior – he will no longer try to cheat fate by triumph in life.

THE EROS OF PARIS AND HELEN

The wrath of Achilles was a disturbance of order. Still, while its generation, course, and dissolution provided the drama of the *Iliad*, it was no more than an episode in the greater disturbance, in the war that had been caused by the fatal attraction of Helen. We shall now turn to the question: Why did the Trojans not prevent the war, or at least end it, by restoring Helen to her husband with customary reparations? And this question is inseparable from the other one: Why did they not deal summarily with Paris-Alexander, that apparently useless individual, who was the more immediate cause of their troubles? Homer unfolded the various aspects of the problem in *Iliad* III, on occasion of the single combat between Paris and Menelaus for Helen and her possessions.

The occasion itself indicates the range and complexities of the problem. The simple legal solution (restoration with compensation) is impossible because the fatality of Paris, besides Helen's, is involved in the disturbance. The next best solution as against a long war between two peoples would be the single combat between Menelaus and Paris, the winner taking the prize. That is the solution on which the belligerent parties agree with enthusiasm in *Iliad* III. Obviously the next question will be: Why did the warring parties not resort to it somewhat earlier? And, finally, the question must be answered as to why this attempt to end the war proves abortive even now. The interweaving of these various problems makes the Third Book of the *Iliad* a masterpiece of artistic construction. Regrettably, a complete analysis is impossible in the present context; we must presuppose the reader's knowledge of this wonderful interpenetration of tragedy and comedy. For our purpose the various strands will be separated, and we shall begin the work by isolating the legal procedure which, as throughout the *Iliad*, furnishes the backbone of the story.

The single combat is the result of a challenge issued by Paris and accepted by Menelaus. The agreement between the protagonists must be, and is, accepted by the commanders on both sides. A formal armistice is concluded, stipulating that the victor in the single combat will receive Helen and her possessions. While the combat is going on, there will be no hostilities. And indeed, as soon as the agreement is reached, the soldiers on both sides break their battle lines, joyously put aside their arms, and form a ring of eager spectators around a clearance on which the combat will take place. No matter who the victor, the combat will end the war between Trojans and Achaeans. It looks like an ironclad agreement, and the end of the war within an hour is in sight.

The actual course of events does not fulfill the expectations. The combat begins, but the sword of Menelaus splinters on the helmet of Paris. Then Menelaus atttacks with his bare hands; he pulls Paris by the helmet and drags him, choking him with the strap; and the combat is practically over. At this moment Aphrodite intervenes, the strap breaks, Paris is whisked away by the goddess to safety in Troy, and Menelaus is left with the empty helmet, furiously looking for Paris. Understandably there is some consternation. Everybody, including the Trojans, help Menelaus in the search for the elusive Paris, but in vain. Nevertheless, there is still hope of a happy end because Menelaus obviously is the victor. Then the gods intervene again. Under divine inspiration, one of the Trojan allied leaders conceives the idea of carving a distinguished career for himself by taking a potshot at Menelaus. Not much damage is done by the superficial wound, but the truce is broken, and the battle is resumed (*Il.* IV, 85 ff.). Even now all hopes for peace are not extinguished, considering that the Achaeans are still ready at any time to accept a fair settlement. In the Trojan council Antenor warns his peers that they are fighting against their oath; he admonishes them to fulfill their obligation, to return Helen and her treasure, and to close the war. But Paris refuses to surrender Helen, though he is willing to part with the treasure; and the council upholds him against Antenor (VII, 345–78). The fate of the Trojans is sealed, for the Achaeans now continue the war with the certainty that the oath-breakers will meet their due fate. Every phase of this longish procedure is gone through by Homer with care until every rational means for ending the war is exhausted. Not a shadow of a doubt is left that this war is not governed by the rationality of politics and law, but by irrational forces which spell the end of civilizational order. The analytical isolation of the disruptive force is, in the case of Helen-Paris, quite as careful as in the case of Achilles.

The irrational force governs the procedure of the combat between Paris and Menelaus from its very inception. The combat and the truce are not the result of rational action (which could have been taken at any time) but of an accident. The lines of the Trojans and Achaeans are moving to battle; in the grim moment before the clash the elegantly garbed Paris does a little parading in front and challenges the best of the Achaeans to fight him. Menelaus happens to notice the show-off and eagerly rushes toward him, with the result that Paris quickly falls back into inconspicuous safety behind the line (III, 15–37). But too late. Hector watched the ignominious scene, and now has a few words to say to his brother. Paris is magnificent to look at, a woman-chaser and beguiler, handsome but without spirit or valor, an object of joyful contempt to the enemy, and a shame and bane to his city; the Trojans must be cowards, indeed, or they would have stoned him long ago for all the evil that he has wrought (III, 38–57). The correctness of the brotherly thumbnail sketch is borne out when, at the end of the combat, the Trojans eagerly join the Achaeans in their search for the miscreant, "for they all hated him like black death" (III, 454); and even the herald to the Achaeans, when mentioning the name of Paris, adds to his diplomatic message the private sentiment "would that he had perished long ago" (VII, 390). But Paris knows why the general contempt and hatred do not translate themselves into action against him. He candidly admits to his brother, and even admires, the justice of the portrait; but with dignity he rebukes him for holding against him the gracious gifts of Aphrodite. Such gifts must be honored, for they are bestowed without human merit, at the discretion of the immortals. Joy and fatality of divine gifts must be respected by men, by the receivers as well as by the community. Nevertheless, he is sufficiently nettled by Hector's contempt to make good his initial boast and to fight Menelaus (III, 58–75).

The accidental combat between the husbands brings Helen on the scene. She hurries toward the Scaean gate where Priam and his council are already assembled in order to watch the event. The elders see her coming and reflect that it is worthwhile to suffer the woes of a long war for a woman who looks like a goddess; but more soberly they add that after all it would be better to let her depart rather than to bring misery on themselves and their children for all the future. And Priam addresses her (like Phoenix Achilles) as his "dear child," nowise to be blamed for the war; it is all the fault of the gods (III, 146–70). The charm of the scene casts its spell today as it has always done, testifying to the greatness of the poet who ennobles disaster by making it transparent for the play of divine forces and who heightens the heroes into tragic figures by letting their human frailty carry the will of the gods. But to isolate the scene, to revel in the attraction of divine beauty and the refined humanity of Priam as a climax of the *Iliad* (as some interpreters do), would be a sentimental indulgence, a great injustice to Homer the clear-headed thinker. In the scenes with Paris and Helen we are coming near to the source of disorder on the Trojan side, and Homer uses these scenes quite deliberately for the purpose of characterizing the disordered sentiments through the ranks of the constitutional hierarchy.

Worst is the king himself; the royal gentleman exonerates the "dear child" completely and puts all the blame on the gods; and in the session of the council, when Antenor exhorts the elders to keep faith with their oath and to surrender Helen and her treasure, it is Priam who overrides the admonition to return to the sanity of order and upholds Paris. Second come the elders who, in spite of their judicious appraisal of divine beauty, are ready to admit that the woman is a bane (*pema*) and, represented by Antenor, have preserved a modicum of responsibility. And third come the people, restrained from action by awe, but expressing open contempt and hatred at least for Paris, and quite willing to send the troublesome pests packing. In the *Iliad* itself the tension between ruler and people does not approach the danger of popular revolt; but in the *Odyssey*, as we shall see presently, the disorderly upper class is rather afraid of a populace whose sense for right and wrong is less deeply corroded. It would be an anachronism to read into the epics an issue of antimonarchism and revolution, but there can be no doubt that in Homer's analysis of political crisis the fish begins to putrefy from the head.

The corrosion of sentiments and actions has its center in Paris and Helen; from this center it spreads over the levels of the constitutional hierarchy. Paris and Helen are the gap in the Trojan order through which a dark force of destruction pours in, as Achilles was the gap in the order of the Achaeans. In the characterization of this force, of the *eros*, Homer uses the same technique of symbolization as in the case of Achilles. The Pelide was isolated from the community by his obsessive fear of death, symbolized by the prediction; it was a peculiar kind of open secret which the hero could freely divulge to others, while the others freely conducted themselves as if they had not heard about it; as a consequence, the conversation assumed the complexion of a dream-play, each figure talking in its own dream while acting out a common fate. In the case of Paris the erotic isolation, the disruption of real contact with the order of social relations is most drastically symbolized by the burlesque ending of the single combat. At one moment, we are still in the order of reality, with Menelaus choking his enemy to death; and at the next moment, Paris is invisible in the erotic isolation of his chamber waiting for Helen, while Menelaus, holding an empty helmet, searches for its former wearer.

The participation of Helen in the isolation of Paris is a nauseatingly profound scene. When Aphrodite has saved her darling from the battlefield, and placed him in his chamber, fresh and fragrant for sweeter combat, she goes to summon Helen who still is on the gate watching the excited search for Paris who by now ought to be dead (III, 385–94). Helen at first can hardly believe the command of the goddess; that breach of order, that outrage to decency is too much for her. She is ready to accept the agreement between the belligerents, to end the war, and to return to Menelaus, thus restoring the rightful order of society. She senses that something terrible is going to happen, and tries to hold it off. She makes a pitiful pretense at suspecting that the goddess has perhaps some lesser evil in store for her, that Aphrodite wants to throw her to some other favorite now that Paris is out of the running, continuing the miserable career of her beauty. Then the pretense falters and the horror begins to sink in. She reviles the goddess; she tells her to leave Olympus and become herself the mistress and slave of Paris if she likes him so much. She bluntly refuses to go and to commit the shameful thing (*nemesseton*) for which all women of Troy would blame her for ever after (395–412). The goddess, however, is inexorable, and her wrath (*cholos*) is now stirred. With the authoritative brutality of an Olympian brothel madame she orders Helen to bed unless she wants to meet an ugly fate that the goddess will provide for her at the hands of both Achaeans and Trojans (413–17). Under such a threat the cowed Helen repairs to the chamber. Desperately, in a last attempt, she tries to stir up some decency in Paris by telling him what sort of a coward and weakling he is, and that she would love to see him dead, but to no avail (418–36). The unimpressed Paris informs her that his mind is obsessed with *eros*; that never, not even on the day when he took her from Sparta, had he wanted her as much as just now; and he gently but firmly compels her submission (437–47). The construction closely parallels the case of Achilles. The Pelide wants to cheat his fate by the great, though ephemeral triumph in life; in the dream play of Paris the goddess cheats fate by transfiguring the imminent death into the embrace of Helen.

The fish begins to putrefy from the head; and at the head — as it becomes increasingly clear — are the gods. From the chamber of Paris and Helen the scene shifts to the ultimate source of disorder, to the Olympians who are assembled and watch the events before Troy with intent interest. Zeus is pleased. In spite of the disappearance of Paris, there is still hope for a happy end that will avert destruction from his beloved Ilion, if only the Trojans will live up to the agreement and surrender Helen. The burlesque end of the combat even adds spice to the situation, and the divine ruler maliciously taunts Hera and Athena with their inactivity while Aphrodite plays a practical joke on their Achaean friends. The taunts precipitate a crisis. Zeus suggests to the council of the gods that this would be the occasion to end the war, if it should be their pleasure. But his mocking remarks have developed in Hera a fine *cholos*; with indignation she rejects the idea that all her sweat and toil for the destruction of Troy should be wasted, and grimly she assures Zeus that not all the gods will give their assent. The subsequent Jovian remonstrations only provoke pointed legal information that Zeus is not the absolute ruler of the world; the Olympian constitution is a limited monarchy, and each of the gods has inalienable rights and privileges. The crisis is overcome by compromise. Zeus cannot overrule the will of Hera to destroy his Ilion, but he can threaten her with retaliation against cities that are dear to her heart. Hera accepts the threat, and in exchange for Troy she will offer no resistance whenever Zeus wants to lay waste Argos, Sparta, and Mycenae. That appears to be a sensible compromise to the gods. They agree on the destruction of Troy as the first step in the larger program, and Athena is dispatched to inspire the previously described breach of the truce (IV, 1–72).

The problem of disorder, thus, is traced to its ultimate source in the council of the gods, and that is as far as the *Iliad* goes. The time to take stock of the results, however, has not yet come. This assembly of the gods whose principal occupation seems to be the destruction of Mycenaean civilization is odd to say the least. Before penetrating more deeply into the mysteries of Homeric theology we shall do well to broaden the basis of the study by the ideas which the *Odyssey* has to contribute to the subject of order and disorder.

THE *ODYSSEY* ON DISORDER

The *Odyssey* opens with an assembly of the gods in a somewhat different mood. The great war now lies ten years in the past; Zeus indulges in remembrance and reflection. Evil there is in the world, like the fate of Aegisthus who slew Agamemnon and in his turn was slain by Orestes. But the mortals are wrong when they say that evil comes from the gods; through their own perversity they create sorrow for themselves beyond their share, as is proven by the case of Aegisthus who was forewarned of his fate if he committed his crimes. Such pious reflections allow Athena to draw the attention of her divine father to the case of Odysseus. He is in the miserable captivity of Calypso on Ogygia, while far away his home is rapidly ruined by the insolent suitors of Penelope. Here is evil without any apparent misdeeds of Odysseus; and one may even say that the gods are its cause. For the goddess Calypso retains him because she wants him as a lover, and Poseidon chases him over the seas relentlessly because he got the better of Polyphemus in quite reasonable self-defense. Zeus admits that the case needs cleaning up if his reflections are to be vindicated. Fortunately Poseidon is absent in a distant country so that the first measures can be taken behind his back; and later he will have to lay by his *cholos* when he sees the other gods united against him. Hermes, thus, is dispatched to Ogygia to inform Calypso that she will have to frustrate her passion and let Odysseus go; while Athena repairs to Ithaca in order to groom Telemachus for resistance to the suitors of his mother (*Od.* I, 31–95).

As far as the gods are concerned the evil that still can be attributed to their little indulgences in *eros* and *cholos* will be liquidated under the new regime of mellow morality. As far as the mortals are concerned, the Jovian reflections are the prologue to the disorders of Ithaca and their punishment by the returning Odysseus. We must dispense with the intricacies of Achaean marriage law (meticulously described by Homer in order to isolate the precise crime of the unwanted suitors), with the subtle degrees of rottenness in the princely suitors, as well as with the colorful story of the return and punishment. We rather must concentrate on the fundamental traits which characterize the disintegration of public order. In describing the symptoms of disintegration Homer uses the same method as in the corresponding description of disorder in Troy, in so far as he traces the symptoms through the ranks of the constitutional hierarchy.

The evil at the royal top of the pyramid is obvious. The king is absent for almost twenty years, while his old father is powerless in retirement. The son, Telemachus, is an unimpressive youth of twenty. His decency, it is true, is not impaired by the embarrassing situation in the house, and he even gives some promise of development under the guidance of Athena, but he will at best grow into a friendly average. Even the goddess shows impatience with his dispiriting insignificance and reflects gloomily: "Few sons grow like their fathers; most are worse, and only few are better" (*Od.* II, 276ff.). With this generalization from the disheartening appearance of Telemachus, Athena continues the reflections of Nestor in the *Iliad* that the generation of Troy is no match to the companions of his youth; the generation of Telemachus is a further decline.

Next in the hierarchy come the nobles of the Cephallenian region. The most distinguished among them should form the constitutional council and see to it that a regency is established in the absence of Odysseus, or that the succession to the kingship be regulated. The older members of the nobility, as far as they have not joined the expedition against Troy, are on the whole decent-minded but few in number and powerless against the trend of the younger generation. And the younger lords are the wastrels who, a hundred strong, have occupied the manor of Odysseus and devour its substance while beleaguering Penelope. They presume Odysseus to be dead but neither do they recognize his son as the king, nor does any one among them have sufficient stature to reach for the kingship himself. The kingdom is in leaderless anarchy. The contrast between the old and the young, for the rest, plays an important role throughout the *Odyssey*. Its meaning appears perhaps most clearly in the figures of the swineherd Eumaeus and the Odysseus in beggar's disguise: The old men of quality are in disguise and low station, while rank and public status belong to the young vulgarity.

The role of the people, finally, as well as its relation to the nobility, is characterized on occasion of the assembly which Telemachus convokes at the behest of Athena. No session of the assembly has been held since Odysseus left for Troy. An old lord (one of whose sons is among the suitors), a friend of Odysseus, presides over the meeting. Telemachus appears, not as king or successor to the kingship, but as a private plaintiff, seeking help from the people against the nobles who destroy his property. The constitutional order as a whole thus comes into play. The noble suitors are incensed by this appeal to the assembly; but they are also afraid, and by heated argument they try to avert the people's attention from the issue. The assembly, however, has not much stomach anyway for armed action, amounting to civil war, that is, for the only action that could dislodge the brazen suitors. The sullen hesitation of the people becomes so nauseating that Mentor puts a curse on them: May no king in the future be kind and righteous, let him be stern and unrighteous, since Odysseus is not remembered by the people over whom he ruled like a father! (*Od.* II, 229–41). The corruption reaches down to the people; if the future should bring a decline from kingship to tyranny they would not deserve any better.

THE AETIOLOGY OF DISORDER

It will be possible now to appraise the theory of order that emerges from the Homeric epics — if, for lack of a more appropriate one, the term theory will be allowed to signify a technique of symbolization which is distinctly pre-theoretical. The appraisal will best commence from a problem that lies at the heart of the Homeric symbolism, that is, from the function of the gods. It has been frequently observed that the reflections of Zeus at the opening of the *Odyssey* are something like a theodicy. The gods are absolved from causing evil in the world. That seems to be a purer, or at least more carefully reflected, conception of the gods than can be found in the *Iliad*; and the apparent advance of religious sentiment and theology is used as an argument for dating the *Odyssey* later than the *Iliad*.

We do not question the later date of the *Odyssey*, but we are inclined to question the premises on which the argument is based. For the argument from increasing purity presupposes that "gods" are something of which one can have purer or less pure conceptions independent of a larger context; that there is a "theological" development in isolation from a general view concerning the order of human existence in society. Such presuppositions, however, will appear dubious as soon as they are examined more closely. Let us assume, as an hypothesis, that there are no more than two sources of evil, *i.e.*, gods and men. In that case a shifting of responsibility from one source to the other can only purify gods at the expense of men, or men at the expense of gods; the purer the one side becomes, the impurer will be the other side. Neither the reality nor the amount of evil are touched by such shiftings; and what precisely is to be gained by locating evil in man rather than in the gods will remain obscure as long as such operations are interpreted under the aspect of their "purifying" results.

The opening of the *Odyssey* will acquire a new significance if we recognize that Homer is concerned, not with purification of the gods, but with the aetiology of disorder. Evil is experienced as real; and the evil forces which disrupt order certainly are disturbing enough to invite exploration of their nature and source. The location, or transfer, of responsibility will become of lively interest if it is understood as a search for *truth* about the source of evil. Truth is Homer's concern rather than purification. And since the "gods" are not self-contained entities but power complexes in the order of being that also embraces man, an increase of truth about the gods will also be an increase of truth about man. What really is at stake, therefore, is not a progress of morality or theology but the genuinely theoretical issue of the nature of being as far as order and disorder of human existence in society are concerned.

If the issue, thus, is restated in ontological terms, the relation between gods and men will appear in a new light. Gods and men are not fixed entities but more or less clearly discerned forces in an order which embraces them both. The primary experience is that of an order of being which permeates man and transcends him. Both relations are of equal importance; there is no clearly circumscribed order of man, over-arched by a transcendent order of the gods; the forces that operate and interact in the comprehensive order of being rather reach into man himself in such a manner that the borderline between human and transhuman is blurred. If in the interplay of forces man is distinguishable as a unit at all, it is by virtue of his bodily existence in space that will be terminated by death. And even this formulation attributes to the complex called man more of a demarcation than it actually has in the epics. For in the language of Homer there are no words for body and soul.

The word *soma* which in later Greek means "body" occurs indeed but it has the meaning of "dead body," "corpse." The living human shape can only be designated by *chros*, skin; and *chros* does not mean skin in the anatomical sense (the skin or pelt that can be skinned off an animal, *derma*), but skin in the sense of a surface that is the bearer of color and visibility. This Homeric visibility of surface (as distinguished from our notion of bodily existence) is an immaterial, intangible quality to which unexpected things may happen. The visible shape may become invisible at the right tactical moment and reappear elsewhere, as in the case of the vanishing Paris. And then again it may expand demonically as in the appearance of Achilles when he frightens the Trojans from the body of Patroclus, with a thick golden cloud around his head and shining flames rising from the cloud, shouting with the sound of a trumpet. Such diminutions and exaltations of visible shape, however, are understood as more than human; they only occur with the help of the gods, an intermediate phenomenon as it were between normal human appearance and the occasional donning of visible shape by the immortals. The conception of a "living body" as it is familiar to us does not exist in the epics; it would presuppose the notion of an animating principle that endows the body with form, the notion of a "soul" — and there is no word for "soul" in the epics.

Again, to be sure, the word *psyche* which in later Greek means "soul" is present as is the word *soma* but it signifies an organ of man rather than the organizing form of a body. Not much information can be extracted about this *psyche* from the epics, except that it means a life-force which leaves man in death and then leads a miserable, independent existence as the shadow, the *eidolon*. And since there is no conception of the soul, such phenomena as "emotions," "stirring of emotions," "thinking," cannot be conceived as functions of the psyche but must be understood (by the terms *thymos* and *noos*) as additional organs of man. The problems of man and his soul are not absent from the Homeric work, as we shall see presently; nevertheless, this peculiar articulation of a man into a bundle of organs and forces compels the poet to treat such questions by means of a symbolism which barely recognizes man as a well-circumscribed, world-immanent center of action.[2]

The Homeric problems of order originate in the uncertainties concerning the nature of man. Only one thing is really certain even about Homeric man: he must die. Hence, "mortal" is the preferred synonym for man, distinguishing his nature without a doubt from that of the immortal gods. For the rest, the transhuman elements of the order of being penetrate so deeply into man or, from the other side, man is yet so imperfectly closed as a self-conscious, reflecting agent, that the status of various phenomena as human or divine must remain in doubt and, in particular, that quite frequently it will not be certain to what extent the actions of man are his actions at all. Homer's difficulties in dealing with these problems, as well as the importance of his partial solutions, can be understood only if we place ourselves in his position. If, on the contrary, we interpret the epics under the assumption that he knew already what gods and men were, his specific achievement in clarifying the nature of man and the meaning of order will be obscured. Hence, we shall approach the problem casuistically by analyzing the two main classes of action as they appear in the epics, that is, first the actions which maintain and restore order, and second the actions which disturb order.

All through the epics run divine interventions which result in human decisions of public importance. A typical case is the energetic action of Odysseus, in *Iliad* II, when he holds back the army that is on the point of boarding ship for home; it is an action at the behest of Athena. The cases of this type are rather frequent. Any human decision, hesitation, or resolution somewhat out of the ordinary is apt to appear as inspired by divine counsel. They are so frequent indeed that sometimes the interventions themselves become a routine; Athena is a ubiquitous lady, especially in the *Odyssey*, arranging the voyage of Telemachus step by step, from pushing the young man into action, to outfitting the ship and getting him on his way. On the whole, however, the interventions effectively serve the purpose of raising the otherwise irrelevant doings of man to the rank of actions which are transparent toward the order of being. Ordinary men, going about their ordinary business, are not favored in this manner; the divine appearances are bestowed on the heroes when the consequences of their action affect public order. Hence, action in this limited sense acquires the more-than-human meaning of a manifestation of divine order; and the hero in the Homeric sense can be defined as the man in whose actions a more-than-human order of being becomes manifest. The Homeric clarification of the meaning of action was continued by Aeschylus. In his *Suppliants* especially, Aeschylus characterized heroic action (that is the only action deserving the name, as distinguished from ordinary doings) as the decision for Dike against demonic disorder; the order of the polis, in so far as it was established and maintained by such action, represented the order of Zeus. Action at the heroic height, thus, is as much human as it is the manifestation of a divine force. And the public order of a society, in so far as at critical junctures it depends on the forthcoming of such action, is precariously maintained in being at the borderline of this meeting of human with divine forces.

The aetiology of order and disorder obviously cannot be reduced to a simple formula. Are the gods who inspire, or the men who obey, responsible for heroic action? And who is responsible for a debacle when a hero did not receive a divine inspiration at the right moment—the god who played truant or the man who embarked on an unfortunate course of action by his own light? And such questions become even more pungent when actions are disruptive. What is the status of *ate* in Homeric ethics? On the one hand, she is blinding passion that motivates actions in violation of just order; on the other hand, she is a goddess, the oldest daughter of Zeus who, on occasion, plays a trick even on her own father. Who is responsible for misdeeds caused by *ate?* A detailed answer to such questions would require a monograph. We can do more than state the principle of Homer's position, supported by a few cases.

Through the *Iliad* the poet seems to be engaged in a subtle polemic against the morality of several of his figures—and the polemic quite probably is also aimed at his social environment which sympathized with the figures. Take the case of Achilles. From Homer's descriptions he emerges as a splendid warrior, useful to have on your side in an emergency, but as a not very appealing figure, almost a pathological case. And the poet leaves no doubt that the trouble stems from toying and tampering with fate, from misusing the divine Thetis for satisfying the hero's childish desires, and from a reluctance to shoulder the burden of humanity. The difficulties fall apart when the burden of fate and responsibility is accepted with humility.

. . .

On the basis of the preceding analysis we can venture to formulate the relation between the two epics. The *Iliad*, so it seems, is much richer in its exploration of the mysteries of action than the second epic. It is hardly permissible to consider the *Odyssey* an advance beyond the *Iliad* with regard to theology or religious sentiments. At most one can say that in the prologue in heaven Homer states in explicit terms the problem that occupied him all through the *Iliad*, i.e., the aetiology of evil. The term "aetiology," hitherto used undefined, does require, and can now receive, some precision. We are using the term because it is Homer's word in dealing with his problem. The question is whether the gods are *aitioi* or not *aitioi* with regard to the evil that befalls man. The meaning of *aitios* (*Il.* III, 164) ranges, in the Homeric contexts, from "guilty" or "blameworthy" to "responsible for" or "being the cause of." When Homer speaks of men who ascribe evil to the gods, he uses the word *aitioontai*, (*Od.* I, 32), with a corresponding range of meaning from "they accuse" or "blame" the gods to "they make them responsible," or see in them the "source" or "cause" of evil. The primary concern of Homer is not a vindication of the gods but the interpretation which men put on their own misconduct. The tendency of his aetiological interest can, therefore, be circumscribed by the following theses:

(1) Man is in the habit of making the gods responsible for his misdeeds, as well as for the evil consequences engendered by his misconduct.

(2) Theoretically, this habit implies the assertion that the gods are the cause of the evil which men do and suffer. This assertion is wrong. It is man, not the gods, who are responsible for evil.

(3) Practically, this habit is dangerous to social order. Misdeeds will be committed more easily if responsibility can be shifted to the gods.

(4) Historically, a civilizational order is in decline and will perish, if this habit finds general social acceptance.

This circumscription of Homer's aetiological concern can be based on the *Iliad* alone. The reflections of Zeus, in the *Odyssey*, do no more than state a part of the problem in direct language, preparatory to the evil which the suitors bring on themselves by their deeds.

The most impressive phenomenon, as always in the decline of an order, must have been the acts of wanton indulgence, due to *eros* and *cholos*, as well as of ambition "beyond the share" (*hyper moron*) (*Od.* I, 35), which break the right order (*themis*) so frequently and so deeply that a society is no longer capable of self-defense. This is the phenomenon which Toynbee has called the suicide of a civilization. Since this is the same phenomenon which Plato tried to analyze in the Hellenic case, it should not surprise us that the Homeric aetiological concern (as set forth in the four theses) bears a remarkable resemblance to Platonic problems.

In the present context, however, the resemblance is less important than the great difference which is due to the fact that Homer wrote before, while Plato wrote after the discovery of the psyche. The Homeric achievement is remarkable as a struggle for the understanding of the psyche with the rather crude symbols that we have studied. Homer astutely observed that the disorder of a society was a disorder in the soul of its component members, and especially in the soul of the ruling class. The symptoms of the disease were magnificently described by the great poet; but the true genius of the great thinker revealed itself in the creation of a tentative psychology without the aid of an adequate conceptual apparatus. Without having a term for it, he envisaged man as having a psyche with an internal organization through a center of passions and a second center of ordering and judging knowledge. He understood the tension between the two centers, as well as the tricks which passion plays on better knowledge. And he strove valiantly for the insight that ordering action is action in conformance with transcendent, divine order, while disruptive action is a fall from the divine order into the specifically human disorder. We can discern the dim outlines of the Platonic anthropology, and even of the Platonic postulate that God rather than the disorderly velleities of man should be the measure of human action.

This strand of Homer's thought, however, had to dangle as a loose end because the theoretical means for weaving it into a consistent conception of order were not available. If we read the famous opening of the *Odyssey* with care, we find Zeus reflecting that men, through their own folly, create sorrow for themselves "beyond their share" (*Od.* I, 34). The gods are not responsible for the evil that men bring on themselves — but who is responsible for the evil that is not caused by man, and apparently not by the gods either? The clean division into divine order and human disorder leaves a considerable residue of evil, symbolized in the epics by various means. First of all, the divine order of the Olympians extends only to the inhabited earth with its human societies; it does not extend to the elemental realm of Poseidon, or the underworld of Hades; Zeus is the highest of the gods and has sovereign prerogatives, but his jurisdiction has definite barriers. In the second place, the Olympian gods themselves are a dubious source of undisturbed order, beset as they are by jurisdictional quarrels of their own and by domestic strife. And, thirdly, there is Moira, Fate, with its decisions beyond the influence of the other gods. Homer did not attempt a theoretical penetration of this wilderness beyond the island of precarious Jovian order. Such symbols as the Platonic creation of the divine puppet player, who pulls the various cords and leaves it to man to follow the right one, were not yet at his disposition.

Nevertheless, as far as the central problem, the breakdown of Mycenaean civilization, was concerned, it was clear that something more was needed by way of an explanation than the misconduct of a few members of the ruling class. Individuals, as for instance Aegisthus or the suitors, could be forewarned that their personal crimes would find terrible retribution. But the historical process in which a society declines, as well as the infinitude of acts which in the aggregate of centuries spell destruction, had a pattern of their own that could not be described in terms of individual misdeeds. Homer had to face the problem that the day-to-day causality of human action will explain the detail of the historical process but not its configuration. His answer to this mystery of the rise and fall of civilizations was the extraordinary Olympian assembly at which Zeus and Hera agreed on their program for the destruction of Mycenaean civilization, including both Trojans and Achaeans. The answer may seem crude today; but again, Homer could not yet invent a highly theorized symbol like the myth of the alternative motions of the universe in Plato's *Statesman*. And if we remember that even a modern thinker, with the experience of two thousand years of metaphysics at his disposition, could do no better than invent the *List der Vernunft* in order to explain the pattern of history, the achievement of Homer in recognizing the problem will command our respect.

Notes

1. On this section cf. Walter F. Otto, *Theophania* (Hamburg, 1956), 28–33, and in general the same author's *Die Goetter Griechenlands* (4th ed., Frankfurt, 1956).

2. For Homer's anthropology cf. Bruno Snell, *Die Entdeckung des Geistes. Studien zur Entstehung des europaeischen Denkens bei den Griechen* (Hamburg, 1946), the chapter "Die Auffassung des Menschen bei Homer."

Image, Symbol, and Formula   Cedric H. Whitman*

It is a commonplace of criticism to observe that Greek poetry is more direct than English poetry, in the sense that the Greek poets, with the notable exception of Pindar and Aeschylus,[1] make far less use of metaphor and other forms of figurative language than do the English. Even English prose of the simplest sort is full of metaphors and metonymy, such as the "flow of time" or a "torrent of abuse," which have, of course, lost nearly all their figurative force and have become mere trite circumlocutions. Rendered into Greek literally, these would be all but unintelligible, for although all the forms of Greek poetry have clichés which are peculiar to their own idioms, they are seldom imagistic. The reason for this fact

*Reprinted from *Homer and the Homeric Tradition* (Cambridge: Harvard University Press, 1958), 102–27, by permission of the publisher.

cannot be found in the neoclassic doctrine of "suitability," which began with Aristotle and culminated in Boileau and Pope. The Greeks were not afraid of bold or far-fetched images; indeed, when they do use images, they generally use bold ones, and some of the metaphoric flights of Aeschylus and Pindar dazzle even the modern reader, when they do not make him wince. One could more easily imagine Aeschylus adopting Eliot's "coils of light spiralling downward to the horror of the ape," than using such a phrase as the "flow of time." Perhaps the latter is too tame. More likely, the Greek poet ordinarily felt no need to transform his language in this way, but used imagery for more specific ends than the general one of keeping his language indirect and poetic. By and large, he presented his thoughts in a language which is as direct as it is concentrated and intense.

Modern criticism tends to find the essence of poetic speech in metaphor, and to regard the art of poetry as primarily imagistic, while the more external elements of the form, meter, rhyme, and even the other rhetorical figures, are purely secondary. If this view is true, a serious question arises about Greek poets, especially Homer: how to account for the power of a poet who has always been found so singularly lacking in metaphor? It has been estimated that there are only twenty-five real metaphors in the whole first book of the *Iliad*, which has six hundred and eleven lines.[2] At the rate of one metaphor in each twenty-four-and-a-half lines, few poems would be effective. Either metaphor cannot be so central, or else Homer has been overestimated. But there is a third alternative, that Homer may be indeed more metaphoric than has been thought. The directness of Homer's language is striking, but it is very far from the directness of prose. If it lacks metaphor in the modern sense, it is nonetheless a tremendous imagistic texture, and metaphoric in the sense that all language is, in a way, metaphoric. In order to make clear what is meant, it will be necessary to explore the meaning of metaphor and of poetic speech in general. It must also be borne in mind that in Homer we are dealing with an oral, traditional style, and that the problem therefore differs somewhat from the problem as found in written literature. This is not to say that the poems do not exhibit many of the virtues found in written literature; they do. Even a purely literary approach reveals many of their profound vistas. But the question of metaphor well illustrates the limits of the method. In the Homeric epic we have to deal with something which established many of the literary assumptions of Western culture, but which in its oral, traditional origins was modally different from all subsequent poetry.

Even on the surface, Homer is by no means lacking in figurative language. The most evident kind is, of course, the great epic simile, rising like a prismatic inverted pyramid upon its one point of contact with the action. Metaphor occurs, though sparsely: when fighters fall, they "sleep the brazen sleep," or "night wraps their eyes." The Achaeans are subdued by the "scourge of Zeus."[3] The somewhat mysterious "bridges of war" may be metaphor.[4] Among the lesser figures, one can find examples of metonymy, synecdoche, apostrophe, anaphora, personification, onomatopoeia, and probably others.[5] But even if these were more numerous than they are, they would not explain the power of the Homeric style which Matthew Arnold described as simple, rapid, and noble. Homer is unique in the ability to call things by their right names — helmet, ship, or shield — and make them strike the ear as rich and strange. Thus what might be called the "first level" of the poems, the rational, factual level, has an intense beauty of its own, which perhaps partly explains Homer's appeal to children. In any case, it makes him the most sensuously vivid of all poets; whatever extended implications may exist, it is never necessary to grasp these before one can feel the poetic fire of a scene. The simplest statements of fact or action have a compact vitality and immediacy which put all naturalistic modes of realism to shame. For all his scarcity of the more familiar types of figurative imagery, except simile, Homer's lines are as sharply imagistic as it is possible to conceive; all is clear, pure, and detailed. What is the secret of such a poetic method, which seems to do without so many of the poetic modes of other literature, and why is there no prosaic dross in these long narratives which seem to have so much to record in the way of plain fact, common action, saga, genealogy, and catalogue? To answer the question, one must examine the components of the epic style itself, and see in what way it is related to the imagistic and symbolic procedures of poetry in general.

It is not easy to find satisfactory definitions for the terms "symbol" and "image" as used in literary criticism. In general, however, the poetic symbol is a word or phrase which carries a larger meaning than that which it denotes, and this larger meaning is determined and limited by the contextual associations of the work in which it stands. Such association is clearly distinct from the "free association" of psychoanalytical method; and similarly the poetic symbol, in being more fluid, is distinct from the more or less fixed Freudian symbolism of dreams, though it may make use of the latter. An image, on the other hand, is primarily a word or phrase devised to evoke sense impression, visual, auditory, or any other. Images may, and easily do, become symbols by association, and how rapidly this can happen is well illustrated by Shakespeare's: "Put out the light, and then put out the light." But the first function of an image is a direct appeal to that part of the mind which recognizes sense-experience.

The term "direct appeal" demands clarification, for it is precisely the direct appeal of Homer's narrative method which is the immediate object of this inquiry. Since both symbols and images appeal directly to the mind — the latter primarily to sense, the former to wider realms of association — it will be necessary to explore briefly the psychology underlying this appeal, and to seek the wider meanings of symbolism. The clearest and most convenient formulation is that of Susanne Langer, in her brilliant *Philosophy in a New Key*. According to Mrs. Langer, the chief function of the brain is to select, classify, and transform by recombination the data of sense-experience. This function, which she terms "symbolic," or "symbolific transformation," terminates in two modes of expression, the discursive and the presentational.[6] The discursive mode is the logical, syntactical symbolism of language, and it relates primarily to the process of logical, rational thinking. Its communications require time, and they depend for intelligibility upon a selective series of articulate sounds and a systematic syntax. The presentational mode is that of the visual arts, whose syntax, if so it may be called, lacks the systematic aspect of language, requires no time to be envisioned whole, and relates primarily to the intuitive side of the mind.[7]

In these two contrasting modes, clearly two contrasting types of symbolism are represented, the one mediated by time, and controlled by the denotative limits of words and the framework of logic, the other immediate, supralogical, and controlled only by the structure evolved by its own intention. It is the latter which is essentially the mode of art, but two major arts offer odd combinations of both modes. Music, though consisting basically of tones, which are presentational, requires time to be heard entire, and employs in the laws of harmony and counterpoint an extended syntax analogous to that of language. And poetry uses, as its only medium, the discursive mode of language. Yet when we speak of the "direct appeal" of an image or symbol, we mean that it appeals as an image of painting or sculpture appeals to the mind, that is, presentationally, and without the intermediate office of any extended, or rational, syntax. We may well ask how, in any art whose entire medium is discursive, it is possible to achieve symbols or images whose effect is presentational. Where the symbol or image consists of a single word, the problem scarcely arises, for no grammatical syntax is involved, and the amount of time required to pronounce one word is scarcely sufficient to intervene between it and the mind's response to its meaning. Indeed, in one of Saroyan's plays, a character writes poems consisting of one word only, such as "Tree" or "Is." But while it must be admitted that this character understood the basic problem of poetry, the amputatory method is not the answer, for poetry aims at more than monosyllabic images. It aims at images in series and in relation to each other, all functioning in the service of a complex total meaning, toward which its vehicle of words and grammar are not by nature ideally conducive.

"All art," said Nietzsche, "aspires to the condition of music," meaning that all art aspires to achieve its end through pure form. In the twentieth century, nonobjective painting and the "nonthinking" school of poets, led by Gertrude Stein, attest the challenge of other arts to music's primacy in the sphere of pure formalism. Yet these answers are somewhat like that of Saroyan's poet. Form in painting implies a struggle with subject matter, and form in poetry implies a reckoning with the intellective reference of words. To remove the problems implicit in the raw materials of an art is not to solve them. The chief symptomatic difference between poetry and prose is that the latter, in using a discursive symbolism to a discursive end, has its problem of the adjustment of form and content already solved: grammatical syntax corresponds to logical (ideational) syntax. The poet's problem is to make grammatical syntax correspond to the presentational syntax of his intended work of art. If grammar wins the day, his work is frigid, or prosaic. The problem is even further complicated by the fact that poetry is not to be divested wholly of its discursive quality, which is implied by the medium. Attempts to do so, such as those mentioned above, are, like the attempts of Bernini and other artists of the Baroque to transcend their media, manneristic. Whatever their success or partial success, they are very foreign to classical Greek poetry, and differ from it in much the same way that Bernini's pontifical tombs, where marble is made to resemble silk, differ from the classical sculptor's acquiescence to his material. The answer is not to annihilate the discursive quality, but to transform it. Any poet, especially an epic poet with a story to relate, must deal with words in grammatical relationships, but these grammatical relationships must constantly create the presentational, formal syntax of the poem, the artistic life and meaning which it must, as poem, possess apart from the strict denotation of its words and the logical sequence of its ideas.

It is by means of the image and the poetic symbol, as defined above, that language is made presentational. Any word alone may be imagistic, except perhaps colorless modal auxiliaries, and any word may be a poetic symbol, hence presentational. But when a group of grammatically related words become presentational, it is because some technique has been employed to suppress their grammatical symbolism in favor of a presentational symbolism. The importance of the time element is consequently also diminished, since the sense of evolving thought is transcended by the imagistic unity of the total phrase. The techniques which so tend to identify groups of words with artistic rather than logical syntax are familiar: metaphor and the other figures, departure from colloquial order of words, actual omission of some grammatical factor which can easily be understood, meter with its effect of contrapuntally modifying the normal sound of words, rhyme which tends to emphasize sound over sense, and finally diction itself. For when we praise a poet's choice of a right or inevitable word, we must remember that it is chosen in reference to the poem's artistic end, and not for its dictionary meaning. Language thus used becomes imagistic and symbolic in a new sense. As a picture of a cat is a symbol of a cat, but not a definition of a cat,[8] so too poetic language is a symbol of the thing represented, but not its definition.[9] It must now be asked, how far can the process go? Can poetic economy be so complete that every word in a poem will be presentational, or must there be always some dross?

In the *Four Quartets*, Eliot seems to have admitted that, in certain poetic forms at least, there must be some dross, a residue of unavoidable discursiveness which one may as well treat as frankly unpoetic. But a glance at three lines from Shakespeare will show that even the humblest words can be drawn by a skilled hand into a symbolic scheme: "O Westmoreland, thou art a summer bird / That ever in the haunch of winter sings / The lifting up of day."[10] Here the isolation of *a* bird of joy against *the* given fact of winter grief completes the metaphor with a special poignancy. If the position of the two articles be exchanged, this poignancy totally disappears, and the image becomes an optimistic one of perfectly expectable, even inevitable, rescue from casual misfortune. The limits of meaning of the definite and indefinite article are here used to frame a psychic attitude characteristic of the aging and guilt-laden Henry IV.

Any word, therefore, even the indefinite article, may become symbolic in a poetic scheme, that is, it may contribute presentationally and not merely grammatically to that scheme. Imagery does so in that its very diction, carefully selected, prompts a unified, though perhaps highly complex and articulated, sensory response. Symbols, in the full sense of poetic symbols, do so by virtue of their accumulated contextual meanings in the poem. To illustrate: in the first book of the *Iliad*, the image of fire occurs in the burning pyres of those dead of the plague.[11] It is simply an image, and a vivid one. But in the course of the poem fire takes on a host of associations, and becomes in a sense the symbol of the chief action of the poem. Such a process is possible only in an art which employs a medium where meaning is both denotative and connotative. In spite, therefore, of the grammatical, discursive problem, words, with their specific denotative force and their power of almost infinite semantic expansion through connotation, offer perhaps the richest soil of all for artistic symbolism. Synonyms, for instance, by virtue of identical denotation, and even homonyms, or near-homonyms, through similarity of sound, may both contribute to the symbolic structure.

To return now to the *Iliad* and the *Odyssey*: it has sometimes been felt that the formulaic, oral style which Homer inherited from the epic tradition could not, since it was not his own creation, have anything to do with his genius, which was to be sought instead in his departures from oral method. But besides the fact that we cannot point to a single certain departure from the method, it must be said that Homer's genius is profoundly involved with the traditional style, and we shall not understand his unique power without first understanding the aesthetics of the style itself. This whole aspect of formulaic verse has been ignored, partly because Parry's studies in epic technique emphasized the functionalism of the formula, and its origin in the long, slow work of multitudinous singers.[12] That the formulae are traditional and functional is granted. What else they are remains to be seen.

One of the chief characteristics of the epic formula is that it regularly occupies a given metrical position in the hexameter. The proper name with its epithet is many times more frequent at the end of a line than at the beginning. The word [*cheír'*], "hand," is very frequent in the *Iliad*; in the nominative or accusative plural, if modified by [*áaptoi*] or [*áaptous*], "invincible," it invariably closes the line; but the phrase [*èn cheíressi*], "in his hands," always begins the second foot of the hexameter. A glance at the Homeric concordance could multiply examples of such practice almost to infinity. A formula is, in fact, a semantic unit identified with a metrical demand, and it is a testimony to the extraordinary strictness and economy of the singers that there are so few duplications, or formulaic alternatives with the same meaning and metric.[13] There are a very few exceptions, and certainly a word changes position more easily than a phrase does, but in general both words and phrases are fixed in definite metrical positions.[14]

Another peculiarity of the epic formula is the semantic unity of its parts. This is especially true of noun-and-epithet combinations, such as "Agamemnon king of men," "swift-footed horses," and "rose-fingered dawn." These are not meant to be heard analytically, but more as names given in full; they are the equivalents of Agamemnon, horses, and dawn, and, often repeated, fall on the ear as units. Yet they are ornamental units also, and richer than the mere nouns alone would be. Furthermore, such unity is not confined to phrases involving nouns with epithets. The battle books of the *Iliad* abound with a bewildering variety of formulae, all metrically different, but all conveying the fall of a warrior who has his death wound: "his limbs were loosened," "he seized the earth with his palm," "night wrapped his eyes," "his armor rattled upon him" (as he fell), and a great many others. All frequently recur, and once their meaning is known, the ear no longer distinguishes the words so much as accepts the phrase whole. "So speaking, he sat down" crystallizes to a single image. Some formulae even fill whole lines, yet their essential unity is not lost: "Thus he spoke, and brandishing hurled a long-shadowing spear." One may break this down into words, but one tends to read it, or hear it, simply as one expression, embodying the act of ceasing to speak and hurling a long spear. The line is a unity, and even the strongly imagistic word "long-shadowing" does not dominate its force, which is kinetic and narrative. The mind's singularly unified response to the formula is observable in the beginning student's frequent ability to translate a formula correctly, though he may have forgotten which word means what. The process can extend even to those passages of many lines, such as the descriptions of a feast, launching a ship, or arming for battle. Such nonanalytic unity of meaning also is functional in origin. The singer wanted a phrase with a certain meaning and devised it; once devised, it could be reused, but only as a whole. To break it up or alter it was possible, but then one made another whole. The formula, not the word, was the epic unit. And the same is true of the longer repeated scenes. They might be lengthened or shortened, but they were units, to be used as such.[15]

One might, therefore, describe the epic formula as an artificially devised unit of semantic, grammatical, and metrical functions. As such, it has clearly transcended the discursive function of speech, and has become a vividly presentational medium, in short, an art form. Whether or not a given formula embodies an actual metaphor, it is nevertheless always imagistic, and appeals directly to the senses. Its artificially devised union of metric and meaning subordinates its grammar and suppresses the time sense, so that from the materials of a discursive symbolism has been made a building block of a presentational symbolism. The formula is functional, therefore, not merely in the sense that it assists in creating verse, but also because it is a sort of poetic atom, a fragment of technically transformed speech whose structure is already that of art, not logic.

Oral epic is not, then, in a sense composed of words at all; its formulae are not the words of speech, but units of poetry and song. The paucity of metaphor is perhaps best explained by this fact alone; for all poetic speech is an artifice aiming at the subordination of logical relationships to the symbolism of artistic form, and the task is equally well performed, if not better performed, by a specially devised series of formulae as it is by metaphor. It appears, in fact, that metaphor is only one of many techniques employed by the formula for making images.

Since our knowledge of ancient Greek oral technique comes from two Homeric poems alone, it is difficult to state with certainty the extent of the formulaic system. For all the fixity of the combinations of noun and epithet, the crystallization of frequent phrases, and the all but complete absence of duplication among formulae, there is also an enormous amount of variation in Homer's phraseology, and the vocabulary of the poems is staggeringly large. It may well be asked how much of all this can be formulaic. It was Parry's conviction that everything in Homeric style was traditional and formulaic, though he recognized that without more evidence certainty was impossible.[16] But two internal facts of the Homeric poems themselves tend to justify Parry's opinion. First, it is clear from the concordances to Homer that, for all the variations, almost every word (not to mention whole phrases) has a preferred position in the line, or two preferred positions, and not more as a rule. In the case of words and phrases occurring only once, of which there are many, the greatest doubt arises. Yet even these phrases are often formed on the analogy of other phrases whose formulaic nature is apparent, and often enough the word which occurs alone but once occurs in an otherwise well-known formula. The second fact which leads one to believe that the whole style is formulaic and traditional is the dialectal mixture. No attempt to separate the various contributions of Aeolic, Ionic, and the others has ever been successful. Any dialectal form may turn up anywhere, which would certainly not be the case had Homer, who presumably spoke one dialect, altered the traditional epic idiom to any appreciable extent.

It is more than likely, therefore, that essentially everything in Homer is formulaic, and that to look for Homer's verbal contribution is vain. He doubtless made some. But creativity of this sort took place totally in terms of formulae, some of which were often the special possession, or even personal creation, of individual singers;[17] it would be most difficult, without the discovery of other contemporary epics, to put one's finger on a single phrase which is Homer's own, though one may suspect the *Shield of Achilles* of containing not a few. But Homer's own genius could not have lain chiefly in the devising of new formulae; in a traditional style there is little premium upon verbal, or even formulaic, novelty. It is the genius of the style itself, more than it is Homer's genius, which appears in the splendor or aptitude of individual phrases.

In actuality, when one considers the extent of the formulaic method, it is clear that the functional purpose which gave birth to it was far transcended in the phase of its greatest development. The wide range of phraseological variation, while it confirms rather than upsets the oral theory, also proves that mere convenience was only a minor consideration to a really skilled singer. Homer could say anything. A poor singer might have only a few formulae, comparatively speaking. But Homer's immense range shows what the traditional style was to one who really commanded it. It was a language within a language, and must have been learned as a language is learned, by ear and use. It was a presentational, imagistic, and highly formalized language also, in which each unit had been turned on the lathe of generations of poetic artificers, into a perfected and inevitable device, satisfying both the functional and the artistic needs of the poet.[18] Grace and accuracy of observation characterize the mosaic pieces of this language, and each is itself the symbol of an idea, an image, or an action. Yet, since the whole is still a language, it conducts in a kind of disguise the necessary minimum of discursiveness.

When words are set to music, they become not merely groups of meaningful syllables, but syllables whose meaning, by being adjusted to a tonal pattern, is modified by the formal effect of the union, and suspended in time until the pattern is complete. Something of the sort happens in the making of words into formulae. And if analogies to the technique of Homer have been found in Serbia and Greece itself, it is difficult to find anything analogous to the effect of Homer, in whom the style achieved an extraordinary degree of perfection. Something similar is perhaps to be found in the style of Mozart. Based as it is on a developed aristocratic tradition, whose compositional elements are largely formulaic, the eighteenth-century manner became in Mozart's hands, through sheer skill of deployment, a medium of surpassing emotional and artistic authority, whose impact is of such intimately combined force and elegance that it is hard to say which predominates.

Oral tradition had already, then, provided Homer with a language which needed no further artistic transformation; it was an art-language, and the analysis of it so far has had little to do with Homer as an individual poet. Yet every singer was a creator within the formulaic limits, and therefore Homer's genius should reveal itself in the same way that any creative genius does, in the use of the medium, and in the propriety of the parts to the whole. Only in Homer's case the limits and possibilities of oral technique must be kept in mind.

In general, the combinations of proper names with their epithets stand in Homer as they must have stood in the tradition, and though every epithet may have sprung from an individual source,[19] it ends as a heroic generality whose reference is to the whole heroic world.[20] Any man might be called "mighty," for instance, and any woman "white-armed." These are ideal abstractions of the heroic view of things, symbolical in a way of the sexes, the one as strength, the other as beauty. If the epithet "good at the war cry" seems to be all but confined to Diomedes and Menelaus, it nevertheless does not indicate their particular ability to shout war cries, for it is used, though rarely, also of Hector, Ajax, and Polites, to answer a metrical need. It happens simply because the names Diomedes and Menelaus are metrically equivalent in Greek, and the whole formula fills the second half of the hexameter after the feminine caesura, and never occurs elsewhere. Some heroes, indeed, tend to appropriate to themselves certain particulars of the heroic apparatus, as a large planet collects families of comets. Thus, partly for metrical reasons, but also by reason of special characteristics, Odysseus is "many-counciled," and Achilles is "swift of foot." These two, incidentally, are metrically equivalent, but never exchanged, and indeed it is no mere chance. Odysseus is not principally famed for his swiftness of foot, and Achilles admits his lack of subtlety in council.[21] These, then, are specific character-epithets. Agamemnon's "king of men" epithet may be of similar kind.[22] But it is a question whether they can be regarded as Homer's characterizations, or, like patronymics, regular and traditional for the most famous heroes.[23] Only a very few epithets, uncommon ones for the most part, seem to be used with reference to the specific context in which they stand, such as "much-traveled," used only twice of Odysseus, and "cowardly," used of Aegisthus.[24] For the most part, epithets merely complete names, and their symbolic force, such as it is, lies only in their relating the names to the large tradition of the heroic past, and giving them thereby an added dimension.

On the other hand, since everything in the epic is formulaic, though highly varied formulaic speech, the functional aspect cannot in the large be the determining factor. Functions are functions of something, and in this case, of the poet's intention. The oral poet, like any other, must plan his lines, and he must have some notion of what the end will consist of when he sings the beginning. It is not beyond the oral singer to do so much. The text of Homer may have its little failures, which are due to traditional intrusion of a formulaic word which is actually not at all appropriate.[25] But Homer won fame not for his noddings but for his triumphs. The problem in oral composition was to to invent a new phrase, at least not as a rule, and certainly not unless it was absolutely necessary. The problem was to adjust the building blocks of the poetic speech with reference to association and design.

Another example of the use of a common formula in an uncommon way can be found in the *Patrocleia*, where Patroclus, attempting to scale the Trojan wall, confronts Apollo, and rushes at him, "equal to a god."[26] The phrase is traditional enough, but here it takes on more than a merely honorific force. Patroclus is struggling with Apollo, and, as appears later, he is anything but Apollo's equal. Yet the poet has made it clear just before that Patroclus' great burst of courage is due to the direct inspiration of Zeus, and that this inspiration is yet a "calling unto death."[27] The heroic association of divine valor with death involving a god is implied in the epithet, which moreover recalls Patroclus' first moment of involvement in the action which led to his death. This is the moment when, summoned by Achilles, he comes out of his tent "equal to Ares," and "it was the beginning of his woe."[28] From here on till his death, Patroclus' epithets take on a divine context. One might multiply instances, but at the risk of seeming to isolate special moments of propriety, and obscuring the all-important fact of Homer's consistent felicity in the arrangement of formulae. Each one that seems singularly well chosen depends for its effect on hundreds of lines of texture which have prepared it.[29] No one, for instance, can fail to notice the effect of the common phrase, "glorious gifts," which ends the *Patrocleia*, as the immortal horses of Achilles, "glorious gifts" from the gods to Peleus, carry the charioteer Automedon to safety, leaving Patroclus dead on the field. Its commonplace ring now takes on a peculiar irony, since all Achilles' glorious gifts hereafter will be vain and stale, mere commonplaces of his heroic position. Here it is almost impossible to draw the line between the poet and the style itself, yet the effect is there, an effect of terrible bitterness. Indeed, the whole line, unnecessary for the action alone, seems to have been added to emphasize the connection of Achilles with the Olympians who have espoused his cause and permitted the death of his friend. In Homer's scheme, instead of wearing themselves out, the formulae keep gaining symbolic weight, like rolling snowballs. Achilles is often compared to a lion, but when he strides out the door of his tent "like a lion" after threatening Priam, the image reflects in particular the helpless king's view of him;[30] it cannot, in that moment, remain mere epic ornament. Even such a cliché as the rose-fingered Dawn, who mounts Olympus, passes from the functional to the symbolic by constant reference to the airy world of the gods and their circumambient scheme of divine scathelessness, against which the deadly human drama is played. As one critic aptly remarked, everything becomes symbolic in the hands of a good poet.[31]

In Homer this transformation is as nearly complete as it can possibly be, partly by virtue of the oral style itself, partly by Homer's use of it.

When one approaches some of the larger forms of Homeric imagery, the hand of the poet himself becomes more distinguishable. The similes, as is usually said, rise from a single point of comparison with the action, and thereafter go their own way. This is partly true, yet their way is controlled by the larger pattern to an extent, for if it were not, the extra clauses which regularly expand the similes would be, for all their formulaic immediacy, hopelessly discursive. To continue with lions, for example, they behave variously. It is like a desperate lion that Odysseus emerges from the underbrush and meets Nausicaa:

> Forth like a lion bred in the mountains he started, trusting in strength,
> One that strides rain-soaked and blown by the wind, his eyes
> Blazing; and forthwith comes among cattle or sheep,
> Or among wild deer; and his belly bids him
> Come to assail the flocks, even to the sturdy steadings.[32]

Here the added details give fullness to the picture, but the image is controlled within the limits of the main characters' situations, the wild, sea-battered, and hunger-driven hero in relation to the domestic and defenceless young Phaeacian girls. This rain-and-wind-lashed lion wins a good deal more sympathy, for all his terror, than does the ravening beast to which Agamemnon is compared when he slays two sons of Priam.[33] And these are but two of many variants on the lion theme. The simile may begin at a pinpoint of external similarity, but it ends in character. When Odysseus is compared to an octopus, his two chief characteristics are implied — tenacity and deviousness.[34] Again, in the Phaeacian episode, where the song of Demodocus makes Odysseus weep like a woman captured in the sack of a city,[35] the long-developed image raises a host of implications. Throughout the whole entertainment held in his honor, the mystery of Odysseus, and particularly his striking difference from the Phaeacians, has been subtly implied. They have been testing him, and have found him singularly sufficient and challenging, but his superiority has remained so far an unexplained, half-hidden fire, which has been slowly revealing itself. Now with the simile of the captive woman, Homer suddenly injects a graphic and terrifying vision of the world from which Odysseus comes, a world of burnt cities, slain men, and women dragged to slavery, the old turbulent Achaean world, which to the Phaeacians is just a song for an evening's amusement.[36] The latter, especially Alcinous, have been trying to impress their guest, but now the tables are turned. Before the shattering reality of Odysseus, the long-sufferer, this fairy-tale world of Phaeacia fades to a humble, attentive background. Alcinous questions Odysseus anxiously, and the hero begins his great narrative. But the simile has brought to a dramatic head the contrast between those who are simply favored by the gods, and those who meet their challenge on sea and battlefield.

Such a dramatic use of the simile at once invades the proper function of the scene itself. Another example is the quiet image of the stars at the end of *Iliad* VIII. There the watchfires of the quiescent but still threatening Trojans are compared to the numberless stars on a clear night; but scene and simile are both night-pieces, and they blend almost imperceptibly, creating a momentary abatement of the intensity of war, and preparing the way for the nocturnal interlude which takes place before the battle is resumed. Here the image is not controlled by character, but by a total dramatic situation. It does not exist wholly for its own sake, handsome as this particular one is. Like a fountain, it rises from its point of comparison, fire and stars, but falls back into the larger basin of meaning. For the fire is a deadly symbol in the *Iliad*, while the stars stand in the world of the gods, the placid air; and images of divine peace alternate throughout the poem with pictures of war and strife. At the end of Book VIII, this intrinsic and consistent contrast unites the image of peaceful stars and the description of the embattled watchfires into a strange union with each other and with the whole poem.

Thus images become action; and the scene is an image dramatized. This process, though common in the epic, is so germane to the more concentrated form of tragedy that one or two examples from the latter will help to illustrate it. The self-blinding of Oedipus for instance is the active climax of a whole series of images dealing with the symbolic implications of sight and blindness; earlier it was dramatized in the scene with Teiresias. The manacles which are put on Philoctetes are simply a dramatized image of the paralyzing volitional paradox in which he finds himself. The net and the sea-purple carpet in the *Agamemnon* are very familiar. In the case of the manacles and the net, the treatment of the plot seems to have bred the symbols. In the *Oedipus*, one might argue that the crucial symbol of sight versus blindness preëxisted, or at least coexisted with the treatment. Epic, with its more diffuse action, offers few examples of imagery so tightly knit with action. But if Homer's method is different, his practice is just as symbolic, and one may see a little into his types of creative association. Women's weaving, for instance, seems to have exercised power over his imagination. Helen's great web is woven with pictures of the war for her sake,[37] and becomes in an instant the symbol of her self-conscious greatness and guilt, paralleling her speeches to Hector, Priam, and Aphrodite. How different is Penelope's weaving, the token of her filial piety toward Laertes and her fidelity to Odysseus![38] And it has been said with insight that Andromache's weaving of a purple fabric with flowers, while Hector is fighting his last battle, does not occur by chance; purple is the epithet of death, and flowers are grave-offerings.[39] It might be added that the flowers are perhaps in character for Andromache. These are weavings with a fatality in them, and they prompt the wish that Homer had described the patterns on Calypso's loom, and Circe's. But perhaps it is just as significant that he did not. Calypso and Circe are goddesses without fatalities, and their weaving is merely decorative. But with Arêtê, the Phaeacian queen, there is middle ground. What she weaves is not described, but her yarn is a "sea-purple," as it should be for the queen of a great seafaring people.[40] And when Helen reappears in the *Odyssey*, spinning, though not weaving, is the motif which signalizes her return to domestic propriety.[41] Her equipment is singularly gorgeous, and she is compared to the most chaste of goddesses, Artemis of the Golden Spindle. It is not perhaps surprising that Homer should have pushed his traditional images of spinning and weaving into fatal or characteristic symbols. Even that early, the Moirai were regarded as spinners; and one "weaves" both trickery and council.[42]

In an age and in an art form where the "stream of consciousness" has not yet become a regular method, the emotional springs of a scene tend to objectify themselves in things and people. Homer does, indeed, use the soliloquy, often with tremendous effectiveness, as in Hector's last reflections by the Scaean Gate. But he also dramatizes mood into action. In the scene where Poseidon comes to the assistance of the Greeks while Zeus slumbers, there is a strange passage where the Greek chiefs put on better armor, giving the inferior arms to inferior people; then Poseidon leads them forward with a sword like lightning in his hand.[43] To describe in such a way the renewed courage of those who have courage to renew is simply to dramatize a simile: "they counter-attacked like fresh men with new armor." It surely has no realistic significance, for the battle was in too desperate a stage to allow time for such maneuvers.[44] It is difficult to know whether the passage ought to be read as action or image. But the real point is that the distinction has broken down, as it often does in Homer. Since all his action is imagistic, it is no surprise to find on occasion that his images also act. Such passages are bold indeed; a few, such as the *Iliad's* Fight in the River, are unintelligible unless read as acting images. They announce the triumph of the poetic scheme over every naturalistic consideration. They are, in a way, like the poet's disregard of time in such a scene as the discovery of Odysseus by Eurycleia. There a flashback of seventy-six lines intervenes between the nurse's recognition of the scar and her gesture of joyous surprise.[45] No attempt is made to convey the quickness of the action. But there is no lack of narrative skill here. The poet solves the problem of describing the instantaneous by disregarding time altogether, and the whole picture of past and present collapses to a single imagistic point in the hearer's mind. Eurycleia's total memory was too big for a single formula, or even several. So Homer simply dramatizes her mental image, complete with speeches and even the boar-hunt, which incidentally she could not have witnessed.

The relation between certain of Homer's scenes and the image contained in a formula is sometimes so close and explicit that some episodes seem to be scarcely more than formulae acted out like charades. In the fourth *Odyssey* Menelaus relates how he was confined by adverse

winds in the island of Pharos for twenty days, until the sea nymph
Eidothea came to his rescue. He asks her which of the gods "shackles and
binds him from his path."[46] The last two words of the formula recur, with a
slight change, in *Odyssey* 5, where Athena stills the winds which have
shipwrecked Odysseus: "Then she bound the paths of the other winds."[47]
The metaphor of being "bound," or prevented from a journey by adverse
winds, or, as in English, wind-bound, is reversed into an image of binding
the paths of the winds, which is the function of a benign and favoring
deity. So far, we meet here only formulaic variations on a basic metaphor.
But in Book 10 of the *Odyssey* the metaphor becomes action, a little scene:

> And he [Aeolus] stripped off the skin of a nine-years' ox,
> Wherein he bound the paths of the blustering winds . . .
> And tied them in my hollow ship with a shining string
> Of silver, that not even a little might breathe through . . .[48]

What was originally a figure of speech is acted out, with the winds
literally tied up in a bag with a silver string, which the companions later
undo, in one of their occasional moments of insubordination. The episode
comments eloquently on the psychological interpretation of metaphor and
magic, poetic speech and poetically conceived action.

Again, the description of Odysseus' landing in Phaeacia and meeting
with Nausicaa strikingly illustrates how a single formula with its image
not only may underlie and mingle with the action, but also may external-
ize or objectify the internal states of the characters and embrace a
dramatic situation whole. After the struggles of the shipwreck, the hero,
exhausted, half-conscious, and vomiting brine, crawls ashore at the river
mouth, in a place free of stones, where there was "a shelter from the
wind."[49] The passage is full of an overwhelming sense of relief and
salvation, but it arises not from anything Odysseus says about it, but from
the nature of the things which he encounters. Of these — the land itself, the
slackened stream, the lack of stones — none is so central to the feeling of
benignity as the image of windlessness, the cessation of all rough elements.[50] The winds have had their will in the shipwreck. One of the two
things Odysseus still fears now is that the wind will blow cold at dawn if
he sleeps on the shore;[51] and he seeks the thicket of wild and domestic
olive, "Which neither the force of the damp-blowing winds/Pierced, nor
the flashing sun struck with his rays,/Nor the rain poured through."[52]
There he falls asleep, like a spark hidden under ashes. This is logical
enough, but it is also magical. A spark under ashes revives with wind, and
presently there are winds; but with a subtle change. Homer is immersed in
images of peace and safety, the focus of which is to be Nausicaa, herself an
image of tender nurturing, peace, and every blessing of civilization. She
cannot be a wind. At the beginning of Book 6, she is asleep, like Odysseus,
but Athena, summoning her to his aid, comes into her safe chamber,
through the closed doors, "like a breath of wind."[53] This wind which

rushes toward the bed of Nausicaa is a presaging token of the impact which the experienced, weather-beaten Odysseus is to have upon the sheltered Phaeacians, especially Nausicaa, an impact which is vividly dramatized in Book 8. This wind has action and danger in it, nicely imaged in the simile of the weatherbeaten lion, when Odysseus comes out of the bushes toward the princess and tells her how wind and water brought him to Scheria.[54] By contrast, Phaeacia, the land blessedly remote from all enemies, is a windless paradise: "Assist his bath," says Nausicaa to her friends, returning to the formula which keeps repeating itself, "where there is shelter from the wind."[55] It is scarcely a wonder, in such an elaborate complexity of weather symbolism, that when Athena finally leaves Nausicaa in charge for the moment, she goes to an Olympus which, though it is much unlike the gods' dwelling as described elsewhere in Homer, is very like the safe thicket where Odysseus sleeps: "Neither by wind is it shaken, nor ever wet by rain,/Neither snow comes near it, but verily clear sky/Cloudless expands, and a white gleam spreads over all."[56] It is a mistake to think that Homer has climbed in this vision of supernal tranquility to a nobler conception of the divine kingdom than he had in the *Iliad*. He is simply following the course of his imagery, and developing in action and description the vision which is most briefly caught in the formula, "where there was a shelter from the wind."

An understanding of this method can sometimes lead to the real purport of a passage. In *Iliad* XX Aeneas tells Apollo how Achilles once chased him all the way down Mount Ida in a surprise raid; Athena, he says, "going before Achilles *made a light*."[57] Here "light," as elsewhere in the *Iliad*, is a metonym for victory; as such it occurs in various formulae.[58] In the beginning of the nineteenth *Odyssey*, however, one finds the scene where Telemachus and Odysseus are removing the arms from the hall by night, in preparation for slaying the suitors:

> And before them Pallas Athena
> Holding a golden lamp made a most beautiful light.
> Then spoke Telemachus to his father swiftly:
> "Father, here is a great wonder I see with my eyes;
> The walls of the house and the fair panels,
> The pine beams and the pillars thrusting upward
> Gleam all round to my eyes as if with blazing fire.
> Surely some god is within, of those who keep Olympus."[59]

Here, as in Aeneas' formula, Athena makes a light go before a hero destined for victory. But the metaphor has turned into a miracle, motivated, however, on the simple, logical level by Eurycleia's earlier question: who will carry the light for you? The essence of both the formula and the scene is the same image of divine light going before, guaranteeing triumph, or better, foreseeing it from the gods' timeless point of view.

Alexandrine critics questioned the genuineness of this passage, because of the impropriety of Athena's doing so menial a task as carrying a lamp.[60] But the lamp is merely a detail, like the silver string tying up the winds, an adjunct to the light of triumph. The ancient objection is transparently foolish in this case anyway, but the formulaic analogy makes the meaning of the passage clear.

A comparable passage occurs at the end of *Odyssey* 20. Here the suitors, guilty now of every possible breach of civilization, are suddenly bewitched by Athena; they laugh "with strange jaws," and weep simultaneously, and the food that they eat seems streaked with blood. The seer Theoclymenus perceives the phenomenon, and more too:

> Ah, wretches, what evil is this you suffer? In night your
> Heads are wrapped, and your faces, and limbs below;
> Lamentation flares out, your cheeks are wet with tears,
> The walls are sprinkled with blood, and the fair panels.
> Full is the forecourt, and the great hall of ghosts,
> Making their way into Erebus under the darkness; the sun also
> Perishes from heaven, and an evil mist spreads over all.[61]

This passage too has been suspected, and called "shamanistic," in that it exhibits clairvoyance, and envisions as finished what is yet to come.[62] But such clairvoyance into things to come, here the deaths of the suitors, merely reflects, as often in Homer, the gods' way of looking at things. The passage corresponds, as darkness corresponds to light, to the passage of Athena with the lamp; if that betokened victory, this betokens death. And again, it is merely the dramatization, in visionary terms, of formulaic motifs familiar enough elsewhere. When Theoclymenus says, "Your heads are wrapped in night," it is precisely parallel to the formulaic line: "Dark night wrapped his eyes about . . ."[63] The metaphor is a frequent one for death, and one which itself is developed in the *Iliad* into literal action when a darkness, caused by mist that blotted out the sun, gathers around the body of Patroclus in the thick of the battle.[64] Here too, the sun "perishes from heaven, and an evil mist spreads." The sprinkling of blood on the walls and meat, moreover, is not an unfamiliar image; it is one associated with impending but as yet unaccomplished doom: twice in the *Iliad* Zeus sheds a rain of blood, once when Sarpedon is about to fall, and earlier when Zeus himself intends "to hurl many brave heads into Hades."[65] All these motifs are recognizable elsewhere. The journeying ghosts, on their way to Hades, may seem to a degree irregular; yet these two lines only summarize what is narrated in the opening of Book 24, the so-called second *Nekyia*. All such use of poetic materials is entirely characteristic of Homer. It rests upon the compression or expansion of images whose smallest unit is the formulaic phrase and whose larger developments may grow to many lines. And in the vision of Theoclymenus, though its effect is unique and its atmosphere somewhat more macabre and uncanny than is usual in Homer, there is nothing innovating or shamanistic, nothing which is not native to the traditional imagery.

Even the uncanniness finds some parallel in the crawling hides and mooing meat of the slain Cattle of the Sun.[66]

The episodes just described, however, contain a great deal more than the images mentioned, and, of course, not every scene can be read backwards into a formula. The character of Nausicaa, for example, is a chef-d'oeuvre quite apart from her symbolic function in the rescue of Odysseus. Her own existence as a poetic creation, a paradigm of the day on which a girl becomes a woman, is an especially appealing example of the genius of the Greek artist for generalizing upon the individual without destroying individuality. But all Homer's characters are equally universalized individuals, and his scenes for the most part dramatize them for their own sakes, within the limits of a totally conceived heroic world. Thus, though the poetic image is the genesis of the dramatic or narrative scene, their dimensions and functions differ.

Yet many of Homer's scenes, apart from their relation to formulae, are just as traditional poetic units as the latter, and doubtless all are modeled to a degree on types.[67] The battle books of the *Iliad* offer a dizzying variety of small combat scenes, whose recurrent motifs are combined and recombined into ever new situations, whose circumstances, like life itself, are always different, yet always coincide with others at certain points. It is a formal design corresponding to, but not specifically imitating, the natural world. Crystallized and formulaic, its life is not naturalistic but generic, its realism is classical, not that of photographic illusionism. The battle books, for instance, have been mistakenly neglected, for quite apart from their intimate connection with the whole structure, they better illustrate in one way Homer's skill with the oral style than do the more famous parts of the poem. Traditional as they are, Homer narrates them as images in a whole design. An image was defined originally as a direct appeal to sensory response, and in the formula, it was stated, a syntactical group of words gains the presentational power of an image through identification with the formal syntax of a fixed rhythmic pattern. When formulae are combined and recombined as they are in Homer's battle scenes, it is like the falling of glass chips in a kaleidoscope. Patterns constantly are formed, always with consistency of color, and always with pieces of the same shape, yet always different and always luminous with surprise. No matter how many are combined, the imagistic impact of formulae is not lost provided they are chosen with relevance to the total design which is aimed at. The poet's mind herein acts like the mirror in the kaleidoscope, constantly rounding the fall of formulae into an organic, larger unit.

The outlines of the larger units are, of course, determined by plot and character. Large scenes, like coral, are agglutinative organisms, made of smaller formulaic pieces. But they are also whole conceptions, subordinated in turn to the whole poem. They do not just grow; they grow by design, each with a presentational life of its own, that is, with the ability to impress the mind as a unit and not as a series. Thus the famous scene between Andromache and Hector has been finely analyzed as an interlocking of two main images, the world of man and the world of woman, which are hopelessly separate save for the unifying presence of a child.[68] This is one view and an important one. But there are also many other ways of looking at it, for when an image is dramatized, it can never again be compressed; it exists in its own right as a scene, an image, but a kinetic one, an image of humanity in action.

But to speak of "images of humanity" leads to the most general considerations, and the question of Homer's ultimate intention as an artist. No mere analysis of the tools and technique of a poet can explain his power. The structural elements of epic, scene, simile, and formula, subserve a total concept which in Homer's case is a vision of the heroic world of the past. Like all else Homeric, it is in part traditional, the keepsake of generations of bards, the long memory of the "glories of men." But it is also molded anew by each new hand for each new poem. It differs a little, though only a little, in the *Odyssey* from what it was in the *Iliad*, and hence it is always a creation, or a re-creation, never a mirrored imitation. It reflects nothing exactly, for it comes to being through the formulae which are not realistically mimetic, but distillates of observation, formalized units standing at a remove from reality in order to present it imagistically. It took centuries to forge this medium, and the pieces date from every generation of singers from the fall of Troy, or before, to the eighth century. Hence it arises that Homer's world is not the Mycenaean world, nor the world of the eighth century. It is the epic world, a visionary structure whose chief pillar is the heroic aspiration. Within that structure, all the elements fit, though they may not correspond precisely to anything outside it. Each refers broadly to the whole, reflecting a composite idea, not a specific one. Parry said that the fixed epithet adorns the whole of heroic verse rather than any specific person.[69] He might have gone father and said that every formula reflects a group of associated notions seen in perspective within the heroic structure. Archilochus lost his own personal shield in battle. In Homer, every shield, even Ajax's big one, is the universal heroic shield, seen through centuries of admiring retrospect. It is "towerlike," or "equal all round," or "well turned" interchangeably, not because Homer forgot which kind of shield Ajax was carrying on a certain day, but because the only shield his Ajax ever had was an epic shield, symbolic of all that a heroic shield must be. It is a shield-metaphor, which changes with perfect unconcern from a Mycenaean body-shield to a round hoplite shield, reflecting any shape which had crept into the conventional speech by sometime being glorified in action. A completely plastic conception, the Homeric symbol, shield, whether it be called [*àspis*] or [*sákos*], is always a metaphor, and in Book XVIII of the *Iliad* it undergoes a tremendous expansion and becomes a metaphor of the whole heroic world.

So too with helmets. For one trained in the bardic tradition, a helmet was conceived according to the metrical space it was to fill. At the beginning of a line it might well be [aulōpis trupháleia]. It seems impossible to identify this particular helmet, and one suspects it of being a composite helmet-image, with no counterpart in armory. It strikes the ear grandly,[70] but it seems to have no factual inevitability. When Apollo knocks the helmet from Patroclus' head, the phrase is used, but the same implement is also referred to as [pēlēx] and [kunéē], which presumably have different meanings.[71] But the distinctions have no importance for Homer. His phrase is a pictorial unit, encrusted with helmet images, the metaphor, not the name, of a helmet.

The two or three really specific descriptions of objects in Homer stand out in great contrast to the host of formulaic things. The boar's-tusk helmet, the cup of Nestor, and perhaps the breastplate of Agamemnon[72] protrude from the texture of the poem as they do just because they are decorative and definite, rather than stock in trade. Somehow, perhaps because they were considered peculiarly remarkable objects, they escaped falling into one generality or another, and their descriptions survive whole. So do the objects themselves, at least two of them. The boar's-tusk helmet has been reconstructed from Middle Helladic fragments — incidentally long antedating the man who wears it in the *Iliad* — and the cup of Nestor, though greatly disputed, is surely to be recognized in the dove-goblet dug up by Schliemann.[73] It is not impossible that Agamemnon's breastplate might somewhere turn up. But no one has ever found a shield like that of Achilles, and no one ever will. Metaphors are not found in excavations.

The answer to the problem of Homer's "directness," his apparent lack of metaphor, is now clear. His whole world is a metaphor, an enormously articulated symbolism of the heroic life. His apparent naturalness is the product of the exact opposite, a highly contrived convention. But poetic truth is artifice, and the more complete the artifice is, the more true is the poem. Frigidity and bathos proceed not from artificial causes, but from rifts and failures in the artifice. If metaphor flags and facts prevail, the presentational is lost, and the poem sinks to prose. But Homer's metaphor cannot ever flag. It is in great part identical with the very language he speaks. For no matter how poor a singer used this speech, there is one virtue he could never lack, the momentary vividness of image after image. He might arrange his images badly, or repeat himself too often and in the wrong way, and thus dull the edge to a degree and fail of any real supremacy. But the epic medium was an extraordinary one, with some special advantages which, in the hands of a great singer, could lead to the *Iliad* and the *Odyssey*. Yet what was required of such a poet, in order to use the epic language to the full and create such poems, still, as in the case of all great artists, baffles analysis. The metaphoric world of the heroes which Homer created lay in fragments like the chips of stone and gold before a mosaic is made. The pieces were ideally suited to the purpose, but it remained to conceive the total design around a central theme, and then, within that design, to set all the formal building blocks in such a way that they would pick up light and shadow from each other in a consistent symbolic scheme. If the scheme is right, everything within it will be symbolic; but everything must be seen symbolically for the scheme to be right. At this point, we must leave it to Homer.

Notes

1. See Finley, *Pindar and Aeschylus*.

2. M. Parry, "The Traditional Metaphor in Homer," *CP*, I ser. 28 (1933): 37. This small figure is due to the severely limited definition of metaphor which Parry uses in this article. His actual intention was to defend Homer from the charge of deficiency in metaphor.

3. XII.37.

4. IV.371, XI.160, VIII.378, 553, etc. The etymology of [*géphura*] is unknown; hence it is impossible to say whether its use here is metaphoric, or represents some real, though vanished, meaning of the word.

5. E.g., metonymy: XIV.387 ([daís], "heat," for "strife"); synecdoche, VI.306; H. Schrade, *Götter und Menschen*, pp. 147f., fails to realize that synecdoche explains his "partial" epiphanies of the gods—hands, thighs, eyes, etc., apostrophe, XVI.693; anaphora, 3.109ff.; personification (Eris), XI.3; onomatopoeia,12.235–238.

6. S. Langer, *Philosophy in a New Key*, 3rd ed. (Cambridge, Mass., 1957), pp. 42ff. See chapters 2 and 4 in general. For this whole discussion of symbolism I am profoundly indebted to Mrs. Langer.

7. But see, in the aforementioned chapter, Mrs. Langer's defense of the whole mind as rational, to which the discursive and presentational modes appeal in ways which differ formally, but which imply no inner mental division between rational and intuitional. The symbolic process lying behind both modes involves the same selection from the steady barrage of sense impressions certain common denominators by which classes and "universal" concepts are formed. Both sense perception and formal reason depend upon such an organon of genus and species; hence ultimately there is no real opposition within the mind of the sensory and rational faculties. Their difference lies in mode of expression.

8. Langer, *Philosophy in a New Key*, pp. 68ff.

9. Schadewaldt's comparison of the Homeric simile to the definitions of philosophy, because of the simile's generic source, but specific relation to the texture, means not that the simile proceeds by the discursive logic of definitions, but simply that presentational symbols, like discursive ones, are comprehensible through classification by genus and species. See *Homers Welt*, pp. 148f.

10. *Henry IV*, part 2, IV.4.

11. I.52.

12. See for instance such a statement as: "Such a system could not be the work of a single poet: it must represent the effort of generations of singers, ever seeking and ever guarding the convenient expression, and using it when found, to the exclusion of all other formulae which could replace it." M. Parry, "The Homeric Gloss," *TAPA* 59 (1928): 242. Note the word "convenient."

13. See M. Parry, *passim*, e.g., *Epithète traditionelle*, p. 114.

14. Parry, *Epithète traditionelle*, p. 227, envisions three stages of stylistic development: (1) when the hexameter had not yet adopted unique noun-epithet formulae, but had an

abundance of metrical equivalents; (2) when it began to adopt unique formulae; (3) when it created some analogical equivalents.

15. See A. B. Lord, "Composition by Theme in Homer and South Slavic Epos," *TAPA* 82 (1951): 71ff.

16. *Formules*, pp. 7–8, 22–23, 61; *Epithète traditionelle*, pp. 99, 103, 125–131.

17. See A. B. Lord, "Homer's Originality: Dictated Texts," *TAPA* 84 (1953): 127.

18. Cf. Parry, *Formules*, pp. 50–51, on the inevitability of the formula.

19. Parry, *Epithète traditionelle*, p. 196.

20. *Ibid.*, pp. 154, 172.

21. 8.230; XVIII.106; cf. XIX.218. Odysseus does win the footrace in XXIII.

22. Parry denies it; *Epithète traditionelle*, p. 185.

23. Parry regards them as entirely traditional—*Epithète traditionelle*, p. 163–164—noting, e.g., how *polúainos*, though used only of Odysseus, is used of him in IX.673 and XI.430, before his adventures had earned the epithet for him.

24. I.I; 10.330 [*polútropos*]; 3.310 [*análkis*]. See Parry, *Epithète traditionelle*, pp. 196–198; 200ff., for a discussion with other examples.

25. A careless use of formulae probably accounts for [*amumōn*] used of Aegisthus, 1.29; cf. the transference of "divine" from [hals], "sea" to [*hals*], "salt" in IX.214 (yet here it is [*theíoio*], never used of the sea, which is [*díos*]). Note also Odysseus felling "dry trees," 5.240, a formula better used of wood already felled and lying seasoned, 18.309.

26. XVI.705.

27. XVI.691, 693.

28. XI.604; cf. 644.

29. See for instance: Hampe, *Gleichnisse*, pp. 20–21, on the significance of the formula "man-slaying hands." Cf. Bowra, *Homer and Forerunners*, pp. 11f., on IV.66f.; 71f.; XXII.92; 2.246.

30. XXIV.572.

31. Schadewaldt, *Homers Welt*, p. 50.

32. 6.130–134.

33. XI.113ff.

34. 5.432f. The octopus takes the color of the rock he is clinging to and is used by Theognis, 213–216, as a symbol of [*poikílon éthos*].

35. 8.523–530.

36. Homer is deeply conscious of the relation between the reality of action and the tradition of song which records it; cf. Helen's remark, VI.358. Action in a way exists for the sake of the poetic landmark, which is another way of looking at heroic [*kléos*]. Action is the road to grandeur and eternity.

37. III.125ff.

38. 19.137–150.

39. See Schrade, *Götter und Menschen*, p. 221, on XXII.440 ff. Purple as death, V.83; XVI.334; XX.477. Helen's web is also purple; the formula is identical in both passages: [*díplaka porphuréēn*]. Helen's web, like her action, influences the web of Andromache as well as her fate.

40. 6.306.

41. 4.121ff.

42. 3.208; 7.197f.; XX.127f.; weaving council: IX.93; trickery: 5.356.

43. XIV.376–383.

44. See Odysseus' remarks earlier, XIV.95–102.

45. 19.392–468.

46. [édēse keleúthou], 4.380; 469.

47. [Katédēse, keleúthous], 5.383.

48. 10.19f.; 23f.

49. 5.443.

50. 5.391, 452.

51. 5.291–296; 328ff.; 331–332; 368ff.; 469.

52. 5.478ff.

53. 6.20.

54. 6.131; 171.

55. 6.210; 212; cf. 7.282.

56. 6.43ff.

57. XX.95.

58. VIII.282; XVIII.102; XV.741; XVI.95.

59. 19.33ff.

60. See Stanford ad loc.

61. 20.351.

62. Wade-Gery, Poet.

63. V.310.

64. XVII.366–376.

65. XVL.459f., XI.53ff.

66. 12.394f.

67. See A. B. Lord, "Composition by Theme," TAPA 82 (1951), for a study of traditional scenic motifs. Also W. Arend, Die typische Scenen bei Homer (Berlin, 1933).

68. See Schadewaldt's excellent chapter, "Hektor und Andromache," in Homers Welt, 2nd ed., pp. 207ff.

69. Epithète traditionelle, p. 172.

70. See Aristophanes' parody, Frogs, 1016.

71. XVI.793–797.

72. X.262ff.; XI.632ff.; XI.19ff., respectively.

73. Lorimer, Homer and the Monuments, pp. 212–219 (boar's-tusk helmet); pp. 328–335 (cup of Nestor). It is surely pedantry to argue about how many doves and handles should be on the goblet, or whether [puthménes] can be the supporting stems of Schliemann's cup. A type is a type, and in Nestor's cup, the Mycenaean type is clearly described, though somewhat enlarged; see reference to Ventris, Chapter XII, n. 48, below. However, for the view that Nestor's cup and Schliemann's have nothing to do with each other, see A. Furumark, "Nestor's Cup and the Mycenaean Dove-Goblet," Eranos Rudbergianus 45:41–53.

[Review of *The Making of Homeric Verse: The Collected Papers of Milman Parry*, Edited by Adam Parry]

George E. Dimock, Jr.*

If we know now much better than we did fifty years ago how the *Iliad* and *Odyssey* were composed, and if we are beginning to appreciate correctly the nature and significance of oral poetry, the credit goes almost entirely to one man, the brilliant American classicist, Milman Parry, who died in 1935 at the age of thirty-three. His work, some of it unpublished, has now been collected and provided with an introduction by his son, Adam, in a volume entitled *The Making of Homeric Verse*, an event for which we can only be most grateful. It is now possible to trace more easily and more completely the thinking which produced and is producing a fundamental change in our notions about poetry.

As early as his M.A. thesis of 1923, here published for the first time, Parry had insisted that Homeric poetry is very different from the art we usually call by that name. Its diction is so rigidly fixed that the word "Athene," for example, occurs in the *Iliad* and *Odyssey* two hundred and twenty-two times as the last word in the line and only eight times in any other position. He explained this and the countless other cases of the same sort by the theory that tradition had provided the poets of Homer's time with an immense stock of metrical phrases of various shapes and sizes in which to tell the traditional stories. These phrases were both useful and beautiful; indeed, they comprised "all the turns of language, all the words, phrases, and effects of position, which had pleased the race"; but the poets who used them, it seemed, must be vastly different from Shakespeare and Dante since both their matter and their manner were so largely prescribed for them by tradition.

The next step was to convince the world of the validity of this theory. It is impossible, of course, to prove that everything in Homer is an inherited formula: many words and phrases occur only once. What Parry did, instead, in his French dissertation of 1928 (translated in this edition) was to demonstrate that one particular group of formulas was organized into systems of such extent and such economy that it seemed impossible that an individual poet could have created them. He showed that for each commonly used noun Homer had, practically speaking, one and one only adjectival element for each metrical situation. Almost without exception Odysseus in the nominative case is "divine" after the bucolic diaeresis, "crafty" after the hephthemimeral caesura, and "divine, much-enduring" after the feminine caesura. Evidently Homer had at his disposal a set of

*Reprinted from *Yale Review* (Summer 1971), 585–90, by permission of the journal.

metrical phrases of different lengths, all meaning "Odysseus," with which to finish his line. Since the same thing can be shown for all the other common names in the *Iliad* and *Odyssey*, and we see furthermore how the less common ones can be substituted in the same systems, it seems inescapable that this part of the diction at any rate is traditional, and a strong presumption exists that the rest of it is also.

At the same time it seemed obvious that the great determinant of Homeric style was metrical convenience, since that is what dictated the poet's choice of epithet in the cases considered above. This observation led to another major step. The similarity between the Homeric poems and the orally improvised poetry of various more recent cultures had already been noted by other scholars, and to Parry it was clear that the demands of such improvisation explained to perfection the subservience of metrical facility which he had discovered in Homeric style. Homer, then, must have been an oral poet, and his formulaic diction must be nothing more nor less than a technique of oral verse-making. This technique furthermore seemed bound to produce what the M.A. thesis had already supposed, the poetry of a poet utterly traditional both in style and content, utterly unlike the poet who could write and so exercise some individual choice in what he would say.

Surprisingly enough this did not mean to Parry that the poetry was worse, but that it was better. In "The Traditional Metaphor in Homer" he writes:

> The making of this diction was due to countless poets and to many generations who in time had found the heroic word and phrase for every thought, and every word in it was holy and sweet and wondrous, and no one would think of changing it wilfully. The Muses it was truly who gave those poets voices sweeter than honey. And those parts of the diction which did not carry the story itself, since their meaning was not needed for understanding, lost that meaning, but became, as it were, a familiar music of which the mind is pleasantly aware, but which it knows so well that it makes no effort to follow it. Indeed, poetry thus approaches music most closely when the words have rather a mood than a meaning. Nor should one think that since the meaning is largely lost it ceases to matter if the meaning is good. Though the meaning be felt rather than understood it is there, as it matters whether music idly heard be bad or good. Of such a kind is the charm of the fixed metaphor in Homer. It is an incantation of the heroic.

Nor did Parry shrink from the claim that only in this way can we understand Homer:

> A traditional poet is good not because of the new that he brings into verse but because he knows how to make use of the traditional. [Realizing] this we have found a charm far beyond any which can be found by men who wilfully wish to read Homer as they would any poetry of their own day. . . . The *Iliad* and *Odyssey* [are] not such

poems as we would ever write, or as Virgil and Dante and Milton wrote; . . . through a study of the oral poetries of peoples outside our own civilization, we have grasped the idea of traditional poetry. There is not a verse in Homer that does not become clearer and greater when we have understood that he too was a traditional poet. This way lies all true criticism and liking of his poems.

Here of course Parry goes too far, and I shall try to say why in a moment, but first let us consider what he has accomplished: he has discovered living counterparts for Homer in the shape of those illiterate bards who in his lifetime still improvised heroic verse in out-of-the-way parts of the world, and he has laid the foundation for the conception of a metrical language which enables them to improvise. In order to study both phenomena he learned Serbo-Croatian, had a special recording apparatus built, and spent much of 1933–1935 in Yugoslavia. His travels resulted in the massive collection of South Slavic song which bears his name in Harvard's Widener Library, and also inspired two of the pieces, one of them hitherto unpublished, now included in this book. Thanks to him much further work has been done since his death, both in these areas and in oral poetry generally. His heroic endeavor to get as close as possible to Homer through his style has made it impossible ever again to ignore the importance of oral, improvising poetry.

As he himself would have wished, the effort to understand the formulaic technique which he mapped has continued. A great advance has recently been made by M. N. Nagler in an extremely important article, "Towards a Generative View of the Oral Formula" (*Transactions of the American Philological Association* 98 [1967], 269–311). Pointing to the lack of success which subsequent workers have had in defining the oral formula, and demonstrating the bewildering variety of ways in which phrases may resemble one another sufficiently to be considered formulaic, Nagler hypothesizes a "mental template in the mind of the oral poet" capable of producing both the particular utterance of the moment and all possible utterances sufficiently like it to belong to the same formula. As we approach the outer limits of likeness in any direction, we will be approaching another template and a new set of similarities. The templates merge at the edges. They are also preverbal, because any one of them can ultimately give rise to totally different sets of words. With this conception, Nagler points out, he reaches something approaching Noam Chomsky's "deep structure," that "knowledge" of our language which, existing in our minds, generates the particular things we say. As is the case with the "deep structure" of any language, the deep structure of an oral poetry is traditional; that is, it is learned. The particular utterances, however, are the speaker's (the poet's) own, however often others may have used the identical words before.

In short, the oral technique of epic verse-making, whose mechanics Parry was the first to describe, is simply a language some of whose rules are metrical. Parry knew this, but did not draw the consequences. His successor, Albert Lord, who actually learned to sing in the South Slavic tradition, has written in *The Singer of Tales* that the accomplished poet moves about in his verse-language as freely as the ordinary person does in ordinary speech. From this valuable observation we may safely deduce what Nagler has already implied, that the poet thinks not just in words but in meter, even though Lord himself does not take this step. So we need no longer think of Homer struggling to fit prefabricated phrases into the pattern of the hexameter, but rather of the pattern of the hexameter in his mind generating the metrical utterances which express his thought. If Achilles is swift-footed, it is essentially because the poet thinks of him that way, however unemphatically, and not because of the meter. By the same token, if the *Iliad* is the greatest poem ever composed, it is because Homer composed it that way and not because of the stereotypes furnished by the tradition, however useful they may have been to him. The poet uses the stereotypes to think with, and therefore the *Iliad* does more than provide heroic mood-music; it shows us our ultimate concerns.

So oral poetry is not so different from the written variety after all. In essence, all poetry is oral since it is impossible to write it without hearing it first, at least mentally. All poetry, oral or written, is first and foremost a matter of thinking in a poetic language. All poets find their verse coming to them in phrases and whole lines rather than a word at a time. The oral poet may be thought to be handicapped by the speed of composition which improvising demands, even if he does, as we believe, think in verse; yet he is not entirely dependent on the moment of performance. There is much evidence in Parry's Yugoslav material that he both practices his songs and sings them over to himself for his own amusement. His very liberation from pen and paper, and, more important, from any idea of a need for word-for-word identity, suggests that he might manage more easily in his mind the great architectural masses of which the *Iliad* and *Odyssey* are made than a poet accustomed to writing could. The important thing about oral poetry then is not that it is essentially different from written; nor, I think, does oral poetry necessarily imply a highly stereotyped diction. I believe that most of it has such a diction because the poets were passionate to make their verses sound as much like the best verses they had heard as possible. Not just the meter but the words and phrases of the tradition *were* the poetry. Homer himself may not have been an oral poet in the sense that he could not write. In fact his poems must have been written by himself or another as he composed them, or we would not have them. What the discovery that there had to be oral poetry behind Homer does do is to show us what pre-alphabetic man could achieve. If Homer or his friend had not written, we would not know his poems, but his audience might have heard the like, perhaps better. It is thrilling to know that behind the "written" poetry of the present and the less remote past, in any or all of the cultures which practice the art, there may loom an oral poetry equally great. Men have had the language to think nobly and deeply about their fate for much longer than we perhaps realize.

On the Iliad

The Shield of Achilles

W. H. Auden*

She looked over his shoulder
   For vines and olive trees,
Marble well-governed cities
   And ships upon untamed seas,
But there on the shining metal
   His hands had put instead
An artificial wilderness
   And a sky like lead.

A plain without a feature, bare and brown,
   No blade of grass, no sign of neighbourhood,
Nothing to eat and nowhere to sit down,
   Yet, congregated on its blankness, stood
   An unintelligible multitude,
A million eyes, a million boots in line,
Without expression, waiting for a sign.

Out of the air a voice without a face
   Proved by statistics that some cause was just
In tones as dry and level as the place:
   No one was cheered and nothing was discussed;
   Column by column in a cloud of dust
They marched away enduring a belief
Whose logic brought them, somewhere else, to grief.

She looked over his shoulder
   For ritual pieties,
White flower-garlanded heifers,
   Libation and sacrifice,
But there on the shining metal
   Where the altar should have been,
She saw by his flickering forge-light
   Quite another scene.

*Reprinted from *Collected Shorter Poems 1927–1957* (New York: Random House, 1967), 294–95, by permission of the publisher.

Barbed wire enclosed an arbitrary spot
  Where bored officials lounged (one cracked a joke)
And sentries sweated for the day was hot:
  A crowd of ordinary decent folk
  Watched from without and neither moved nor spoke
As three pale figures were led forth and bound
To three posts driven upright in the ground.

The mass and majesty of this world, all
  That carries weight and always weighs the same
Lay in the hands of others; they were small
  And could not hope for help and no help came:
  What their foes liked to do was done, their shame
Was all the worst could wish; they lost their pride
And died as men before their bodies died.

  She looked over his shoulder
    For athletes at their games,
  Men and women in a dance
    Moving their sweet limbs
  Quick, quick, to music,
    But there on the shining shield
  His hands had set no dancing-floor
    But a weed-choked field.

A ragged urchin, aimless and alone,
  Loitered about that vacancy, a bird
Flew up to safety from his well-aimed stone:
  That girls are raped, that two boys knifed a third,
  Were axioms to him, who'd never heard
Of any world where promises were kept,
Or one could weep because another wept.

  The thin-lipped armourer,
    Hephaestos hobbled away,
  Thetis of the shining breasts
    Cried out in dismay
  At what the god had wrought
    To please her son, the strong
  Iron-hearted man-slaying Achilles
    Who would not live long.

Imitation
James M. Redfield*

THE MUSE

The poet of the *Odyssey* is, among other things, the first great critic of the *Iliad*. By his collapse of the epic distance he is able to dramatize the problematic of his narrative art. He points to narratives suspended between reality and unreality, between history and fantasy, claiming the merits of both. The poet is free to tell us whatever he likes without losing his claim to actuality; he is in a sense inventing the world he describes.

The archaic Greeks resolved this problematic mythologically, by reference to the Muse. A sacred authority was conferred on the poet, and it was thereby declared that everything in his poem was just as it should be. The poets were figures with a special status, parallel to that of the priests, whom, in this relatively unpriestly society, they to a large extent replaced. Poets were central, integrative figures within archaic culture; in fact they held this position among the Greeks until, toward the beginning of the fourth century B.C., they were forced to give way to the philosophers.

In Homer and Hesiod the work of the bard is said to be like the work of the orator. Public speech that is proper is *kata kosmon*, "ordered" (II.213–14); the bard also sings *kata kosmon* (VIII.489). Both create order in others—the orator in public space, where he puts an end to strife, the bard in the private heart, where he heals distress so that "gladness fills the folk" (IX.6). Hesiod goes so far as to say that the two are inspired by the same Muse . . . in his praise of Calliope, leader of the Muses. . . .

Both the king and the bard are praised, not because their words are true but because they are effective. Both have authority, and both draw their authority from Zeus, the divine source of authority. Both create a common world and thus make it possible for men to live in the world and with one another. The bard and the king are thus parallel figures, and poetry is firmly established as a public fact with public uses. The heroic world is kept alive by the bards as the common possession of the public; heroic epic secures the public by giving it a world alternate to its own, a world between unreality and reality which its members can contemplate in common. From this point of view the epic is a social institution, and the Muse is appealed to, as a god is so often appealed to in culture, to legitimate the institution. When the bard speaks of his inspiration by the Muse, he objectifies his own capacity—dependent as much on the responsiveness of his audience as on his own skill—to create among the folk a

*Reprinted from *Nature and Culture in the Iliad: The Tragedy of Hector* (Chicago and London: University of Chicago Press, 1975), 39–68, by permission of the publisher and the author.

second reality, a poetic world which has a standing parallel to that of objective fact.

The heroic world was thus a "collective representation." The reality of the heroic events was a reality secured and validated by the recurrent collective experience of successful poetry. In this experience the audience felt the presence of the poet's god.

Mythological solutions do not answer questions; they merely set them aside by shifting them to a level at which they cannot be answered. For this reason mythological answers cannot survive criticism; they presume, rather, the absence of criticism. But the Greeks were nothing if not critical. The history of Greek culture after Homer can be seen as a progressive "demystification" of the world — of poetry with the rest. By "poetry" the Greeks meant always, before anything else, the *Iliad*, so the question can be put in this form: What is the standing of Homer once he has been deprived of the authority of his Muse? In tracing this question we shall come, by way of Socrates' quarrel with the sophists, to Aristotle's *Poetics*. We shall see that Aristotle answers, not a new question, but this old question — which he is for the first time in a position to make explicit. Since we also live in a demystified world, since for us also the Muse can be only a metaphor, Aristotle's question must be our question. It is the question of the human meaning of imaginative narrative art — in particular, as a leading example, the *Iliad*.

.   .   .

IMITATION AS A MODE OF LEARNING

Aristotle's treatment of poetry is characteristically eclectic and to some degree synthetic of previous thought. Aristotle extends or renews the Homeric tradition by identifying the central organizing principle of the poem as the story — no longer called *kleos*, but *muthos*, "plot." Aristotle follows the sophistic in treating poetry as a *technē*, "craft," and by finding the special power of that *technē* exhibited in the *pathos* felt by the audience. Aristotle has his own characteristic interest in the kinds and history of human things; he is interested in the development of poetry and wants to define clear genres. All these elements are in the definition of tragedy: "Tragedy is, then, an imitation of an action serious and complete, which has magnitude, in pleasure-giving language, different kinds in the different parts, done by actors and not reported, through pity and fear achieving the purification of these emotions." (*Poetics* 1449b24–28). A tragedy, that is, tells a story having a certain kind of content and with certain formal characteristics; it uses certain means, which are prescribed by the tradition of the genre; and it produces a specifiable effect on its audience. Of "purification" — *katharsis* — we shall say more later. Here I note that Aristotle shows himself the heir of Plato by calling the play an "imitation" (*mimēsis*). He is concerned to rescue this term from the pejorative connotations inflicted on it by Socrates:

> It would seem that, in general, two causes produced poetry, and these by nature. In the first place, imitation is bred into man from childhood (this is the very point in which he differs from the other animals — in that he is most imitative — and he makes his first learnings through imitation), as is the pleasure everyone takes in imitation. And a sign of this is what happens in fact; for things which give us pain when we see them give us pleasure when we look upon the most accurate images of them, for example, shapes of the most despised animals and of corpses. And the cause of this is as follows: learning is delightful not only to the philosophers but to men in general, although they have some smaller share of it. That is why they take pleasure in seeing the images; for it happens that, when they look upon them, they learn and reason out what each thing is, for example that this is that. (But if one has not actually seen the thing before, then it is not *qua* imitation that it produces the pleasure but through workmanship or color or some other cause.)
>
> Imitation being natural to us, as are also harmony and rhythm (for the meters are obviously parts of rhythm), from the beginning those most naturally so inclined, proceeding by small steps, produced poetry out of improvisations. (*Poetics* 1448b4–24)

Aristotle goes down to the ground of nature because, for him, nature does nothing in vain; an activity specific to man and usual among men in general must be an activity whereby men are human. Obviously, not all men are poets, but Aristotle finds the roots of poetry in universal tendencies — tendencies seen even in those still-to-be-developed human beings we call children. Children from infancy dance, chant, and sing; we have some innate tendency to use our bodies and voices to structure space and time. Thus the music of poetry has primitive roots. So also does the imitative content; man is the most imitative of the animals. No doubt this has to do with his power to manipulate symbols. A man can make of himself a symbol, as when the child says, "I'm a vampire, and I'm going to eat you," and thus becomes a performer. And the child, like all of us, takes pleasure in recognizing imitations; thus he becomes an audience. Aristotle grounds imitative poetry on the most primitive sort of recognition: the child who looks at a picture book and says "cow." Aristotle says that the child thereby has some share of the philosophical pleasure of learning.

But here we have a problem. What does the child learn? That a thing can be an imitation? But the child does not point and say "picture of cow"; he says "cow." He recognizes, not the imitation, but the original. And the original — cow — he already knew; otherwise he would not have recognized it in the imitation. So in what sense can he be said to learn anything?

The key word in Aristotle's passage is *sullogizesthai*; Aristotle says that "we reason out" what each thing is. The learning occurs in this process of reasoning out, which itself occurs because the imitation presents us with a problem. A picture of a cow is really very little like a cow. In fact, an imitation must be unlike the original to be an imitation; an imitation cow which was just like a cow would be a cow. Imitation implies certain likenesses in a context of unlikeness. A picture of a cow shares with a cow certain common features; by these features we recognize the model. We identify horns, udder, tail — and we say "cow." That is the syllogism: we say, "Everything with these features is in some sense a cow. This thing has those features. Therefore this thing is in some sense a cow." The content of our learning is not "cow" but "features-of-cow." A mere sketch of these features properly arranged on the page is enough to prompt our recognition; we thus learn something about what we mean by a cow. For purposes of recognition, at least, these few features define a cow. The picture is thus a kind of concept; it presents us, not with a whole cow, but with some basic or underlying cow.

The essence of imitation (to borrow a term from Claude Lévi-Strauss) is reduction, or, as Socrates says, the imitator "makes everything because he only lays hands on some small part of each thing" (*Republic* 598b). Socrates should have added, however, that the corollary of reduction is form. The imitation is qualitatively simpler than the original; thereby it can be more coherent; being less complex, it can be more intelligible. So in a certain sense the imitation is more of a cow — that is, more obviously a cow — than a cow is. That is why the imitation is pleasant — more pleasant than the original. Being made for us, it speaks to us far more directly than anything can in nature. In a certain sense the picture shows us a cow so that we can really see it.

From this point of view, imitation is the discovery of form in things. But we must remember that the form thus revealed to us, while it is really (because recognizably) a form of the object, is in no sense a definitive or absolute form. There is no question of the painter presenting us with some Platonic cow-in-itself. Just as there is no upper limit to the description of an actual cow — there is always more detail to be supplied, more relevant relations to be stated — so there is a potentially infinite number of different valid imitations of a cow. It was a principle of the Picturesque that "a cow is never out of place in a landscape"; the cows imitated by the painters of this genre were ornaments within a humanized natural world and were quite different objects from those presented under C in the child's alphabet. No imitation replaces any other imitation; and while each in its own way reveals some formal knowledge of the original, the aggregate of all imitations does not constitute any systematic knowledge of the cow; each in its own way remains a certain picture of the whole cow, monadic and independently valid. Thus, while the pleasure of imitative art (from this point of view) lies in learning, the artist does not thereby become a teacher. He does not explain anything to us. Rather he sets us a soluble problem, a problem which always remains to be solved over again in some new way the next time it is set.

The artist thus (and Lévi-Strauss saw this point also) is opposite to the scientist. Science explains the whole in terms of its parts and explains typical effects in terms of typical causes. Imitative art, which is in a certain sense more superficial than science (since it deals in appearances), is in another sense more profound; whereas science deals with abstracted elements, categories, and processes; an imitation states (in some specific way) the whole being of the thing. Each imitation rises from some inclusive, if schematic, intuition of the patterns found in experience. By the vision of the imitator, the parts are reduced to a whole, and their wholeness is revealed, perhaps for the first time. As Aristotle puts it: "This is why poetry is more philosophical and more serious than history; poetry speaks rather of the universal, history of the particular. Now it is a universal that a certain kind of person turns out to do or say a certain kind of thing in accordance with probability or necessity; this is what poetry aims at, although it gives the persons proper names. But the particular is what Alcibiades did or suffered" (*Poetics* 1451b5–11).

THE PROBABLE AS THE UNIVERSAL

But (and here we must catch ourselves up again) the distinction between poetry and history is not really relevant to what we have said so far. Of particulars too there is a universal which makes them recognizable and imitable; from such imitations something can be learned. A portrait of Alcibiades might well reveal to us some essential or underlying Alcibiades. The story of Alcibiades could be told with fidelity to literal fact and yet in such a way that the rhythm and form of the events stood revealed. The responsible narrative historian tries, in fact, to do just that. In terms of what we have said so far, history is simply a narrative imitation written under a special discipline: that it must be literally true. But everything recognizable is an equally valid imitation.

Thus the position, as interpreted so far, does not really meet the Socratic indictment. It is not enough that we learn something; we must also learn something important — something more important than Alcibiades or cow. Aristotle is ready to make this claim as well, and, interestingly enough, he is more ready to make it for fiction than for history.

Fiction is a new term — or rather it is not yet a term; there is no word in Aristotle which can be translated just this way. Fiction was in Aristotle's day a new genre, just emerging. The Homeric epics, as we saw, stood between history and fiction; there was no other place for them to stand, for the two had not yet been distinguished. History and fiction evolved in relation to each other and at the same time. History comes to full self-consciousness in Thucydides' Introduction (I.20–22), where he firmly turns his back on the storytellers and the legends which have "won their way into the world of myth." Self-conscious fiction begins with Agathon's *Anthos*, in which "the events and the proper names are made up, and nonetheless it pleases" (*Poetics* 1451b22–23). The problematic of narrative fiction can for the first time be explicitly stated by Aristotle because in Aristotle's time it had for the first time become clear that the meaning of a story need not have anything to do with the actuality of the events narrated.

For Aristotle — and we shall see that this point is crucial — the heroic stories derived from epic are located firmly in the category of fiction. If the audience believes that they actually happened, this belief is merely (so to speak) one of the poet's rhetorical resources. . . . Fiction shows us what sort of thing is possible, probable, or necessary.

The key term here, "probable" (*eikos*), is borrowed by Aristotle from fifth-century rhetorical theory. In a pleading, the litigant told the story of the case — of course in the form most favorable to himself. He might call witnesses to the truth of his narration or cite evidence which supported him. The rhetoricians taught him to take a further step: he could argue that his version of the story was the sort of thing one can expect to happen, while his opponent's version was inherently improbable. Rhetorical instruction thus led to inquiry into the kind of story that men find probable and are generally prepared to believe, and this inquiry laid the ground for the emerging craft of fiction. For Aristotle, the poet of fiction collapses the argument from probability into the narrative itself; instead of telling a story and then defending its truth on the grounds of its probability, he tells us a story which we do not have to believe to be true but which we do believe to be the sort of thing that "is likely to happen in accordance with probability or necessity."

Probability and necessity have to do with the relations between cause and effect and between events and the conditions of events. Whereas the rhetorician takes the conditions and consequences and uses them to reconstruct the event, the poet of fiction begins from the event and constructs around it appropriate conditions and consequences. The rhetorician says: "The accused had motive, means, and opportunity; we conclude that he (probably) committed the crime." The poet starts out to tell the story of a crime and says to himself: "I must provide my criminal with (probable) motive, means, and opportunity." The rhetorician says: "You know that this sort of man does such things; you should believe that this man did them." The poet asks himself: "What sort of man shall I make my criminal? What sort of man is likely to do such things?" The rhetorician says: "You know that criminals generally run away; the accused demonstrates his guilt by the fact that he left the city." The poet says: "After he has committed the crime, what will my criminal do? I suppose he will run away."

The poet, for Aristotle, has made a single *muthos*, a plot, when he has made a chain of events with this sort of internal logic. The perceived relations of cause, condition, and event, as we say, "hold the plot together." Probability and necessity are the sources of unity.

> Tragedy is the imitation of a complete and whole action having some magnitude. . . .
>
> To give a simple definition; it is of such magnitude that when things happen in sequence according to probability or necessity it turns out that there is a change from good fortune to ill fortune or from ill fortune to good fortune. (*Poetics* 1450b24-25 and 1451a11-15)

The change in fortune requires magnitude; it takes a certain scale to accommodate change. But the plot will not be "whole and complete" unless the change is probable or necessary. Aristotle goes on:

> Plot is not, as some suppose, a unity because it is about one person. There are many and unlimited things which happen to a single person; there is, of some of them, no unity. Thus there are many actions of a single person from which no unity of action arises. So all those poets seem to have been wrong who have composed Epics of Heracles and of Theseus and such poems. For they think that, since Heracles was one, there is a single plot about him. But Homer, just as he excels in other respects, also seems to have seen this clearly, whether by art or nature. When he composed his *Odyssey*, he did not include everything that happen to [Odysseus], such as being wounded on Parnassus or pretending to be insane at the gathering of the host — there being no probability or necessity that, when one of these things happened, the other would happen; rather, he constructed his *Odyssey* around a single action of the kind we mention, as also his *Iliad*. (*Poetics* 1451a16-29)

Homer found stories about Odysseus in his tradition; he told, however, not those stories, but the story of a plot he had himself invented. Stories can be borrowed, plots cannot; the invention of a plot is the essence of the invention of a (narrative) poem (*Poetics* 1451b27-29). The plot is the story conceived in a certain way, in terms of relations between conditions and events, causes and consequences. One story can give rise to many plots as the story is reconceived. The poet can borrow his stories from anywhere — from other poets, from history, from his own memories and dreams. He can make his stories up. His power as a narrative poet is his power to conceive the story as unified by an internal logic of probability and necessity and to convey this conception to us. That, for Aristotle, is the characteristic wisdom of the narrative poet.

The poet, in making his plot, discovers a form in the story, an internal logic. He then tells us the story in such a way that we also see the inner logic of it. When we "get" the plot — when we recognize its unity — we do so because we recognize the probability or necessity of the sequence. We "believe" the poet, we call a story "true to life," when we are led to say that, yes, such a man would indeed say or do such things under such conditions and with such consequences. On the premises the poet has set before us, his story does indeed follow.

The premises can be absolutely outlandish; the characters can be placed anywhere—in Hell, in outer space, in fairyland. Fiction is a thought-experiment and is hypothetical. We are quite ready to suspend our disbelief, in the sense that we are ready to grant the poet the premises he needs for his plot. Frequently a premise involves the introduction of an impossibility into the familiar world. What if the actual god Dionysus should appear in a rather ordinary Greek town? What if a rather ordinary Athenian citizen succeeded in making a private peace with Sparta? From these hypotheses develop consequences; the poet displays these consequences in such a way that we recognize their causes.

But there is then a paradox about the poet's display of causes. Insofar as he traces the event back to its first cause—to his own premise—he has shown us nothing, for the first cause is by fiat. If Iago is absolutely evil, he is not interesting as a character, for there is nothing to be explained about him. So we do not ask: Why does Iago do such evil acts? He does them by definition. Iago's significance within the story lies rather in the impact of this unconditioned evil on a world recognizably like our own. From the premises, that is, develop intermediate causes; the poet inquires into these intermediate causes and resolves his inquiry when he shows us that the consequences of his premises develop according to probability or necessity.

The first causes are for the sake of the intermediate causes; the poet sets the stage in order to tell us a story. The story develops by an interplay among thought, character, and action. As the characters confront the events, they change, and the changes that occur within them give rise to further events. These changes are like changes we know. The poet creates his world, but he does not create it just as he wishes. The beginnings are invented, but the consequences follow as they really would. In this sense, fiction presents an unreal world which is about the real world. In this sense also, the principle of all fiction, however fanciful, is realism. The poet is an imitator, not of actual events, but of events which have real (that is, recognizable) causes; the story is probable, not because it tells of the kind of events we would expect to see, but because it shows us the kind of action which, once the poet has explained it to us, we would expect to happen under the conditions he has set.

We can thus define fiction as the outcome of a hypothetical inquiry into the intermediate causes of action, an inquiry which has led the poet to the discovery and communication in a story of some universal pattern of human probability and necessity. The characteristic learning, the "this is that," is the recognition of this universal. The poet does not teach us this universal; in order to recognize it, we must already know it. We are all familiar with the shock of recognition narrative art can bring us, the sense of having brought to the surface some intimately held and perhaps unwelcome truth, as when we say: "Yes, given Othello, Iago, and Desdemona, it could not be otherwise." The poet thus shows us something more about something we already knew; he picks out of the pattern of probability certain characteristic features which, in his presentation, enable us to recognize it as a pattern.

PLOT AS KNOWLEDGE

Aristotle's treatment of fiction, with its emphasis on the inner logic of plot, may seem curiously one-dimensional. Obviously there are other sources of form and unity in narrative art. There is, for example, what we might call rhetorical form, the unity imposed by a poet who is careful to command and control his audience's attention, to excite in them just those expectations he intends to fulfill, and to provoke them to ask just those questions he intends to answer. There is what we might call musical form, form produced by the interplay of symmetry and asymmetry, dissonance and harmony. There is what we might call thematic form, in which incident is connected to incident through the common content of the notions and meditations they provoke in us. All these kinds of form can be characteristic of what Aristotle calls the "episodic plot, where the episodes follow one another without probability or necessity" (*Poetics* 1451b34–35). This sort of plot Aristotle says is the "worst," yet Odysseus' narration, *Odyssey* ix–xii, is of this kind, and we do not think of it as an inferior fictional narrative. The incidents of Odysseus' narration are not connected to one another by probability or necessity—there is no inner logic which determines that they should occur in just this order—but the narrative is formed and unified in other ways.

I do not think that plot is central in all fiction. A work of fiction is often as much about its author ("implied" or actual) as its characters; it may show us how one man sees the world or be a unified reflection upon the process of fictional creation itself. What would Aristotle have made of *Tristram Shandy?*

I suspect that Aristotle's argument is sharpened and limited by his desire to respond to the arguments of the *Republic*, Book Ten, and that he pins his case to the inner logic of plot because in this way he can argue that fiction is a source of knowledge, knowledge which we absolutely require and which we have no other way of acquiring. In other words, that fiction enables us to recognize patterns of probability and necessity gives fiction an ethical standing. In order to make this point, it will be necessary to turn from the *Poetics* to the *Ethics*, and specifically to Aristotle's account of happiness:

> But perhaps that happiness is best is a formulation which obviously commands agreement; one would be glad, however, to be told more clearly what it is. Perhaps we could get at it this way, by stating the function [*ergon*] of a human being. Just as in the case of a flute-player,

sculptor, or any craftsman, or of anything that has a function or action [*praxis*], the good of it and the doing-it-well [*to eu*] are thought to be in its function, so one might have the same thought about a human being—if indeed he *has* any function. Are we to say that of a shoemaker or a carpenter there is a function and action, while of a human being not, but he is by nature functionless [*argon*]? Or just as there is an obvious function of the eye and the hand and the foot and in general of each part, so should one propose some function of the human being also, beyond all these? But then, what in the world can it be? Life is something obviously shared, even by plants, but we are looking for something particular. So one must set aside the capacity for nurture and growth. Next comes the capacity for perception, but this is obviously shared even by a horse or an ox or any animal. There remains some kind of capacity for action which belongs to a creature capable of speech [*or* reason: *logos*].

But this latter can be meant in one of two ways; we must state that we mean the capacity in its actual functioning [*energeia*]—for this seems to put it more adequately. If the function of a human being is an actual functioning of the soul according to reason, or not without reason, then exactly this is man's specific function, and it also is the function of a serious [*or* excellent: *spoudaios*] man, just as the lyre-player and the excellent [*spoudaios*] lyre-player have [the same function], and, in a word, it is generally so; the superlative achievement with relation to the [relevant] virtue [*aretē*] has to do with the function. Of a lyre-player, this is to play the lyre; of an excellent [*spoudaios*] lyre-player, to play it well [*to eu*]. If so, then the human good is an actual functioning of the soul in accordance with virtue. (*Ethics* 1097b22–98a16)

The most important terms common to the *Ethics* and the *Poetics* are *praxis*, "action," and *ēthos*, "character." In both books, character is for the sake of action—but differently. In fiction, character is explanatory of action; we believe the poet because we believe that such a man would do such things. In ethics, character is praised or dispraised by reference to action; we want our sons to be such men because of the actions such men do. In neither sphere does character have any standing by itself. The poet shows us nothing of importance when he draws a character sketch without reference to an action, for the same reason that there is no merit in possessing a good character which is not enacted. Character is the potentiality which comes to actuality in action.

The poet, when he imitates an action, shows us a picture of the actual functioning of human souls. When the imitation has a unified plot, we see that the action follows by probability or necessity from the premised characters and conditions. The poet thus shows us a reduced and clarified (although not at all definitive) picture of the causes and conditions of human happiness and unhappiness; as we recognize the probability of his plot, we come to know certain features of those causes and conditions.

There could be no knowledge more important to a "creature capable of speech."

We should not, however, confuse the kind of knowledge gained from fiction which the kind of knowledge gained from ethics. . . . Ethics and fiction have a common subject matter — *praxis*; but they approach it from opposite directions. Ethics, which is a science, "replaces . . . an effect by its cause," while fiction, which is an art, produces an image "homologous with the object." Ethics is about the conditions of happiness; it treats happiness only potentially. Fiction is about unreal happiness and unhappiness, but it treats these in their actuality. We should not conclude that fiction is unconcerned with the causes of happiness. Ethics works from actor to action and prescribes; it says that such a man will live in such a way and that that is good. Fiction works from action to actor and describes; it shows us that such an action could have been done by such a man, that it is probable. Fiction shows us particular instances of happiness and unhappiness in such a way that we can see the causal relations between the actor, his situation, and the event.

Ethics is about *praxis*, but ethics never achieves an understanding of *praxis*; or, to put the point another way, because happiness is in the fortunate interplay between virtue and circumstance, happiness is finally unintelligible. The success or failure of an action is known only by its results, and since every result leads to a further result, the final result is never before us. Hence the dilemma: Shall we call no man happy until he is dead? But if happiness is an actual functioning and the dead are not actual at all, how can they be happy? Besides, it is possible for a man to live happily and yet become unhappy after death through "dishonors and the misfortunes of his children and descendants in general" (*Ethics* 1100a20–21). The actor commits himself to the future and thus never knows his own act; since the future is without limit, there is no moment when the returns are in.

Similarly action, since it is with others, is never self-contained. Having said that happiness is a certain kind of self-sufficiency, Aristotle goes on: "The self-sufficiency we mean does not belong to man by himself, to a man living his life in solitude, but with parents and children and a wife and in general friends and fellow citizens. . . . But of these things one must set a certain limit. As one reaches out to one's parents and their ancestors and to one's friends' friends, it goes off into infinity" (*Ethics* 1097b8–13). No man is an island, but to treat his fate as inextricably entangled with the present condition and future adventures of the entire continent is to rob him of personal identity altogether. Some limit must be set, even though the limit be to a degree arbitrary. Action, to be intelligible, must be perceived to occur within a definite social field and to have definite consequences. Such limitation of our perception in life is analogous to the discovery of narrative form in fiction. By the imposition of limits we discern, in both cases, the pattern of a *praxis*.

Praxis I have here translated (as is customary) "action." The word might equally be translated "accomplishment" or "event." *Praxis* means, among other things, a transaction in commerce or an action at law. The word has implications of completeness, of activity rounded to a definite outcome.

Litigation and commerce, like games, impose limits on our interactions; within these limits we know how we are obligated and to whom, and we can measure acts against their consequences. The situation so delimited defines which actors are more or less successful than others. Such limits give our choices meaning. Where the limits are not set by rules, however, we must discover them for ourselves. We thus impose a form upon our understanding of human things. We do not hold that men are responsible for or involved with the fortunes of all those with whom they might have come in contact. We speak of happiness as bounded by birth and death, or even in smaller units; we say that such a one had a successful college career, a good war, a rewarding working life. Thus we construct around the central actor or actors an intelligible pattern of events, with a beginning, middle, and end, and a listable cast of characters. We make a life, or some part of a life, into a story. Only in this way can we form any judgment of it. Similarly we must think of ourselves as actors in a story. We must perceive our relations as finite and our acts as testable against some definitive outcome; otherwise our ethical situation "goes off into infinity" and the will is puzzled.

Storytelling thus rises directly from the need for ethical intelligibility. . . . Narrative history rises from a reflection on the experience we already have — a reflection not analytic but synthetic. In telling our own story we gain control of our experience; we give it form and share its meaning with our audience. Thus Odysseus and Penelope tell each other the whole story of their twenty-year separation (XXIII.300–343); this is a necessary completing step in the reconstruction of their marriage. Storytelling is a way of knowing and sharing knowledge of the matter of life.

When the story is told for its own sake, however, as fiction, there must be a further forming of experience. History forms events into a plot; fiction starts with an idea for a plot and generates events. The form of the action, which was in history the conclusion of the thought process, is in fiction the beginning. History is a response to experience; fiction is a response to some idea of experience. That is what Aristotle means when he says that poetry is "more philosophical" than history. He does not mean that the poet is a philosopher. Narrative remains on the level of the particular: it tells of these men in this place. In this sense, fiction, like all imitative art, remains "mid-way between schema and anecdote." The poet is more philosophical only in that he founds his claim to our attention, not on the literal matter of his story, but on the human universal there revealed. The sequence is clearest in the case of historical fiction, when the poet, captivated by the story of Alcibiades, retells that story as the Tragedy of Alcibiades. He will then tell us what "a certain kind of person turns out to do or say . . . in accordance with probability or necessity." The facts about Alcibiades are then no longer important (although the poet may choose to adhere to them either as a special discipline on his art or to help enlist our belief in his narrative); frequently the poet will be ruthless with the facts. He has in effect constructed a new Alcibiades, who is what he is in relation to the poet's plot. For Aristotle, and for us, the *Iliad* is historic fiction of exactly this kind.

In this way Aristotle resolves the problematic of narrative, between truth and falsehood: it can be false in its particulars, he says, yet true to life universally. By taking this step Aristotle also — almost incidentally — resolves the problem of epic distance. The heroic world for him consists of a set of premises on which fictions can be founded; these premises, being the collective possession of the literary tradition, have the special merit of being familiar. Troy fell, the heroes spoke with the gods, Achilles was brave — all these things are known to the audience. The poet, when he creates a plot, shows us an action which follows — given these premises — in accordance with probability or necessity. Thus the *Iliad* appears to be about things very far away and long ago, but what we learn from it is a universal which applies also to ourselves.

Aristotle is able to call the poet both philosophical and instructive without making him into either a philosopher or a teacher. The poet does not teach because he does not, primarily, concern himself with his effect on his audience. As a maker of plot, he must seek out the intermediate causes within the world and for a while consider his characters more real than his audience. No wonder he appears to his audience inspired or possessed.

The poet, further, does not ask general questions; he does not ask: What is justice? loyalty? forgiveness? He asks instead: How was it that Achilles refused the gifts? What would he say in refusing them? He answers these questions concretely; he is not making an essay but a story. Once he has conceived situation and character so clearly that he can speak for Achilles, he is done. He has said what he had to say in telling his story. No wonder any passerby can say more about his poem than he can.

THE EFFECT ON THE AUDIENCE

Aristotle's focus on the inner logic of plot sets a program for criticism. We — the passersby — can ask: How is it that this story is probable and necessary? What universal patterns can be discerned in it? How does the action follow from the premises? . . . It is only fair to say, however, that this is not Aristotle's own program. In the *Poetics* he does not explore the meaning of texts; he examines only the general kinds of things which in a dramatic text engross and move us. The emphasis remains (and in this Aristotle shows himself the heir of the sophistic) on the *pathē*, the emotions produced in us by fiction — and especially the tragic emotions, pity and fear.

. . .

Yet it remains true that for Aristotle a dramatic text moves and engrosses us when we recognize in it some comprehensible pattern of causes — and that it moves us most when this pattern comes to us unexpectedly and thus extends our understanding. Aristotle says: "The imitation is not only of a complete action but of things pitiable and fearful; such things most happen when they happen contrary to expectations because of one another [*di' allēla*]" (*Poetics* 1452a1–4). Casual events, however horrific, do not move us to pity and fear; those emotions are excited by a narrative with meaning. The best kind of meaning is that of the inner logic of the events, the *di' allēla*. When these events are "contrary to expectation," when they reveal to us a pattern of causal relations which we had not seen before, then we are most shaken and enthralled. So the characteristic *pathē* of the plot cannot be separated from its characteristic learning; *pathē* and learning together constitute the characteristic value to us of a well-made narrative.

I suspect that Aristotle meant by *katharsis* exactly this combination of emotion and learning. Aristotle himself has nothing to say about *katharsis* in the *Poetics*; the word occurs once only, in the definition of tragedy. On this one word an enormous body of commentaries has arisen. Since Aristotle gives us no other guide (with the exception of an obscurely related passage in the *Politics*), we can interpret *katharsis* only by interpreting the *Poetics*. Here I notice only that the objects of imitation mentioned in *Poetics* 4, "the most despised animals and corpses," are the typically impure or unclean things; Aristotle there says that we take pleasure in imitations of them because from the imitation we learn something. So perhaps learning itself purifies.

Tragedy, says Aristotle's definition, purifies pity and fear through pity and fear. This appears to be a paradox until we remember that the play is something we both experience and know. The *pragmata*, the events of the story, work on us in certain ways. But as we come to perceive the unity of the plot, its inner logic, we reconceive our own emotions as the necessary conditions of our comprehension of a formally coherent order. We set our own emotions at a certain distance from ourselves; like the story itself, they stand between reality and unreality and are purified as we come to conceive them within the formal order which the work provides.

. . . In connection with the *Iliad*, . . . purification takes place through the comprehension of a unified structure and is equivalent to the discovery that the work is in fact perfectly founded on its own premises.

Hector   Rachel Bespaloff*

Suffering and loss have stripped Hector bare; he has nothing left but himself. In the crowd of mediocrities that are Priam's sons, he stands alone, a prince, born to rule. Neither superman, nor demigod, nor godlike, he is a man and among men a prince. He is at ease in a kind of unstudied nobility that permits neither pride in respect to the self nor humbleness in respect to the gods. Loaded as he is with favors, he has much to lose; and there is something in him that sets him above the favors, the natural endowments — his passion for defying destiny. Apollo's protégé, Ilion's protector, defender of a city, a wife, a child, Hector is the guardian of the perishable joys. The zeal for glory exalts but does not blind him; it sustains him when hope has left him. "For I know well in my entrails and my heart, a day will come when holy Troy will perish." He has learned "to be brave at all times," "to fight in the first ranks of the Trojans." These are his privileges as a prince, which all Andromache's tender urgency cannot make him renounce. And yet he is far from insensible to her plea. It is on Andromache's account, more than on his people's, his father's, his brothers', that the thought of the future tortures him. The very image of the brutal fate that awaits her makes him wish for death. "But as for me, may I be dead, and may the earth have covered me before I hear you cry out or see you dragged away into slavery." Standing there on the threshold of war, Hector clasps with a last look the true goods of life, exposed suddenly to attack, naked as targets. The pain of this leave-taking does not modify his decision which has already been made. "Men will watch in war," and Hector first of all among those who were born in Troy.

Achilles pays for nothing; to Hector everything comes dear. Yet it is not Hector, but Achilles, whose insatiable rancor feeds even on victories, and who is forever "gorging himself with complaints." The man of resentment in the *Iliad* is not the weak man but, on the contrary, the hero who can bend everything to his will. With Hector, the will to greatness never pits itself against the will to happiness. That little bit of true happiness which is more important than anything else, because it coincides with the true meaning of life, will be worth defending even with life itself, to which it has given a measure, a form, a price. Even in defeat, the courage of Hector does not give way before the valor of Achilles, which has been nurtured on discontent and irritable anxiety. But the capacity for happiness, which rewards the efforts of fecund civilizations, puts a curb on the defender's mettle by making him more aware of the enormity of the sacrifice exacted by the gods of war. This capacity, however, does not develop until the appetite for happiness has been stilled, the appetite that

*From *On the Iliad*, trans. Mary McCarthy, Bollingen Series 9, pp. 39–49. Copyright 1947, © renewed by Princeton University Press. Reprinted by permission of Princeton University Press.

drives the aggressor, who is less civilized, on toward his prey and fills his heart with "an infinite power for battle and truceless war."

Death, for Hector, means consigning everything he loves to a life of punishment and torture; flight, on the other hand, is a denial of the thing that transcends him, that "glory" that will some day be the subject of a song and bring Ilion back to life in the centuries to come. Before the walls of Troy, preparing himself to meet Achilles, shaken by premonitions of defeat and by the entreaties of Priam and Hecuba, Hector experiences a kind of ultimate hesitation. Why not keep "peace with dignity" by promising Achilles Helen and half the wealth of Troy? But quickly he gets hold of himself: the war is not in Achilles' hands. Achilles is as deaf to arguments, promises, and human feeling as a hurricane. "Better to meet him at once and have it over with." And now, for the first time perhaps, Hector feels weakness seize him; when he catches sight of his leaping adversary, he is no longer master of his terror. Time after time he has turned the tide of battle, he has taken the measure of Ajax and the very bravest of the Achaians; yet now he, the dauntless, "leaves and takes to flight." Homer wanted him to be a whole man and spared him neither the quaking of terror nor the shame of cowardice. "Ahead flees a brave man, but braver still is he who pursues him at top speed." And this flight, short as it is, has the eternity of a nightmare. "As a man in a dream cannot catch the one he is chasing and as he, in his turn, cannot flee faster than the other pursues, so Achilles that day could not overtake Hector nor could Hector escape him." Homer, here, reaches across history to the very substance of the horror that has neither issue nor redemption. Not around the walls of Troy but in the cosmic womb itself does the ravisher's pursuit prolong endlessly the victim's flight. "And all the gods looked on." Hector makes a last effort, which would have to be called superhuman, did it not precisely define the height and breadth of man's powers: he turns and faces his enemy, having first mastered himself. "I no longer wish to flee you, son of Peleus. . . . It is over. . . . I will have you or you will have me." What he fled from, what he now confronts, is not the "gigantic Achilles," but his own destiny; he meets the appointed hour when he will be sent to pasture in Hades. At least he will not die without a struggle, and not without glory. Dying, he begs Achilles for a last time not to give his body to the dogs. And for a last time his conqueror, drunk with cruelty, is obdurate to his plea. Achilles, at this moment, is aware of not being a man, and admits it: "There are no covenants between men and lions. . . . It is not permitted that we should love each other, you and I." Agony sets Hector free; he recognizes his mistake and yields himself simultaneously to truth and to death: "Yes, I see what you are. I could never have persuaded you. A heart of iron is in you for sure."

In the absence of God, fate becomes the agent of retribution. Hector has to pay for Patroclus' inglorious death, just as Achilles, later on, will pay for the death of Hector. "Ares is just; he kills those who kill." In the excitement engendered by bloodshed, Hector himself forgets the code of honor. The idea of degrading a fallen enemy is no more repugnant to him than it is to his rival. Both of them pushing revenge to the point of impiety, desecrate the victim's body so as to kill straight through to the soul. Between the two scenes in which a conquered man's body is outraged, a most rigorous parallelism is kept. "Death and imperious fate" are announced to Hector by Patroclus, and Hector predicts to Achilles his "death at the Scaean gates." War devours differences and disparities, shows no respect for the unique. Call him Achilles or Hector, the conqueror is like all conquerors, and the conquered like all the conquered. Homer does not spare us this sight. But at the same time he sees warlike emulation as the fountainhead of creative effort, as the spring of individual energy and of the manly virtues in the community. Through it the appetite for glory takes hold of individuals and peoples and transforms itself into a love of immortality. Yet, throughout the *Iliad*, the pride of omnipotence is also the thing that invites the reprisals of destiny. Outside all sanctions of the moral order, outside all imperatives of divine origin, the vengeance of the Nemesis of antiquity *makes an act appear guilty in retrospect that at the time of its commission was not considered a sin.* When the Father of the Gods take out his golden scales to learn fate's decree, the Killer is free to accomplish his sacred mission: he is under the protection of the Immortals. And yet this immunity lasts but an instant; he has hardly fulfilled his allotted role, the force in him is still unspent, when once again he becomes vulnerable.

Force revels only in an abuse that is also self-abuse, in an excess that expends its store. It reveals itself in a kind of supreme leap, a murderous lightning stroke, in which calculation, chance, and power seem to fuse in a single element to defy man's fate. Herein lies the beauty of force, which is nowhere so well shown as in Homer — with the exception, possibly, of the Bible, which glorifies it in God alone. When Homer celebrates the beauty of his warriors, he does not intend to stylize or idealize them; Achilles and Hector are beautiful because force is beautiful, and because the beauty of omnipotence, converted into the omnipotence of beauty, can make man acquiesce utterly in his own destruction, can exact from him that flat submission that delivers him over to force, prostrate in the act of worship. Thus, in the *Iliad*, force appears as both the supreme reality and the supreme illusion of life. Force, for Homer, is divine insofar as it represents a superabundance of life that flashes out in the contempt for death and the ecstasy of self-sacrifice; it is detestable insofar as it contains a fatality that transforms it into inertia, a blind drive that is always pushing it on to the very end of its course, on to its own abolition and the obliteration of the very values it engendered. To illustrate the illusion of omnipotence, Homer chooses not, as one might expect, Achilles or Ajax, but the prince of wisdom himself. A fleeting triumph befuddles Hector; he loses the power of reflection, the sense of proportion; he is no longer aware of the existence of obstacles. When Polydamas counsels prudence, he angrily rejects his advice and threatens him with death for holding defeatist ideas. But Polydamas is surely right to accuse Hector of being always the same in council and in war, unable to brook contradiction: "There is only one thing that pleases you, the perpetual increase of your authority." In Homer, the hero himself, even Achilles, cannot set himself above the human plane. Hector has nothing, courage, nobility, or reason, that is not bent and sullied by war, nothing except that self-respect that makes him human, comes to his rescue at the end, steadies him before the inevitable, and brings him his clearest vision in the instant of death.

Hector, then, has but this way to glory, "the tale of which will pass on to men yet to come." And for Homer's warrior, glory is not some vain illusion or empty boast; it is the same thing that Christians saw in the Redemption, a promise of immortality outside and beyond history, in the supreme detachment of poetry. Achilles ravens on Hector's remains. Every day, starting at dawn, he devotes himself to his lust for reprisal; three times in succession he drags his unfortunate rival's body around the tomb of Patroclus and then leaves it there, stretched out in the dust. His insatiable spleen vents itself both on Patroclus' murderer and on that defeated being, now out of his reach, who reminds him of the futility of victory and the approach of his own death. The gods, however, who took everything else that belonged to Hector, have neither the power nor the wish to deprive him of the beauty that outlives force. Stretched out prone in the dirt, he remains beautiful: "Apollo spares his body all pollution . . . Aphrodite, night and day, keeps the dogs from him." And, intact thus in his young warrior's beauty, he will be given back to Priam. On this point Hermes reassures the old man, who questions his guide anxiously before approaching Achilles: "You would marvel yourself if you were to come and see how dewy he lies there, the blood around him washed away, without a sign of pollution, and all his wounds closed. So the blessed gods care for your son, even in death, for he was dear to their hearts."

Not the wrath of Achilles, but the duel between Achilles and Hector, the tragic confrontation of the revenge-hero and the resistance-hero, is what forms the *Iliad*'s true center and governs its unity and its development. Despite the gods, despite necessity, there is enough freedom here to leave both the reader and Zeus, the divine watcher, in a state of suspense. The changing rhythm of the battle pits the defenders' valor against the invaders' fury in a constantly shifting relation which makes every contestant uncertain of the future. This fluctuation of fortune, however, does not stop the Achaians and the Trojans from calculating, with a kind of muffled lucidity, their respective chances in the "indefinite series of duels" whose ensemble is the Trojan War. Whatever befalls them, the petty pirate kings never lose faith in their own invincibility; Ilion's princes, on the contrary, cannot, even on the brink of victory, shake off a premonition of defeat. By the time Hector dares to face Achilles without despairing of victory, he has already used up the better part of his strength in winning a prior victory over himself. Achilles' mission is to renew, amid these scenes of devastation, the sources and resources of vital energy; Hector's is to preserve, by the gift of himself, the sacred trust whose maintenance assures to life its profound continuity. But these roles, these functions, do not reveal themselves in their true light until the crucial moment of combat when Hector's courage matures into a sovereign act of self-mastery and Achilles' anger mounts into murderous ecstasy. In this light the destinies of the two men appear to be permanently interlocked in struggle, death, and immortality. Where history showed us only ramparts and frontiers, poetry discovered a mysterious predestination that makes two adversaries, whose meeting is inexorable, worthy of each other. And Homer asks no quarter, save from poetry, which repossesses beauty from death and wrests from it the secret of justice that history cannot fathom. To the darkened world poetry alone restores pride, eclipsed by the arrogance of the victors and the silence of the vanquished. Others may blame Zeus and marvel that he permits "the good to be ranked with the bad, those whose souls turn toward justice with those who are given over to violence."[1] With Homer there is no marvelling or blaming, and no answer is expected. Who is good in the *Iliad?* Who is bad? Such distinctions do not exist; there are only men suffering, warriors fighting, some winning, some losing. The passion for justice emerges only in mourning for justice, in the dumb avowal of silence. To condemn force, or absolve it, would be to condemn, or absolve, life itself. And life in the *Iliad* (as in the Bible or in *War and Peace*) is essentially the thing that does not permit itself to be assessed, or measured, or condemned, or justified, at least not by the living. Any estimate of life must be confined to an awareness of its inexpressibility. This pliable wisdom, consubstantial with existence itself, has very little in common with the parade drills of Stoicism.

Sprung out of bitterness, the philosophy of the *Iliad* excludes resentment. It antedates the divorce between nature and existence. Here the Whole is no collection of broken pieces put back together with indifferent success by reason; on the contrary, it is the active principle of interpenetration of all the elements that make it up. The inevitable slowly unfolds, and its theatre is the heart of man, and, at the same time, the Cosmos. Against the eternal blindness of history is set the creative lucidity of the poet fashioning for future generations heroes more godlike than the gods, and more human than men.

Note

1. Compare this text from Theognis with the words of Habakkuk: "Thine eyes are too pure to see evil. And Thou canst not look at iniquity. Why shouldst Thou look with favor on the false-hearted and be silent when the wicked man devours one juster than himself?"

Some Possible Indo-European
Themes in the *Iliad*   C. Scott Littleton*

[*Editor's note*: This article is predicated on the theories and methods
of Georges Dumézil, who has demonstrated that the ancient Indo-
European speaking communities shared a common, tripartite ideology
based on three canonical principles, or "functions." At the apex of this
ideology was the "first function," or the maintenance of cosmic and
juridical sovereignty; next came the "second function," or the exercise of
military prowess and other activities associated with warfare; at the base
of the system was the "third function," that is, all those phenomena and
activities associated with the provision of nourishment, the maintenance
of physical well-being, health, wealth, etc. These three "functions"
pervade the ancient Indo-European pantheons and mythological texts,
from the Icelandic *Eddas* to the Indian *Vedas*, and are also expressed in
the structure of society itself (e.g., the three Aryan or "twice-born" castes
of classical and later India) as well as in the behavior of heroes and demi-
gods, such as may be found in Roman pseudo-history (e.g., the early
sections of Livy's *History*) and the ancient Indian epical texts (e.g., the
Mahābhārata). Littleton suggests that the *Iliad* can be analyzed from this
perspective.]

It is fair to say that, of all relevant ancient Indo-European traditions,
that of the Greeks presents by far the greatest number of difficulties to
contemporary students of Indo-European myth and epic. For the common, tripartite ideological inheritance, so clearly demonstrated by
Georges Dumézil and his colleagues in the myths and epics of the Indic-,
Iranian-, Italic-, and Germanic-speaking communities,[1] is all but absent
in the Greek tradition — despite the fact that this tradition is certainly the
most voluminous and best preserved of the ancient Indo-European traditions. As Dumézil puts it, ["Greece — undoubtedly because of the 'Greek
miracle' and also because the most ancient Aegean civilizations had too
strongly influenced the invaders from the North — contributes little to
comparative studies; even the most considerable traits of the (Indo-
European) heritage have been profoundly modified there."][2]
    Yet here and there, tucked away in a variety of contexts, a few bits
and pieces of the common Indo-European ideology have come to light,[3]
proving that the Greeks were not altogether ignorant of the ideology to
which, as Indo-European speakers, they were heirs. One of the more
recent (1964) and significant additions to this meager store of evidence
concerning the persistence of the Indo-European ideology in the Greek

*Reprinted from *Myth and Law among the Indo-Europeans*, ed. Jaan Puhvel. (Berkeley:
University of California Press, 1970), 229–46, by permission of the publisher.

tradition is A. Yoshida's[4] suggestion that it is expressed in the embellishments on the shield of Achilles, as described by Homer in Book 18 of the *Iliad*. The purpose of this paper[5] is to build upon this foundation and comment upon the extent to which the *Iliad* as a whole may perhaps reflect the common Indo-European ideology. This is, of course, a matter that cannot possibly be dealt with adequately in a paper of this scope. Yet given the high probability that Yoshida is correct in his interpretation of the shield of Achilles (I had come to similar conclusions before encountering Yoshida's article), a few observations relative to the epic's chief figures and events are in order, if only to point the way for further investigation.

First, however, let us hear what Yoshida has to say about the shield.

Pointing out that Homer begins his description of the embellishments with images of the earth, the sky, and the constellations (center of the shield), and ends it with an image of the sea (outermost rim) — images that, he suggests, reflect a conventional cosmogonic scheme — Yoshida goes on to assert that

> [On the contrary, between these two ensembles the artist has carved a series of scenes describing the life of mankind. Moreover, this description is divided into three clearly distinct parts, dedicated, respectively, to activities relevant to one of the three Indo-European functions.
>
> The image of a city at peace (490–508) depicts a marriage (490–496) and then a trial (497–508), two of the major manifestations of the juridical domain, that is to say, of the first function.
>
> The image of a city at war, which follows (490–540), is composed essentially of combats, that is to say, the most typical expression of the second function.
>
> These antithetical tableaux of urban life are complemented by those of rural life: first, agricultural labors, then those of pastoral activities, that is to say, the two principal elements of the provision of nourishment, which [in turn] is one of the principal aspects of the third function; furthermore, in the *korós* scene which follows (590–606) some beautifully and richly garbed young men and girls execute, hand in hand, a joyous dance, much to the admiration of the immense crowd that surrounds them: youth, beauty, richness, popular joy — all these elements also belong to the complex third function.][6]

The third-function character of the final scene, Yoshida suggests, is strengthened by its mention of Ariadne, ["the great Minoan goddess of vegetation"]. To this I might add that there is also a great deal of evidence for the association of dancing with a host of third-function figures, especially the divine twins, in other Indo-European traditions.[7]

It should be emphasized that this interpretation of the shield of Achilles is phrased in thematic, contextual terms, and does not pretend to be predicated upon any set of philological premises, other than the fact that the author of the tradition was an Indo-European speaker. Nevertheless, as mentioned earlier, it does seem to me that Yoshida is correct in his assumption that the tripartite Indo-European ideological principles are expressed here and that their expression unfolds in the canonical order so frequently found in Indic, Iranian, Roman, and Norse materials. The uniqueness of *this* expression is itself an interesting phenomenon, for if we examine that other famous Greek shield, the shield of Herakles as described by Hesiod, no clear parallels emerge. Although Hesiod's description of the Theban hero's shield is perhaps modeled after the Homeric passage in question, and despite certain very specific points of similarity, notably the wedding sequence on the shield of Herakles, wherein people "were bringing the bride to the groom, and the loud bride-song was arising" (line 274), the general character and order of the scenes depicted are distinct from those on the shield of Achilles.

Why Hesiod failed to organize his description in terms of the Indo-European ideology is a moot question, especially in view of the strong probability that he was a younger contemporary of Homer (or at least of the author of the *Odyssey*).[8] Lattimore suspects that the bulk of the description of the shield of Herakles (from line 57 on) may well be the work of a late interpolator.[9] If this view is correct, then perhaps by the time these later lines were composed the hold of the Indo-European ideology had largely given way, although there is nothing in the first fifty-six lines that would clearly indicate its presence. The problem is further complicated by the fact that in most other contexts Herakles is, as Dumézil has shown,[10] one of the most "Indo-European" of Greek figures.

Withal, despite Hesiod's failure to express the common Indo-European ideology in a closely analogous context, its presence in at least one important Homeric passage raises the question of whether or not the *Iliad* as a whole reflects this ideology.

Although it is certainly correct to assert that the *Iliad* is concerned primarily with the behavior of Achilles, his withdrawal and subsequent return to the fray, and only secondarily with the siege of Troy, it must never be forgotten that it is against this latter backdrop that the events relative to Achilles' "wrath" take place. Indeed, it is against this backdrop of internecine military conflict that *all* the events described by Homer take place. Therefore, it seems fitting to begin by asking whether there are any other Indo-European mythic (or quasi-mythic) counterparts to such internecine strife.[11] The answer is, of course, yes: to name but a few samples, the conflict between the Pāṇḍavas and the Kauravas, as described in the *Mahābhārata*; the conflict between Aesir and Vanir, which forms an important element in the Norse tradition; the conflict between the Romans and the Sabines, as described by Livy, *et al.*[12] In all such cases one segment of the society comes into conflict with another segment; even though these segments may be formally distinguished, as in the case of the Romans versus the Sabines.

Now among the more interesting of Dumézil's suggestions as to the character of the proto-Indo-European mythology is that it contained a myth concerning a conflict or "war" between representatives of the first two functions and those of the third.[13] The clearest reflexes of this assumed protomyth are to be found in the Norse and Italic conflicts just mentioned. In the Norse case it is certain that the Aesir, the dominant group of gods, to which Odin, Týr, and Thor belong, are representatives of the first two functions, and that the Vanir, the losers in the struggle, to which Freyr, Njördr, and Freyja belong, are third-function figures. In the Italic case, the Romans, under the leadership of the warlike Tullus Hostilius (second function), and after the successive reigns of Romulus and Numa (first function), engage in a conflict with their neighbors, the Sabines, who, as devotees of luxury, "la tranquillité," and "la volupté," are manifestly representatives of the third function.[14] In both cases, the representatives of the third function — Vanir and Sabines — are defeated and eventually integrated into the social and / or supernatural system, rendering it complete. (Elsewhere, I have suggested that this theme of a "war between the functions" might well serve to explain, or sanction, perhaps, the lowly position of the cultivator in Indo-European society; he was the last to be admitted to it.)[15]

Assuming Dumézil is correct in his interpretation of these two mythical (in the Roman case quasi-mythical) conflicts, is it possible to view the conflict between the Achaeans and the Trojans in the same light? The answer depends upon the extent to which it is possible to assert that Homer, or at least the tradition upon which he drew, conceived of the Trojans in third-function terms.

To begin with, there is the famous Judgment of Paris, which, according to Dumézil, contains perhaps the clearest single Greek expression of the tripartite ideology.[16] At the behest of Zeus, Paris agrees to award the golden "apple of discord" to the fairest of the goddesses. The choice is between the regal Hera, the warlike Athena, and the voluptuous Aphrodite. So as to influence him in his choice, each goddess, seen by Dumézil as representative of one of the three functions, offers Paris a gift: Hera offers world sovereignty (first function); Athena promises military prowess (second function); and Aphrodite tenders the gift of earthly pleasure (third function). Paris chooses Aphrodite, and thus, by alienating Hera and Athena (i.e., the first two functions), he sets the stage for what is to come. It is quite clear that, in making this choice, he has aligned himself and his people with a third-function divinity. Indeed, throughout the epic, the *only* divine being firmly committed to the Trojan cause is Aphrodite; the other two former contestants in that prototypical beauty contest never waver in their commitment to the Achaean cause.

Further evidence of the extent to which the Trojans, both individually and collectively, manifest third-function characteristics can be seen in Homer's descriptions of the city and its inhabitants. The city itself is consistently depicted as a center of wealth and a rich prize waiting to be sacked (cf. 2.133, 9.278, 22.116–118, and elsewhere); indeed, one of the reasons why Achilles withdraws from the fight is his expectation that he will be shortchanged when the spoils are distributed (1.164–171). Evidence of third-function characteristics can also be seen in the emphasis among the Trojans upon family life and the relationship therein. Perhaps the best example of this can be found in Book 6, wherein Andromache, her infant son in her arms, implores Hector to withdraw from the war (390 ff.). With the bitterness of one who prefers peace to war, Hector tells his wife that he must continue to fight; yet before taking leave of his family he finds the time to kiss and fondle his offspring (465–481). Moreover, throughout the conversation between Hector and Andromache there is the implication that the cause is lost and that she and all the rest of the Trojan women will be carried off by the victorious Achaeans. Here, of course, we can compare the fate of the Sabine women.

In this connection it may be recalled that Dumézil has suggested that third-function figures, although primarily concerned with the maintenance of tranquillity and physical well-being, are often depicted as armed in a protective capacity. Typically, they do not instigate conflicts, but they are not exempt from them should they arise or should the domestic peace be threatened. The Roman figure Quirinus is often referred to as Mars *qui praeest paci*, and there are *arma Quirini*. The Norse Freyr is armed with a sword, and the Indian epic heroes Nakula and Sahadeva (projections of the Aśvins) carry weapons and engage in battle.[17] Although the chief Trojan figures, especially Hector, are depicted as doughty warriors, their prowess is displayed solely in defense of their homes and families; they are never portrayed as aggressors.

Turning to a consideration of the principal Trojan figures themselves, it is possible that Hector and Paris are projections of the twin third-function figures so frequently encountered in the pantheons of the ancient Indo-European-speaking communities (e.g., the Vedic Aśvins, the Greek Dioscuri). In order to support this contention, it is necessary to consider two of the chief figures in that other Indo-European epic, the *Mahābhārata*. Some years ago (1947) Stig Wikander was able to demonstrate that the principle protagonists of the Indian epic were transpositions of the major Vedic divinities, and as such reflected the three Indo-European ideological functions.[18] Yudhiṣṭhira was seen to be a projection of Mitra and thereby a representative of the first function; Arjuna and Bhīma, respectively, were projections of the warrior divinities Indra and Vāyu; while Nakula and Sahadeva were projections of the twin Aśvins. In 1957, Wikander focused his attention upon the latter two figures and sought to differentiate them in terms of their respective roles in the narrative.[19] Nakula, for example, is handsome, fearless, and a breaker of horses; Sahadeva is defined as peace-loving, an indifferent warrior, and a keeper of cattle. Furthermore, although together they clearly serve as representatives of the third function, the differences between them would align Nakula more closely with the second function, while his brother is more firmly a representative of the third. In the *Rig-Veda*, common epithets reflecting the third function are used to refer to the Aśvins, although these epithets invariably occur in pairs, and almost always in the same order. This order parallels the epithets used individually in the *Mahābhārata* for Nakula and Sahadeva. Moreover, many post-Vedic texts refer to one of the twins as Nāsatya and the other as Dasra. Wikander concludes that this distinction goes back to Proto-Indo-European times (or at least to the period of Indo-European unity).[20]

If we examine the epithets and characters of Hector and Paris, some interesting parallels emerge. The most common epithet of Hector is *hippódamos*, "breaker of horses." Paris, however, is never so characterized; indeed, in his youth he was associated with the care of sheep, having been weaned by a band of shepherds.[21] Hector's character is that of a valorous and chivalrous warrior; Paris, despite his chief epithet, Alexandros ("Warrior, Champion"), is characterized as an indifferent fighter (e.g., his duel with Menelaus, wherein he survives only with the aid of Aphrodite), and as a man devoted to the maintenance of physical well-being (or at least to his own sensual enjoyment). In short, the distinction between the two Trojan princes is broadly reminiscent of that between Nakula and Sahadeva.

Yet if Hector's principal epithet and character resemble those of Nakula, his name would seem to be derived from the same Indo-European source as Skt. *sáha-* (cf. Avestan *hazah-*, Gothic *sigis*; from Proto-Indo-European **seǵh-*, "to withstand, to uphold").[22] One possible explanation of this metathesis, so to speak, is that at some point before Homer crystallized the tradition, the name of the Nakula figure had disappeared, and his epithets and personality came to be assumed by the surviving Sahadeva figure, that is, Hector. At the same time, it would appear that the *theme* of a functional distinction between the two did manage to persist, and that many aspects of the Sahadeva figure—though by no means all—were transferred to a new figure whose name has no connection with the Indian version, that is, Paris. One aspect that did not shift was the association with cattle-keeping. It is remotely possible that the epithet "Alexandros," together with the curious equine simile that occurs in connection with Paris near the end of Book 6 (506–512), wherein his movements are likened to "some stalled horse who has been corn-fed at the manger . . . ," may be dim survivals of an earlier identification with the Nakula figure. By the same token, despite his epithet and military prowess, certain aspects of Hector's character would seem to reflect Sahadeva; he is, as we have seen, a man who prefers peace to war, a man who would much prefer to live in harmony with his neighbors. Like Sahadeva, Hector is also a would-be peacemaker, and this, too, may be a survival of his former identification.

Whatever the reasons for this transposition, it seems to me that the very existence of a philological connection between Hector and Sahadeva, coupled with the thematic parallels that can be demonstrated between the two sets of heroic siblings, are sufficient to make a strong case for the assumption that Hector and Paris are reflexes of the common Indo-European twin figures. The absence of any lineal connection between the Trojan pair and their divine counterparts (Kastor and Polydeukes), a connection that, as I have said, can be demonstrated in the Indian tradition, does not appear to be an insurmountable obstacle here.

Indeed, the Dioscuri can be brought into the picture, for as the daughter of Leda, Helen is their sister.[23] Thus, while Kastor and Polydeukes are not seen as lineal kinsmen of the Trojan princes, the implication of an affinal relationship seems quite clear. Elsewhere among the ancient Indo-European traditions associated with the twins there is usually a close female relative present, oftentimes a sister, less frequently a spouse; compare, for example, Sarasvatī, Freyja, and, as Donald Ward has . . . suggested, Kudrun and Sītā.[24] That Helen, sister of the Dioscuri, and wife to Paris, fits this pattern is a distinct possibility.

In sum, the Trojans, individually and collectively, seem to represent the third function. If this is correct, then the next task is to consider some possible Achaean candidates for the honor of representing the first two functions.

By all odds, the most logical candidate for the second-function honors is the wielder of the shield discussed previously, Achilles — or, more properly, Akhilleus. He is far and away the most warlike figure in the epic. But what is more, his recalcitrant behavior, as described by Homer, generally conforms to what appears to be a common Indo-European pattern when it comes to warrior figures. Like Indra, Starcatherus, and Herakles, he is culpable. In his *Aspects de la fonction guerrière*,[25] Dumézil suggested that the Indo-European warrior typically commits three characteristic "sins," each of which is a violation of one of the three ideological principles. Indra, for example, is an accomplice in the murder of a Brahman (the three-headed son of Tvaṣṭar, chaplain of the gods), displays cowardice in the slaying of Namuci (with whom he had sworn a treaty), and commits adultery with Ahalyā, wife of Gautama. Starcatherus (Starkadr), as described by Saxo Grammaticus in Books 6–8 of the *Gesta Danorum*, commits a similar set of "sins": he strangles a king (Wicarus of Norway), displays cowardice in battle, thereby causing a war to be lost, and, for a price, agrees to kill the Danish king Olo while the latter is in the act of bathing and thus unable to defend himself.[26] In the case of Herakles, "le seul héros panhellénique," as Dumézil calls him, the sin against the first function involves the murder of his children in defiance of the command that he perform the twelve labors, a command issued by his sovereign, Eurystheus, and confirmed by the Delphic Oracle. His sin against the second function involves the cowardly slaying of Iphitos, who had come to claim his broodmares. His sin against the third function involves his abduction of Astydamia and, subsequently, of Iole. Like Indra, whose powers wane with each "sin," Herakles becomes impotent and eventually succumbs as a result of his misdeeds.

Although the parallels are admittedly imperfect, Achilles, too, commits a set of sins against the established order of things. To begin with, he defies the authority of his commander-in-chief, Agamemnon, and withdraws from the war. Moreover, the immediate cause of his defiance is the command that he give up a slave girl (Briseis). Thus, in this one brief but crucial sequence (1.130 f.) can be seen all the elements in the culpability of the Indo-European warrior. Achilles defies authority (first function); he withdraws from the conflict (second function); and he falls victim of his sexual desires (third function). The Achaean hero's defiance of authority and refusal to fight, to say nothing of his concern with his own sensual enjoyment, are themes that occur over and over as the epic unfolds. In the case of the latter theme, it is clear that during his withdrawal he lives in a manner far more suited to a third-function figure than to a representative of the second function. He has become concerned with his own physical well-being to the exclusion of any concern with the proper performance of his warrior role. A good example of this can be seen in the famous interchange between Achilles and Odysseus, wherein Odysseus, acting as Agamemnon's emissary, offers vast riches, women, and so on, if only he will return to the war (9.252 f.). It would appear that in this context, at least, Achilles is treated *as if* he were a third-function figure.

Another aspect of Achilles' career which bespeaks the third function is his transvestitism at the court of Lykomedes of Skyros. The story, not contained within the framework of the *Iliad* proper (cf., for example, Apollodorus 3.174), is that Thetis had dressed her son as a girl and had hidden him among Lycomedes' women, her purpose being to spare him from certain death in the then imminent war. Achilles' location does not long remain a secret, however, and in what would appear to be an adumbration of their later embassy, Odysseus and Diomedes trick the transvestite into joining the expedition by leaving his armor in the women's quarters. His excessive interest in these warlike appurtenances betrays his true sex, and he eventually joins the fleet at Aulis.[27]

Unlike the other culpable heroes previously discussed, Achilles does manage to redeem himself. He returns to the war bearing the trifunctionally illustrated shield, overcomes Hector, and materially advances the Achaean cause—which, as I have suggested, in essence appears to be the cause of the first two functions. Yet Achilles, too, is doomed; his invulnerability does not last indefinitely. Although his death does not occur within the framework of the *Iliad* proper, it is clear that it is imminent. In Book 18, for example, when Achilles announces his decision to avenge Patroklos' death, Thetis "spoke to him letting the tears fall: / 'Then I must lose you soon, my child, by what you are saying, / for since it is decreed your death must come soon after Hector's" (18.94–96).[28] Later on we learn from Xanthos, Achilles' chariot horse (whom Hera had given the power of speech), that this "decree" had come from " 'a great god and powerful Destiny' " (19.410), or, in other words, from the divine representatives of the first function.

That Achilles, like Herakles *et al.*, does eventually pay the supreme price for his defiance of sovereign authority is congruent with what appears to be a major aspect of the common Indo-European ideology: the ambivalent position of the warrior, especially vis-à-vis representatives of the first function. For he is at once vitally necessary and a threat to the maintenance of the social order. Malinowski once suggested that myths are fundamentally created to serve as pragmatic "charters" for behavior.[29] If this dictum be correct, then in the case of the Indo-European warrior the charter would appear to read: be valorous in battle, but never forget that you are ultimately subject to the authority of your sovereign, for if you do, you are doomed. That such a charter is implied in the account of the "wrath" of Achilles seems quite probable.

. . .

When it comes to candidates for first-function honors, the most obvious is Agamemnon, King of Argos, and commander-in-chief of the Achaean forces. The Argive king's overall sovereign position is continually underscored by such epithets as "wide-ruling" (1.102), "lord of men" (2.612), and "shepherd of the people" (19.35). Although he engages in battle, his prowess as a warrior is rarely emphasized; rather, emphasis is continually placed upon his overlordship. In all this Agamemnon resembles Yudhiṣṭhira, eldest and leader of the Pāṇḍavas, whom Wikander has identified as a first-function figure.

Yet problems arise when we attempt to make a more precise identification, when we attempt to classify the Argive king as Varunaic or Mitraic. For it will be remembered that one of the cornerstones of Dumézil's thesis is the idea of the joint or dual sovereignty, the idea that the Indo-European conception of sovereignty was divided into two complementary aspects: the cosmic and the juridical, personified in the *Veda*'s, respectively, by Varuna and Mitra.[30] In the *Iliad* the evidence is by no means clear as to *which* aspect of sovereignty Agamemnon represents. Like Varuṇa, he is the ultimate sovereign; yet like Mitra, he is very much concerned with the affairs of men and serves (or attempts to serve) as an arbiter of disputes. On balance, however, I would suggest that he is more Varunaic than Mitraic. One reason for this suggestion is the curious impotence exhibited by Agamemnon, especially in times of crisis. Although never abdicating his position as commander in chief, he is by no means decisive and must continually rely upon others to rally his spirits and to prop him up. That impotence — admittedly more physical than mental — is a Varunaic characteristic was long ago pointed out by Dumézil.[31] More recently, in following up Wikander's analysis of the first function in the *Mahābhārata*, Dumézil has suggested that Pāṇḍu himself, "pale and impotent," yet exercising ultimate sovereignty over his offspring, can be equated with Varuṇa, and that Yudhiṣṭhira, as an incarnation of the principle of *Dharma,* is more clearly linked to Mitra.[32]

If Agamemnon is Varunaic, who then might be suggested as the Mitraic representative of the first function? The most promising set of candidates are those figures who most frequently serve as the Argive king's props and counselors: Diomedes, Odysseus, Kalkhas, and Nestor. Diomedes can be ruled out by virtue of his previously discussed second-function characteristics. Odysseus, though manifestly a shrewd and sagacious counsellor, is too clearly a trickster figure; he presents too many parallels to Loki, Syrdon,[33] *et al.*, to be taken seriously as an incarnation of the juridical principle. When it comes to Kalkhas and Nestor, however, the matter becomes more complex. Both figures serve as counselors; both are renowned for their wisdom rather than for their fighting abilities. Yet the contrast between them would seem to reflect that typically found between representatives of the two halves of the function in question. Kalkhas is characterized principally as a seer, as a prophet whose counsel is rooted in a supernatural ability to divine; it is he, for example, who predicts the war's duration and the role that Herakles' arrows will play in its successful conclusion. This concern with prophetic insight, with things supernatural, would seem more Varunaic than Mitraic. In contrast, Nestor is the arbiter par excellence, the adjudicator (or would-be adjudicator) of disputes among mortals; one of his principal epithets is "fair spoken." Rarely if ever does he have recourse to the kind of supernatural modus operandi employed by Kalkhas. On balance, he would appear to be much more concerned with the immediate affairs of the community than Kalkhas, and this, of course, is one of the distinguishing characteristics of the Mitra figure. Indeed, Kalkhas' relationship to Agamemnon presents some broad parallels to the relationship, as expressed in the *Rig-Veda* (cf. *Rig-Veda* 10.72.3–5), between Varuṇa and Dakṣa (or perhaps Aṃśa; cf. *Rig-Veda* 10.31.3), wherein the latter is primarily concerned with ritual relationships and (in the case of Aṃśa) with the distribution of divine fate.

In short, although Kalkhas and Nestor present a great many generalized first-function characteristics, I suggest that Nestor comes closest to meeting the requirements of a representative of the juridical half of this function.[34]

These, then, are some possible Indo-European themes in the *Iliad*. If there be any validity to them, the trifunctional character of the illustrations upon the shield of Achilles, so convincingly demonstrated by Yoshida, is by no means an isolated survival of the common Indo-European ideology in Greek epic. Rather, the presence of these themes would seem to indicate that the overall tradition relative to the siege of Troy — or at least those aspects of it upon which Homer drew — was thoroughly infused with this ideology. To those who object to this conclusion on the grounds that the traditions surrounding the siege of Troy may well reflect an actual historical event, one may counter that it would not be the first time such an event has been subject to ideological reinterpretation. Gerschel, for example, has ably demonstrated that the Roman interpretations of the fall of Carthage, an undoubtedly historical event, were typically phrased in terms of the common Indo-European ideology[35]—to which the Carthaginians, as Semitic speakers, were most likely not a party.

If in fact the Trojan War did take place, it seems certain that those who took part in it were themselves the products of a tripartite social system. The Pylos tablets have yielded a picture of a society composed of three hierarchically ordered, functionally differentiated social strata: ["Thus, at present, one may be able to assert that the Mycenaeans conceived of their society as essentially composed of a sacerdotal class (the collective name of which is not yet known), the *lāwós*, a warrior class, and the *dāmos*, a producing class, and that this trifunctional structure was also found at the highest echelon of the hierarchy in a kind of triumvirate constituted by the *wánax*, the *lāwāgétās*, and the *dāmokólos*, each of whom was attached to one of the three social orders."][36] In the light of the evidence for the persistence of the Indo-European ideology in the structure of Mycenaean society, it is not unreasonable to assume that this ideology persisted in other areas of Mycenaean culture, and that, as in the much later Roman case just noted, it could have been brought to bear on the characterization of an event such as the defeat of a major commercial rival, that is, Troy.

By Homer's time the tripartite character of Greek social organization, so clearly evidenced in the Pylos texts, had largely disappeared. This disappearance seems to have owed in large measure to the disruptive effects of the Dorian invasions, the subsequent growth of Phoenician and other Near Eastern influences, and perhaps, as Dumézil phrases it (see above), the beginnings of "le miracle grec." Yet the apparent absence of social tripartition does not in itself mean that the common ideology had wholly given way. It does not mean that this ideology had necessarily disappeared in the oral traditions relative to the exploits of Achilles, Hector, *et al.*, upon which Homer must have drawn in the composition of the epic. Indeed, given the generally conservative nature of oral traditions (the *Rig-Veda* and the Irish *Lebor Gabála* are excellent examples of such conservatism within the Indo-European domain), it is entirely possible that these traditions had managed to preserve more than a modicum of their original tripartite character. Thus, though not himself the product of a tripartite society, Homer may very well have fallen heir to a body of tradition that took initial shape centuries earlier in a far more "Indo-European" social and intellectual context, that is, Mycenaean society, as revealed by the Mycenaean tablets.

There are, of course, some purely philological and stylistic grounds for assuming a connection between the *Iliad* and other Indo-European epic narratives, and these should be noted, if only in passing. For example, in Jaan Puhvel's opinion there are very sound philological reasons for deriving the Homeric hexameter from Indo-European metrical sources. An interesting stylistic correspondence can be seen in the extent to which the typical Homeric enumeration, which characteristically applies an epithet to the last item or person enumerated, parallels Indic epical enumerations: for example, "These were the dwellers in Kynos and Opoeis and Kalliaros, and in Bessa, and Skarphe, and *lovely* Augeiai" (*Iliad* 2.531–532; italics mine), and "Drona, Karna, Bhūriśravas, Śakuni, the son of Sabala, and Bāhlika the *great car-warrior* (*Udyogaparvan* 5.149.1–5; italics mine).[38] The etymological tie between [*Hector*] and Sanskrit *sáha-* has already been noted.

In sum, although it is, as I have previously pointed out, impossible to deal adequately with a subject of this magnitude in a brief paper such as this, I do think that a strong case can be made for the Indo-European character of the *Iliad* and its principal characters and events. At the very least, the interpretations suggested here, coupled with those of Yoshida relative to the shield, would certainly seem to warrant a great deal more attention to possible Indo-European ideological themes in Greek epic than has heretofore been given.

Notes

1. Perhaps the most succinct statement of Dumézil's thesis can be found in his *L'idéologie tripartie des Indo-européens* (Brussels, 1958), p. 31. For a comprehensive discussion of Dumézil's work, together with that of his disciples and critics, see my *The New Comparative Mythology: An Anthropological Assessment of the Theories of Georges Dumézil* [3rd ed. Berkeley and Los Angeles, 1982].

2. Dumézil, *op. cit.*, p. 91 [translation mine].

3. See Dumézil, *Jupiter, Mars, Quirinus* (Paris, 1941), pp. 257–260, wherein the tripartite character of Plato's *Republic* is discussed; 'Les trois fonctions dans quelques traditions grecques," *Hommage à Lucien Febvre* (Paris, 1953), II 25–32; *Aspects de la fonction guerrière chez les Indo-Européens* (Paris, 1956), pp. 93 ff., wherein the career of Herakles is discussed from an Indo-European standpoint. Others who have applied Dumézil's theory to Greek data include F. Vian, "La triade des rois d'Orchomène Étéocles, Phlégyas, Minyas," *Hommages à Georges Dumézil* (Brussels, 1960), pp. 215–224, and A. Yoshida, "La structure de l'illustration du bouclier d'Achille," *Revue Belge de philologie et d'histoire* 42:5–15 (1964); "Survivances de la tripartition fonctionnelle en Grèce," [*Revue dé l'histoire des religions*] 166:21–38 (1964): "Sur quelques coupes de la fable grecque," [*Revue des études anciennes*] 67:31–36 (1965): "Piasos noyé, Cléité pendue et le moulin de Cyzique: Essai de mythologie comparée," *RHR* 168: 155–164 (1965); "Le fronton occidental du Temple d'Apollon à Delphes et les trois fonctions," *RBPh* 44:5–11 (1966). [For a discussion of the problems presented by Greek mythology, see Littleton, "The Problem That Was Greece: Some Observations on the Greek Tradition from the Standpoint of the New Comparative Mythology," *Arethusa* 13:141–159 (1980)].

4. "La structure de illustration du bouclier d'Achille."

5. I should like to thank Professors Jaan Puhvel and Donald Ward for their most helpful comments and suggestions relative to this paper. Special thanks are due Professor Atsuhiko Yoshida who, although not a participant in the symposium in which this paper was initially

read, has nevertheless contributed a great deal to its final form through his invaluable criticisms and suggestions.

6. Yoshida, "La structure de l'illustration du bouclier d'Achille." pp. 7–9 [Translation mine].

7. For a discussion of this point, see Donald Ward, *The Divine Twins: An Indo-European Myth in Germanic Tradition* (Berkeley and Los Angeles, 1968), pp. 50–51.

8. Cf. Richmond Lattimore, *Hesiod* (Ann Arbor, Mich., 1959), p. 13.

9. *Ibid.*, p. 9.

10. Dumézil, *Aspects de la fonction guerrière*, pp. 93 ff.

11. That the Achaean-Trojan confrontation was internecine seems certain; see for example Helen Thomas and F. H. Stubbins, "Lands and Peoples in Homer," in A. J. B. Wace and F. H. Stubbins, eds., *A Companion to Homer* (London, 1963), pp. 283–310, esp. 285–288.

12. For a discussion of the Indo-European character of the conflict between the Romans and the Sabines, see Dumézil, *La religion romaine archaïque* (Paris, 1966), pp. 79–84.

13. *Ibid.*, see also Littleton, *op. cit.*, pp. 12–13.

14. Dumézil, *ibid.*

15. Littleton, *op. cit.*, p. 13.

16. Dumézil, "Les trois fonctions dans quelques traditions grecques."

17. G. Dumézil, "Remarques sur les armes des dieux de 'troisième fonction' chez divers peuples indo-européens," *Studi e materiali di storia delle religioni* 28:1–10 (1957).

18. Stig Wikander, "Pāṇḍava-sagan och Mahābhāratas mytiska förutsättningar," *Religion och Bibel* 6:27–39 (1947).

19. S. Wikander, "Nakula et Sahadeva," [*Orientalia Suecaug*] 6:66–96 (1957).

20. *Ibid.* Further evidence can be found in the *Avesta*, wherein there is only a single demon, Nanhaithya, whose name corresponds to Nāsatya. The more benevolent twin seems to have survived demonization and persists, Wikander believes, in the person of Atar, son of Ahura Mazdāh; see also Ward, "The Separate Functions of the Indo-European Divine Twins," above, pp. 194–195.

21. Cf. Apollodorus 3.148. Paris' childhood conforms to the general heroic pattern, as delineated by O. Rank, Lord Raglan, and J. Campbell: although born of Priam and Hekabe, he was exposed at birth on Mount Ida as a result of prophecy that he would bring about Troy's ruin. Like Oedipus, however, he was reared by shepherds, and it was only after reaching manhood that he was able to claim his birthright. The etymology of his name is obscure. H. Frisk (*Griechisches etymologisches Wörterbuch*, II [Heidelberg, 1965], p. 275) suggests that it is perhaps Illyrian in origin.

22. Cf. J. Pokorny, *Indogermanisches etymologisches Wörterbuch* (Bern, 1959), p. 888.

23. They do, of course, have separate fathers: Kastor is generally viewed as the son of Tyndareos; Polydeukes and Helen are fathered by Zeus.

24. D. J. Ward, "Kudrun: An Indo-European Mythological Theme?" *Indo-European and Indo-Europeans* (Philadelphia, 1970).

25. *Op. cit.*; also in *Heur et malheur du guerrier* (Paris, 1969).

26. This action, although it lacks the sexual component, does involve both money and bathing, and the act of bathing is conducive to a sense of physical relaxation and well-being. To kill a bather is to kill one who, for the moment at least, is neither a sovereign nor possessed of effective physical prowess, and would seem to relate to the third function (cf. Littleton, *The New Comparative Mythology*, p. 124–125).

27. This episode has a number of counterparts elsewhere among the Indo-European

traditions relating to second-function figures; cf., for example, the episode in the *Mahābhārata*, Book 4 (the *Virātaparvan*), wherein Arjuna, posing as a eunuch, becomes a dancing master in the harem of King Virāta. See Dumézil, *Mythe et épopée* (Paris, 1968), pp. 71–72.

28. This and other English translations of Homer are taken from Richmond Lattimore, *The Iliad of Homer* (Chicago, 1951).

29. B. Malinowski, "Myth in Primitive Psychology," in *Magic, Science, and Religion* (New York, 1955), p. 101.

30. Dumézil, *Mitra-Varuna: Essai sur deux représentations indo-européennes la souveraineté* (Paris, 1940; 2d ed., 1948. [See also Dumézil, *Les dieux souverains des Indo-Européens* (Paris, 1977).]

31. [Ibid.]

32. Dumézil, *Aspects de la fonction guerrière*, p. 75.

33. An Ossetic trickster figure; cf. Dumézil, *Loki* (Paris, 1948).

34. Professor Yoshida suggests (personal communication, April, 1969) that Nestor's character may also contain some elements reflecting what Dumézil has termed "les dieux premiers": figures who are trifunctional in definition and who serve to introduce (or to complete) canonical lists of the representatives of the three functions; e.g., Dyauh, Janus, Heimdallr (cf. Dumézil, *Tarpeia*, [Paris, 1947], pp. 97–100; see also "La tripartition indo-européenne," *Psyche* 2:1348–356 [1947], where Dumézil terms the divinities in question ["the spine of the system"]. Like Heimdallr *et al.*, Nestor belongs to an earlier generation; he is far and away the oldest of the major Achaean figures. Moreover, he is curiously removed from the sphere of action, serving typically as a mediator and counselor rather than as an active co-sovereign. Despite his advanced age he survives the war and continues to play an important part in subsequent events; even his name may be significant here, as it can be translated "The Returner, He Who Returns." A case, too, can be made for a trifunctional character in that he is at once a counselor of the sovereign, is typically characterized as a horseman, and is described as the ruler of one of the wealthiest and most prosperous of the Achaean cities. Nevertheless, even if, as I suspect, Yoshida is correct in identifying these traits as appropriate to a "dieu premier," this would not rule out a double identification as far as Nestor is concerned, for, as we have seen, a good case can also be made for assigning him to the role of juridical counterpart of Agamemnon.

35. L. Gerschel, "Structures augurales et tripartition fonctionnelle dans la pensée de l'ancienne Rome," [Journal de psychologie normale et pathologique] 45:57–78 (1952).

36. Yoshida, "Survivances de la tripartition fonctionnelle en Grèce," *op. cit.*, p. 35 [translation mine]. See also M. Lejeune, "Prêtres et prêtresses dans les documents mycéniens," *Hommages à Georges Dumézil* (Brussels, 1960). pp. 129–139. For earlier interpretations see L. R. Palmer, *Achaeans and Indo-Europeans: An Inaugural Lecture* (Oxford, 1954), pp. 1–22; M. Ventris and J. Chadwick, *Documents in Mycenaean Greek* (London, 1956), pp. 119–125.

37. Personal communications, January, 1967.

38. This translation is taken from C. V. Narasimhan, *The Mahābhārata* (New York, 1955), p. 113.

King Eëtion and Thebe as
Symbols in the *Iliad*   John W. Zarker*

The role of King Eëtion and Thebe in the *Iliad* is a small but continuing and significant one. This paper suggests that Homer intended for his auditors to think along certain lines and to experience certain emotions when either the king or his city were mentioned. The effect upon the modern reader, who is not experiencing the epic orally, is different; he tends to read and to evaluate the Greek epic in the light of his own literary experience. This paper proposes that the effect of the allusions to Eëtion and Thebe is similar to that achieved when a modern author consciously weaves certain themes and symbols into his writing.

It seems logical to assume with Leaf, and more recently Wade-Gery, that there was probably a pre-*Iliad* poem about Achilles, especially about his "Great Foray" to the south of Mount Ida, Thebe, and Lyrnessos.[1] Leaf, referring to the "Great Foray," states that when the passages relating to it are collected[2]

> we see at once that they all belong to a consistent whole — the story of a raid by Achilles along the southern Troad to the very head of the Gulf of Adramyttium. They are, besides, so allusive in character, so graphic and yet so imperfectly told, that they can only be understood as references to a story, the main themes of which were quite familiar to those for whom the *Iliad* was composed. It is indeed possible to reconstruct the outline of the tale. It was evidently a famous epic poem — whether complete in itself, or only an episode in a larger work, is now beyond our power to say. . . . We will call it the poem of the Great Foray.

The evidence as deduced by Leaf appears to me to be eminently sound. There might well have been such an epic poem or episodes in a larger epic describing the exploits of Achilles around Troy. Homer's auditors, upon hearing of King Eëtion and Thebe, would think of Achilles' attack, taking, and subsequent treatment of Thebe and its inhabitants as related in oral epics.

The reader of today, however, does not have these earlier poems or episodes to which he can relate the references to Eëtion and Thebe. Often the allusions to the tragic events at Thebe are completely overlooked because the frames of reference are missing. The tragic overtones of Thebe for the characters and occurrences in the *Iliad* are, so to speak, beyond our wave length. It is the purpose of this paper to draw together the allusions to Thebe and Eëtion and to suggest the nature of emotional and rational response involved in their employ.

*Reprinted from *Classical Journal* 61 (December 1965):110–14, by permission of the journal.

The most extensive passage about Eëtion is found in the speech of Andromache to Hector in Book 6. Andromache is described (6.395–8)[3]:

> Andromache, the daughter of high-hearted Eëtion;
> Eëtion, who had dwelt underneath wooded Plakos,
> in Thebe below Plakos, lord over the Kilikian people.
> It was his daughter who was given to Hektor of the
>   bronze helm.

Since my argument is based primarily upon the relationship of Eëtion, Hector, and Andromache, it is necessary to quote *in extenso* the narrative of the fall of Thebe and Achilles' magnanimous treatment of the defeated on that occasion (6.411–30):

> . . . for there is no other
> consolation for me after you have gone to your destiny—
> only grief; since I have no father, no honoured mother.
> It was brilliant Achilleus who slew my father, Eëtion,
> when he stormed the strong-founded citadel of the Kilikians,
> Thebe of the towering gates. He killed Eëtion
> but did not strip his armour, for his heart respected the dead man,
> but burned the body in all its elaborate wargear[4]
> and piled a grave mound over it, and the nymphs of the mountains,
> daughters of Zeus of the aegis, planted elm trees about it.
> And they who were my seven brothers in the great house all went
> upon a single day down into the house of the death god,
> for swift-footed brilliant Achilleus slaughtered all of them
> as they were tending their white sheep and their lumbering oxen;
> and when he had led my mother, who was queen under wooded
>   Plakos,
> here, along with all his other possessions, Achilleus
> released her again, accepting ransom beyond count, but Artemis
> of the showering arrows struck her down in the halls of her father.
> Hektor, thus you are father to me, and my honoured mother,
> you are my brother, and you it is who are my young husband.

Here Achilles is pictured as the heroic chivalric epic ideal. He slew the king and his sons but did not dishonor the king by taking his armor; he ransomed the queen mother.[5] Whitman comments[6]: "This was the way chivalric warfare should be, magnanimously endowing even defeat and death with an honorable beauty." This passage in Book 6 reveals the Achilles before the Wrath and as he will be again after receiving Priam and returning the body of Hector.

Andromache in the long passage just quoted would seem to be speaking rhetorically while trying to persuade Hector to defend Troy from the walls; she had stated that he was her father, mother, and brother. This brings to light an apparent inconsistency later in the *Iliad*. Podes, a son of Eëtion, is twice mentioned in Book 17. He is portrayed as a rich man who was the friend of Hector and who shared his table. Podes might well be the brother of Andromache and the brother-in-law of Hector. The inconsistency can be removed in one of two ways. A first and less satisfactory solution is to imagine another Eëtion; this is possible since there is no specific identification of Eëtion here in Book 17.[7] This does not explain the close companionship between Hector and Podes. A second and more logical solution is that Podes was actually dead when Andromache spoke to Hector in Book 6 and that Homer is once more relating out of chronological sequence an individual incident in the fighting during the nine-year period.

It is definite that Andromache had been wed to Hector before the fall of Thebe or she too would have been a captive like Chryseis, the daughter of Chryses, priest of Apollo. In speaking to Thetis, Achilles describes Chryseis (1.366-9):

> We went against Thebe, the sacred city of Eëtion,
> and the city we sacked, and carried everything back to this place,
> and the sons of the Achaians made a fair distribution
> and for Atreus' son they chose out Chryseis of the fair cheeks.

Chryseis is the first cause of the quarrel between Agamemnon and Achilles. Briseis is, to be sure, the actual catalyst for the wrath of Achilles. Cogent details can be learned from consideration of the lot of the captive Briseis (2.690-93),

> whom after much hard work he had taken away from Lyrnessos
> after he had sacked Lyrnessos and the walls of Thebe
> and struck down Epistrophos and Mynes the furious spearmen,
> children of Euenos, king, and son of Selepios.

In the passage just quoted, Homer joins together the fates of Lyrnessos and Thebe, of Briseis and Chryseis. Briseis comments most poignantly upon her fate when she finds Patroclus dead after returning from the tent of Agamemnon (19.290-99)[8]:

> So evil in my life takes over from evil forever.
> The husband on whom my father and honoured mother bestowed me
> I saw before my city lying torn with the sharp bronze,
> and my three brothers, whom a single mother bore with me
> and who were close to me, all went on one day to destruction.
> And yet you would not let me, when swift Achilleus had cut down
> my husband, and sacked the city of godlike Mynes, you would not
> let me sorrow, but said you would make me godlike Achilleus'
> wedded lawful wife, that you would take me back in the ships
> to Phthia, and formalize my marriage among the Myrmidons.

Here Homer makes the equation between the fate of the captive Briseis of Lyrnessos, whose husband was slain before the city by Achilles, and of Andromache of Troy, who will lose her husband in the same way by the same hand. Homer seems to be spinning a web of foreboding and ultimate destruction over Troy by intermittent references to Achilles' earlier exploits at Lyrnessos and Thebe.

When Achilles answers Odysseus during the embassy, he refers to all the possessions which he has won during the Trojan War thus far $(9.364-7)$[9]:

> I have many possessions there [at home in Phthia] that I left behind
>   when I came here
> on this desperate venture, and from here there is more gold,
>   and red bronze,
> and fair-girdled women, and grey iron I will take back;
> all that was allotted to me.

The grey iron is mentioned again in the final reference to Eëtion which comes in Book 23 of the *Iliad*. In the funeral games for Patroclus, the lump of iron is both contest and prize for the shot put. The value of the iron is described by Achilles $(23.832-5)$:

> For although the rich demesnes of him who wins it lie far off
> indeed, yet for the succession of five years he will have it
> to use; for his shepherd for want of iron will not have to go in
> to the city for it, nor his ploughman either. This will supply them.

The wealth of Thebe and the physical prowess of Eëtion himself are also attested $(23.826-9)$:

> Now the son of Peleus set in place a lump of pig-iron,
> which had once been the throwing-weight of Eëtion
>   in his great strength;
> but now swift-footed brilliant Achilleus had slain him and taken
> the weight away in the ships along with the other possessions.

Among the other possessions is the horse Pedasos. Archaelogists have suggested that, together with weaving, the wealth of Troy may have been derived from horses, their breeding and training.[10] Pedasos, taken when Thebe fell, is placed in the traces with Achilles' own horses (16.152–3). Pedasos becomes in one way a symbol in himself. When alive, he symbolizes the actions of Achilles at Thebe, his success in storming and taking it as well as his kindness and mercy afterward in burning Eëtion in his armor, and in ransoming Andromache's mother. The horses lead Patroclus beyond the ditch and are accomplices in his forgetfulness of the warnings of Achilles. Sarpedon in aiming at Patroclus hits Pedasos (16.468–9)[11]: "the horse, who screamed as he blew his life away, and went down / in shrill noise into the dust, and the life spirit flittered from him." The fall of Pedasos into the dust foreshadows the fall of Achilles' crest from the head of Patroclus and the imminent death of Achilles.[12] With the death of Pedasos the final rage and madness of Achilles caused by the death of Patroclus is also foreshadowed. No longer is Achilles to be noble, kind, and merciful. His spirit becomes hardened by the fire of his wrath transferred from Agamemnon to the Trojans and Hector; the chivalric treatment of the defeated is to become a thing of the past. Yet the theme of Eëtion and Thebe suggests to the reader or auditor that Achilles will not always be wrathful, since he was not so in the past. By use of this theme, in the incident of Pedasos the horse, Homer prepares his audience for the changes to be wrought in the character of Achilles in Books 23 and 24, for Achilles' return to normality.

Hector speaks directly to his horses (8.185–97), urging them to repay all the care and attention which Andromache, the daughter of Eëtion, had given them. One would suppose that these were Trojan since Troy was famous for horses. It is possible that Hector's horses are part of the dowry of Andromache and originally came from Thebe, especially in the light of the reference to Pedasos. Most probably the horses of Hector were Trojan and cared for by Andromache at Troy, and Pedasos was a Trojan horse given by Priam or Hector to Eëtion to win Andromache (22.472).

Another of the former possessions of Eëtion can be observed when the embassy arrives to try to persuade Achilles to reenter the battle and to become reconciled with Agamemnon (9.186–9)[13]:

> and they found Achilleus delighting his heart in a lyre, clear-sounding,
> splendid and carefully wrought, with a bridge of silver upon it,
> which he won out of the spoils when he ruined Eëtion's city.
> With this he was pleasuring his heart, and singing of men's fame. . . .

Once again Homer is evoking the Achilles of the past, the Achilles who was the heroic chivalric ideal, fearless, invincible in battle, kind and humane in victory.

The significance of all these references to Eëtion and Thebe becomes clear in the words of Andromache as she observes Achilles dragging the body of her husband around Troy. At this point in the *Iliad* the chief defender of Troy, Hector, whose son they called Astyanax since his father "alone saved Ilion" (6.403), has been slain and all that is good, pure, and noble in Troy is now doomed. As this paper began with the most extensive quotation about Thebe in the conversation of Andromache and Hector, it now reaches its conclusion with Homer recalling Book 6 by having Andromache lament as she happens to be wearing the circlet (22.470–72): ". . . which Aphrodite the golden once had given her / on that day when Hektor of the shining helmet led her forth / from the house of Eëtion, and gave numberless gifts to win her." The reader recalls what had happened to the house of Eëtion and the numberless gifts; the shining helmet evokes the magnificent scene in Book 6, where Astyanax was afraid of his father because of his shining helmet, and this caused both Andromache and Hector to laugh, a light naturalistic touch in a tragic scene. Now the sight of Hector being dragged about causes her to faint; upon recovering, she laments (22.477–81):

> Hektor, I grieve for you. You and I were born to a single
> destiny, you in Troy in the house of Priam, and I
> in Thebe, underneath the timbered mountain of Plakos
> in the house of Eëtion, who cared for me when I was little,
> ill-fated he, I ill-starred.

Andromache makes the obvious equation. The fate of both Hector and Andromache is the same, as is that of Thebe and Troy. What happened to Thebe and the other cities of the Troad will happen to Troy. What happened to Chryseis, Briseis, and other captive women will happen to Andromache. Only now Achilles' wrath is stronger, and he is no longer the man he was at Thebe. Troy, instead of the kind treatment and noble respect for the dead and captured as at Thebe, will suffer the fate of Pedasos and Lykaon. Achilles' taking of Thebe is the dramatic foreshadowing of the fall of Troy.

This paper, in studying the references to Eëtion and Thebe, has shown the relationship between the character of Achilles before his wrath and during it; it motivates the change in Achilles after the wrath when he returns the body of Hector. More important, the use of Eëtion and Thebe as symbols in the *Iliad* emphasizes the single destiny, the interlocking fate of Eëtion, Hector and Priam, of Chryseis, Briseis, and Andromache, and of Thebe and Troy.

Notes

1. H. T. Wade-Gery, *The Poet of the Iliad* (Cambridge 1952) 85.

2. Walter Leaf, *Troy: A Study in Homeric Geography* (London 1912) 242–3; see his Appendix D for a listing of passages referring to the "Great Foray" (pp. 397–9). Leaf does not cite 9.328–30 in Appendix D.

> But I say that I have stormed from my ships twelve cities
> of men, and by land eleven more through the generous Troad.
> From all these we took forth treasures, goodly and numerous.

Nor does Leaf cite 9.664–5; see below n.9 for Quintus of Smyrna, who gives evidence of separate lays on Achilles' exploits around Troy. It is surprising how well Leaf's theory on an epic escapes conflict with the much later theory of Parry and Lord on oral epic.

3. I wish to express gratitude to the University of Chicago Press for their kind permission to quote from Richmond Lattimore's translation of the *Iliad* (Chicago 1951). All translations from Homer here are his. For the Greek text I have used Monro and Allen's 3d ed. (Oxford 1920). Also valuable were A. Gehring, *Index Homericus* (Leipzig 1891) and C. E. Schmidt, *Parallel-Homer* (Göttingen 1888).

4. T. B. L. Webster, *From Homer to Mycenae* (London 1958) p. 165, comments on the burial of Eëtion with his armor and contrasts Elpenor, who died in Circe's house and begged Odysseus to bury him with his arms (*Od*.11.74).

5. See the incident of Lykaon (20.34ff). Achilles even a relatively short time before had ransomed a captive taken on a night expedition. The text suggests a time lapse of twelve days. Since this conflicts with the time lapse of the first book of the *Iliad*, one must assume that

Lykaon had been free and home only twelve days. See also the Adrestos incident in *Iliad* 6.42–65. Achilles' mercy in ransoming the queen mother, known to be the mother-in-law of the chief defender of the Trojans, is particularly intriguing, since the Greeks had been besieging Troy for some years. It is indicative of Achilles' attitude towards war; especially unusual is his refusal to bring other than economic and military pressure against his chief adversary. See also *Iliad* 11.104–6, where Agamemnon slays two sons of Priam, Isos and Antiphos, whom Achilles had captured previously and released for ransom.

6. C. H. Whitman, *Homer and the heroic tradition* (Cambridge, Mass. 1958) p. 189; see also p. 198 for reference to Achilles' humanity evidenced in the treatment of Eëtion and the captives of Thebe.

7. See 21.43 for reference to Eëtion of Imbros.

8. See also 19.59–60 and 20.89–96 and 187–194, where reference is made to Achilles' expeditions to Lyrnessos and Pedasos. Aeneas was nearly captured by Achilles but escaped into Lyrnessos which was taken (20.193–4): "and [I, Achilles] took the day of liberty away from their women / and led them as spoil. . . ."

For Pedasos see Leaf (n.2) pp. 221–3, where he cites *Il.*6.33–5 on the death of Elatos from Pedasos, slain by Agamemnon; also 21.87 refers to Altes who holds Pedasos. Leaf also cites a late story found in the scholia on 6.35. Other towns taken by Achilles include Lesbos 9.128–30, 270–72 (seven maidens offered by Agamemnon to Achilles who had taken their town), Skyros 9.666–8 (Iphis), Tenedos 11.624–5 (Nestor's Hekamede). The mention of Diomedes at the end of Book 9 does not seem to agree with Achilles' professions of love for Briseis (9.334–43) and Patroclus' suggestion of legitimate marriage (19.297–9).

9. Although the evidence of Quintus of Smyrna is deservedly suspect, it is interesting to note that he believed that there were separate poems, concerning Achilles' exploits in the Troad, his taking of twelve cities by sea and eleven by land. Thebe is mentioned specifically (4.144–53 and 14.121–30). Quintus, in describing the lamentation at the death of Achilles, includes the female captives taken at Lemnos and Thebe (3.545–50).

10. See D. L. Page, *History and the Homeric Iliad* (Berkeley 1959) 57–8, 70, 252. It may be significant that in the funeral games of Patroclus, Diomedes won, driving the Trojan horses taken from Aeneas. Further, the preeminence of the Trojans in horsemanship and horse training may have occasioned the selection of a horse as the way to take Troy.

11. See Whitman (n.6) p. 245, who states that the horses of Achilles are "the only figures who are so involved in both eternity and time as conflicting yet inseparable forces are confined to the context of Achilles. They are the symbols of Achilles' foreknowledge and tragic suffering."

12. Whitman (n.6) pp. 201, 202, does not note this possibility.

13. See Whitman (n.6), who states (p. 193) that "the practice of epic singing was profoundly involved with the roots of early self-consciousness, the estimate of oneself in the light of the future's retrospect."

The *Iliad* or the Poem of Force   Simone Weil[*]

The true hero, the true subject, the center of the *Iliad* is force. Force employed by man, force that enslaves man, force before which man's flesh shrinks away. In this work, at all times, the human spirit is shown as

*Translated by Mary McCarthy. Pendle Hill Pamphlet #91. Pendle Hill Publications, Wallingford, Pennsylvania 19086. Used by permission.

modified by its relations with force, as swept away, blinded, by the very force it imagined it could handle, as deformed by the weight of the force it submits to. For those dreamers who considered that force, thanks to progress, would soon be a thing of the past, the *Iliad* could appear as an historical document; for others, whose powers of recognition are more acute and who perceive force, today as yesterday, at the very center of human history, the *Iliad* is the purest and the loveliest of mirrors.

To define force — it is that x that turns anybody who is subjected to it into a *thing*. Exercised to the limit, it turns man into a thing in the most literal sense: it makes a corpse out of him. Somebody was here, and the next minute there is nobody here at all; this is a spectacle the *Iliad* never wearies of showing us:

> . . . the horses
> Rattled the empty chariots through the files of battle,
> Longing for their noble drivers. But they on the ground
> Lay, dearer to the vultures than to their wives.

The hero becomes a *thing* dragged behind a chariot in the dust:

> All around, his black hair
> Was spread; in the dust his whole head lay,
> That once-charming head; now Zeus had let his enemies
> Defile it on his native soil.

The bitterness of such a spectacle is offered us absolutely undiluted. No comforting fiction intervenes; no consoling prospect of immortality; and on the hero's head no washed-out halo of patriotism descends.

> His soul, fleeing his limbs, passed to Hades,
> Mourning its fate, forsaking its youth and its vigor.

Still more poignant — so painful is the contrast — is the sudden evocation, as quickly rubbed out, of another world: the faraway, precarious, touching world of peace, of the family, the world in which each man counts more than anything else to those about him.

> She ordered her bright-haired maids in the palace
> To place on the fire a large tripod, preparing
> A hot bath for Hector, returning from battle.
> Foolish woman! Already he lay, far from hot baths,
> Slain by grey-eyed Athena, who guided Achilles' arm.

Far from hot baths he was indeed, poor man. And not he alone. Nearly all the *Iliad* takes place far from hot baths. Nearly all of human life, then and now, takes place far from hot baths.

Here we see force in its grossest and most summary form — the force that kills. How much more varied in its processes, how much more surprising in its effects is the other force, the force that does *not* kill, i.e., that does not kill just yet. It will surely kill, it will possibly kill, or perhaps it merely hangs, poised and ready, over the head of the creature it *can* kill, at any moment, which is to say at every moment. In whatever aspect, its effect is the same: it turns a man into a stone. From its first property (the ability to turn a human being into a thing by the simple method of killing him) flows another, quite prodigious too in its own way, the ability to turn a human being into a thing while he is still alive. He is alive; he has a soul; and yet — he is a thing. An extraordinary entity this — a thing that has a soul. And as for the soul, what an extraordinary house it finds itself in! Who can say what it costs it, moment by moment, to accommodate itself to this residence, how much writhing and bending, folding and pleating are required of it? It was not made to live inside a thing; if it does so, under pressure of necessity, there is not a single element of its nature to which violence is not done.

A man stands disarmed and naked with a weapon pointing at him; this person becomes a corpse before anybody or anything touches him. Just a minute ago, he was thinking, acting, hoping:

> Motionless, he pondered. And the other drew near,
> Terrified, anxious to touch his knees, hoping in his heart
> To escape evil death and black destiny . . .
> With one hand he clasped, suppliant, his knees,
> While the other clung to the sharp spear, not letting go . . .

Soon, however, he grasps the fact that the weapon which is pointing at him will not be diverted; and now, still breathing, he is simply matter; still thinking, he can think no longer:

> Thus spoke the brilliant son of Priam
> In begging words. But he heard a harsh reply:
> He spoke. And the other's knees and heart failed him.
> Dropping his spear, he knelt down, holding out his arms.
> Achilles, drawing his sharp sword, struck
> Through the neck and breastbone. The two-edged sword
> Sunk home its full length. The other, face down,
> Lay still, and the black blood ran out, wetting the ground . . .

Perhaps all men, by the very act of being born, are destined to suffer violence; yet this is a truth to which circumstance shuts men's eyes. The strong are, as a matter of fact, never absolutely strong, nor are the weak absolutely weak, but neither is aware of this. They have in common a refusal to believe that they both belong to the same species: the weak see no relation between themselves and the strong, and vice versa. The man who is the possessor of force seems to walk through a non-resistant element; in the human substance that surrounds him nothing has the power to interpose, between the impulse and the act, the tiny interval that is reflection. Where there is no room for reflection, there is none either for justice or prudence. Hence we see men in arms behaving harshly and madly. We see their sword bury itself in the breast of a disarmed enemy who is in the very act of pleading at their knees. We see them triumph over a dying man by describing to him the outrages his corpse will endure. We see Achilles cut the throats of twelve Trojan boys on the funeral pyre of Patroclus as naturally as we cut flowers for a grave. These men, wielding power, have no suspicion of the fact that the consequences of their deeds will at length come home to them—they too will bow the neck in their turn. If you can make an old man fall silent, tremble, obey, with a single word of your own, why should it occur to you that the curses of this old man, who is after all a priest, will have their own importance in the gods' eyes? Why should you refrain from taking Achilles' girl away from him if you know that neither he nor she can do anything but obey you? Achilles rejoices over the sight of the Greeks fleeing in misery and confusion. What could possibly suggest to him that this rout, which will last exactly as long as he wants it to and end when his mood indicates it, that this very rout will be the cause of his friend's death, and, for that matter, of his own? Thus it happens that those who have force on loan from fate count on it too much and are destroyed.

But at the time their own destruction seems impossible to them. For they do not see that the force in their possession is only a limited quantity; nor do they see their relations with other human beings as a kind of balance between unequal amounts of force. Since other people do not impose on their movements that halt, that interval of hesitation, wherein lies all our consideration for our brothers in humanity, they conclude that destiny has given complete license to them, and none at all to their inferiors. And at this point they exceed the measure of the force that is actually at their disposal. Inevitably they exceed it, since they are not aware that it is limited. And now we see them committed irretrievably to chance; suddenly things cease to obey them. Sometimes chance is kind to them, sometimes cruel. But in any case there they are, exposed, open to misfortune; gone is the armor of power that formerly protected their naked souls; nothing, no shields, stands between them and tears.

This retribution, which has a geometrical rigor, which operates automatically to penalize the abuse of force, was the main subject of Greek thought. It is the soul of the epic. Under the name of Nemesis, it functions as the mainspring of Aeschylus's tragedies. To the Pythagoreans, to Socrates and Plato, it was the jumping-off point of speculation upon the nature of man and the universe. Wherever Hellenism has penetrated, we find the idea of it familiar. In Oriental countries which are steeped in Buddhism, it is perhaps this Greek idea that has lived on under the name of Kharma. The Occident, however, has lost it, and no longer even has a word to express it in any of its languages: conceptions of limit, measure, equilibrium, which ought to determine the conduct of life are, in the

West, restricted to a servile function in the vocabulary of technics. We are only geometricians of matter; the Greeks were, first of all, geometricians in their apprenticeship to virtue.

.   .   .

Thus violence obliterates anybody who feels its touch. It comes to seem just as external to its employer as to its victim. And from this springs the idea of a destiny before which executioner and victim stand equally innocent, before which conquered and conqueror are brothers in the same distress. The conquered brings misfortune to the conqueror, and vice versa: "A single son, short-lived, was born to him. / Neglected by me, he grows old—for far from home / I camp before Troy, injuring you and your sons."

A moderate use of force, which alone would enable man to escape being enmeshed in its machinery, would require superhuman virtue, which is as rare as dignity in weakness. Moreover, moderation itself is not without its perils, since prestige, from which force derives at least three quarters of its strength, rests principally upon that marvelous indifference that the strong feel toward the weak, an indifference so contagious that it infects the very people who are the objects of it. Yet ordinarily excess is not arrived at through prudence or politic considerations. On the contrary, man dashes to it as to an irresistible temptation. The voice of reason is occasionally heard in the mouths of the characters in the *Iliad*. Thersites' speeches are reasonable to the highest degree; so are the speeches of the angry Achilles:

> Nothing is worth my life, not all the goods
> They say the well-built city of Ilium contains. . . .
> A man can capture steers and fatted sheep
> But, once gone, the soul cannot be captured back.

But words of reason drop into the void. If they come from an inferior, he is punished and shuts up; if from a chief, his actions betray them. And failing everything else, there is always a god handy to advise him to be unreasonable. In the end, the very idea of wanting to escape the role fate has allotted one—the business of killing and dying—disappears from the mind: ". . . We to whom Zeus / Has assigned suffering, from youth to old age, / Suffering in grievous wars, till we perish to the last man." Already these warriors, like Craonne's so much later, felt themselves to be "condemned men."

The wantonness of the conqueror that knows no respect for any creature or thing that is at its mercy or is imagined to be so, the despair of the soldier that drives him on to destruction, the obliteration of the slave or the conquered man, the wholesale slaughter—all these elements combine in the *Iliad* to make a picture of uniform horror, of which force is the sole hero. A monotonous desolation would result were it not for those few luminous moments, scattered here and there throughout the poem, those brief, celestial moments in which man possesses his soul. The soul that awakes then, to live for an instant only and be lost almost at once in force's vast kingdom, awakes pure and whole; it contains no ambiguities, nothing complicated or turbid; it has no room for anything but courage and love. Sometimes it is in the course of inner deliberations that a man finds his soul: he meets it, like Hector before Troy, as he tries to face destiny on his own terms, without the help of gods or men. At other times, it is in a moment of love that men discover their souls — and there is hardly any form of pure love known to humanity of which the *Iliad* does not treat. The tradition of hospitality persists, even through several generations, to dispel the blindness of combat.

> Thus I am for you a beloved guest in the breast of Argos . . .
> Let us turn our lances away from each other, even in battle.

The love of the son for the parents, of father for son, of mother for son, is continually described, in a manner as touching as it is curt: "Thetis answered, shedding tears, / 'You were born to me for a short life, my child, as you say. . . .' " Even brotherly love: "My three brothers whom the same mother bore for me, / So dear. . . ." Conjugal love, condemned to sorrow, is of an astonishing purity. Imaging the humiliations of slavery which await a beloved wife, the husband passes over the one indignity which even in anticipation would stain their tenderness. What could be simpler than the words spoken by his wife to the man about to die?

> . . . Better for me
> Losing you, to go under the earth. No other comfort
> Will remain, when you have encountered your death-heavy fate,
> Only grief, only sorrow. . . .

Not less touching are the words expressed to a dead husband:

> Dear husband, you died young, and left me your widow
> Alone in the palace. Our child is still tiny,
> The child you and I, crossed by fate, had together.
> I think he will never grow up . . .
> For not in your bed did you die, holding my hand
> And speaking to me prudent words which forever
> Night and day, as I weep, might live in my memory.

The most beautiful friendship of all, the friendship between comrades-at-arms, is the final theme of The Epic: ". . . But Achilles / Wept, dreaming of the beloved comrade; sleep, all-prevailing, / Would not take him; he turned over again and again." But the purest triumph of love, the crowning grace of war, is the friendship that floods the hearts of mortal enemies. Before it a murdered son or a murdered friend no longer cries out for vengeance. Before it — even more miraculous — the distance between benefactor and suppliant, between victor and vanquished, shrinks to nothing:

> But when thirst and hunger had been appeased,
> Then Dardanian Priam fell to admiring Achilles.
> How tall he was, and handsome; he had the face of a god;
> And in his turn Dardanian Priam was admired by Achilles,
> Who watched his handsome face and listened to his words.
> And when they were satisfied with contemplation of each other . . .

These moments of grace are rare in the *Iliad*, but they are enough to make us feel with sharp regret what it is that violence has killed and will kill again.

There may be, unknown to us, other expressions of the extraordinary sense of equity which breathes through the *Iliad*; certainly it has not been imitated. One is barely aware that the poet is a Greek and not a Trojan. The tone of the poem furnishes a direct clue to the origin of its oldest portions; history perhaps will never be able to tell us more. If one believes with Thucydides that eighty years after the fall of Troy, the Achaeans in their turn were conquered, one may ask whether these songs, with their rare references to iron, are not the songs of a conquered people, of whom a few went into exile. Obliged to live and die, "very far from the homeland," like the Greeks who fell before Troy, having lost their cities like the Trojans, they saw their own image both in the conquerors, who had been their fathers, and in the conquered, whose misery was like their own. They could still see the Trojan war over that brief span of years in its true light, unglossed by pride or shame. They could look at it as conquered and as conquerors simultaneously, and so perceive what neither conqueror nor conquered ever saw, for both were blinded. Of course, this is mere fancy; one can see such distant times only in fancy's light.

In any case, this poem is a miracle. Its bitterness is the only justifiable bitterness, for it springs from the subjections of the human spirit to force, that is, in the last analysis, to matter. This subjection is the common lot, although each spirit will bear it differently, in proportion to its own virtue. No one in the *Iliad* is spared by it, as no one on earth is. No one who succumbs to it is by virtue of this fact regarded with contempt. Whoever, within his own soul and in human relations, escapes the dominion of force is loved but loved sorrowfully because of the threat of destruction that constantly hangs over him.

Such is the spirit of the only true epic the Occident possesses. The *Odyssey* seems merely a good imitation, now of the *Iliad*, now of Oriental poems; the *Aeneid* is an imitation which, however brilliant, is disfigured by frigidity, bombast, and bad taste. The *chansons de geste*, lacking the sense of equity, could not attain greatness: in the *Chanson de Roland*, the death of an enemy does not come home to either author or reader in the same way as does the death of Roland.

Attic tragedy, or at any rate the tragedy of Aeschylus and Sophocles, is the true continuation of the epic. The conception of justice enlightens it, without ever directly intervening in it; here force appears in its coldness and hardness, always attended by effects from whose fatality neither those who use it nor those who suffer it can escape; here the shame of the coerced spirit is neither disguised, nor enveloped in facile pity, nor held up to scorn; here more than one spirit bruised and degraded by misfortune is offered for our admiration. The Gospels are the last marvelous expression of the Greek genius, as the *Iliad* is the first: here the Greek spirit reveals itself not only in the injunction given mankind to seek above all other goods, "the kingdom and justice of our Heavenly Father," but also in the fact that human suffering is laid bare, and we see it in a being who is at once divine and human. The accounts of the Passion show that a divine spirit, incarnate, is changed by misfortune, trembles before suffering and death, feels itself, in the depths of its agony, to be cut off from man and God. The sense of human misery gives the Gospels that accent of simplicity that is the mark of the Greek genius, and that endows Greek tragedy and the *Iliad* with all their value. Certain phrases have a ring strangely reminiscent of the epic, and it is the Trojan lad dispatched to Hades, though he does not wish to go, who comes to mind when Christ says to Peter: "Another shall gird thee and carry thee whither thou wouldst not." This accent cannot be separated from the idea that inspired the Gospels, for the sense of human misery is a pre-condition of justice and love. He who does not realize to what extent shifting fortune and necessity hold in subjection every human spirit, cannot regard as fellow-creatures nor love as he loves himself those whom chance separated from him by an abyss. The variety of constraints pressing upon man give rise to the illusion of several distinct species that cannot communicate. Only he who has measured the dominion of force, and knows how not to respect it, is capable of love and justice.

Andromache's Headdress   Kenneth Atchity*

If the name of Andromache at once calls to mind the image of her tearful smiling, then Homer's song of memory has preserved the essence of her character. Never in the *Iliad* is Andromache far from tears. Once only does she smile. Yet, despite this quantitative disproportion, the paradox of her role is balanced. The smile is as important to Homer's definition of

*Reprinted from *Homer's "Iliad": The Shield of Memory* (Carbondale: Southern Illinois University Press, 1978), 75–81, by permission of the publisher.

Andromache's character as are her countless tears. Against the disorder of all her other social ties represented by the tears, Andromache's unique smile symbolizes the order of her existence that has been established through her perfect marriage to Hektor. One man gives her existence meaning which one smile expresses. Yet precisely because she values, so much more strongly than others whose identities are defined through multiple relations, the orderliness which her husband embodies, Andromache must let Hektor risk his life — and so her own life as well — in order to preserve it. Even the single smile is mingled with tears.

Unlike Helen, Andromache is voluntarily and naturally defined only as a Trojan in the *Iliad*. Her affinity with Helen's galaxy of images and characters is more circumstantial than essential; it is expressed in Andromache's divided loyalties, more toward husband than toward city, which have resulted from the disorder of current Trojan circumstances. But Homer wasn't interested in expressing the aversion Andromache might well have felt toward the society for which her husband — whose ambiguous motivation the poet does explore exhaustively — fought; we never hear her speak against Troy in general, or Paris in particular. Rather, the composer of the *Iliad* consistently emphasizes Andromache's singleminded and unswerving dedication to Hektor, as a contrast with Helen's more evenly ambivalent attitude. Homer let his listeners draw their own conclusions about her silence concerning anything outside her family. Andromache speaks, in the *Iliad*, to no one but her husband.

Andromache is related to Helen through the images of the loom, the bed, the headdress, and memory. The thematic importance of the meeting on the wall in Book 6 is defined by Andromache as much as by Hektor. To begin with, Homer emphasizes the family's appearance together by juxtaposing it dramatically with the furious battle; dramatic impact is enhanced by the fact that the scene immediately follows the encounter between Glaukos and Diomedes. In the context of that exchange Homer revealed the way in which personal experience, the genealogically-revealed relationship between the two warriors' families, might relegate war temporarily to the background of man's concern. But the poet quickly reasserts the major theme by showing the even closer relationship between Hektor and Andromache overshadowed, and unalterably influenced, by the presence of war: when Astyanax is terrified by his father's helmet. Battle and death, suspended temporarily in the understanding between Glaukos and Diomedes, once again prevail.

Andromache is a figure whose total propriety heightens our recognition of Helen's unnatural position. She, like Helen, is shown on the Trojan wall, but for such different reasons, such unmixed emotions. Andromache is absorbed in her husband and home. Hers is not the selfish attitude of Paris, nor the communal motivation of her Hektor, nor the transcendent perspective of Helen; hers is purely familial: Andromache is wife, mother, and widow. So comphrensively domestic is her relationship with Hektor that she even tends his horses (8. 187). Andromache's singular mode of behavior is explained by the fact that she is, like Helen, an expatriate — an element in Andromache's characterization which has the widest implications, associating her also with Chryseis and Briseis. Achilles was responsible for the alienation of all three women from their homelands. Andromache's formal introduction as the daughter of Eëtion (6. 395) contrasts the normal multiplicity of her former identity (as sister, child, and princess) with the present one-sided definition she possesses as a guest-bride in a foreign society.

The relationship between Andromache and Hektor in Book 6 contrasts strikingly with that between Helen and Paris in Book 3. The superficial resolution of the disorderly marriage in Book 3 (recalling the equally superficial resolution implied in Hera and Zeus' bedding-down at the end of Book 1) is very different from the fatally interrupted orderly marriage in Book 6. Hektor's two references to the loom symbolically frame the possibilities for Andromache. His first mention of the artifact, when he predicts that Andromache will serve at the loom of an alien warrior (6. 456), makes it an image of their disrupted domestic harmony. In fact, Andromache is not found at home where Hektor expects her (6. 371); her absence from the household is ominous.

Hektor's second mention of the loom marks a momentary alteration in his doomsday outlook to a more hopeful one, no doubt explained by his wish to alleviate Andromache's grievous reaction to his prophetic speech. Here the artifact symbolizes the stability of the family and the order of their marriage (6. 491); Hektor includes weaving in his delineation of the appropriate duties for women within an orderly society (6. 492–93). Since their relationship has produced a son who may continue their orderly mode of action, Hektor's optimism may have some ground. Neither he nor Andromache knows for sure at this moment which of the two outcomes, symbolized by each image of the loom, will in fact occur. In the meantime Hektor fights for the preservation of order; and Andromache must return to her loom which is still her orderly work. The scene concludes with the tacit agreement that each will persist in unselfish activity. Helen and Paris come together, Hektor and Andromache go apart, when, in each case, the movement should be the opposite. Andromache complies with her husband's decision, although she does not share the process of its making. Andromache plies her loom, not self-conscious of her own importance, but solely in the hope that her beloved domestic stability will continue — through Hektor's political success.

Andromache is at her loom when she receives the dreaded news of Hektor's death; the imagistic continuity is an example of the psychology of memory, leaving us with the impression that in the time that has passed between their meeting in Book 6 and the events here in Book 22 Andromache hasn't once moved from the family hearth, where, obeying her husband, she persists in maintaining domestic order. Now there is no doubt which symbolic meaning of the artifact has been realized on the plain:

> but the wife of Hektor had not yet
> heard; for no sure messenger had come to her and told her
> how her husband had held his ground there outside the gates;
> but she was weaving a web in the inner room of the high house,
> a red folding robe, and inworking elaborate figures.
> She called out through the house to her lovely-haired handmaidens
> to set a great cauldron over the fire, so that there would be
> hot water for Hektor's bath as he came back out of the fighting;
> poor innocent, nor knew how, far from waters for bathing,
> Pallas Athene had cut him down at the hands of Achilleus.
> She heard from the great bastion the noise of mourning and sorrow.
> Her limbs spun, and the shuttle dropped from her hands to the ground.
> (22.437–48)

It is pathetically ironic that Andromache is introduced here simply as "the wife of Hektor" (22. 437) at the very point when she has lost her primary identity, and it is tragically ironic that Hektor's wife is the last to know about his death. Homer emphasizes Hektor's compulsion to act on behalf of his nation by having the news come first to king and queen. Hektor's death, after all, signals the end of Troy. Only after the representatives of society have expressed their initial grief does Homer turn to narrate the reaction of Andromache. But how much more fully he elaborates her reception of the news, how much more extensively he concentrates upon her actions! As if to compensate her somehow for being the last to know, the poet employs the strangely equivocal adjective *etētumos* ("true, truthful, real") to describe the messenger *who did not come* to Andromache. The impression so created is that Hektor's wife possessed the knowledge of his death mysteriously, but no less certainly, through some extraordinary manner of cognition. Her first words all too accurately reflect the reality which she has feared for so long (22. 449 ff.).

Yet despite her premonitions, Andromache has persisted in her weaving. Homer portrays her pursuing a course of action no less futile, with respect to family well-being, than are Hektor's own final acts, with respect to social stability. Quietly reflecting her husband's pursuit of transcendent glory, Andromache becomes herself the symbol of wifely devotion (like Penelope, whose patient weaving has a happier reward). Without elaborating its subject matter, Homer makes the robe she weaves nevertheless special, as a symbol of her dutiful fulfillment to her husband's exact wishes; her subsequent orders for the building of the bath-fire indicate that her obedience is complete — extending to Hektor's general wishes as well as to his detailed commands. Long before, Hektor had outlined the proper behavior for all Trojans to pursue (8. 517–20), dictating that each wife, in her own house, should kindle a fire. He did not mention, then, what purpose their fires should serve; here, at the most dramatic moment possible, their function is emphatically familial. As it washes the soil of battle from the weary soldier, the household bath simultaneously cleanses him of his outside, national responsibilities. The tragedy of Hektor's conflicting loyalties is that he fell "far from waters for bathing" (22. 445). The attentive efforts of his wife have been in vain; the narrator's comment heightens the poignancy of Andromache's futile preparations (22. 445).

Andromache drops the shuttle from her hands (22. 448). The sudden interruption of the artifact's creation directly reflects not only the disruption of the marriage, now final, but also of Andromache herself who is, by Hektor's death, undefined. The composer's attention to this particular detail of the image—the actual cessation of the weaving—is another contrast with his treatment of the loom of Helen. The loom of Andromache is meant to be associated particularly with the dissolution of the family; with the husband and father dead, the loom's function, both actual and symbolic, ends. Helen's loom, on the other hand, symbolizes the general breakdown of human society—Trojan and Achaian together.

Still, the two Trojan wives (in Book 3, and in Books 6 and 22) behave in similar ways. Both women, for example, are shown twice at the wall. Helen was led there, the first time, by Iris to witness the hoped-for restoration of order, through the arrangement of the truce and duel; and order was the keynote of Andromache's first appearance on the wall with husband and son. Now, however, the wife of Hektor leaves her household behind once more, but this time with symbolic finality; the potential of order has been lost, the probable disorder realized. Instead of a living Hektor she sees at the wall a husband dead and cruelly dishonored (22. 462 ff.). Andromache reflects her husband's mortality, so allied with her identity, when she faints (22. 467). Andromache's swoon is the physical gesture that complements the namelessness with which Homer had introduced her in this scene. In much the same manner Helen was led away by Aphrodite from her position next to Priam on the wall; here, too, the movement is from the unrealized potential of order to the renewal of actual disorder, in the daemonically enforced bedding-down with Paris. The relationship between the two wives, with respect to their appearances on the wall, is that of cause and effect: Helen's involuntary reaffirmation of disorder leads directly to Andromache's brokenhearted experience of domestic disintegration. Helen's return to her unnatural home has caused Andromache to be separated forever from her natural one. So house is set against house, bed against bed.

In the lines that follow the fainting scene, Homer associates another artifact, the headdress, with Andromache, to form an image that serves to focus her present grief in a gesture, to recall the depth of her emotion in a history of the artifact's origin, and to heighten the emotional impact of the poem's major theme by evoking our visual memory of a similar artifact treated in a similar way for an entirely different reason — Hektor's shining helmet. Her first experience of grief recalls to Andromache her wedding:

> The darkness of night misted over the eyes of Andromache.
> She fell backward, and gasped the life breath from her, and far off
> threw from her head the shining gear that ordered her headdress,
> the diadem and the cap, and the holding-band woven together,
> and the circlet, which Aphrodite the golden once had given her
> on that day when Hektor of the shining helmet led her forth
> from the house of Eëtion, and gave numberless gifts to win her.
>
> (22. 466–72)

First the poet reiterates Andromache's imitation of her husband's death (22. 466–67), reminding us of Hektor's identifying role in their intimate marriage. Her ritual despoilment of the headdress recalls the previous dropping of the shuttle, but even more strikingly, Hektor's voluntary removal of *his* headgear for the benefit of their son. But Homer contrasts the two acts with precision. Here is no careful displacement to signify, in the case of Hektor, a retention of respect and value for the object; instead, the headdress is relinquished definitely, forever — its usefulness, like that of the loom, at an end. In the visual imagination, the difference between the two gestures is as stunning as it is precisely drawn.

Yet even displaced, the headdress works mnemonically to associate Andromache with Aphrodite, with her wedding, and with her expatriate status. The manner in which she left the house of Eëtion, through the propriety of Hektor's "numberless gifts" (22. 472), stands in sharp contrast with the disorderly abduction of Helen by Paris. Hektor's wooing is the exemplary standard by which others, like Othryoneus' of Kassandra, or even Achilles' of Briseis, are to be judged; and Andromache is the symbol of ideal marriage. Andromache's newly symbolic role, on the essential human level, is confirmed in the image of her almost ritual elevation: "And about her stood thronging her husband's sisters and the wives of his brothers / and these, in her despair for death, held her up among them" (22. 473–74). The gesture of her in-laws seems to say, Look what war has wrought upon the family!

When Andromache recovers from her swoon, her speech expresses explicitly what the imagery has implied. Recalling the temporary disruption of her family in the scene in Book 6, she declares, in the superfluous catechism of extreme emotion, that the reciprocal relationship between father and son is now destroyed conclusively. Hektor can no longer help Astyanax; nor can the son serve his father (22. 485–86). Her prophecy of his certain fate is vivid (22. 488 ff.). And her speech ends with a poignant evocation of lost domesticity, focused on the same art-images associated with her bath-fire at the opening of the episode: " 'But now, beside the curving ships, far away from your parents, / the writhing worms will feed, when the dogs have had enough of you, / on your naked corpse, though in your house there is clothing laid up / that is fine-textured and pleasant, wrought by the hands of women. / But all of these I will burn up in the fire's blazing, / no use to you, since you will never be laid away in them' " (22. 508–13). Her carefully prepared fire will now fulfill a purpose very different from that for which it was originally intended. All images of the peaceful hearth are inverted. Sure that Hektor will have no honorable funeral, Andromache resigns herself to carrying out the ultimate duties of a loyal wife. Priam's faith in human nature and his ability and determination to test it are not granted to Andromache. She finds no consolation in the discovery of a new, meaningful way of acting; yet she remains stolidly content in the knowledge that her symbolic gestures will be meaningful enough. Because of Priam's unexpected success, however, Andromache will appear one last time with her dead husband, in Book 24. Homer recapitulates her characterization in her bedside attention to Hektor. The image of the funeral bed reverses the order of thematic implications which had been suggested by the headdress in Book 22. There the death of Hektor led to recollection of their wedding; here the wedding bed has become the funeral bier.

Andromache finally stands juxtaposed with Kassandra, whose outcry over her greatest brother defines in the most general terms the political role of the primary Trojan warrior: "She cried out then in sorrow and spoke to the entire city: / 'Come, men of Troy and Trojan women; look upon Hektor / if ever before you were joyful when you saw him come back living / from battle; for he was a great joy to his city, and all his people' " (24. 703–6). What Kassandra only implies in her own general social role, as futile as that of Hektor, Andromache will make explicit. She, like the others, recognizes the national importance of Hektor's death and of the role he played in life. But when the meeting between Priam and Achilles reveals that it is the familial structure which will survive the particular catastrophes of history that conclusively destroy one society or another, we understand that Andromache's view is closer to the heart of Homer's vision. So Andromache speaks of the widow and the orphan, who will bear the sufferings of social disruption. Because Troy must now fall, Astyanax will die. And she reminds us that Hektor's protection of the city was just the general way of referring to his defense of individual wives and children who must now be separated from their nourishing and identifying habitat (24. 725–43). For humankind experiences anguish only when the individual human being is touched by pain and grief. The disaster of social disorder is, then, in the last analysis, intelligible only in the sorrow of each person who has been separated unnaturally from the stability of a social system. Andromache's lament concludes with the image of the marriage bed deprived of its natural occupant. It is in this way that Homer communicates his characteristically social perspective: that war ends, as it begins, with conjugal disorder.

On the Odyssey

A Valediction:
Forbidding Mourning

John Donne

As virtuous men pass mildly away,
　　And whisper to their souls, to go
Whilst some of their sad friends do say,
　　The breath goes now, and some say, no:

So let us melt, and make no noise,
　　No tear-floods, nor sigh-tempests move,
'Twere profanation of our joys
　　To tell the laity our love.

Moving of th' earth brings harms and fears,
　　Men reckon what it did and meant,
But trepidation of the spheres,
　　Though greater far, is innocent.

Dull sublunary lovers' love
　　(Whose soul is sense) cannot admit
Absence, because it does remove
　　Those things which elemented it.

But we by a love, so much refin'd,
　　That our selves know not what it is,
Inter-assurèd of the mind,
　　Care less, eyes, lips, and hands to miss.

Our two souls therefore, which are one,
　　Though I must go, endure not yet
A breach, but an expansion,
　　Like gold to airy thinness beat.

If they be two, they are two so
　　As stiff twin compasses are two,
Thy soul the fix'd foot, makes no show
　　To move, but doth, if th' other do.

And though it in the center sit,
    Yet when the other far doth roam,
It leans, and hearkens after it,
    And grows erect, as that comes home.

Such wilt thou be to me, who must
    Like th' other foot, obliquely run;
Thy firmness makes my circle just,
    And makes me end, where I begun.

The World as Meditation   Wallace Stevens*

J'ai passé trop de temps à travailler mon violon, à voyager. Mais l'exercice essentiel du compositeur — la méditation — rien ne l'a jamais suspendu en moi . . . Je vis un rêve permanent, qui ne s'arrête ni nuit ni jour.

                                                        Georges Enesco

Is it Ulysses that approaches from the east,
The interminable adventurer? The trees are mended.
That winter is washed away. Someone is moving

On the horizon and lifting himself up above it.
A form of fire approaches the cretonnes of Penelope,
Whose mere savage presence awakens the world in which
    she dwells.

She has composed, so long, a self with which to welcome
    him,
Companion to his self for her, which she imagined,
Two in a deep-founded sheltering, friend and dear friend.

The trees had been mended, as an essential exercise
In an inhuman meditation, larger than her own.
No winds like dogs watched over her at night.

She wanted nothing he could not bring her by coming
    alone.
She wanted no fetchings. His arms would be her necklace
And her belt, the final fortune of their desire.

*Reprinted from *Collected Poems of Wallace Stevens* (New York: Alfred A. Knopf, 1954), 520–21, by permission.

But was it Ulysses? Or was it only the warmth of the sun
On her pillow? The thought kept beating in her like her
    heart.
The two kept beating together. It was only day.

It was Ulysses and it was not. Yet they had met,
Friend and dear friend and a planet's encouragement.
The barbarous strength within her would never fail.

She would talk a little to herself as she combed her hair,
Repeating his name with its patient syllables,
Never forgetting him that kept coming constantly so near.

Archery at the Dark of the Moon   Norman Austin*

To discover an order as of
A season, to discover summer and know it,
To discover winter and know it well, to find,
Not to impose, not to have reasoned at all,
Out of nothing to have come on major weather,

It is possible, possible, possible. It must
Be possible.

— Wallace Stevens, "Notes Towards a Supreme Fiction"

Odysseus, aroused back to his senses by his restless comrades, begs Kirke to grant him passage home. She tells him he must first travel the road to the house of Hades and dread Persephone, to consult the *psyche* of Teiresias. At that his heart breaks, for it "no longer wished to live and look upon the light of the sun" (10.498). Odysseus travels to that realm of *zophos* [the east] where the sun's rays never penetrate, and there Teiresias prophesies a safe homecoming for him if he will but reverence the sun. Odysseus returns from the darkness to Kirke's island, "where are the house of Dawn, and dancing floors, and the risings of the sun" (12.3–4). He continues on his journey, past Sirens, the Clashing Rocks, Skylla and Charybdis, until he reaches the sacred island where the sun pastures his sacred days and nights. There Odysseus' comrades perform their sacrilege on the inviolable property of the sun and are hurled from the light of the sun forever. Odysseus alone is saved from the storm by finding, "with the rising sun" (12.429), a cave above Charybdis. There he clings to an olive tree through the livelong day like a bat, until the time when a hungry

*Reprinted from *Archery at the Dark of the Moon* (University of California: Berkeley, 1975), 239–53, by permission of the publisher.

judge goes home for his dinner, when Charybdis vomits up the mast of his ship. Jumping aboard his mast he is carried out to sea for nine days, and on the tenth night he finds refuge with the nymph Kalypso, who hides him away from the sight of man and god for seven years.

"When the year came round in the circling of the seasons [*eniauton*] which the gods, in their spinning, had marked as the time of his return. . . ." So begins the poem with a simple, almost formulaic, temporal notation, which gains in significance when we realize that the circling seasons bring around simultaneously Telemachos' maturity, Penelope's remarriage, and the return of the man absent for twenty years, lost at sea and presumed dead for ten years. We are not put *in medias res*, when the poem opens, but *in ultimas res*.

If Odysseus is to return to the light of the sun, it is now or never. But Athena, the divine architect of the poem, is not perturbed by any sense of urgency. To the contrary, she delights in dancing around the urgency. She introduces Odysseus' name quite casually into the conversation on Olympos when Zeus is musing on the fate of that evil suitor Aegisthus. She contrives to have Hermes sent to start Odysseus on his way, while she goes to Ithaka to create further complications. At the time when the pressures on Penelope are the most severe, she leads Telemachos to undertake a voyage across the sea. Odysseus is justifiably angry to hear that Athena has sent his son away at such a time (13.417–419); it seems a gratuitous cruelty for Athena to dispatch the boy into perils at sea, while leaving his mother and his property at the mercy of villains. But an eleventh-hour crisis holds no threat for Athena. It merely enhances her orchestration of time and persons. While events move swiftly to their culmination, she darts in and out, back and forth, now as a dream, now as a bird, now as a young man, a young girl, a wise old man, busy but ever insouciant, full of pleasure in her weaving of individual times into the cosmic time.

Odysseus starts out from Kalypso's island to look once more upon the sun, to regain his time. He steers his ship from Ogygia by the stars, by the Great Bear, the Pleiades, and "late-setting Boötes" (5.272–3). As we have seen in chapter 3, the stars give Odysseus his spatial orientation, which he has lacked since arriving years before at Kirke's island where he could not distinguish *zophos* from *eos*, east from west, darkness from light. But the stars give him also a temporal notation. From Hesiod, as from many other sources, we learn what the constellation of the Pleiades meant for agricultural and seafaring Greeks. If the sun was one hand on their chronometer, the Pleiades were the other.[1] For both farmer and sailor the Pleiades by their risings and settings announced the times for both beginning and closing the essential activities of the year. For the sailor, the rising of the Pleiades signified the start of the sailing season in the spring and their setting the end of the sailing season just before winter. Odysseus sails from Kalypso's island when the Pleiades are visible during the night;

this would put his journey very late in the sailing season, just about as the season is to close. The year is far advanced.

Since Homer is wont to give his spatial or temporal notations by two coordinates, we are pleased to find him making the time of the journey precise by balancing the Pleiades with "late-setting Boötes." The expression "late-setting Boötes" has prompted various interpretations, none persuasive. It has been argued that Boötes is "late-setting" because it sets after more southerly constellations that rise simultaneously with it. This is unsatisfactory, because the only star that could bear this relation to Boötes is Spica in Virgo, a constellation not named in Homer. Furthermore, the Pleiades and half a dozen other constellations are close to the declination of Arcturus in Boötes, and could just as well be called "late-setting" as Boötes. Arcturus and the Pleiades, differing some twelve hours in right ascension at the present time, are balanced like a pair of scales in the sky. As Boötes sets, the Pleiades rise. To say "setting Boötes" is the reverse of saying "the rising Pleiades." In their complementary balance, surely, lies the clue to Homer's epithet for Boötes. Odysseus cannot watch both Boötes and the Pleiades simultaneously, or not for very long, since the visibility of one implies the invisibility of the other. Odysseus must watch Boötes as it sets at dusk, while the Pleiades are rising, and he would continue to steer his way through the night by the "late-rising" Pleiades until Boötes returns to take up his post in the early hours of the morning when the Pleiades sink below the horizon. "Late-setting" would mean, by this interpretation, the evening, or acronycal setting.

From the reference to Boötes and the Pleiades we can place Odysseus' journey from Kalypso's island between the evening rising of the Pleiades and their morning setting, in that period which in 432 B.C. would fall between 19 September and 8 November on the Julian calendar.[2] From Hesiod we learn that the morning setting of the Pleiades (8 November in 432 B.C.) marks the end of the sailing season; at their setting, winter storms break out and it is time to beach the ships for winter (*WD* 619ff.). Hesiod pinpoints the onset of winter as the coincidence of the falling of the Pleiades and the rising of all the winds — as the Pleiades plunge into the misty sea the blasts "of the winds" arise (*WD* 619–622). Several centuries later an epigram commemorating a death at sea echoes Hesiod's warning (Theocr. *epigr.* [XXV] Gow).[3]

The twenty-five days in which Odysseus builds his ship and completes his journey to Scheria are the last sailing month of the year. For seventeen days he crosses the open sea, enjoying calm and a favoring wind, but suddenly, on the eighteenth day of his voyage, a violent storm arises which shatters his ship and lashes him mercilessly for two full days. Odysseus becomes, in Homer's simile, a thistle tossed across the plain by gusts of the autumnal north wind (5.328). Poseidon's savage storm can be none other than Hesiod's first winter storm. There are close parallels between Hesiod's and Homer's descriptions. In Homer, Poseidon rouses the storm thus (5.292–296):

> [(he) troubled the sea, and roused all blasts of all manner of winds, and hid with clouds land and sea alike; and night rushed down from heaven. Together the East Wind and the South Wind dashed, and the fierce-blowing West wind and the North wind, born in the bright heaven, rolling before him a mighty wave.]

That the storm is a joined battle of all the winds Homer continues to emphasize throughout the passage (cf. 304–5, 317), most notably in verses 330 to 332, where Notos and Boreas alternate with Euros and Zephyros in hurling Odysseus' ship back and forth. When the ship is nothing but flotsam, scattered like chaff in the wind (vv. 368–369), the winds subside except for the violent north wind which continues to bluster for another two days until it brings Odysseus in sight of Scheria. The *Odyssey*'s battle "of all the winds," following hard on the reference to the autumnal sky, is poetic amplification of what is a brief almanac date in Hesiod. It corresponds also with the dissolution of the covenant of the winds, which is the mythopoeic way the old Norse work *Konnungs Skuggsjá* describes the beginning of winter.[4]

Odysseus reaches Scheria at the very close of the sailing season. He was, in fact, caught in the dreaded first storm of winter. Had he dallied longer on Ogygia he would have had to wait out the winter and Penelope would have remarried. The Phaiakians' extraordinary sailing skill now assumes a new significance. Their supernatural power might seem superfluous when Odysseus has already eluded every kind of peril by his own wits, but Homer's maritime audience would have enjoyed the coincidence that the storm that closed the paths of the sea for the year should have cast Odysseus among a people whose skills were happily not subject to the season. The Phaiakians secure Odysseus' passage across the treacherous winter sea because the weather has now made human navigation suicidal.

From this point several references confirm the meteorological evidence. When the storm casts Odysseus ashore on Scheria he is in a quandary whether to expose himself to the night frost near the river or to find himself a warmer spot in the woods, and thus chance an attack from wild animals (5.466–473). Choosing the latter course, he beds down beneath a dense heap of leaves, autumn's debris, "sufficient to protect two or three men in the winter season, even if winter should be unusually severe" (5.483–5). Later in Ithaka, during the first night of Odysseus' stay in Eumaios' hut, a rain storm blows all night and Odysseus invents a story of how he had tricked a soldier out of his cloak one winter's night in Troy. Eumaios understands the hint: he moves Odysseus' bed close to the fire, spreads sheepskins on it, and throws over Odysseus his own specially thick cloak, designed for protection against harsh winter storms (14.457–522). Eumaios himself spends the night out on the ground near the pigs; for protection against the cold he takes another thick cloak and a goat's fleece, and finds himself a snug shelter against the north wind (14.529–533). In Odysseus' palace the servants heap logs on the fire to give both light and warmth (19.63–64). The nights are long, says Eumaios; there is time enough for both story-telling and sleep (15.392ff.).[5]

In Ithaka, the chronology begins to narrow down from seasons to days. Odysseus twice swears a solemn oath, once to Eumaios and later to Penelope, by Zeus and by the hearth of Odysseus which has given him asylum that "Odysseus will return at this very *lykabas*, when one moon is waning and the other waxing" (14.160–162; 19.305–307):

> [Verily all these things shall be brought to pass even as I tell thee. In the course of this self-same day [year] Odysseus shall come hither, as the old moon wanes, and the new appears.]

In later Greek *lykabas* signified "year," but its etymology is uncertain and scholars divide on whether to take it as year, season, month, or day in the Homeric passages.[6] It is surely not a synonym for *etos* or *eniautos*, the customary and general words in Homer for year (or season), but something more precise since the reference to the moon's cycle seems epexegetic. Also, it would be contrary to the poem's progressive concern for exact chronology that Odysseus make at this point safely vague predictions about an event sometime within the twelvemonth. The solemnity of Odysseus' oath suggests that he is not hiding behind comfortable generality but staking his life on a very precise and, therefore, daring prediction. *Lykabas* must surely be either "this particular month" or, even better, the dark of the moon, a meaning that could accommodate either the etymologies linking *lykabas* with *lyk-* (light) or those linking it with *lykos* (wolf). Maas, for example, understands *lykabas* as winter, the season "when wolves run," but his etymology might just as well apply to the dark of the moon, that period almost universally considered of sinister aspect. Whether *lykabas* be year or month, however, makes little difference in the circumstances, for the year has practically run its course: "this year" and "this month" are, at this point in the poem, synonymous.

During the conversation between Odysseus and Penelope in Book 19, Odysseus swears that Penelope's husband will be home at the dark of the moon. A few moments later Penelope proposes to hold a contest for her remarriage on the morrow. The stranger immediately assures her that "Odysseus, wily man that he is, will be home before the suitors stretch the bowstring and wing an arrow through the iron" (19.586–587). Thus does he confirm what events in the next books will reveal, that Penelope's morrow and the stranger's dark of the moon are one and the same. Behind their veiled language the two exchange concrete and precise information as to what will happen and when, Penelope would grasp at once the import of the stranger's talk of the dark of the moon, for preparations were about to begin for the feast of Apollo which, as the scholiast remarked, must be the feast of Apollo Noumenios, Apollo of the New Moon. Odysseus' first night in Ithaka is a "moon-obscured night" (*nyx skotomenios*), which brings a vile storm of rain and wind.[7] It could be argued that all night storms obscure the moon, but in Homer storms obscure the sky. This is the only storm in Homer in which the disappearance of the moon is emphasized. It was not the storm that hid the moon, but the dark of the moon that brought the storm.

On the following day Eurykleia busies herself and her staff with the preparations for the lunar feast; the suitors gather in their usual way. Ktesippos demonstrates the suitors' ignorance of both marksmanship and sacral moments by aiming an oxhoof at Odysseus' head and hitting the wall instead. Before Penelope can produce the bow to give him his second chance at Apollonian skills, Theoklymenos has a harrowing vision of death. Heraklitos Rheter interpreted Theoklymenos' vision, which occurs, as he notes, on the day "which the Athenian youths call "[*hénēn te kainéan*]," as a description of a solar eclipse that can occur only at the time of the new moon.[8] Modern critics, their lives no longer regulated by the lunar calendar, might reject such an interpretation as an anachronism for Homer, but for a people whose livelihood was dependent on the cycles of sun and moon, who, moreover, sanctified every new moon with religious ceremony, the connection between new moon and solar eclipse must have been apparent from a very early time. Theoklymenos' vision remains a vision and not a literal eclipse; the *Odyssey* is not an almanac, but it incorporates almanac data into its dramatic exposition. The suitors laugh at Theoklymenos' wild fantasy, but Homer's audience, knowing their calendar, would have understood what Theoklymenos meant when he said on the eve of the new moon: "Your heads are shrouded in night, the walls run red with blood, the sun has perished from the sky, and a murky gloom has settled over everything" (20.351–357). Theoklymenos' prophetic vision is one more announcement of the exact moment of the denouement, an announcement of the most emphatic sort, for it describes that calamitous and awe-inspiring event that can happen in that moment of equilibrium between one moon and the next.

Wilamowitz, who understood *lykabas* as the day that in the Athenian calendar was called [*hénē te kaì néa*], interprets Odysseus' oath to mean ["*Odysseus comes today*"], but goes further to suggest that it is a particular new moon, the new moon that begins the new year.[9] Although there is no explicit statement to this effect in the poem, the air suddenly becomes alive with intimations of spring. Penelope, recounting her grief to Odysseus, likens herself to the nightingale which sings its beautiful song in early spring, perched amid the thick foliage on the trees (19.519–520):

> [(the nightingale of the greenwood) sings sweetly, when spring is newly come, as she sits perched amid the thick leafage of the trees.]

Shortly before Penelope's conversation with Odysseus, he had replied to Eurymachos' insults by suggesting that the two men compete in field work "in the spring season when the days are long" (18.367). At the moment of vengeance the tokens of spring become unequivocal. The bowstring in Odysseus' hand "sang out fair like a swallow's note" (21.411). In the midst of the fray, Athena taunts the suitors in Mentor's shape and then darts up to the rafters in the form of a swallow (22.240). Moments later the suitors are routed in panic like a herd of cattle goaded by the gadfly "in the season of spring when the days are long" (22.299–301). Autumnal and winter pictures which had accompanied Odysseus' journey from Scheria to Ithaka — the windblown chaff, night frosts, fallen leaves, bitter storms — give way, on the day of vengeance, to the sounds and sights of nightingales, swallows, farmers breaking the soil or cutting grass, and pasturing cattle.

The association of swallows with spring is almost universal wherever the swallow is known. In extant Greek literature swallows appear infrequently, but in most cases they come as harbingers of spring.[10] Aeschylus, it is true, likens barbarian tongues to the twittering of swallows (*Ag.* 1050, fr. 450) and Eustathius inclines towards this association in his discussion of the Odyssean passage (see his Commentary, 1914–20ff.). But if the sound of the bowstring is barbarous, it is barbarous only to the suitors, who turn pale with fear at the note. For Odysseus and his family it is a beautiful omen, *kalon* as Homer calls it. The sound of the bow and Athena's metamorphosis into a swallow that perches beneath the rafters can mean nothing else but the arrival of spring.

Tradition has preserved from antiquity a certain type of popular song which celebrates the annual return of the swallow. In the Rhodian song *Chelidonismos,* as recorded by Athenaeus (VIII.360b), and in the Samian *Eiresione,* attributed to Homer's authorship in the *Vita homeri herodotea* (chap. 33), children impersonate swallows and make a tour of houses, standing at the doors to demand entrance and promising prosperity on the house in return for gifts and threats if no gifts are forthcoming. "The swallow has come bringing lovely seasons and lovely years," the Rhodian song begins, and concludes after a set of promises and threats, "open up, open up the door to the swallow. We are not old men, but children." The Samian song, according to the *Vita,* was one that Homer, accompanied by the local children, used to sing at the doors of the most prosperous houses when he wintered one year in Samos. The occasion of the song was exactly the occasion of the swallow's song in the *Odyssey,* the new-moon festival in honor of Apollo. The song wishes prosperity on the house, and concludes. "I come, I come yearly as the swallow who perches with bare and nimble feet in the forecourt. Give something if you will; but if not, we will not stay. We did not come here to remain with you."[11]

Sir James Frazer, in an article citing examples from Greek literature as well as from contemporary folklore, offered further clarification of the

Rhodian swallow song by showing that the swallow is often welcomed into houses since it is a good omen for the swallow to make his nest in the rafters.[12] In both the Rhodian and Samian versions the children imitate the behavior of swallows: if invited into the house and given gifts they will assure prosperity; if rejected they will work harm and pass on to a more hospitable house. They impersonate, it is obvious, the harbingers of spring.

The pseudo-Herodotean *Vita*, in reality less *vita* than hagiograph, attempts, as do the other *Vitae*, to make Homer an honorary citizen of as many cities as possible, particularly those that claimed to be his birthplace. In the *Vita*, Homer is a wandering minstrel who goes from one city to another, accepting work where he finds it and rewarding his hosts with song in proportion to their hospitality. Superficially he has become a mendicant poet, but in reality a hero figure whose prowess lies in his gift for song. Like other hero figures he suffers misfortune, performs exploits, though these are in song, and undergoes periods of servitude. For weapons he has his incantations, with which he blesses or curses according to the treatment he receives — his arrival at a city brings either prosperity or calamity. Many of the songs and epigrams in the *Vita* are undoubtedly local products which tradition attributed to Homer, but the structure of the *Vita* is clearly an extrapolation from the *Odyssey*. Mentor, Mentes, and Phemius, for example, the *Vita* transforms into the helpful friends and teachers of Homer whom he gratefully immortalized in his poem. By a method familiar to all students of literary criticism, the *Vita* has read the *Odyssey* as cryptic autobiography of the poet. There are no wandering bards in the *Odyssey* but there is a wandering hero who pays high compliments to bards, and in fact entertains his hosts with song in return for their hospitality. In the *Vita*, bard and wandering hero merge into a single figure. It is the poet who travels, both from financial necessity and from a desire to explore the world, who arrives at a house or city and appeals for the rights of hospitality and for outright gifts. The *Vita* owes its most apparent debt to the Phaiakian episode of the *Odyssey* and to the last part of the poem when Odysseus arrives at his palace in Ithaka, that is, to those episodes where the emphasis is on Odysseus as an indigent guest, who entertains the company with tales in return for clothes and supplies. In his own house he plays the mendicant, praying for the good health of those who treat him kindly and threatening those who mistreat him with the vengeance of heaven. The owners of the house receive him kindly; Penelope, in fact, after one evening's conversation with him, treats him as next of kin.[13]

The connection of the Samian *Eiresione* with Homer's name is not coincidental. The song itself probably has no connection with Homer but it lends itself readily to inclusion in a Homeric hagiography. Homer sang the song, says the *Vita*, at the new-moon festivals for Apollo during a winter in Samos. But the swallow song, celebrating the arrival of the swallow, would be apt at only one new-moon festival of winter, namely, the new moon marking the end of winter and the beginning of spring.

The *Odyssey* is, in fact, our earliest *Chelidonismos*, in an amplified and dramatized version. Celebrations of the annual arrival of the swallow seem to have been a custom widely practiced in Greece and no audience could fail to notice the *Odyssey*'s use of the popular tradition. The arrival of the hero, who is both beggar and itinerant "poet," signals the end of disintegration and the beginning of reconstruction. The itinerant in disguise, like the children disguised as swallows, makes his rounds to test each man's hospitality and dispenses rewards accordingly. He is even barefoot and shabby, as the children seem to be in the Samian *Eiresione*. He arrives in winter and takes his vengeance at the feast of the new moon in honor of Apollo. At the moment of vengeance his bow sounds the swallow's note, the first note of spring, and Athena, the miracle worker, perches in the rafters in a swallow's disguise, a good omen for a prosperous new year. Athena is the first swallow of the season.[14]

Northrop Frye has reminded us that comedy has its roots in the celebration of spring's victory over winter, the New Year's conquest of the Old.[15] So it is in the *Odyssey*, our earliest comedy. Odysseus, put back into time, sails on his last voyage in the autumnal season, becoming one with the season, chaff blown by the autumnal wind. He survives the first storm of winter, arrives at Scheria when there is frost on the ground, and buries himself beneath the year's fallen leaves. It is dead of winter when he arrives in Ithaka to warm himself at Eumaios' humble fire. He proceeds to his palace and there vows vengeance at the dark of the moon. There Theoklymenos sees a solar eclipse on the day of the Old and the New — instant of transition between waning and waxing, ending and beginning, point of equilibrium pregnant with potential for either good or bad. The suitors mock his talk of darkness, for had not Eurymachos already joked that there was light enough in the hall (18.353–355): "Not without god comes this man into the house of Odysseus, for most bright is the light shining from his head, since there is not a hair on it." Odysseus has become the only light there is in the house.[16]

Penelope institutes her contest on that day of contraries. Odysseus' bow sounds the swallow's note and his arrow, *hora* made visible, threads the twelve axes with the same deadly accuracy as nimble Odysseus threads the calendar. The gods' destined plan comes to fruition with not a moment to spare. Accurate in timing as in marksmanship, Odysseus, with a prayer to Apollo — god of both timing and marksmanship — fulfills his vow and the gods' plan on the last day of the appointed year, in the last hours of the last day. A swallow darts in among the rafters; the suitors, personification of waste and dissolution, are routed like cattle stung by the gadfly in the long days of spring. Winter in Ithaka is at an end. As we expect in comedy, the rout of winter calls for a feast. "Now is the hour come to set a banquet for the Achaians in the light, and then to turn to song and the lyre, which are the glory of the feast" — so Odysseus triumphantly calls out to his son (21.428–429). The feast begins. The bard takes up his lyre, the halls resound with the noise of the lyre and the feet of men and women dancing, and passersby exclaim: "Ah, then someone has married the long-courted queen" (23.143–149).

Once every twenty-nine days or so the moon moves into conjunction with the sun, when it is veiled from our sight. It then travels on its orbit slowly out from the sun until full moon, when it stands in opposition and greets the sun from afar. As it continues its orbit it wanes and approaches the sun until it surrenders once again to the sun's embrace. The monthly dance of sun and moon is repeated on a vaster scale by sun and stars. Constellation after constellation disappears behind the sun and then moves outward in its orbit. Conjunction and opposition in a ceaseless cycle is the visible pattern of order in the universe.

Such are the ceremonies in the heavens on which Homer's courtly hexameters rest, the phases of sun and moon moving in quiet harmony, the phases of sun and star crossing paths once every year, the phases of the winds merging with the phases of the stars, the swallow by day, the nightingale by night heralding to farmer and sailor the completion of one phase and the start of another. Set in the midst of this dance of all creation is man, than whom, as Odysseus says, "earth nourishes nothing more frail" (18.130). At the mercy of those beings that live at their ease in courtly disport, man is swept from prosperity to poverty, from joy to despair, from life to death — "such is the *noos* of men on the soil" (18.136). Sun, moon, and stars move in their majestic circuits, while beneath them man is wracked by storm, war, disease and age.

But Odysseus chooses for himself the lot of man. He returns home "to accept in silence the gifts of the gods, whatever they might give him" (18.142). His acceptance of mortal fortune is the opposite of passive resignation; it is a ceaseless effort to build with hand and mind a world that the gods may — no will — sooner or later destroy. Odysseus builds a world of objects around him — houses, furniture, ships, arms — and builds too a world of people attuned to his mind. And his mind, despite what he says through his beggar's mask, is not fixed on his belly. His is the mind that has seen a nymph who can change men into other species, and another who can offer him immortality. It has looked upon the property of the sun and the property of Hades. It has looked into its own birth and death, and into the realms in between. When Odysseus returns to his obscure little island to create *homophrosyne* [harmony] there, he has already begun to create *homophrosyne* between his mind and the heavenly paradigms. Thus he enters into a courtship, which he had performed many years before, in phase now with the courtship of sun and moon.[17] The courtship on earth coincides precisely with the courtship in heaven. Such is the *Odyssey*'s definition of *hora*, the right season, and its definition too of mind, a definition vaster than that bequeathed to us by our tradition of the individual body housing an isolated soul, man set in an adversary position towards the universe.[18]

Penelope alleges that the burial shroud she weaves is for her father-in-law. We are not fooled. It is for Odysseus, not Laertes. In weaving and unraveling the shroud Penelope lays her husband in his grave by day and raises him, Lazarus-like, from the dead by night. She too performs her daily ceremony of opposition and conjunction, accepting her husband's death and from his death creating his life anew, in a ceaseless process of waxing and waning.[19] What is her weaving but the rhythm of the life of the man who moves between the realms of Hades and Helios, now disappearing from the light, now coming into being once more? And in her weaving is the paradigm too of Homer's poetics. For man, build as he will his own microcosm, must as inevitably leave the splendor of the sun, and his microcosm must disintegrate with him. Only in the weaving and unweaving of Homer's formulas into hexameters can Odysseus hope for anything beyond a momentary affirmation of his frail existence. The singer is like the gods in speech, and there is no purpose of greater grace than when banqueters sit to listen to their singer — so Odysseus says to the Phaiakian artists: Of the gifts the gods give, the greatest in the *Odyssey* is song.

Notes

1. For the importance of the Pleiades in the measurement and regulation of the year among agricultural peoples, see M. P. Nilsson, *Primitive Time Reckoning* (Lund, 1920), pp. 274–276, and *RE*, s.v. "Pleiaden," Bd. XXI.2.2486–2523. See also Athen. XI.489ff. for his discussion of the importance generally of the Pleiades, and specifically for their place in Hesiod and Homer. For the time of Odysseus' sea journey from Ogygia see, for example, the edition of Ameis-Hentze-Cauer at *Ody.* 5.272ff. . . .

2. See *RE*, s.v. "Fixsterne," for risings and settings in 432 b.c. There would be some adjustment in dating to conform to the time of the *Odyssey*'s composition, but the minor adjustment need not concern us here.

3. This epigram is in Gow's two-volume edition of Theocritus (Cambridge, 1965).

4. In confirmation of the time of Odysseus' voyage, the scholiast at *Odyssey* 5.171 says that Odysseus hesitates to accept Kalypso's offer of a passage home because he fears the dangers of the season. The same autumnal storm lashes earth in the simile at *Iliad* 16.384ff. On the connection between the autumnal storm in the *Odyssey* and that in Hesiod, see Cuillandre, *La droite et la gauche*, p. 176.

5. See J. van Leeuwen's edition at *Odyssey* 5.467ff. for a fuller citation of references to wintry weather conditions in the *Odyssey*. . . .

6. See Stanford's note at 14.161 for some discussion of the possible interpretations. Manu Leumann, *Homerische Wörter* (Basel, 1950), p. 212, is probably the best source for the etymology and meaning of *lykabas*.

7. *Odyssey* 14.457. The night is not only moon-obscured but vile, such a night as never was elsewhere in Homer. Richmond Lattimore, *The Odyssey of Homer* (New York, 1965), translates v. 457: "A bad night came on, the dark of the moon."

8. Heraklitos *Alleg. hom.* chap. 75. See Felix Buffière, *Les mythes d'Homère* (Paris,

1956), pp. 226ff. A. Shewan, "Two Ancient Eclipses," *CW* 21(1928):196–198, not only accepts Theoklymenos' vision as a description of a solar eclipse, but proceeds to date it to 1178 B.C.

9. Wilamowitz, *Heimkehr*, p. 43, and *Der Glaube der Hellenen* (Berlin, 1931), vol. 2, p. 29.

10. In *Poetae Melici Graeci*, ed. D. Page (Oxford, 1962), references to swallows in Stesich. 211, Simon. 597, Carm. pop. 848, are all tokens of spring.

11. Though only two examples of the swallow's song of spring have survived, it was a type of song of wide dispersion and practice. See *Vitae Homeri et Hesiodi*, ed. U. von Wilamowitz-Moellendorff (Berlin, 1929), for parallels. See also Plut. *Thes.* 22; schol. Arist. *Equites* 720.

12. James G. Frazer, "Swallows in the House," *CR* 5(1891):1–3, a short but invaluable article for folk customs and ceremonies that elucidate the pattern of the *Odyssey*.

13. E. Meyer, "Homerische Parerga," *Hermes* 27(1892):359–380, is one scholar to see the importance of the connection between the *Odyssey* and the *Vita herodotea*. See particularly his pp. 376–377, where he argues that the *Vita* 33 indicates that Apollo's feast in the *Odyssey* falls on the *Noumenia*. On Apollo's new moon feast in the *Odyssey* see also George Thomson, "The Greek Calendar," *JHS* 63(1943):52–65, especially p. 57, n. 40, and Einar Gjerstad, "Lunar Months of Hesiod and Homer," *Opuscula Atheniensa I. Acta Instit. Athen. Regni Sueciae*, series 4 (Lund, 1953), pp. 187–194.

14. Franz Dirlmeier, *Die Vogelgestalt homerische Götter* (Heidelberg, 1967), p. 28, takes Athena's swallow shape here as her very self, "das heisst in ihrer eigentlichen Gestalt". . . .

15. Northrop Frye, *The Anatomy of Criticism* (Princeton, 1957), pp. 163ff., 182–183. Readers of Frye's pages on the mythos of comedy can find much of value for a structural understanding of the *Odyssey*. That the *Odyssey* conforms to the comic mode was recognized in antiquity. See Hermogenes, *Peri Heur.* 177–178, for a brief comparison of Homer with Menander, and Eustathius 1745.30.

16. Light and fire imagery play insistently around Odysseus as the poem approaches its peripety. Howard Clarke, *The Art of the Odyssey* (Prentice-Hall, 1967), pp. 73–75, notes such instances as Odysseus' adopted name *Aithon* ("Blazes") at 19.183, and the comparison of Odysseus to the bright sun in the simile at 22.384–389. We have here, however, not merely imagery or metaphor, but something so entirely physical as to be almost beyond the reach of our metaphysics. Odysseus, descending into his death with winter's decline of the sun, and emerging into life anew with the sun's spring ascent, so aligns the microwaves of his organism with the macrowaves of the sun that, when once in phase with the cosmos, he becomes the focus that gathers the sun's rays and directs them in one piercing beam on to the little island of Ithaka, to shed there its light, its warmth, and its restorative powers. Odysseus' brilliant bald pate at 18.354–355 is the focal lens for the sun's fierce intensity. Through that lens, in Odysseus' answer to Eurymachos' foolish jest, we glimpse the first signs of the change in the season (v. 367). . . .

17. The conjunction of sun and moon is a particularly propitious time for marriage. See Roscher's *Ausführl. Lexicon der griech. und Röm. Mythologie* (Leipzig, 1894–1897) vol. 2, pp. 3159ff., s.v. "Mondgöttin," for a discussion of the association of marriages with the new moon. See also Margarete Bieber, "Eros and Dionysos on Kerch Vases," *Hesperia*, suppl. 8(1949):31–38, on new-moon marriages. . . .

18. The significance of the calendrical indicators in the *Odyssey* was clear enough to such scholars as Wilamowitz, or Gilbert Murray who, in *The Rise of the Greek Epic*, 4th ed. (Oxford, 1934), pp. 201–212, connects Odysseus' return in the nineteenth year with the cycle of Meton's *Eikosieteris*, which was a coordination of solar and lunar cycles. . . .

19. Ludwig Radermacher, "Die Erzählungen der Odyssee," *Sitzungs-berichte d. Kaiserl. Akad. d. Wissenschaften in Wien, Phil.-hist. Kl.* 178(1915):32ff., considers briefly Penelope as a lunar figure, and her weaving and unraveling as the pattern of the waxing and waning moon. . . .

[The Tales Odysseus Told Alkinoos, and an Akkadian Seal]   E. A. S. Butterworth*

The story of Polyphemus, as Professor D. L. Page points out in *The Homeric Odyssey*,[1] is a tale which is widely spread over Europe and beyond. No less than 125 examples of it have been collected, of which few, if any, are derived from the *Odyssey*. However widely-spread a folk-tale may be, it would be quite wrong to assume that it originated in a mere-story-teller's fiction. There is a great deal more behind folk-tales than that, and the only point at which I should venture to differ from Professor Page (and other classical scholars) is at his view of Homer as simply a grand story-teller in the medium of epic poetry. It seems to me certain that the poet (or poets) of the *Odyssey* had a purpose in mind beyond that of telling the story of the epic itself.

The true nature of the Odyssean Cyclops has not, as far as I know, hitherto been recognised. Homer makes of the Cyclops an absurd and barbarous figure inhabiting the world of fairy-tale. This is not the place to set out the elaborate, and startlingly successful, attempt of the *Odyssey* to ridicule, disguise, and destroy a movement, or element, of the earlier world, which, originating in Asia, had apparently been active in Greece also in early times. It must however be said that the *Odyssey*, as we now have it, was a part of the educational, or propagandist, aspect of the Olympian revolution, which derived its immense scope and significance from the fact that it was in part a political and social movement.[2] Homer's treatment of the story of Polyphemus bears this out.

The Greek word [*kúklos*] from which "Cyclops" is formed, means a circle or wheel. The Sanskrit word *cakra* has the same meaning, as well as having its special sense of a bodily centre of concentration in the practice of yoga. In itself, this would not be a matter for comment, but when it is seen in the light of the truth about the Cyclopes, the degree of identity of meaning in the two words begins to arrest our attention. According to Hesiod[3] the Cyclopes gave thunder, lightning and the blazing "thunder-bolt" [*keraunós*] into the hands of Zeus. Apollodorus[4] says the same and adds[5] that Apollo slew them. They were therefore beings of some consequence and as victims of Apollo belong to the pre-Olympian world. . . . The thunderbolt of Zeus . . . is a symbol of ultimate reality, human consciousness and the natural universe which is still understood to-day in India and, until recently, was so in Tibet. The Cyclopes therefore are not barbarian monsters but are intimately connected with the conception of the *vajra*, as was the Cretan Zeus.

Homer, in the ninth book of the *Odyssey*, prefaces the account of Odysseus' visit to the Cyclops with that of the visit to the land of the Lotus-eaters, who eat flowers for their food. The Lotus-eaters were

*Reprinted from *The Tree at the Navel of the Earth*. (Berlin: Walter De Gruyter and Co., 1970), 172–84, by permission of the publisher.

apparently peaceable, even friendly, people,[6] who gave to the three companions whom Odysseus had sent to reconnoitre the land the fruit of the lotus to eat. "Whoever ate the honey-sweet fruit of the lotus no more wished to send back news or to return, but desired to remain there with the lotus-eating men, feeding on the lotus, and to think no more of returning." It is implied that they no longer wished to interest themselves in practical affairs or see their families. So too, as we have already remarked, did Calypso, daughter of baleful Atlas, in the first book of the *Odyssey* keep Odysseus on her island at the omphalos, the navel, of the sea; with soft and winning words she sought to bring him to forget his Ithacan home. To live isolated from the world, eating the honey-sweet lotus, as we shall see, is not here a description of indolence but of the monastic life of the contemplative yogi. The flowery food [*anthinon eidar*] of the lotus-eaters must have been ambrosia and nectar,[7] if, as will be suggested, we have to take "lotus" here in its sense of "blissful condition of ecstasy."

Odysseus compels his companions to return to the ship. They come to the land of the Cyclopes. The Cyclopes are arrogant and without laws [*athemiston*]. They take what heaven sends, neither planting nor ploughing; grain and the grape grow of themselves in abundance. They herd sheep and goats. They hold no councils nor courts, but dwell, each family by itself, in caves in the mountains. They are thus, as the *Odyssey* emphasizes, not a political group at all. The implication is, for the Greek hearer, that they are a primitive, uncivilised people, for Odysseus goes on to say that they build no ships in which to visit the cities of men, they use no ploughs, they do not exploit the abundance of their island. In this they closely resemble the Lotus-eaters. To another hearer than a Greek caught up in the Olympian revolution and, particularly, the Apolline movement, there are other ways of regarding this settlement of families: they had cut themselves off from politics and commerce to pursue, for some reason not yet explained, a life of independence and pastoral simplicity. For Odysseus, however, the dearest and trustiest of his comrades on this occasion was *Polites, Citizen* [*Od.* 10.224f].

We notice in passing that Odysseus likens the Cyclops to no "bread-eating man, but to a wooded peak standing up alone, apart from the others" [*Od.* 9.190ff]. One may speak of a "mountain of a man" in English, and Homer could have done much the same in Greek, but why the wooded top? A thick thatch of hair? Nothing in the text bears out so quaint a notion. We may ask, without answering our question, but remembering the association of the Cyclopes with the "thunderbolt," whether behind the curious simile lies the image of the tree, or grove, on the top of a mountain. . . . That foothills are commonly forested, and probably were so more commonly in ancient Greece than to-day, hardly explains the image.

When Odysseus sets out for the cave of the Cyclops he is careful to emphasize his veneration for Apollo and the favour shown him by Apollo's priest [*Od.* 9.197ff], but he tells us also that he took with him the twelve best [*aristous*] of his companions [*Od.* 9.195]. The account of the gift of wine by Apollo's priest, fifteen lines long, follows immediately on the statement that the hero had chosen his twelve "best" companions to go with him to visit the Cyclops. Elsewhere[8] I have drawn attention to the possible religious significance of the group of a leader and twelve followers, and here it is right to recall the twelve "rays" on the scarab from Gaza bearing the omphalos-signs or cakras linked by the channel of the *suṣumnā*. The suggestion was made[9] that the rays represented twelve disciples of the kilted man in the centre of the design. The original purpose of the visit to the Cyclops may then have been to make a pilgrimage to a spiritual leader. The length of the passage which describes the wine as a gift of Apollo's priest, following immediately, as it does, on that which mentions the choice of twelve companions, invites reflection: does Odysseus protest Apollo's patronage too strongly? After all, Apollo is said to have slain the Cyclopes: did Odysseus and his twelve companions originally come as friends of the Cyclopes, to Polyphemus as a master, or as emissaries of a political, Apolline, world, to destroy him? Alkinoos tells us that the Cyclopes, like the Phaeacians and the Giants, were known for the closeness of their relationship to the gods [*Od.* 7.201ff]. Cyclops says that he has no fear of the gods; he thinks nothing of aegis-bearing Zeus [*Od.* 9.273ff], and the blessed gods, for the Cyclopes are stronger. If one considers carefully the implications of these statements, and the original possession by the Cyclopes of the "thunderbolt" with the *bindu*, or point of the Void, which is the source of the universe, at its centre, one must surely come to the conclusion that the Cyclopes held a distinctive doctrine about things spiritual. If we may argue from the *bindu*, in which the knowing subject in the act of awareness and the generation of the universe are equated, it made no distinction between the central essence of human nature and ultimate reality itself.[10] A man was therefore potentially "divine." Man himself is capable of attaining liberation from birth and death, of knowing immortality. There is no world of "gods" separate in kind from the world of men. The Olympian religion however made precisely this division of the universe between Gods and men. To the ignorant its denial might appear as arrogance. The sin of Tantalus was that he taught his followers the mysteries of the gods and shared with them the divine ambrosia.

I know of no possible explanation of the "eye" in the forehead of the Cyclops if is it not the Ājñā-cakra of a form of yoga. Yoga is often practised against the background of the Advaita doctrine, and issues, as we saw in the last chapter, in a regenerate or "enlightened" man. Odysseus, as I suggest, in grinding out the "third eye," shows, in our *Odyssey*, his antagonism to any such view of man. We have already raised the question whether, in the source from which Homer drew the elements of the story, Odysseus was a foe of the Cyclops or a visitor in quest of enlightenment. We shall not attempt to answer it, but must draw attention instead to the real significance of Odysseus' naming of himself as "No man" in his answer to the stupefied Cyclops. To name oneself "No Man" or "Nobody" is something that needs explanation in itself, quite apart from the consequence of the lie for the Cyclops.

We have spoken of the tradition that the Cyclopes were the original possessors of the "thunderbolt" of Zeus, and have just reminded ourselves that the centre of the thunderbolt was a representation of the Void which was at once the Self and the potential world as an object of consciousness. It is not known how far back this conception reaches into the past of Indian spiritual thinking: it is found in Buddhist tradition, but much that is emphasized in Buddhism has its origin in earlier doctrines. Sunya, the Void, as we have seen, is an integral part of Indian doctrines associated with yoga.

. . . The enlightened man is aware that his nature is not his own: "Even and upright his mind abides nowhere."[11] Such then are the consequences of the doctrine of the Void, which is symbolised by the centre of the Cyclopean "thunderbolt." However improbable it may seem at first sight, this is the ultimate significance of the [keraunos]. The myth of the Cretan Zeus and Hellenistic representations of the thunderbolt both point to a common source with the Indian tradition. Mrs. David-Neel likewise tells us in *Initiations and Initiates in Tibet* that the Lamaist mystics of Tibet deny the existence of an ego.[12]

This then is the meaning of Odysseus' reply to the Cyclops' enquiry after his name: he is No-man [*Oûtis*] for no man [*oûtis*], as the Cyclops well knows, has an identity that can be seized and maintained through time by a word or name. It is mockery of the Cyclopean doctrine of what is real, and the torment of the Cyclops at the hands of Odysseus may be seen as something like Dr. Johnson's rebuttal of Berkeleyan idealism. It may be tentatively suggested that the cannibalism so surprisingly attributed to this solitary shepherd, in that he devoured the companions of Odysseus, is a brutalised rendering of the methods by which the Cyclopes destroyed in their disciples the conviction of a continuous individual identity. If we may judge by the traditions of the Zen school of Buddhism, these may have included paradox, nonsensical problems, psychological shock or even a blow if its meaning could be conveyed with it. A ruthless concentration and a "fierce technique," "scornful of the usual apparatus of religion"[13] certainly marks that school, and the stories of Bodhidharma make it probable that at one time they characterised the Indian circles from which he came. Esoteric Lamaist masters similarly make very severe demands upon their disciples, which in legend (but only in legend) may include their deaths.[14]

If the symbol of the Void was known in the traditions about the Cretan Zeus,[15] and the *cakras* were represented on the scarab of the earlier second millennium B.C. found at Gaza, the possibility of the reflection of such doctrines in our *Odyssey* is clearly to be taken seriously. Nor can the [*koanon*] of the three-eyed Zeus at Argos be overlooked, a deity who may, as we have remarked, be equated with the Danaid Chrysaoreus, and, if so, was as much Poseidon as Zeus. This reflection of doctrines and practice becomes the more probable if they met with antagonism in the Greek world, as they seem to have done when the political current that bore the cult of Olympian Zeus and Apollo with it started to flow in strength.

The Cyclops' lord is not Zeus but Poseidon, whose trident, like those of Śiva and of Asiatic shamans, is, as I have sought to show elsewhere,[16] a mark of superhuman powers associated with ecstasy. Poseidon is not a ruler of gods and men, like Olympian Zeus: he is not a political deity but a figure of the powers which may become accessible to man. It is this that explains the gigantic stature of Polyphemus. The Cyclops is [*pelórios*], he is like a mountain-peak standing up alone among the hills. Odysseus overcomes him, not by main force but by low cunning, [*dólō*], when he stupefies him with wine. It is in the structure of thought that lies behind the ascetic practice of yoga, which is the true source of the Odyssean figure of the Cyclops, that the reason is to be found for the presentation of Polyphemus as a man of enormous size.

In the earlier stages of yoga the novice yogi aims at transforming the fragmented chaos of psychophysiological life into a cosmos.[17] The goal is autonomy, and the method of achieving it involves control of the breath. Through this controlled breathing and the accompanying bodily postures and acts of mental concentration, the yogi acquires his own centre; his blind participation in the becoming and passing away of the universe is suspended. He becomes a universe in himself, his centre an adamantine axis which is assimilated to the axis of the world, which is the Tree of Life. "Exactly as Indra, who personifies the axis of the Universe, separates day from night, the Earth from the Sky, and makes the Cosmos 'be' — so does the unified breath play its part as the pillar of the human body."[18] The breaths are identified with the cosmic winds, correspondences to sun and moon are found in the body of the yogi. The spinal column is equated with Mount Meru, the cosmic axis.[19] This is, to be sure, only an intermediate stage in the development of the yogi: in the final stage of liberation, he withdraws from the cosmos, becoming autonomous and free. During this intermediate stage, however, man is, as Eliade puts it, recast "in new, gigantic dimensions," he becomes a "macranthropos." It was for this reason, I suggest, that Polyphemus stood up alone like a mountain-peak among the hills. . . .

The sequence of tales told by Odysseus in the hall of Alkinoos and Arete, from that of the Lotus-eaters to the disaster of the herd of Helios, is . . . a series of scenes illustrating different aspects of an ecstatic discipline which sometimes appears to be shamanist, sometimes to be drawn from the practice, doctrine and imagery of yoga. . . . Yoga and shamanism have in fact both points of contact and differences.[20] The *Odyssey* is in no way sympathetic to either discipline, the eastern origins of which seem to be certain. Homer was committed to the Olympian revolution and to a political world. . . .

Notes

1. Oxford (1955, corrected London and Beccles 1966), p. 3.

2. One aspect of this in the *Odyssey* has been set out in Chapter III of *Some Traces of the Pre-Olympian World in Greek Literature and Myth* (Berlin, 1966).

3. *Theog.*, 501–6.

4. 1.2.1. and 3.10.4.

5. 3.10.4.

6. 9.92 f.

7. It is worth noticing that the fruits on long stalks held by the goddess seated under the fruit-bearing tree of life on the gold ring found by Schliemann at Mycenae (Pl. XXII [b]) are not, as is commonly held, poppy-heads but the seed-heads of *Nymphaea lotos*, or a closely-related species, as anyone who takes the trouble to visit a botanical garden can see for himself.

8. [*Some Traces* etc., p. 130, n. 70.]

9. [Ibid., p. 167.]

10. [Ibid., p. 170.]

11. [Christmas Humphreys, *Buddhism* (3rd. Ed., Harmondsworth, 1962), p. 186.]

12. 2nd. Edition, English transl. (London, 1958), p. 19. *Cf.* p. 198.

13. Humphreys, *op. cit.*, p. 179.

14. Alexandra David-Neel, *op. cit.*, pp. 53 f. See also W. Y. Evans-Wentz, *Tibet's Great Yogi, Milarepa* (O. U. P. paperback, 1969, reproducing 2nd. Ed. of 1951), p. 107.

15. See pp. 129–32.

16. *Some Traces* etc., pp. 149–53 with plates III–XV.

17. Eliade, *Yoga*, p. 97.

18. M. Eliade, "Cosmical Homology and Yoga" in *The Journal of the Indian Society of Oriental Art*, V (1937), p. 192.

19. Eliade, *Yoga*, p. 235. See also the passage from the *Corpus Hermeticum* (XI. 20) cited by R. Reitzenstein, *Di hellenistischen Mysterienreligionen*, 3rd. Ed., p. 167.

20. See Eliade, *Yoga*, pp. 311–41.

The *Odyssey* and
Primitive Religion

Richard J. Sommer*

"Men die because they cannot join the beginning to the end."
— Alcmeon of Croton

This essay. . . . will attempt a reading of the [*Odyssey*] which may account for the existence of the many demonstrable parallels between episodes in the [poem] and features of primitive religious belief and practice. It will suggest that these episodes and their corresponding cultic features did not find their way into the poem by sheer chance; that they bear coherent relations to one another which can be adequately explained only by reference to the religions of a Mediterranean world anterior to the composition of the *Odyssey*. The parallels cannot be ignored, and although few of the questions they raise can be permanently settled, the suggestions made here may provide a unifying hypothesis for further interpretation.

Let us begin *in medias res*. Despite the greatness of Odysseus's achievement in visiting and returning from the Grove of Persephone as a mortal and yet-living man, and despite the fact that all the rest of his adventures group themselves with a startling symmetry around this central point in the epic,[1] the episode in Book XI remains curiously diffuse and non-climactic. Homer's Circe explains it as a necessary visit — which it is not[2] — to obtain Teiresias's prophecy, yet this office is fulfilled almost immediately, leaving three-quarters of the book to trail along as best they can. Extraordinary resemblances have been demonstrated at various points between the *Odyssey* and the Assyrian-Babylonian *Gilgamish Epic*, and the climax in the corresponding section of the earlier poem seems to fall on a revealed truth[3] closely equivalent to Achilles' famous "I would rather be plowman to a yeoman farmer on a small holding than lord paramount in the kingdom of the dead."[4] Yet with equal ease and more immediate purpose, we may concentrate our attention upon another encounter which takes up more lines than those with either Teiresias or Achilles, the meeting between Odysseus and Agamemnon which takes place after the so-called Catalogue of Heroines.[5] The appearance of Agamemnon climaxes a series of references in the early books of the *Odyssey* to his murder by Aegisthous and Clytemnestra, the former his usurper and member of a rival branch of the same family,[6] the latter Agamemnon's wife and first cousin to Penelope.[7] Athena herself first refers to the murder in Book I, and calls the attention of Telemachus to the admirable example set for him by Orestes, Agamemnon's avenging son. Nestor tells the story again (Bk. III) in somewhat more detail, and again

*Reprinted from *The Odyssey and Primitive Religion* (Oslo: Norwegian Universities Press, 1962), 4–36, by permission of the publisher.

the parallel is drawn between Orestes and Telemachus. Finally Menelaus gives a longer version (Bk. IV) told to him by Proteus, the Old Man of the Sea, who had directly followed this disclosure with news of Odysseus's imprisonment. The indication is, then, that the fate of Agamemnon is comparable to that of Odysseus and that the poet has deliberately introduced the terms of the comparison.

Nor can there be much serious question any longer that the story of Agamemnon's death originally referred to a ritual event, probably repeated at regular intervals, or to a radical change in the character of that event worthy of being recorded in the mythological annals of the tribe. Elements of the plot are familiar enough to the anthropologist who does not insist on looking the other way: the old king is disposed of by his queen and an outsider who takes the throne to rule by matrilinear right; the avenger, however, is the son of the old king, claiming patrilinear right to the crown. It is significant, in my opinion, that the *Odyssey* relates only this much of the story, and makes no mention of the punishment for matricide exacted from Orestes by the Erinnyes; like the Roman king Tarquin the Proud, this young rebel did not escape from the certainly older matrilinear order scot-free, though the *Eumenides* of Aeschylus makes it quite clear that his insurrection, approved (and this is worth remembering) by Athena, was to have been ultimately successful.

In this light the conversation between Odysseus and Agamemnon takes on new meaning. The parallel existing between them is strengthened, particularly when Agamemnon, understandably vehement, warns Odysseus: "Never be too kind even to your wife. Never tell her all you have in your mind; you may tell something, but keep something to yourself. However, *you* will not be murdered by your wife, Odysseus. She is full of intelligence, and her heart is sound, your prudent and modest Penelopeia."[8] Penelope is never in the *Odyssey* obtrusively other than this, yet Agamemnon has raised the question, and proceeds to deepen the shadow he has cast upon her integrity by advising Odysseus to bring his ship to the shore of his native land secretly, not openly, "for there is no longer any faith in women."[9]

Let us stop for a moment and see in exactly what terms the situations of Agamemnon and Odysseus are parallel. Both are kings. One has been murdered — clad in special robe, Aeschylus tells us, and killed by his wife and usurper-successor at the sacrificial altar he had approached on a crimson carpet designed, we are informed, for the tread of gods, not men.[10] The other is in danger of such a death at the hands, perhaps of his wife, and certainly of men who aspire to the kingship of Ithaca by marriage to her.[11] Agamemnon fought nine years at Troy and returned home in the tenth. Following this, Odysseus wandered for nine years and in the tenth year (the twentieth year all told) is returning to face the same crisis. This is the setting of his epic triumph. What remains for us is to establish the character of that triumph, for which we must turn to other quarters.

The forces that converge upon Odysseus's victory and dictate its nature have their beginnings so far back in the pre-history of Eurasian primitive culture that they will never be open to more than educated speculation. A few things we can be relatively sure of, the first being that in Eurasia generally, the first religions centered about a Goddess rather than a god,[12] and the reason of that worship was to promote the fertility, which the Goddess embodied, of fields and flocks and the tribe. Several writers have insisted that the eminence of the female deity in this early age reflects a similar state of affairs in the structure of the primitive societies, that, in short, matriarchy preceded partriarchy in the general development of man. There are no certain answers to this hypothesis, however, and its truth or falsity is much less important for our present purposes than our recognition of the force of the evidence upon which the theory has been grounded. Whether women in ancient Eurasia were in positions of political, social, economic power over their men-folk or not, it cannot be disputed that they were numinal centers, with their strange discharges of blood, and mysterious creative powers, for the magical and religious attention of the tribe. Women were objects of veneration and fear, sources of life—and of death as well. In the early stages the Goddess, as a projection of this numinal power, seems to have reigned alone. Later, perhaps when the role of the male in producing children had been recognized and cultic practice had been adjusted to accommodate the fact, a consort God appears at the side of the Goddess and shares a portion of her prestige, suffering seasonal death and rebirth under the loving and deadly shadow of his powerful protectress.[13] This associaton provides the pattern for the relationships of Athena, Hera, and Aphrodite, among many others, to Odysseus, Jason, and Paris.[14] The festivals of the religious pattern involved center about a "mimic marriage of the powers of vegetation"[15]—the Goddess and God, emergent from a sacred tribal queen and her chosen king—designed to increase by imitating the fertility of flocks and crops. It has been suggested that Odysseus shows marks of having at one stage in the development of his story been one of these Dying Gods or, as Thomson suggests, a solar Year-Spirit, an Eniautos-Daimon associated with Hermes or Poseidon Hippios or with Helios,[16] who is "thought to die and come to life again, or to be obscured for a season only to reappear in renewed splendour."[17] As Thomson explains, "Eniautos means, not so much a measured space of time, as the completed cycle of the seasons, at the moment of its completion."[18] This Daimon, then, is more in the nature of a regularly recurring "momentary deity," to use a phrase promulgated by Cassirer, a god who becomes real at certain critical junctures in the primitive calendar, who gains a sudden though regular importance in what we know as "rituals of passage." The adventures of

Odysseus, occurring as they do in sudden episodic concentration with only the most perfunctory attention paid to interstitial time-lapses, show marked resemblance to this pattern. Aside from the obvious fact, however, that the Homeric Odysseus is not a god but a human being and emphatically says as much several times in the course of the epic,[19] his simple identification with the dying Eniautos Daimon raises certain immediate difficulties, since Odysseus does not die in the poem and is not absent for a single seasonal cycle but for twenty . . . and the pattern by itself, distinct from the Homeric energy and cast of opinion exerted upon it, is not sufficient to explain the full scope of the story's final form.

The most curious and significant feature of the worship of the Goddess and her consort appears to have been a cultic practice parallel to the death of the God: in so far as he was considered a deity or embodied divine characteristics, the sacred king of the tribe was ritually murdered — whether in actuality or effigy may scarcely now be distinguished — or deposed when his powers began to fail.[20] Frazer himself, whose work on this savage rite remains the most exhaustive, should be allowed to explain the reasons for it:

> People feared that if they allowed the man-god to die of sickness or old age, his divine spirit might share the weakness of its bodily tabernacle, or perhaps perish altogether, thereby entailing the most serious dangers on the whole body of his worshippers who looked to him as their stay and support. Whereas, by putting him to death while he was yet in full vigour of body and mind they hoped to catch his sacred spirit uncorrupted by decay and to transfer it in that state to his successor. Hence it has been customary in some countries, first, to require that kings should be of unblemished body and unimpaired mind, and second, to kill them as soon as they begin to break up through age and infirmity. A more stringent application of these principles led in other places to a practice of allowing the divine king or human god to live and reign only for a fixed period, after which he was inexorably put to death. The time of grace granted to limited monarchs of this sort has varied from several years to one year or even less.[21]

Fragmentary evidence for the existence of this practice through many parts of the Mediterranean area is much too frequently met and too complicated in its reconstruction to make citation practicable. Yet we may, for example, simply ask as Stanford does,[22] under what circumstances Odysseus's father Laertes retreated into an agrarian isolation tantamount to deposition or exile, leaving his son to reign alone. Homer does not explain.

Other incidents in the *Odyssey* likewise display a curiously disjointed resemblance to the dangerous reign of the sacred king. The boar, for instance, seems to have been seen as the Dying God's enemy and killer, both in the Mediterranean region and to the east.[23] Adonis was killed by a boar, as were Tammuz, perhaps the Zeus of Crete, Arcadian Ancacus,

Lydian Carmanor, and the hero of Irish epic, Diarmuid.[24] Similarly, the Egyptian god Seth was out hunting wild boars when he found the body of his enemy-brother Osiris and tore it into fourteen pieces, and later he fought Osiris's son Horus in the guise of a black pig.[25] In the *Nekyia*, Agamemnon describes his and his comrades' murder as the slaughter of "white-toothed swine" (Bk. XI, 413ff) at a marriage feast, thus reversing the situation; then, in Book XIX of the *Odyssey*, we are told how Odysseus happens to have a scar on his leg: he received it as a boy from the tusk of a wild boar while hunting with his maternal grandfather Autolycus. The importance of the incident lies not so much in the fact that it follows the ritual pattern,[26] but rather that Odysseus *escapes* the fury of what may well have been a holy killer.

We should keep in mind as we explore the implications of another story about Odysseus's last years which Homer does not mention at all, and ask whether his silence is merely due to ignorance of the incident, or whether the poet expurgated it from his work on grounds of unsuitability, as he did frequently. The story is contained in the lost *Telegoneia* of Eugammon, a minor epic poem of which a short résumé by Proclus remains, as follows:

> After the burial of the suitors Ulysses sacrifices to the nymphs and then goes to visit his herds in Elis, where he is entertained by Polyxenus. The stories of Trophonios, Agamede [sic], and Augeas are related. After returning to Ithaca to perform the sacrifices prescribed by Teiresias, Ulysses goes to the country of the Thesprotians, marries their queen Callidice, and leads them in a war against the Brygi, in which Ares takes part on behalf of the Brygi, and Athene for Ulysses, while Apollo intervenes as a mediator. On the death of Callidice, Polypoetes, son of Ulysses, becomes king, and Ulysses returns to Ithaca: then Telegonus son of Ulysses by Circe, who had been seeking for his father, makes a descent upon Ithaca. Ulysses comes to repel the attack and is killed by his own son. Telegonus finds too late what he has done, and takes his father's body, with Telemachus and Penelope, to his mother Circe, who makes them immortal. Finally, Telemachus marries Circe, and Telegonus Penelope.[27]

So much for Teiresias's prophecy that "from the sea shall thine own death come, the gentlest death that may be, which shall end thee foredone with smooth old age, and the folk shall dwell happily around thee."[28] Assuming for the *Telegoneia* story a genuinely ancient source, Homer's omission of any reference to the details it relates is perfectly understandable: he would not tolerate the murder of a hero by his son nor the placid matrimonial tangle which terminates the minor poem.[29] We may note a tradition supposed to have been voiced, among other places,[30] in Aeschylus's lost *Psychagogi*, to the effect that Telegonus kills Odysseus with the poison spear of a sting-ray.[31] If this was one of the ritual forms of the sacred king's murder,[32] we would have reasonable grounds for assuming that the death

Odysseus undergoes in this version is a cultic one. Homer mentions it not at all, and substitutes a suspiciously similar and harmless "gentle death from the sea." And he similarly disregards alternative and current traditions which claim that all or some of the suitors shared Penelope's affections with Odysseus,[33] and that she made love to Apollo or bore Arcadian Pan to Hermes.[34] The only remains of these anecdotes in Homer are an awkwardly explained incident in Book XVIII in which Penelope is prompted by Athena "to show herself to the wooers, that she might make their heart all flutter with hope, and that she might win yet more worship from her lord and her son than heretofore,"[35] and the general situation of many men living in a house with one woman which is reminiscent of a polyandrical household.[36] Homer seems to have transferred the faithlessness attributed to Penelope to the twelve maids[37] — among them the most noticeable reversed image of Penelope herself, ungrateful Melantho, lover of Eurymachus, whom Telemachus hangs as penalty for having "gone the way of shame."[38]

A definite pattern to these Homeric omissions and modifications emerges, a pattern which becomes clearer if we accept, with certain qualifications, the thesis that the Homeric epics "were composed for a race with patriarchal institutions out of materials derived from an older matrilinear society."[39] Once again, we cannot emphasize strongly enough that what is meant is exactly a "matrilinear" organization, for which evidence is plentiful enough in Greece and surrounding areas in the early stages of Mediterranean culture,[40] and not "matriarchal," for which very little satisfactory evidence can be found. Reckoning of descent through the female line is common enough in peoples with a recent or incomplete grasp of the concept of paternity, and it is easy to see why among such peoples the woman remains the mysterious and dangerous center of the tribe's ritual activity: she is the sole link between the successive generations and the sole source of life to all. The sacred danger of Woman haunted Greece throughout her greatest age, a fact to which Aeschylus's play *The Eumenides* stands ready witness, and in no matter how depressed a status the Greek maintained his women, behind all his restrictions upon them, whether in the seventh century or in the fifth, lay a primitive terror of their sacred power. Every attempt to deny this power was made, including, if we may judge by *The Eumenides*, the denial to the woman of any role of consequence in the act of generation, and of any claim to representing a vital link between grandfather and father and son. Nothing, in this repressive mood, could seem more dangerous or disreputable than the reminiscences of the ritual murder of a king who was quickly replaced by another, in marriage to a queen whose permanent cultic regency would not have been questioned. That the male should enact the short life and fleeting of a changeable Dying God, that a female should remain after the dreadful murder to reign again, perhaps even participate in it, was a condition intolerable to the Greek consciousness, and the vital core of

Greek literature was formed under this intolerance half-cognizant of its origins. The Homeric epics, the aristocratic "literature of chieftains, alien to low popular superstition,"[41] share — in so far as the materials could be purged of their ancient confusion and blood[42] — this patriarchal vehemence,[43] and the all-embracing theme (Book XIV) of the *Odyssey* is whether or not "the race of godlike Arceisius [Odysseus's paternal grandfather] may perish nameless out of Ithaca."[44]

Before we pass on to an examination of the major episodes of Odysseus's travels, we should observe the framework into which they are set. First of all, the *Odyssey* is concerned with not one journey, but two: Books I–IV are largely devoted to Telemachus's increasing awareness of his inadequacy to deal with the situation in Ithaca without his father, and to his journey outward to find Odysseus or receive word of him. James Joyce seems to have been unusually sensitive to this aspect of the poem, since in *Ulysses* almost equal weight is given to each of the two principal characters, Stephen and Bloom, and the real climax of the novel occurs in their meeting, in the father-son society which they create between themselves. Secondly, Telemachus is the first member of Odysseus's family to greet Odysseus (Book XVI) upon his return to Ithaca, and plays a major role in his revenge upon the suitors. Thirdly, the last book of the poem deals with the reunion of Odysseus and his father Laertes, who is convinced of his son's identity when Odysseus shows him the scar of the boar-wound on his leg; the book ends with the three of them, grandfather, father, and son, standing side by side to defend "the race of godlike Arceisius" against those who have come to avenge the suitor's death.[45] And upon Athena's prompting, Laertes is first to cast his spear and kill his man. Odysseus has been the missing link in the patrilinear descent; both his son and father are helpless without him. Now, with his survival and return, the dynastic honor is joyfully restored, Telemachus comes into his manly strength, and sufficient virile power returns to old Laertes to drive a spear through a man's armor and body and out the other side. The triumph of a poem and way of life are bloodily complete.[46]

It remains for us to show how Odysseus's survival — the episodic "fairy-tale wanderings," as Finley puts it — relates to this patriarchal triumph. In explanation, we may refer to Robert Graves' summary account: he sees in Odysseus a rebellious sacred king who refused to be murdered and replaced by another consort for the queen. "Lotus-land, the cavern of the Cyclops, the harbour of Telepylus, Persephone's Grove, Siren Land, Ogygia, Scylla and Charybdis, the Depths of the Sea, even the Bay of Phoreys — all are different metaphors for the death which he evaded."[47] With some allowance for Graves' habitual overstatement of a case, this is true, though, as in the adventure in the cavern of Polyphemus, the ritual from which any episode derives may be comparable to the others only in the more general features common to the vast majority of Mediterranean cultic practices. What will mainly concern us in each case is that it show the marks of the critical juncture of a ritual cycle, a rite of passage; that it show a possibility of death and a consequent rebirth; that Odysseus's commendable aim is to enjoy the revivifying effects of each episode without suffering the concomitant crudities; and that, in each case but one, the thematic connection of these adventures with Odysseus's final trial against the suitors for re-marriage to Penelope is strengthened by the appearance of a threatening female figure strongly associated with the more obviously ritualistic elements in the story. . . .[48]

. . .

After their two-fold encounter with Aeolus in Book X, the mariners sail into the harbor of Telepylus, land of the Laestrygonians. Here again Odysseus's mariners bear the brunt of the disastrous adventure in what, as in the cave of Polyphemus, appear to be substitute sacrifices for Odysseus himself. One of them Antiphates snatches up immediately, and in the attack which he organizes, all but one of the twelve ships — the usual number for sacrifices[49] — are demolished, and in this one Odysseus escapes. The episode is curtly related, and only two small features need further interest us. One is the fact that the first person the exploring mariners meet on shore who gives them any notion of the great size of the Laestrygonians in general, is not the daughter of Antiphates who directs them to the palace, and whose bulk occasions no comment whatever, but Antiphates' wife whom they meet inside the house: "she was huge of bulk as a mountain peak and was loathly in their sight."[50] Only after seeing her with this curious immediate hatred, do the mariners describe any of the Laestrygonians as gigantic. Her tremendous stature provides slim pickings for the traditional view that Telepylus is the Land of the Midnight Sun, its inhabitants tall Nordic fjord-dwellers,[51] and we should remember that size in primitive representations, as in Indian, Greek, Egyptian, and medieval European art, is often governed by religious or political importance of the figure represented. The Ithacans meet Antiphates' queen *inside* the palace, and after calling her husband she takes no further part in the action; it is not impossible that she was originally the ubiquitous Goddess herself, in a barbarian and terrible form, and that Homer's humanizing tendency transformed idol and temple into queen and palace. The second feature to be noted is that the introduction of the mariners to the Laestrygonians grotesquely foreshadows the arrival of Odysseus among the Phaeacians: they are met by the king's daughter, corresponding to Nausicaa, near the shore; by each girl's help, the respective travellers arrive at the palace; and in each case the first and most imposing figure to be met is the queen. The two receptions are very different, to be sure, and except for the juxtaposition of stone-throwing incidents in each case with the departure of ships . . . the stories from that point on are decidedly divergent; but is it not possible that in these episodes we detect two differing aspects of the same or kindred ritual patterns? In any case, the first person in Telepylus to threaten the adventurers is huge, female, and inspires an immediate hatred or terror in them for which Homer gives no reasons.[52]

The visit to Circe, which follows, displays far more clearly the characteristic elements of the ritual struggle which we have claimed to be the dominant theme of the *Odyssey*. It has been convincingly argued that Circe herself is a minor solar goddess of the general type of Ishtar, the alternately cruel or beneficent courtesan-divinity of oriental origin.[53] She changes Odysseus's mariners into nine-year-old swine; we have already noted the part played by the boar in sacrificial ritual, and in addition may observe that swine played an important role in the Thesmophories, festival of the Athenian cult of Demeter, and in the Eleusian Mysteries,[54] in both places serving evidently as emblems of fertility. Because of the isolation of Circe's dwelling,[55] the transformed animals surrounding it, the singing, and the chalice shared by all, as well as the subsequent details of the metamorphosis and rescue, Germain argues that the cultic origin of the episode lies in a ceremony of initiation.[56] At some stage in its development this may likely have been the case, yet the narrative is internally discontinuous enough to suggest a multiple origin, and in the account of Odysseus's rescue of his men (with which neither Germain nor Carpenter deal at any length) the story shows strong liaisons with the seasonal fertility-ritual of the type we have described. Let us attend closely to the sequence of events in this rescue, the importance of which may be measured by the fact that it is the first encounter of Odysseus himself with the goddess. The hero starts out and is intercepted by Hermes, who gives him the magic herb *moly* and tells him exactly how to protect himself from Circe's enchantments. We have already noticed that Hermes, perhaps as a double of Odysseus,[57] was reputed a lover of the faithful Penelope[58] whom he visited — interestingly enough in view of the Polyphemus episode — in the form of a ram.[59] In addition, his was a very ancient divinity[60] following the general type of the Eniautos-Daimon[61], and he was represented by a crude stone phallus guarding every doorstep in Athens, assuring fertility to those within the house.[62] In this capacity and when the phallic Herm guarded a tomb, he represented the chthonic "power that generates new lives, or, in the ancient conception, brings the souls back to be born again."[63] Yet when he appears to aid Odysseus, it is in the far different form of the beautiful anthropomorphic god of the Homeric pantheon, thoroughly assimilated to the spirit of a patriarchal Olympus, and the help he gives Odysseus is in full accord with his transformation.

Odysseus proceeds to Circe's dwelling. There she offers him a golden cup[64] containing the charmed potion and, according to his instructions, Odysseus drinks it without harm. When Circe taps him with her wand, he draws his sword and rushes at her as though he intended to kill her. She clasps his knees in supplication and in the same breath, asks him to put his sword in its sheath and to lie with her.[65] He agrees — and this, too, is by

Hermes' instruction — only after her solemn oath not to harm him when he is stript, because otherwise, as Hermes has warned him, "she may unman you and make you a weakling."[66]

These details show a curiously disjointed resemblance to the fertility symbols of chalice, lance, and sword made familiar to us by Miss Jessie L. Weston's famous study of the Holy Grail legends, *From Ritual to Romance*.

> Lance and Cup (or Vase) were in truth connected together in a symbolic relation long ages before the institution of Christianity . . . They are sex symbols of immemorial antiquity and world-wide diffusion, the Lance, or Spear, representing the Male, the Cup, or Vase, the Female, reproductive energy.
>
> Found in juxtaposition, the Spear upright in the Vase . . . their signification is admitted by all familiar with "Life" symbolism, and they are absolutely in place as forming part of a ritual dealing with the processes of life and reproductive vitality.[67]

Miss Weston then devotes a full chapter to the sword (which figures again in the evocation of ghosts in Persephone's Grove, and in the encounter with Scylla), used as a similar emblem of male virility in the fertility ritual of the sacred king or Dying God throughout Europe, Asia Minor, and India.

Yet Homer's use of these sacred objects — if we may identify them as such — represents a highly significant deviation from the ritual. He has separated the cup and the sword, ordinarily found together, and has placed them in the respective hands of the two protagonists, one female, the other male, as potential weapons.[68] The sword of Odysseus triumphs, and he then agrees to lie with the goddess only if she promises not to emasculate him — for that is the only meaning the passage and word [*anánora*] can reasonably yield. The highly appropriate death-wound given to the god and sacred king who embodied the principle of fertility and were destroyed when it waned, would frequently have been that of castration,[69] for which we find an historical counterpart in the self-emasculation practiced by the priests of Cybele in imitation of her divine consort Attis.[70] In later expurgated accounts of this sacred death, the wound would of course be transferred to other parts of the body, hence the scar on Odysseus's leg from a boar's tusk, referred to above.

If this is not sufficient indication of a methodically distorted basis for the Homeric story in a ritual of the general pattern with which we are concerned, we may notice further that when the mariners are restored from their shapes of nine-year-old swine, they become "men again, younger than they were before, and far comelier and taller to look upon."[71] Not only does Circe return them to their original condition, but she makes them younger as well, and this rejuvenation, we may suspect, is directly relatable both to the pattern of the original ritual whatever it may have been, and to the Homeric rearrangement of its details. Not only does Odysseus triumph over the tyrannical rite, but he makes use of its restorative magic as well, on his own terms. We need not suppose that Homer understood the meaning of the scene, or any of the others supplied him by tradition, *as ritual*; the chances are slim, in fact, that he could have comprehended directly the foundation in cultic practice of the material which he altered. It is very difficult for us to realize the unitary response ancient man must have made toward his experience. Ritual supplied to him a certain very limited number of *formulations* of human or anthropomorphic divine behavior, with which he could interpret his experience. The species of myth which we know, from present-day savage parallels[72] to have been recited simultaneously with the cultic performance as corroboration and substantiation for it, provided the first verbal reinforcements of these formulations. Yet ancient man, unlike us, could hardly have confined them — the image of the Dying God and his death among them — to a "religious" area of experience separated from a "secular" verbal tradition. Orally transmitted legends would have burgeoned in secondary growth far beyond the limits of specific ritual performance or its accompanying recitation,[73] yet a glance at the body of Eurasian mythology is sufficient to show that it is largely tied down to variations upon a few basic formulations with demonstrable parallels in ritual practice. This secondary growth of myth is speculative: each variation upon the ritually-oriented original pattern is a violation and an adventure in thinking beyond the limits of the collective tribal consciousness. The image of the Dying God is an assertion of that collective awareness, and Homer's Odysseus is a violation of it. What makes Homer's speculative deviation so remarkable is that it is repeated with fair consistency within the epic, and that the issue of *deviation itself* is integrated, as more obviously in the *Iliad*, into the vital center of the poem's action. Odysseus insists upon living as a man, not dying into divinity, with all that that insistence implies of an individual consciousness emergent from the confines of collective understanding.

The adventurers stay on Circe's island for a year, "for the full circle of a year . . . and the seasons returned as the months waned, and the long days came in their course,"[74] according to the ritual calendar, in other words, up to the season when it would be time for Odysseus's ordeal to be repeated.[75] Comparisons of the *Odyssey* at this point with Gilgamish's descent into the underworld appear to indicate that the Shiduri-Circe figure was, from the beginning, closely related to the hero's adventure in the land of the dead: 'the two goddesses each respectively advise the heroes at the moment of this enterprize.'[76] Therefore it should not afford us much surprise to find Circe prescribing a voyage to Persephone's Grove as the occasion of his next ritual trial, particularly since such a visit was — as instanced in those of Dionysus, Theseus, and Heracles[77] — "an essential scene in the drama of the Eniautos-Daimon"[78] and his counterpart, the sacred king. Having met Agamemnon and returned to the island of Circe, who greets the mariners properly as "men overbold, who have gone alive into the house of Hades, to know death twice, while all men else die once for all,"[79] they are ready for their next ordeal, the Sirens. However little we may know concerning these enigmatic creatures, they appear to take their place in our pattern. Their name is closely related to that of the wild bee or wasp,[80] and priestesses of various goddess-cults — particularly those of Demeter and Persephone, and Artemis of Ephesus — were frequently identified with this insect.[81] Phrygian Cybele was worshipped as a queen-bee, her priests practising self-emasculation as her drones; Aphrodite loved the unfortunate Anchises on Mount Ida while they were surrounded by a swarm of bees, and there is said to have been a golden honey-comb displayed at the goddess's shrine on Mount Eryx, reputedly the gift of Daedalus.[82] The bee also appears in later Greek religious thought as a symbol of the renascent soul,[83] but this symbolism must have had its primitive foundations in earlier cultic practice, connected in some way with the observations of seasonal rebirth upon which that practice was almost invariably based.

In addition to this hint as to the character of the Sirens, we observe two closely juxtaposed elements in the episode. First, the Sirens are unquestionably associated with death, since they are surrounded by heaps of bones, presumably of those whom they have drawn to listen to their song. Secondly, the Sirens promise knowledge, above all: Circe has warned the mariners that anyone who draws near "in ignorance" [àidreíē] will never return (XII. 41–6), and the Sirens tell Odysseus in their song that "we know all the toils that in wide Troy the Argives and Trojans endured through the will of the gods, and we know all things that come to pass upon the fruitful earth."[84] The reader is strongly, perhaps justifiably tempted to view these two elements as integrally related one to the other, just as they are in *Genesis:* the fruit of the Tree of Knowledge threatens death to Adam and Eve (2:17), "for in the day that thou eatest thereof thou shalt surely die." In both stories the knowledge granted appears to be god-like, as befitting a god; Yahweh observes (3:22) that "the man is become as one of us, to know good and evil," and probably Adam's acquisition was not, in its origin, specifically limited to moral knowledge, any more than that offered to Odysseus.[85] Yet both are associated with death, and in the *Genesis* account at least, with the possibility of a subsequent immortality (3:22–4) akin to a god's. The sacred king of primitive Greece and surrounding areas would have been deliberately confused with the god, and would have been mated with the queen-goddess and sacrificed only in his divine identity, and with promise of a consequent immortality. Many stories, like that of Actaeon, associate the ritual death directly with "knowledge" of the goddess herself, in the proverbially Biblical sense of that word, and *Genesis* still equates the eating of the fruit with Adam's and Eve's subsequent knowledge of their nakedness (3:6–7). In light of these comparisons, then, we may conjecture that the knowledge promised by the Sirens, like that afforded by the Tree of Knowledge[86] originally referred to the sacrifice of a sacred king as god, or as the fertile embodiment of divine power.

Just as in Odysseus's encounter with Circe, Homer has distorted and rearranged the elements of what we may assume to be the original ritual, in order that Odysseus may claim its benefits while escaping the savage reality of sacrificial death which it had implied. As they pass the Sirens Odysseus, with appropriate irony, puts "honey-sweet wax"[87] in the ears of his crew so that they may not hear "the voice sweet as the honeycomb,"[88] and has himself tied to the mast so that he can hear and yet not die. We may even guess that this confinement, viewed in the Homeric poem as a safeguard, initially referred to the posture of the sacrifice itself, and that at the ritual stage in the development of the story the mariners, bedaubed with beeswax, represented participants in the ceremony. If this approximates truth, we should be struck, as in the story of Circe, with the remarkable method and deliberation of Homer, in his conversion of a story whose original meanings would have been available to him less through factual certitude than through a strange and ghostly intuition of the past.

Possibly because of their legendary geographical location in the Straits of Messina, however, the figures of Scylla and Charybdis have assumed a character in customary interpretation as embodiments of natural phenomena, as vividly imaginative representations of the dangers of the sea. Yet however great the Homeric imagination, it did not function that way, though on the other hand the account in the *Odyssey* of this unpleasant pair is sufficiently abbreviated to render interpretation in more feasible terms difficult and tenuous. All we may be sure of is that the monsters are female, and deadly. Nor can we conclude much from their genealogical connections, no matter how interesting these may appear, for fear of falling into the unwarranted syncretism habitual to Greek mythographers from Herodotus onward.[89] Yet another approach yields more fruitfully to our speculative efforts. Certain motifs occur in repetition throughout the *Odyssey*, and find their counterparts in this episode as well. The first of these is the cave. Polyphemus is encountered in a cave; Scylla lives in one, Circe's description of which is significant: "a dim cave, turned to the West, toward Erebus, even where you shall steer your hollow ship, glorious Odysseus."[90] This chthonic orientation—for the West, the end of the sun's journey, the direction of Elysium, the abode of the primordial night-god Erebus, can mean only that[91]—seems to indicate, particularly in conjunction with the monster's murderous aspect, that her cave is to be compared with Calypso's as the residence of the Goddess of the Underworld. Finally, Odysseus awakes from a mysteriously deep sleep on the shore of Ithaca near a strange cave with two entrances, one for mortals and one for gods, and inhabited by female spirits.

The second motif is the tree, or branch. The olive spit plays an important part in the struggle with Polyphemus,[92] Circe's dwelling is in deep forest, "sacred glades,"[93] Odysseus is to know Persephone's Grove by its poplars and willows, he is saved by the "fig tree with rich foliage"[94] over Charybdis; alder, poplar, and cypress grow around Calypso's cave,[95] Odysseus falls asleep under a curious double olive tree on the Phaeacian shore, covered with leaves[96] and later covers his nakedness from Nausicaa with a leafy branch;[97] finally, he awakes on the Ithacan shore under a sacred olive tree, and we are already familiar with his olive-tree bed.

The third motif is that of the entrance, the gate, the threshold.[98] Polyphemus is prominently concerned with the entrance to his cave, which he guards and controls (see fn. 92). All of the ships which passed through the mouth of the harbor at Telepylus are destroyed; Odysseus alone has moored his outside the entrance-way (characteristically) and so escapes death. Circe's island is both Gateway to the Sun and the last point of departure on the journey to the underworld. Scylla sits at the entrance to her cave, and the passage between her and Charybdis is itself a gateway. Both in Telepylus and in Phaeacia, entrance to a palace is immediately followed by an encounter with an imposing queen. The curious double entrance to the cave on the shore of Ithaca has already been noted. And finally, Odysseus kills the suitors from the "great threshold"[99] of his own home.

These three elements are combined in the encounter with Scylla and Charybdis, in a fashion which invites comparison with similar forms in myths and rituals recorded from areas of wide geographical separation. G. R. Levy, in *The Gate of Horn*, traces the cave-cult and its Megalithic architectural developments from northern Europe through southern Eurasia to the practices of present-day Stone Age societies in Melanesia, and it is there that the living force of this ancient species of religious belief may be most clearly understood. A terrible goddess, known as Le-hev-hev on Vao,[100] is associated with the entrance of the cave (see fn. 92) which leads to the underworld, and which is indiscriminately associated with the various rebirth-transformations which everywhere constitute the group of what we call rituals of passage.[101] Like the Scorpion Man[102] and Woman who guard the Cave of Death in the *Gilgamish Epic*,[103] and like Scylla herself, Le-hev-hev is imagined "as a Rock . . . crab, spider, or megalopod."[104] The function as guardian of the cave's entrance, and her multibrachiate nature, receive strengthened significance from an account of ritual practice among the devotees of Le-hev-hev:

> *The Journey of the Dead*, as mimed in the ritual dances of Vao, bears the closest relation to the literary legends of our own civilisation, suggesting some common foundation in a universal ritual descended from the Stone Age of Europe and Asia. In Vao the newly-dead man is believed to arrive before the entrance to a cave on the seashore, where he encounters the dreaded Guardian Ghost. In front of the cave-mouth is a design called "The Path," traced upon the sand by Le-hev-hev. At his approach she obliterates the design, which the dead man must complete or be devoured . . . After half completing the design, he must tread its

mazes to the threshold of the cave, where he may now offer the tusked boar which was sacrificed in the mortuary rites performed after his burial.[105]

The goddess is then prevailed upon to admit him to the underworld. In the Wala version the dead man carries a branch of weed on his voyage, and gnaws "the bark of a 'milk-bearing' tree" as a sign of his transformation to an infantile condition.[106] An observer of the Australian labyrinth-dances associated with this pattern and derived from the same level of culture concludes that they are, first, inevitably concerned with death and rebirth; secondly, without exception have to do with a cave or the constructed equivalent of one; thirdly, always have a maze before the entrance; and fourthly, the central figure in the rite is inevitably a woman.[107]

Let us apply the elements of this ritual pattern to Odysseus's adventure. He and his mariners approach Scylla who is sitting in the entrance to her cave, like Le-hev-hev's, facing the sea. Both possible outcomes of the confrontation of the goddess have similarly their parallels in the *Odyssey*: six mariners, doubles of Odysseus, are snatched up and devoured, while the hero himself "searched out the paths of the sea."[108] The phrase, which does not occur elsewhere in the *Odyssey*, appears to have transferred the maze-design found at the entrance of the cave in the Melanesian ritual, to the difficult sea-passage itself, between Scylla and Charybdis. What is important, and characteristic of Odysseus, is that the treading of the maze, however successful, does not lead to the cave — and the underworld — but away from it. Once again the basic elements of a ritual situation have been rearranged and subverted to the purposes of a hero in search of human life rather than immortality in death, a hero determined not to subordinate himself to a dominance of the female principle over that life.

In order to arrive at an intelligent hypothesis concerning Odysseus's returning encounter with Charybdis, we must add to our Melanesian parallels another, drawn out of [a] region almost equally remote from Greece, yet bearing traces of origins in the same cultural stratum. Beowulf, prince of the Geats, struggles and conquers a female monster in a setting remarkably similar to the Ithacan king's escape from Charybdis. Grendel's mother, in no matter how Christian a poem she appears, is unquestionably a relic of prehistoric pagan mythology. It is explicitly said of her and her son that "they have no knowledge of a father, whether any had been begotten for them in times past, among the mysterious spirits."[109] Which is usually taken to mean simply that they were creatures without history, unable to reckon their lineage, but which may quite as easily imply an ignorance of paternity.

Their lair is described in terms reminiscent of Homer's setting for the Odyssean episode: it is found in an "unknown land . . . dangerous fen-paths, where the welling stream under the mists of headlands goes down, a flood under the earth."[110] By comparison, Homer mentions the two high cliffs[111] in which dwell Scylla and Charybdis, and remarks that over Scylla's there is an eternal mass of clouds which never clears away.[112] Other elements present a much stronger parallel, however: the lair of Grendel's mother is reached through water, a lake "over which hang frosted groves; the wood rooted fast overshadows the water."[113] When Beowulf finds the lair, he recognizes it by the sight of these "mountain trees hanging over grey stone."[114] This latter detail, twice insisted upon in *Beowulf*, has its direct parallel in the fig tree, rooted on the cliff over Charybdis,[115] to which Odysseus clings in order to avoid being drawn down when Charybdis sucks in the waters of the sea. Finally, Charybdis's maelstrom is itself echoed in the curious behavior of the lake in *Beowulf*: "thence surging water rises up, darkly to the clouds, when the wind stirs evil storms, until the air turns misty, the heavens weep."[116]

Each passage sheds light on the other. The she-monster in *Beowulf* is definitely a divinity in the *Odyssey*, whereas the localized form of Grendel's mother tells against the interpretation of Charybdis as a vague representation of a simple whirlpool, or general manifestation of natural powers. The crucial role of the fig tree in the *Odyssey* suggests that a greater significance than the Anglo-Saxon poet conveys, is to be attached to the grove over the lake. And whereas Charybdis's vortiginous action reveals to Odysseus only the black sand of the sea-bottom,[117] for Beowulf it is the entrance to an underworld lair, in which he will meet a more or less anthropomorphic female monster. We are again confronted with the pattern of a goddess who is associated with the opening to an underworld, with the addition of a fig tree, "rich with foliage," or grove of trees, hanging over the watery entrance. To understand these we must refer back to the Melanesian "milk-bearing tree," the full significance of which we shall have occasion to discuss when we deal with the olive tree forming the foundation of Odysseus' bed. For the moment it must suffice to say that the many Mediterranean and Eurasian parallels for this peculiar tree indicate that it is a manifestation of the Goddess herself, in a beneficent, fertile aspect; in this embodiment she is the Mother and Guardian of Birth, rather than the Goddess of Death.[118] Charybdis is both of these, and her aspects are separately embodied in the two images of whirlpool (if that is what it is) and fig tree. When Odysseus approaches her, he clings to the fig tree, associated with the powers of rebirth,[119] rather than descending as Beowulf does[120] with his sword[121] into the flame-lit[122] den of the she-monster. Again it appears that Homer has altered the essential images of the original ordeal, viewing the tree as a separate means of escape rather than another form of Charybdis herself, in order to allow his hero to enjoy the beneficial effects of a passage through death to rebirth without suffering the consequences which full participation would entail.

The theft of Hyperion's cattle and the mariner's consequent punishment, though like the Cyclopian incident and the encounter with Scylla showing evidence of a substitute-sacrifice in place of the king himself, approaches the repeated theme of the epic from a somewhat different angle. On the analogy of the theft of Apollo's cattle by Hermes, a prototype of Odysseus, it would seem likely that the mariners, in stealing Helius's cattle, are acting simply as doubles for Odysseus himself, as they elsewhere do. The crime is his, or was, since the whole tenor of the Homeric epic is uncongenial to a guilt-motif of this sort, which finds a place more properly in Tragedy, and Homer does his best to transfer the stigma. Yet guilt was involved in the cycle of the dying god. As Gilbert Murray tells us, "the life of the Year-Daemon, as it seems to be reflected in Tragedy, is generally a story of Pride and Punishment. Each Year arrives, waxes great, commits the sin of Hubris, and then is slain. The death is deserved; but the slaying is a sin: hence comes the next Year as Avenger, or as the Wronged One re-arisen."[123] In the course of the poem Odysseus plays both roles: here, in the form of his mariners, he suffers the deserved death, yet lives on in his own person, in order to stand as Avenger (of a different yet the same crime) upon the threshold of his own home, during the festival of Apollo Neomenius,[124] a god derived, like Helius himself, from an ancient sun-Daimon.[125]

This episode and the remaining two which follow it in chronological order, differ in an important respect from those which precede it. While it, too, repeats in small the escape-from-death which is the central concern of the epic as a whole, it is the first incident in the poem to point forward to Odysseus's Ithacan revenge, the major action. For the first time, there is less emphasis on Odysseus's refusal to die as consort to the Goddess, than on the establishment of a *phase* in the ritual cycle which will find its completion only in his ultimate refusal to succumb before Penelope and the suitors. Here Odysseus suffers loss more certain than ever before, in the destruction of *all* of his companions and his ship, and if we are correct in assuming that the victims of Zeus are merely types of Odysseus himself, we may further assume that a longer ritual measure, contrapuntal to the repeated escape-metaphor, has been introduced, and that the shadowy god-king standing behind the mortal Odysseus has been put to death, not to rise again until the festival day of revenge and reunion with Penelope.

This counterpoint is maintained in the following adventure, Odysseus's sojourn on the island of the cave-goddess Calypso. On the one hand, she is the "Concealer,"[126] that is, as Goddess of Death she harbours the dead god during the time when, as the feeble winter sun or as the sun during its nocturnal disappearance, he is dormant and obscured.[127] On the other hand, traces remain of an escape from death similar to the others, in Odysseus's refusal to accept immortality at Calypso's hands. The immortality which she promises can most coherently be explained as meaning one thing: an immortality *beyond* death, originating perhaps in an apotheosis and devout reverence post-humously accorded a sacrificed king.[128] But Odysseus does not wish the immortality of a semi-divine here; he wants a life, the life of a mortal man.

In both capacities, as Concealer and Temptress, Calypso suitably appears with fragmentary trappings of a chthonic goddess,[129] and we notice that when Calypso complains to Hermes about the gods' jealousy concerning "mixed marriages" between mortal and immortal, the example she uses — Eros and Orion, Demeter and Iasion — as parallels to herself and Odysseus, are not stories of goddesses forced to relinquish their mortal lovers, but of men destroyed for presuming to mate with a goddess. We may, in fact, entertain suspicions that at one time these examples were more appropriate than they appear to be in the Homeric poem. But Homer's Calypso is safely subservient to the Olympian deities, and must let her lover go on his way.[130] . . .

Notes

1. Gabriel Germain, *Essai sur les Origines de Certains Thèmes Odysséens et sur la Genèse de l'Odyssée* (Paris, 1954), p. 333.

2. Rhys Carpenter, *Folk Tale, Fiction and Saga in the Homeric Epics* (Berkeley, 1958), p. 146. New light has been shed, however, upon the necromantic rites which Odysseus performs in the underworld. On April 12, 1960, *The New York Times* carried a special from Athens announcing the discovery by Greek archaeologists of a large Necromanteion (Oracle of the Dead) at the confluence of the Kokytus and Acheron rivers in Epirus, in the northwest region of Greece. In this massive structure were found evidences of libations of honey and white barley, together with burnt sacrifices of sheep and bulls. Among the artifacts uncovered were a small clay statue of Persephone and one of Cerberus. The inner temple room, used for oracular consultation with the dead, is reached by a complicated and dark labyrinth with three arched gates. These details will have important bearing on later discussion in this chapter. The Necromanteion itself dates from the third century B.C., but was reared on the site of another much earlier building used probably for similar purposes. The use of honey and mention of it in the Homeric account may have some relation to the episode of the Sirens, and hints of labyrinthine structures appear in several of the others including the story of Charybdis. Honey appears also in the sacred cave in the Bay of Phoreys, the place where Odysseus is finally deposited at his return to Ithaca.

3. Germain, pp. 368–370. See, however, Morris Jastrow and Albert T. Clay, ed. *An Old Babylonian Version of the Gilgamesh Epic* (New Haven, 1920), introd., p. 40. This appears to indicate that the pronouncement of Enkidu (and, likewise, that of Achilles) is a later teaching attached — no matter how early this was done — to a popular tale which at one time existed for a much different purpose. Much that we know of the formation of myth corroborates their opinion of the formation-sequence of these elements in the story.

4. *Odyssey*, xi, 488ff., trans. W.H.D. Rouse (New York, 1951), p. 125.

5. All whom, incidentally, appear to be pre-Hellenic, testifying to the antiquity of their place in the *Nekyia*. See Germain, p. 332; Denys Page, *The Homeric Odyssey* (Oxford, 1955), p. 39., finds the meeting with Agamemnon one of the original episodes of a visit to the underworld.

6. See the legend of the feud between the houses of Atreus and Thyestes. This relation by blood (in a double sense) between Aegisthous and Agamemnon establishes their point of strong resemblance to the Celtic king-and-tanist, to Cain and Abel, Gilgamesh and Enkidu, Castor and Polydeuces, and the hundreds of other stories of fratricide or severe twin-rivalry associated with ritual and royal succession, which together with stories of patricide and

succession to the father's throne, fill the world's mythologies. See Lord Raglan, *The Hero* (New York, 1956), p. 194.

7. Since Ikarios and Tundareos were brothers, Penelope daughter to the former, Clytemnestra to the latter.

8. *Odyssey*, xi, 442ff., trans. Rouse, p. 124.

9. *Odyssey*, xi, 454–456. These lines are missing in many of the ancient editions of the epic. The possibility that they are late, perhaps Athenian interpolations, offers no great hindrance to our hypothesis to be suggested in this article. Recent criticism, especially that of Professor Cedric Whitman, tends to indicate a greater degree of Athenian modification of the epic than hitherto supposed. This Athenian attitude seems completely in accord with the Homeric transformation of the original ritual elements of the poem, and it is true, also, that even if the *Nekyia* as a whole is a late addition to the poem, the *catabasis* which it relates is one of the oldest elements to be found in the traditional literature and legendary annals of Eurasia and Africa. In short, we can hardly accept the view of the *Odyssey* (presented by D. Page and others) as a poem ready to fly apart and disappear into patches and pieces at the least examination of linguistic and vocabularly characteristics. The paradoxical youth-and-age of the *Nekyia* is a case in point, showing up the futility of this kind of disintegrative criticism.

10. *Agamemnon*, 915ff.

11. There can be little question that this is their underlying motive in besieging Penelope. For the argument and evidence, see George Derwent Thomson, *Studies in Ancient Greek Society*, Vol. I, *The Prehistoric Ægean* (New York, 1949), p. 424.

12. E.O. James, *The Cult of the Mother-Goddess* (London, 1959), passim.

13. Also see G.R. Levy, *The Gate of Horn* (London, 1948), p. 86ff.

14. J.A.K. Thomson, *Studies in the Odyssey* (Oxford, 1914), p. 165.

15. J.G. Frazer, *Lectures on the Early History of the Kingship* (London, 1905), p. 161.

16. J.A.K. Thomson, p. 58.

17. Ibid., p. vii.

18. Loc. cit.; see also Martin P. Nilsson, *Primitive Time-Reckoning* (Lund, 1920), p. 97.

19. For instance, XVI 172ff. It is interesting, however, that Homer seems almost to protest too much, and the fact that Odysseus is taken for a god on these occasions may be indicative of an aura of divinity which the poet uneasily felt must be rendered innocuous. See Gilbert Murray, *The Rise of the Greek Epic* (Oxford, 1911), pp. 158–159, and *Five Stages of Greek Religion* (London, 1935), p. 62.

20. Leonard Cottrell, *The Anvil of Civilization* (New York, 1957), p. 23; G.D. Thomson, p. 158.

21. Frazer, pp. 291–292.

22. W.B. Stanford, *The Ulysses Theme* (Oxford, 1954), pp. 60–61.

23. Germain, p. 137.

24. Robert Graves, *The Greek Myths* (Harmondsworth, 1955), 18.7; see also Levy, p. 154ff.

25. Germain, pp. 136-7.

26. Cf. Lord Raglan, pp. 187–188.

27. Quoted in J.A.K. Thomson, pp. 104–105.

28. S.H. Butcher and Andrew Lang, trans. *The Odyssey*, in *The Complete Works of Homer* (New York: Modern Library, no date), p. 166; *Odyssey*, xi. 134–137. Classicists sometimes find it convenient to dismiss the Telegoneia as an imitative post-Homeric fancy, but the extract we have given seems to indicate very ancient sources indeed, and we would do well to follow the hint thrown out long ago by Andrew Lang, that the cruder, more incomprehens-

ible forms of a story are far oftener the more primitive forms, rather than degenerations of a highly developed version. (See Andrew Lang, *Custom and Myth* (London, 1898), pp. 178–179.) It seems unlikely that Eugammon would have been ignorant of the Homeric story or would have disregarded it if he wrote after Homer, though the discrepancies between the two accounts are obvious (J.A.K. Thomson, p. 106), unless Eugammon, whether writing before or after Homer, were in contact with a genuine alternative tradition.

29. Eugammon's poem itself, one is inclined to suspect, shows evidence of superficial expurgation or a misunderstanding of traditional materials; we may even wonder (J.A.K. Thomson, p. 59) if originally Telemachus, as another consort-lover-son-god, married Penelope, and Telegonus Circe. Other lands, other customs.

30. E.g., Dictys, *Journal of the Trojan War*.

31. J.A.K. Thomson, p. 106.

32. Graves, p. 18.

33. Stanford, p. 88.

34. Pindar and Herodotus. See J.A.K. Thomson, p. 46–47, who accepts the tradition as ancient and authentic; also Pausanias, viii. 12. 5–6.

35. *Odyssey*, XVIII. 158–162. trans. Butcher and Lang, p. 283.

36. See, however, G.D. Thomson, pp. 71–72.

37. Twelve is a number applied most frequently to sacrificed animals or slaughtered human beings, in the *Iliad*; here it may thus indicate a cultic origin for the hangings. In a similar fashion, Scylla has twelve tentacles, and Odysseus tells us in Book IX that his ill-fated ships originally numbered twelve, as did the men who followed him into the cave of Polyphemus. Gabriel Germain, *La Mystique des Nombres dans l'Epopée Homerique et sa Préhistoire* (Paris, 1954), pp. 17–18; for a parallel hanging of twelve maidens, with strong indications of its possessing the character of sacrifice, see Aeschylus, *Suppliants*, 465; also Elizabeth Hazelton Haight, *The Symbolism of the House Door in Classical Poetry* (New York, 1950), p. 21.

38. *Odyssey*, XXII. 424; Butcher and Lang, trans., p. 351.

39. J.A.K. Thomson, p. 169.

40. Cf. Pausanias, i. 2. 6; and G.D. Thomson, pp. 98–99, 113, 140–143, 146, 149–150, 154 and passim; who regularly confuses the two, despite protestations to the contrary.

41. Gilbert Murray, *Five Stages*, p. 59.

42. Ibid., p. 61.

43. Ibid., p. 58.

44. *Odyssey*, XIV. 180–182; trans. Butcher and Lang, p. 214. Lines 174–184 were apparently suspect to Aristarchus, since Eumaeus would have been ignorant of the ambush. These seem like tenuous grounds for rejection, but if they are interpolations, we are entitled to employ the same argument used in fn. 9, to deal with another set of lines similar in their almost programmatic intent. (See A.T. Murray, trans. *The Odyssey* (Cambridge, Mass., 1953), vol. II, p. 46, fns. 1, 2.)

45. *Odyssey*, xxiv. 502ff.

46. Although see D. Page, pp. 101–102, 114.

47. Graves, 170.1; for a similar view of the episodes as repetitions of a single basic ritual pattern, see Levy, fn. 2, p. 268.

48. Pages 14 to 17 of the original essay have been deleted. In them Professor Summer discusses connections between the myth of Polyphemus and ancient ritual.

49. Germain, *Nombres*, pp. 17–18; this situation and the cannibalism in the land of the Cyclops may be compared with that of the Athenian youths and maidens presented to the Cretan Minotaur every nine years; the story is evidently told of a stage in the emancipation of the sacred king in which an *interrex* or similar figure was substituted for him in the periodic

sacrifice, allowing the king to retain his powers for another like period. Even this substitute-sacrifice is interrupted by Theseus, just as Odysseus blinds Polyphemus after he has eaten only six of the twelve companions. See Murray, *Rise of the Greek Epic*, fn. p. 157, and Plutarch, *Vit. Theseus*, XV.

50. *Odyssey*, x. 112–113; trans. Butcher and Lang, p. 147; the epithet ἰφθίμη as applied to the king's daughter is not "stalwart" or "huge," as A.T. Murray points out, because it is elsewhere used of Penelope and other women. A.T. Murray, vol. I, p. 352, fn.

51. It is more likely that the lengthened daylight in their country is due to sketchy connections with the Scorpion-Men, Guardians of the Sun's Portals in the *Gilgamesh Epic*. See Germain, *Genèse*, pp. 414–417.

52. The monstrous queen appears very briefly in the corresponding episode in the story of Gilgamesh; see *Gilgamesh Epic*, Tablet IX.

53. Germain, *Genèse*, pp. 272–273.

54. Ibid., pp. 139–140.

55. See, however, Levy, pp. 102–106.

56. Germain, *Genèse*, pp. 131–132.

57. J.A.K. Thomson, pp. 28–29; see also Pausanias, viii. 4. 6.

58. See further, Charles Seltman, *The Twelve Olympians* (London, 1952), p. 75.

59. Graves, 26.b; see Pausanias, ii. 3, 4; Herodotus, ii. 145; for the variety of attributions of the paternity of Pan, see Scholion to Theocritus I. 3. With the supplementary material collected by C. Wendel, *Scholia in Theocritum Vetera* (Leipzig: Teubner, 1914), pp. 27–32; for the version that Hermes in the form of a ram begot Pan on Penelope, see Philarg. Verg. Buc. *II*. 32 (Wendel, p. 30); Servius Danielis on Verg. Aen. II. 44 (Wendel, p. 32), however, makes the transformation not to a ram, but a goat (*in hircum*).

60. G.D. Thomson, pp. 172–173.

61. J.A.K. Thomson, p. 29.

62. Charles Seltman, *Women in Antiquity* (London, 1956), p. 99.

63. Murray, *Five Stages*, p. 55; see also D. Page, p. 117., for Hermes as Psychopompos.

64. Shidura — or Sabitum — in the *Gilgamesh Epic* is repeatedly referred to as "cup-bearer," though the meaning of the epithet is even more obscure than here. See William Ellery Leonard, *Gilgamesh, Epic of Old Babylonia* (New York, 1934), p. 46–50., Tablet X.

65. *Odyssey*, x. 333–335; the juxtaposition is obviously meaningful.

66. *Odyssey*, x. 299–300; trans. Rouse, p. 111.

67. Jessie L. Weston, *From Ritual to Romance* (Garden City, 1957), p. 75.

68. If we assume that Circe's wand represents the lance, then she would be in possession of the two symbols ordinarily juxtaposed; Odysseus's sword would make a hostile third. For evidence that in the Grail legends the sacred objects were sometimes separated, though not in this unfriendly fashion, and borne in procession each by a youngster of the sex they represented, see Weston, p. 76. Not only in Gottfried's redaction of the story of Tristan and Isolt, but as well in a portion of the far earlier Sigurd story in the Poetic Edda (from the *Sigrdrífumál* through the *Brot af Sigurðarkviðu*, pieced out with the equivalent passages in the *Volsunga Saga*), we see the sword used in the same ambiguous representation found in the *Odyssey*: Sigurd takes the shape of his foster-brother Gunnar in order to ride through a circle of magic fire and claim Brynhild as his (Gunnar's) bride; once within the circle, the Sigurd-Gunnar sleeps three nights with Brynhild, but places the naked sword — ambiguously representative of Sigurd's sexual and other powers, as well as of his hostile renunciation of the sexual act — *between* their bodies. They then return to the outside world. Sigurd changes shapes with the real Gunnar, and the latter weds Brynhild. Sigurd does not fare as luckily as Odysseus, however. Brynhild eggs Gunnar on to kill Sigurd, and only afterward tells her husband of the sword between them. She is the humanized Deadly Female here, to be sure;

and it is worthy of note that in her former aspect as the valkyrie Sigrdrifa (in the *Sigrdrífumál*) she shares the pedagogic character of Circe and the Sirens, in teaching Sigurd runic wisdom.

69. Weston, pp. 22–23, 44–45; for possible Gilgamesh parallel, see Haupt's theory, summarized in Morris Jastrow and Albert T. Clay, *An Old Babylonian Version of the Gilgamesh Epic* (New Haven, 1920), p. 49.

70. E.g., see Pausanias, vii. 17. 10–12.

71. *Odyssey*, X. 394–395. (trans. Loeb, A.T. Murray).

72. See Bronislaw Malinowski, *Magic, Science and Religion* (New York, 1948), p. 107ff.

73. Malinowski's category of *Kukwanebu* seems to show this type in transition from ritual utility; pp. 102–104.

74. *Odyssey*, x. 469–470; trans. Butcher and Lang, p. 158.

75. Cf. Gilgamesh's repudiation of Ishtar in Tablet VI, Jastrow and Clay, p. 50.

76. Germain, *Genèse*, p. 357.

77. Graves, 27.k; 103.5–6; 134.1.

78. J.A.K. Thomson, p. 30.

79. *Odyssey*, XII. 21–22; trans. Butcher and Lang, pp. 181–182.

80. For the full argument, see Germain, *Genèse*, p. 388.

81. Ibid., pp. 388–389; although see H.J. Rose, *A Handbook of Greek Mythology* (London, 1958), p. 130, fn. 48. Classical literature of the later patriarchal period, to be sure, refers to the queen-bee as male, but this does not prove that earlier matrilinear societies possessed of imperfect knowledge, if any, of the reproductive function of the male, would have held the same view.

82. Graves, 18.f; 18.3.

83. Germain, *Genèse*, p. 389.

84. *Odyssey*, xii. 189–191; trans. A.T. Murray. For the association of oracular knowledge with bees in a cult-center which shows other strong connections with Odysseus and Penelope, see Pausanias ix. 40. 2; also ix. 39. 2–14; viii. 10. 1–4.

85. Germain, *Genèse*, p. 386.

86. Even if we do not take into account the wide-spread place, claimed by Graves, of apple and serpent in the ritual of sacrifice; Graves, p. 21. See also the discussions later in this chapter of the identification of fruit-bearing tree and Mother-Goddess; also Levy, passim.

87. *Odyssey*, xii. 47–49; trans. Butcher and Lang, p. 182.

88. *Odyssey*, xii. 187; trans. Butcher and Lang, p. 186.

89. A habit the beginnings of which appear in Hesiod's synthesis of external resemblances between deities in terms of divine genealogies. One such chain involves Scylla: she was the daughter of Phorcys and Hecate, transformed to the monster seen in Homer by Amphitrite for having an affair with the latter's husband Poseidon. The attendant beasts of Circe and Hecate's hell-hounds, a common feature of Eurasian fertility goddesses, are faintly suggested in Scylla's voice, that of a puppy. The relation between these three is otherwise strengthened through Medea: she is spoken of as calling upon Hecate and as being a witch in her own right, and is of course the niece of Circe through her father Acëtes. The only conclusion from this is pallid enough, and readily granted: that these ladies share the chthonic and sexual aspects of the ubiquitous Goddess. (H.J. Rose, pp. 64, 121–2, 202, also 235–6.) Polyphemus is also of the family, being grandson of Phoreys (*Odyssey*, i. 71–3.)

90. *Odyssey*, xiii. 80–83; trans. A.T. Murray.

91. See *Odyssey*, x. 526–530; Odysseus is instructed to turn the heads of his sacrificial victims "toward Erebus," i.e., toward Persephone's Grove, the Land of the Dead; while he is

to turn himself backward, settling his face "towards the streams of the river," i.e., toward the land of the living, to which he is determined to return. The action is of course highly appropriate and characteristic of him, if our theory is correct. Notice too, that Odysseus and his sacrificed sheep are in parallel circumstances: presumably the direction of their heads guarantees the passage of their vital powers to the underworld; the position of Odysseus's ensures that his will not do likewise. The danger to his life is implicit in the nature of the instructions. The legend of Orpheus leading Eurydice up from the underworld has an element analogous to this. For more detail concerning this sacrifice and the place in which it was done, see fn. 2.

92. See D. Page, p. 13; though as usual in the Homeric stories the specific identity of Polyphemus remains obscure, his general type is well represented by close parallels both in ancient times and in present-day Stone Age cultures. No one appears to have noticed his obvious associations with the *entrance* to the cave; these may, however, be compared to the attributes of other entrance-deities. A Melanesian parallel is the Guardian-Ghost Le-hev-hev, admittedly regarded by natives as sexless or female, but given power of admission through the cave-entrance to the other world, like Cerberus and possibly Polyphemus conceived as the Devourer of the Uninitiated Dead, and is identified in the New Hebrides with the tusked boar. Polyphemus's single eye is probably, as A.B. Cook has contended, representative of the solar disk; and this is further confirmed by his association with the ram. The Golden Fleece story seems to corroborate this relation, and the author of the present work has in his possession several Egyptian amulets, one at least identifiable with Ammon-Ra, showing a ram's head with a rayed solar disk between the horns, in a position easy to conceive of as a "single eye." Polyphemus is then of the Solar-Earth Spirit type, Guardian of the Entrance, and associated with the chthonic Goddess. Besides its resonant association with the olive of Athena, Odysseus's olive-stake appears to play a role in this episodic distortion of ritual similar to the golden bough of Aeneas, the branch covered with precious stones in the story of Gilgamesh's descent, the "branch of weed" in the Wala Melanesian voyage of the dead man, the branch of the Egyptian and Mesopotamian milk-yielding sycamore or other species, and countless others which which any reader of Frazer will be familar. The difference in the *Odyssey* is that while Odysseus uses the olive-stake for protection in the time-honored way, he does *not* use it for entrance to the other-world, but for the disruption of the ceremony and re-escape to the living world by the same entrance through which he entered. (For references to Melanesia, see Levy, pp. 154–157.)

93. *Odyssey*, x. 275.

94. *Odyssey*, xii. 103.

95. *Odyssey*, v. 63–64.

96. *Odyssey*, v. 474ff.

97. *Odyssey*, vi. 127ff.

98. See Elizabeth Hazelton Haight, *The Symbolism of the House Door in Classical Poetry* (New York, 1950), Chapts. I–III, IV and passim.

99. *Odyssey*, xxii. 2; for another association of threshold and bow, see Haight, p. 24.

100. Levy, p. 154.

101. Ibid., p. 160; for parallel Greek associations of the woman with entrances, see Haight, pp. 43 and 54ff. The sexual symbolism of the gate as respective female organ, the act of passing through the entrance as both birth and generative impregnation, is too universal and obvious to require explanation; the necessity of a guard at the gates will be likewise clear.

102. Corresponding to Taghar, Le-hev-hev's daimon-consort; Levy, p. 155.

103. Levy, fn. 2, p. 155.

104. Loc. cit.

105. Ibid., p. 156.

106. Ibid., pp. 156, 161.

107. Ibid., p. 157.

108. *Odyssey*, xii. 259.

109. C.L. Wrenn, ed. *Beowulf, with the Finnesburg Fragment* (Boston, 1953), vv. 1355–1357.

110. Ibid., vv. 1357–1361.

111. Comparable in their juxtaposition with the Goddess's cave to Mt. Mashu, "the lost ancestral mountain" of the Sumerians, from which the ziggurat-architecture is supposed to have emerged; see Levy, p. 168ff.

112. *Odyssey*, xii. 73–76.

113. *Beowulf*, vv. 1363–1364.

114. Ibid., vv. 1414–1415.

115. *Odyssey*, xii. 103. For a similar Greek juxtaposition of sacred grove and under-world entrance, see Haight, pp. 34–35. The association is common in classical literature. The author remembers having seen several others (one in Apuleius) though unable to relocate them. They appear to indicate regularly the sacred precincts of a Goddess. For those of Athena, see *Odyssey*, vi. 291ff.

116. *Beowulf*, vv. 1373–1376.

117. *Odyssey*, xii. 242–243.

118. See p. 66ff.

119. As indicated by the Melanesian parallel (see Levy, pp. 120ff. and passim.), and also represented with admirable clarity in the burial chamber of Tuthmosis III, Thebes, where a sycamore tree is depicted offering the breast to the king; see the Skira edition, Arpag Mekhitarian, *Egyptian Painting* (New York, no date), Eg. 18, p. 38.

120. Carpenter, p. 137.

121. *Beowulf*, vv. 1441ff. and 1557ff.

122. See Levy, p. 161; and cf. *Beowulf*, vv. 1570–1572.

123. Murray, *Five Stages*, p. 33; although see Levy, p. 329.

124. Einar Gjerstad, "Lunar Months of Hesiod and Homer," *Opuscula Atheniensia* I (Lund, 1953), p. 191.

125. Murray, *Five Stages*, p. 50; or Sisyphus as the sun-god (Graves, 67.1) from whom Odysseus's maternal grandfather Autolyeus stole cattle also. See the discussion of the similar double role of Joyce's hero, embodied in Stephen and Bloom, of Creator and scapegoat god, in Kristian Smidt, *James Joyce and the Cultic Use of Fiction* (Oslo, 1955), pp. 49–50 and passim.

126. W.J. Woodhouse, *The Composition of Homer's Odyssey* (Oxford, 1930), p. 216.

127. J.A.K. Thomson, p. 30; Gilgamesh likewise displays characteristics of a sun-divinity, in the opinion of Jastrow and Clay, pp. 48–49.

128. Without which no willing victims could have been found to satisfy the Goddess, if the king-sacrifice was ever more than an effigy in human shape or a proto-dramatic representation of such a death. Compare the immortality conferred on Hercules after he ascended his own funeral pyre while still alive. Compare Hera's promise to make Medea's children immortal if the latter would lay them on Hera's sacrifical altar, whereupon the Corinthians stoned them to death. Compare also two accounts of what seem to be immortalizing ceremonies interrupted: a) Demeter's attempt to make Demophoön immortal by holding him over the fire, when his mother entered and broke the spell; and b) Thetis's attempt to make her son Achilles immortal like herself by burning his flesh in the fire, as she had done successfully with her other six children; her husband Peleus interrupted her when only Achilles' ankle-bone remained untransformed. See Graves, 24.e; 81.r; 145.f; 156.d.

129. Though his sources, as usual, are exasperatingly unspecified, Graves tells us that the alder surrounding her cave was sacred to the Pelasgian death-god Cronus, as were the sea-

crows perching in the branches; the owls and falcons were emblematic of herself; parsley is a sign of mourning, and iris was the flower of death (Graves, 170.8.). The poplar found here is also to be found in Persephone's Grove; it signifies the autumnal equinox, and Plautus evidently uses it in his *Casina*—"Sed manendum, tum ista aut populina fors aut abiegina tua."—as a symbol of the loss of hope. (Graves, *The White Goddess* [London, 1948]). p. 176.) Cypress has long been associated with funerals and mourning, (*Shorter Oxford English Dictionary* (1955), p. 447.) though possibly did not have this meaning in the classical world.

130. [In the remainder of his essay, not reprinted here, Professor Sommer discusses Odysseus's trip to the land of the Phaeacians, time, ritual cycle, and the symbolism of Odysseus's and Penelope's bed, hewn from a tree.]

The Renaming of Odysseus   Alice Mariani*

> There is no one among mankind goes nameless,
> High or low, from the moment of his birth,
> But to every man his parents give a name, as soon
> as he is born.
> —*Odyssey* VIII. 552–554

THE NAME AND THE SCAR

"No man alive," the Phaeacian king comments, trying to discover the name his tight-lipped [*xeînos*] goes by, "is anonymous; his parents give him a name as soon as he's born." In the scene in which Odysseus, once again a nameless stranger, inadvertently makes himself known to his old nurse Eurycleia, Homer brilliantly links the hero's identifying, individuating name—the name that is every man's heritage from his parents, and marks his emergence from anonymity into his own mortal existence—to the pain that is part of his identity.

Starting from his identification scene with Telemachus, in which the son raised "Far from the Battle" relives his helpless adolescence and anticipates the dangerous maturity of the approaching Slaughter, all of Odysseus' revelations of himself in Ithaca involve his peculiar gift of trouble. He announces the stranger's identity to the suitors wordlessly by shooting one of them dead with an arrow from the great bow that he alone can bend, then proclaims to the rest that Odysseus has returned to repossess all that is his by killing their whole company. The other citizens of Ithaca learn who the stranger is when the grisly news of the slaughter is bruited about, and the suitors' avengers recognize their former compatriot when he comes screaming down upon them intent on battle. To establish his identity in Ithaca—assert to the usurpers, that is, his true roles as husband and head of his household—Odysseus must cause pain in this

*From "The Forged Feature: Created Identity in Homer's *Odyssey*" (Ph.D. diss., Yale University, 1967), pages 111–38, by permission of the author.

obvious sense. But he identifies himself to those he loves in Ithaca as well, by subtler revelations of his gifts of pain, and as the trouble he brings to Telemachus suggests, such pain may be a necessary and not always destructive one. The medium for all but one of the latter identifications is the famous boar scar on Odysseus' thigh.

THE CONTEXT OF THE BOAR SCAR STORY

One of the most memorable scenes in the *Odyssey* is the vivid and moving passage in Book XIX in which Eurycleia, washing the feet of the wretched stranger in the light of his own hearth, knows him by the scar revealed by that light as her master and nurseling. Into the split second between her recognition of the scar and her exclamation of his name in amazement and joy, Homer inserts an astonishing "digression" of seventy-four lines, almost as long as the whole scene with Eurycleia which it divides. So rich in meaning within its context does this passage seem that one is inclined to take it less as a "departure" from the main action[1] than as an artful focus of the thematic development of Odysseus' identity, dramatically *framed* as it were by the carefully structured whole of that scene.

I do not entirely agree with Erich Auerbach's well-known analysis of the boar scar passage in the first chapter of *Mimesis*, and it might be well to digress here for a moment to examine his account of the "digression."[2] For it is as such that he sees the passage. Comparing the Homeric style with that of the Old Testament as opposing modes of the "literary representation of reality in European culture," Auerbach finds the "basic impulse" of the former in its need "to represent phenomena in a fully externalized form, visible and palpable in all their parts, and completely fixed in their spatial and temporal relations" (p. 4). This is an illuminating speculation, but in Auerbach's application of it to the passage he has chosen as representative of the Homeric style, "basic impulse" seems equated, despite his own passing distinction, with total poetic effect. To say that when the scar "comes up" in his narrative "Homer's feeling simply will not permit him to see it appear out of the darkness of an unillumi-nated past," (p. 4) is to imply that the story of the origin of the scar is introduced in and for itself, that its relations to the dramatic scene it interrupts are either fortuitous or non-existent. If I understand him correctly Auerbach would seem to favor the latter view, that there are no significant relations between the scar episode and the scene with Eury-cleia. Arguing from the syntactical construction which sets off the episode and from the omission of any indication that the story is a recollection of Odysseus himself, he concludes that a "subjectivistic-perspectivistic proce-dure, creating a foreground and background, resulting in the present lying open to the depths of the past, is entirely foreign to the Homeric style; the Homeric style knows only a foreground, only a uniformly illuminated, uniformly objective present" (p. 5).

It is certainly significant in the context of Auerbach's comparative argument in his first chapter that Homer does not specifically press a "perspectivistic connection," but he seems to me to have oversimplified the way in which the episode really functions in this case. The absence of obvious suggestions of the relations of the episode to the total action surely does not preclude the existence of such relations. The story of the boar wound seems, for the moment it comes alive under our eyes, an "independent and exclusive present," but this is because in Homer the moment at hand is seen with such great intensity and is so valued in its own vivid life at the *same time* as it is held in a larger pattern in which perspective and the interrelation of past and present are vital elements.

Odysseus' identification scene with Eurycleia is unquestionably one of the most important ones in Ithaca, in some ways equalling those with Penelope and Laertes. Surprisingly, perhaps, Homer gives it more dramatic importance than the comparable scene with Telemachus. One might speculate that the reason for this lies in the fact that Odysseus and Telemachus are in some sense abstractions for each other, represent respectively the *idea* of a father, the *idea* of a son; as such each is a powerful element in the life situation of the other, but they do not know each other as persons at all. On the other hand, for Odysseus his nurse, his wife, his father are part of the remembered life he returns to in Ithaca, have formed his identity and so in a sense recreate it in their recognition; while he for them is of course by the same token a remembered *person*, around whom a thousand memories cluster. In the identification scenes with all three, the memory of significant events in Odysseus' past plays a vital part.

The importance of the scene with Eurycleia is underscored in several ways. We recall, for one, that this is the first of the identifications in the poem by a person who has actually known Odysseus already — for whom, that is, he is not merely a famous name. It is the first, moreover, to take place inside Odysseus' home, and indeed beside his own hearth, which gives it *per se* a kind of symbolic weight, marking the moment as *the* moment of Return. Nor is it going too far, I think, to understand Eurycleia as serving here as a kind of surrogate mother, and the bath she gives him as marking a sort of rebirth.

Odysseus' mother, Anticleia ("equal to fame" or "confronting fame") is of course dead, and Eurycleia ("wide fame"), whose name matches hers so closely, and whom Odysseus' father "honored in his home as equal to his dear wife" (*Odyssey* I.432), supplies the place of an old mother in the family group to which Odysseus returns. To delineate the relationship more precisely, she *combines* the roles of midwife, nurse, and mother, and attention is called to her delivering, nurturing and cherishing the hero — even to her resemblance to Odysseus in character — in the two sections of the scene which frame the story of Odysseus' birth, naming, and coming to manhood.

When the stranger requests that only some "discreet and understanding" old woman bathe him, "one whose spirit has perhaps undergone as much as mine," Penelope replies seemingly rather indirectly with lavish praise of her *guest*'s wisdom, discretion and understanding; then proceeds to observe that she has just such a one as he has asked for, an old woman with a mind "for discretion and wise counsel," the one

> *Who nursed and brought up wisely that unfortunate*
> *one* [Odysseus],
> *Receiving him into her hands at the moment his*
> *mother bore him.*
>
> (*Od. XIX.* 354–355.)

The last line strongly implies that Eurycleia acted as midwife; it might, not too fantastically, suggest as well the buried image of her washing the newborn child, an image which slides over into the bath she gives him now. The bath follows, introducing the story of the naming of the newborn Odysseus and the winning of his scar; immediately after this "digression," in the conversation between Odysseus and Eurycleia which completes the frame, her nurse-mother-midwife associations are again stressed. "You're Odysseus! his very self!" are the first words her "mingled joy and pain" permit her to speak, formally giving him his name once more after the naming and coming-into-one's-name of the Autolycus story. "Dear child," she repeats a few lines later, "my child." "And I didn't know you before, before I had felt all my lord's body all round [*pánta . . . amphaphásthai*]." Her verb here, surely greatly exaggerated for the brief touch she has given the scar, is poetically rather than factually exact, a poignant evocation of the long intimacy of their relationship which compresses into one phrase the years she has tended these limbs, this body, now ageing, once received into her hands at birth and cared for through its growth into young manhood. Odysseus, who before the boar passage has addressed Eurycleia as "old woman," now shifts to *Maîa*, which means variously "nurse," "mother," "foster-mother," "midwife"; he acknowledges her further in reminding her that "you nursed me yourself at this very breast of yours," and to emphasize the extreme danger of his position threatens, should she give him away, to harm her "my nurse though you are."

I have laid so much stress on these elements in the framing context of the boar passage because they seem to me to point toward the particular significance of the passage. The "digression" of book XIX comes at that point of the poem (the night before the slaughter) in which Odysseus is about to reclaim his home and his wife by revealing simultaneously his identity and his fatal marksmanship to the usurping suitors — and so come fully into his identity in the larger sense. Coming at this point, the story of Odysseus' naming and the gaining of his scar is in itself a revelation of identity, an exploration of who Odysseus is which reaches back into the beginnings of selfhood.

THE GIFT OF THE SCAR

It may be useful here to sketch in the incidents of XIX.393–466 briefly. The story of the boar scar literally breaks into Eurycleia's experience of recognizing it, snatching away the word "scar" in the middle of a sentence—"and at once she recognized / The scar—" and bearing us off with it into the long story of where and how and why Odysseus got it: ". . . which once the boar drove in with his white tusk / When he went to Parnassus with Autolycus and his sons. . . ." Autolycus is identified (still in the same sentence appropriated from Eurycleia) and the story leaps backward from the boar to recount Autolycus' arrival at his daughter Anticleia's home just after the birth of Odysseus, where he is ceremoniously asked to name the child. He tells the parents to name him Odysseus and "when he has reached man's estate" to send him to Parnassus, Autolycus' home, where the grandfather will give the young man gifts out of his own possessions. "It was for this Odysseus went," the narrative continues, moving forward abruptly, "that he might get those splendid gifts." At Parnassus Odysseus gets more than perhaps he bargained on. After the feast which welcomes him comes a boar hunt; in the watching circle of his relatives the young man is the first to rush in upon the ferocious boar at bay and receives a deep thigh wound, after which he kills the boar. The wound is healed with magic songs, Odysseus receives his gifts from Autolycus and returns to Ithaca where his parents rejoice to see him and ask him all about his visit and how he got his scar. The two lines which describe Odysseus telling them the story repeat almost word for word the opening lines of the passage: "[he told them] how, hunting, the boar drove in with his white tusk / When he went to Parnassus with the sons of Autolycus." The story thus neatly closed off, the poem returns to Eurycleia and the recognition of the scar, picking up (although beginning a new period) with exactly the same word [tèn,] "which," "this") on which it had left her.

The technical devices by which frame and story are joined give an extraordinary sense of deliberately crafted relevancy to the boar passage — which fits into its place in the Eurycleia scene as closely as the doors of Odysseus' bedchamber fit their frames, skillfully joined and hung by Penelope's true husband, or as a fragment of intarsio shaped and trimmed with careful art fits perfectly into the whole of a design even as it calls attention to itself *as* something so shaped and trimmed. To determine just how it is relevant we should look more closely at the two events of the boar passage — the naming and the hunt — and their interconnections.

The meaning of the name Autolycus gives his grandson is by no means entirely clear. What seems plain is that he intends the name to be an augury for the future character and experience of his grandchild, eventually a kind of descriptive monicker, name and epithet in one: *ŏnom'* . . . as he says, "name and nickname." 'Epōnumos means specifically, "named after some person or thing," or, "of a name given in commemoration or remembrance of something," adding the implication, verified by the context, that Autolycus is in a sense naming the child after himself, giving him in the name he hopes will identify his grandson a kind of inheritance from his own store of personal "gifts." Eurycleia has tactfully suggested a "significant name"[3] for the child, Polyaretos, "Many prayers," when she sets him on Autolycus' knee with the remark that "he's the child we've prayed for so much [*poluárētos*]." The old man ignores this blandly pious proposal and evidently makes up a pungent and original name on the spot, supplying its etymology and urging its adoption:

> Gambròs èmòs thugátēp te, tí thesth' ŏnom' hótti ken èípō.
> polloîsin gàr ègō ge òdussámenos tód'hikánō,
> àndrásin edè gunaixìn ànà chthóna poulub'oteiran.
> tōi d'Oduseùs ŏnom' ĕstō èpōnumon.

> Son-in-law, daughter, give him the name I tell you.
> For since I've odysseussed many on my way,
> Both men and women in this wide world,
> Then let his name and nickname be Odysseus.   .
>   (*Od.* XIX.406–409)

L.-S.-J. define *òdússomai* as "to be wroth against, hate," but, as George Dimock observes,[4] this does not seem quite exact for the context. Autolycus has been carefully identified a few lines above (395–398) as "surpassing all men in unscrupulous dealing [*kleptosúnēi*] and lying [*ŏrkōi*], literally 'in oaths,' i.e. breaking his word and / or wording his oaths so craftily as not to commit himself)"; he is a great favorite of Hermes, the trickster god, god of the roads and of thieving, who himself gave Autolycus these peculiar "gifts."[5] The grandfather is mentioned as a thief in *Iliad* X, where Odysseus is involved in a characteristically equivocal exploit, combining great daring and presence of mind with some rather ugly breaking of faith (note the treatment of Dolon), theft, and the ruthless murder of sleeping men. During this adventure Odysseus is wearing an odd cap of boar's tusks (1) which originally, the poem notes, had been stolen by Autolycus, "boring into the owner's strong-built house." It seems probable, Dimock concludes, that what the grandfather-godfather has in mind in *òdússomai* is not so much "wrath" as his rogue's hostility against one and all, "a hand and mind against every man, by nature, or as a matter of policy."[6] Note Autolycus' stress on numbers: "many," "both men and women," "on this populous earth"; he appears to be boasting, in short, that there's trouble wherever he goes. *'Odússomai* is cognate with *òdúnē*, "pain," "suffering," and Autolycus, unrepentant, unsentimental wolf in wolf's clothing (*his* name means "Lone Wolf," or "The Wolf Himself") frankly wants his grandson to be able to dish it out to all and sundry.[7]

    What perhaps he cannot see is the ambiguity of the name he is wishing on Odysseus: "Troublemaker"[8] may mean that the child will make a lot of trouble for himself while making it for others, will perhaps have to endure the pain and trouble brought upon him by gods angry at his troublemaking (which is how *òdússomai* is used of Poseidon's revenge for the Cyclops, *Odyssey* v. 340, 423) — will have in short to live out all the implications of his name. Which is, in fact, the experience of Odysseus in his eponymous poem: to suffer and to make others do so.

Immediately after naming his newborn grandson, Autolycus promises him gifts when he shall have come of age:

> When he has come to manhood and comes to the
> great home
> Of his mother's people at Parnassus, where my
> possessions are,
> I will give him of these things and send him on
> rejoicing.
>
> (*Od.* XIX.410–412)

The promise of the gifts serves of course to move the action on from the incident of the naming to the boar hunt at Parnassus: "It was on account of these gifts that Odysseus came there, that he might receive the shining gifts"; and indeed the whole matter of the naming is technically quite unnecessary, "interferes" between the first mention of the scar when Eurycleia sees it in line 393 and line 413 when Odysseus finally goes to Parnassus where he is to get the scar. But as we have seen the naming incident is in fact vitally relevant to the identification scene with Eurycleia, and in turn the relation between the naming and the scar is itself of central importance. The naming is there not merely as an incidental detail to explain how Odysseus happened to go to Parnassus — but to suggest that the winning of the boar scar is a kind of achievement of his name and of all it implies, an "Odysseusing," a coming into himself. As the bestowal of the curious name is the first "gift" of Autolycus to Odysseus, the boar scar is itself one of the "shining" or "splendid" gifts that the young man come of age "receives" in Parnassus. The actual gifts of gold and bronze are carefully noted as a patrimony, given from among Autolycus' own possessions; and as the name has derived from his grandfather's life experience, so the scar is a kind of inheritance of the continuous life experience of the race — into which Odysseus comes at the moment of coming into his own manhood and his own individuality. Like the external possessions he is given, the scar is a formal recognition that he is Odysseus; and will serve in turn, with deep propriety, as a mark by which he is recognized as himself by Eurycleia.[9]

The wounding of Odysseus is worth looking at closely. Preceded by a day-long feast, the hunt seems at once part of a ceremonial honoring of his coming to man's estate, and a trial of it or an initiation. In the full company of his grandfather's family but leading them all ("close behind the hounds"), Odysseus is "the first of the first" to confront the boar with all the "sons of Autolycus" evidently watching him; he is wounded by it and in turn "wounds" the animal. This verb, *oútáō*, which is used twice in the passage to describe what Odysseus does to the boar, seems a strange one for the single fierce strike which kills the animal outright. It suggests an effort to convey the *mutuality* of the act: Odysseus wounds and is wounded (the word used of the gash he gets above the knee, *ōteilḗ*, is derived from *oútáō*) in a fierce exchange in which the two strikes are all but simultaneous. Many details of the encounter, in fact, suggest a contest of equals. The verbs used of both combine the meaning of a rushing forward motion with an eagerness for the kill: Odysseus "drove on avidly" (*ĕssut'*), the boar "charged in eagerly" (*aíxas*), but the boar "got his blow in first" (*phthámenos*); the effect is quite like that of two warriors rushing upon one another on a battlefield, perhaps in one of the familiar contests of peers in which the others stand apart to witness, springing into action only afterward, to bind up the wounded, drag off the dead as the sons of Autolycus do here. The onrushing heaviness and ferocity of the boar is brilliantly rendered in Homer's swift details, caught as if by the opponent's eye as the animal charges toward him, of the bristling back and the "fire flashing from his eyes"; that fierce flashing is met at once by the "flashing" point of Odysseus' spear and we think suddenly perhaps of the "shining" gifts he has come here to Parnassus for. The boar having driven his tusk in deeply, the young man's spear point drives "clear through" and the body of the animal "fell in the dust screaming, and the life force fluttered out," a formula whose elements are used word for word in the *Iliad* numerous times to describe the death of a warrior in battle.

Inevitably one thinks of the various similes in the *Iliad* which compare warriors to wild boars, XII.471ff. on Idomeneus, for example, and in particular XI.414ff. where Odysseus himself, at bay in a circle of Trojans, is likened to one. The mature Odysseus as we know him in the *Odyssey*, in fact, is not unlike this boar through which he comes into manhood, or which marks his arrival: the characteristic stance, at bay before a hostile world; the solitariness; the oblique, *likriphís* [wolflike] thrust of his defense; the cunning concealment in a *pukinós* lair. *Pukinós* combines the literal sense of dense, tightly woven foliage with the widely used metaphoric meaning "guarded," "cautious," "shrewd," "cunning"; the boar's lair is thus applicable metaphorically to Odysseus as we have known him, and its description (440–443) follows word for word that of the hero's "lair" in the olive trees of Phaeacia (V.478ff.), itself a darkly clear and powerful image of the intricate intelligence and caution by which Odysseus manages to preserve his identity against the forces which threaten it.[10]

Immediately after receiving the wound and killing his boar Odysseus—who in the passage up to this point has been referred to as simply "Odysseus" (four times) or *dîos* ["noble," "good"] Odysseus," a very common and rather colorless epithet—achieves a string of resounding formal epithets, *ònómata epṓnuma*, which are used again and again of the mature Odysseus of the poem: the sons of Autolycus bind up *ōteilèn d'Odusèos àmúmonos èntithéoio*, "the wound of blameless, godlike Odysseus."

Giving him the "shining gifts" which recognize the parallel achievements of his Odysseusing and his encounter with — his odysseusing of — the boar, Autolycus and his sons send Odysseus on his way "rejoicing," *chaíronta*, a form which can apply to both the young man and his hosts; he is similarly received in Ithaca by his father and mother, *chaíron*, "rejoicing." The joy in both instances and on both sides, it is clear, extends beyond the material gifts in which Homer's Greeks frankly delight, to include a joy in the achievement of manhood marked by the boar hunt, the coming into a self presaged in his name and crowned now by the achieved eponyms of his maturity.

THE MARK OF IDENTITY

The language of the final lines of the boar passage confirms the deliberated relevance of the "digression" and its two interrelated events. Bearing his Parnassian gifts, the shining presents of Autolycus, and the scar, Odysseus comes back "rejoicing to his own dear native land,"

> To Ithaca. There his father and noble mother
> Rejoiced at his joyous homecoming and asked him
>   about everything,
> The scar he had gotten; and he told them his
> story well. . . .
>
>   (*Od*. XIX. 462–464)

To read of this ur-Return is to be confirmed in the sense that Odysseus' adventure at Parnassus is the ur-Adventure, a prototype of his life experience in the poem — or, more modestly, at least a clear anticipation of it: he goes out from home in quest of the achievement of his name (and gifts), causes pain and endures it, narrowly escapes death, returns home ([*nostéō,*] the verb that re-echoes throughout the *Odyssey*) to the dear land of his fathers (*phílēn ès patríd'*) with joy and is received with joy by his family, shows his scar, is eagerly questioned about his experience and tells his story. Odysseus' parents ask him, on his return, about "everything, / The scar that he suffered," and it may not be over-interpreting Homeric economy of detail to find in this curious apposition the implication that the scar indeed is or includes "everything" that happened to Odysseus at Parnassus in the crucial experience of his coming of age. Later, the kind of give and take symbolized in the boar hunt will be, if not "everything," certainly a central and pervasive quality of the hero's mature Adventures.

That Odysseus finds his identity in giving and enduring pain is, I take it, the central thesis of George Dimock's short but extremely suggestive essay on the *Odyssey*, to which I have referred earlier and to which my reading of this and other episodes owes a good deal. Dimock traces the significance of Odysseus' name throughout the poem from its origin in Autolycus' obscure verb, and finds the name an index to the hero's total experience. Odysseus *causes*, he points out, as much suffering as he undergoes. But the "ultimate object" of the pain is "recognition and the sense of one's own existence, not the pain itself." From this point of view, he continues, Athene's punning question early in Book I provides its own crucial answer. *Tí nú oì tósonodúsao, Zeû;* she asks, "Why do you odysseus him so, Zeus?" The action of the poem is just that, the odysseusing of the hero: evil and suffering are a reality — although not the only reality — in the world through which he must move; and he is enabled to become himself through his encounter with them. "In exposing Odysseus to Poseidon," Dimock concludes, "in allowing him to do and suffer, Zeus is odysseusing Odysseus, giving him his identity. In accepting the implications of his name, Trouble, Odysseus establishes his identity in harmony with the nature of things."[11] Pain, like Odysseus' name, like his scar, is a kind of gift.

To cause pain, then, in the mature experience of the hero, is a simple necessity of existence; neither inflicted brutally and at random nor shrunk from, it is closely bound up with pain endured, accepted simply and sensed as among the conditions of human existence. Both can be occasion for rejoicing as they mark our perpetually renewed entrance into the continuum of human life and in so far as they are among the means by which our vitality is asserted and the depth and resonance of our encounter with life is felt. In this sense the boar episode is an anticipation of all Odysseus' later experience, even a kind of arch-Adventure, placed by design with a crucial identification scene of his final Adventure.

The scar that serves in many of those scenes in Ithaca as the "manifest sign" of Odysseus' identity, has as such a further significance. I have called the hero's departure from Calypso's island an option for, even an insistence on, his mortality, and found this insistence an important element of Odysseus' sense of himself.[12] The boar scar, it seems to me, is at one and the same time a token of triumphant heroic achievement and a mark of the hero's mortality. The scar Odysseus will carry in his flesh as long as he lives is a reminder of his close brush with death, and of his mortal vulnerability, the thousand natural shocks that flesh is heir to. The gods' flesh bears no scars. The hero's characteristically human limits are at least foreshadowed at the very outset of his career, in the sign that wins him his name and will later mark him as unquestionably Odysseus.

To appropriate the terms used by Thomas Greene in his study of the classical and Renaissance epic, the wound that earns Odysseus his name in his first Adventure is a sign of both the hero's control and his mortal limits. We might fairly say of Odysseus that his inescapable limitations are at least foreshadowed at the very outset of his career, in the sign that wins him his name and will later mark him as unquestionably Odysseus.

THE RELATION OF SCENE AND STORY

Thus the revelation of the scar in the present time of the narrative, in which it serves as Odysseus' "manifest token" in almost every identification of himself to his family and familiars, is far more than the disclosure of an external sign. The "digression" of Book XIX has identified the scar for us as the mark of what Odysseus is, of his specifically mortal existence, of the mingled joy and pain he experiences and causes others to feel.

For this reason the reaction of Eurycleia to her discovery strikes us as perfectly expressive of her recognition. "Joy and pain together gripped her," and she sings out his name. A second later Odysseus, himself "Joy-and-pain," literally grips her, in a gesture perfectly expressive of himself: the poem notes that one hand grasps her throat, but the other draws her nearer to him, and apparently in a half-embrace, not in order to whisper, for the verb (phōnéō) usually means to speak aloud and clearly. Of necessity menacing, he threatens her with death (exaggerating probably to impress the garrulous old woman with the need for absolute discretion); yet his tone is roughly tender at the same time, as he remembers her nursing him and slips into the caressing and intimate maîa he has called her since childhood. The whole moving dimension of time in the relation between the two, glanced at in Penelope's reference to the presence of Eurycleia at Odysseus' birth, and in the naming episode of the boar scar story, comes briefly but sharply into focus. The identifying scar reveals Odysseus' mortal ageing, his human subjection to time, even as, an unchanging mark in mortal flesh, it asserts the persistence of individual identity through time. Eurycleia assures him of her loyalty, brings new water to replace what has spilled from the basin when she dropped his leg, in the shock of recognition, and bathes her "dear child"; Odysseus hides the scar beneath his beggar's rags, and as if this were a formal gesture of withdrawing again beneath his disguise, the identification scene between them is over.

The exchange (lines 467–507) constitutes the closing half of the "frame" around the boar scar story (lines 393–466); it is difficult to imagine a more sensitive and illuminating adjustment of part to part. The image of picture and frame, in fact, is quite inadequate. The relation between the story and its context is fully dynamic: each deepens the other's significance; indeed their interaction creates that significance.

Notes

1. Much less is it merely a suspected "interpolation," a device for "suspense," or a naïve and "exasperating" postponement of the climax, which is all that Stanford (*Odyssey*, Vol. II, p. 332) notes as having been said of it.

2. *Mimesis: The Representation of Reality in Western Literature* trans. Willard Trask (Garden City, N.Y., 1957), pp. 1–20.

3. See Stanford, *Odyssey*, Vol. II, pp. xxi–xxii, on this Homeric phenomenon; also Vol. II, p. 332.

4. "The Name of Odysseus," in *Essays on the Odyssey: Selected Modern Criticism*, ed. Charles H. Taylor, Jr. (Bloomington, Indiana, 1963), pp. 54–55.

5. In view of Odysseus' claim to renown for all kinds of deceptions and cunning stratagems, Hermes is an appropriate patron to have in his background, even once-removed.

6. *Op. cit.*, p. 55.

7. For an almost entirely different view of the meaning of Odysseus' name, see W. B. Stanford, "The Homeric Etymology of the Name Odysseus," *Classical Philology* (1952), 209–213. Stanford discusses the relative justifications for taking *odussámenos* in *Odyssey* XIX.407 as passive or active, i.e., as meaning either "having incurred the anger of many," "hated," or "having been angry at," "irascible." He decides for a primarily passive meaning, a reference to the odium of the gods (with a suggestion of undeserved human hatred for the hero). He concludes that Odysseus (by suffering the worst that gods and men could do) *surmounts* the nemesis of his name, whereas Dimock's point is that Odysseus *lives up to* his name, which he takes to refer centrally to the hostility he shows, the pain he brings to others. Stanford's view in this article is repeated in his book, *The Ulysses Theme: A Study in the Adaptability of a Traditional Hero*, 2nd ed. (New York, 1964), pp. 10–12.

8. Dimock (p. 59) proposes "Trouble" as "perhaps as good a translation of Odysseus' name as any."

9. For an interesting general view of the relation between the epic hero's name and his experience, see Thomas Greene, *The Descent from Heaven: A Study in Epic Continuity* (New Haven and London, 1963). It seems to me that some of Greene's observations about the "norms of epic" in general might be applied very particularly to the boar scar episode which I will propose we take as a kind of norm for Odysseus' mature experience. In his remarkable formulation, "the epic tries to define the relation between the hero's name and his death." Discussing the epic hero as a distinctly human figure, Greene relates the importance of the hero's name to his control over his world, and both to the mortal limitations of that control:

> Why is it necessary that the hero bear a name? The right to a name means that a man can commit acts which vary qualitatively from another man's acts. Man in his middle state shares with the animals his mortality, and with the gods his right to bear an individual name. A man's name is very important in heroic poetry; it becomes equal to the sum of his accomplishments. . . .
> Epic narrative in other terms is a series of adjustments between the hero's capacities and his limitations. His life as a hero is devoted to informing his name with meaning. Because, unlike an animal he can accomplish a distinctive, personal thing, and unlike a god, he has no past accomplishments, the hero must discover and demonstrate at the outset what meaning his name may have. He is impelled to act, and, as action among men is agonistic, he is plunged into a contest of *areté*, *virtus*, capacity — a struggle to impose his being on his world. He can do this by demonstrating his control over a piece of his world: by subduing another man or men or a monster, or by pitting himself victoriously against some natural hazard of his environment. To remain a hero he must continue to demonstrate control, and so his career imitates the expansiveness of the epic imagination. But at the end of that movement, implicitly or explicitly, his inescapable limitations await him. (p. 16)

The wound that earns Odysseus his name in his first Adventure, I will attempt to demonstrate, is a sign of both the hero's "control" *and* his mortal limits, which in Odysseus' experience are unified rather than opposed. See below for my view of the scar as a sign of mortality.

10. The association of the olive tree lair with Odysseus' identity suggests itself

naturally, but it is developed and strengthened by the fine simile of V.488–491 which follows the description of the lair. Odysseus asleep in the tightly woven, inextricable unity of wild and cultivated olives, two trees "from a single stem," is compared to the "seed of fire" banked in black ashes by an isolated upland farmer to preserve it, a brilliant image for the tiny spark of selfhood which the floods of the formless sea and its salt terrors have not been able entirely to engulf and extinguish, stubbornly preserving itself to flare out next day in the Phaeacian encounter.

    11. "The Name of Odysseus," p. 72.

Ithaka C. P. Cavafy*

As you set out for Ithaka
hope your road is a long one,
full of adventure, full of discovery.
Laistrygonians, Cyclops,
angry Poseidon — don't be afraid of them:
you'll never find things like that on your way
as long as you keep your thoughts raised high,
as long as a rare excitement
stirs your spirit and your body.
Laistrygonians, Cyclops,
wild Poseidon — you won't encounter them
unless you bring them along inside your soul,
unless your soul sets them up in front of you.

Hope your road is a long one.
May there be many summer mornings when,
with what pleasure, what joy,
you enter harbors you're seeing for the first time;
may you stop at Phoenician trading stations
to buy fine things,
mother of pearl and coral, amber and ebony,
sensual perfume of every kind —
as many sensual perfumes as you can;
and may you visit many Egyptian cities
to learn and go on learning from their scholars.

Keep Ithaka always in your mind.
Arriving there is what you're destined for.
But don't hurry the journey at all.
Better if it lasts for years,
so you're old by the time you reach the island,

*From Edmund Keeley and Philip Sherrard, trans., *C. P. Cavafy: Collected Poems*, ed. George Savidis (Princeton: Princeton University Press), 67–68. Translation © 1975 by Edmund Keeley and Philip Sherrard. Reprinted by permission of Princeton University Press.

wealthy with all you've gained on the way,
not expecting Ithaka to make you rich.

Ithaka gave you the marvelous journey.
Without her you wouldn't have set out.
She has nothing left to give you now.

And if you find her poor, Ithaka won't have fooled you.
Wise as you will have become, so full of experience,
you'll have understood by then what these Ithakas mean.

SELECTED BIBLIOGRAPHY

Books and articles collected in this volume are included in this bibliography (marked *) without annotation. All entries, whether annotated or not, are recommended.

TEXTS

Homeri Opera. Edited by David B. Munro and Thomas W. Allen. 2 vols. 1902. 3d ed. Oxford, England, 1957.

The Iliad. Edited by Walter Leaf. 2 vols. London, 1886.

The Iliad. Translated by A.T. Murray. 2 vols. London, 1924.

The Iliad. Translated by Robert Fitzgerald. Garden City, New York, 1974.

The Iliad of Homer. Edited by Walter Leaf and M.A. Bayfield. 2 vols. 1895. 2d ed. London, 1962.

The Iliad of Homer. Translated by Richmond Lattimore. 1951. Reprint. Chicago, 1967.

The Iliad of Homer, Edited by M. M. Willcock. Classics Series (Macmillan Educational Series), Basingstoke, England; Macmillan, 1978. Cf. *Greece and Rome* 26 (1979): 87.

The Odyssey. Translated by A.T. Murray. 2 vols. London, 1919.

* *The Odyssey*. Translated by Robert Fitzgerald. Garden City, New York, 1961. "On Translating Homer" is abridged from Fitzgerald's end-notes.

The Odyssey of Homer. Translated by Richmond Lattimore. 1965. Reprint. New York, 1967.

CRITICISM

Abercrombie, Lascelles. *The Epic: An Essay*. London, 1922. Abercrombie's intuition of the Homeric epics is so accurate that his work is hardly outdated.

Allen, Thomas W. *The Homeric Catalogue of Ships*. Oxford, England, 1921.

Amory Anne. "The Gates of Horn and Ivory." *Yale Classical Studies* 20 (1966):35–40.

———. "Omens and Dreams in the *Odyssey*: A Study of the Relationship between Divine and Human Action." Ph.D. diss., Radcliffe College, 1957.

Anderson, O. "Odysseus and the Wooden Horse." *Symbolae Osloenses* 52 (1977).

The wooden horse is not only Odysseus's first exploit, but also prefigures the events that take place on Ithaca.

Andreae, B. & Flashar, H. "Strukturaequivalenzen zwischen den homerischen Epen und der frühgriehischen Vasenkunst." *Poetica* 9 (1977):217–65. In the *Odyssey*, secondary motifs are attached to the principal theme on the same basis found in subgeometric vases.

Andreev, J. V. "Könige und Königsherrschaft in den Epen Homers." *Klio* 61 (1979):361–84.

Aristotle. *Poetica*. Translated by W. Hamilton Fyfe. 1927. Cambridge, England, 1965.

Armstrong, James I. "The Arming Motif in the *Iliad*." *American Journal of Philology* 79 (1958):337–54. The treatment of Patroklos's arming is especially interesting.

Arnold, Matthew. "On Translating Homer." In *The Poetry and Criticism of Matthew Arnold*, edited by A. Dwight Culler, 217–32. Boston; 1961.

Atchity, Kenneth John. "Achilles' Sidonian Bowl." *Classical Outlook* 51 (November 1973):25–26.

*———. *Homer's Iliad: The Shield of Memory*. Carbondale and Edwardsville; 1978. Examines images connected with artistic creativity in the Iliadic world and the relationship of memory, cognition, and action in the epic. The theme of the *Iliad* is the relationship between order and disorder from personal to cosmic levels. The *Iliad* is a poem about human love, the announcement of Homer's insight that the love between two individuals, a love overleaping bonds of blood and politics, provides the basis for the achievement of the noblest humanity.

———. "Iris in *Iliad* 18." *Arethusa* 7 (Fall 1974):221–22.

———. "Teucer in the *Iliad*." *Classical Outlook* 52 (February 1975):62.

———. "The Power of Words in the *Iliad*." *Classical Outlook* 53 (September 1975):5–6.

———. "Homer's Ultimate Vision." *Classical Outlook* 53 (May 1976):98.

———. "Structure in *Iliad* 3." *Classical Outlook* 54 (March 1977):74–75.

———. "The Omen in *Iliad* 2." *Classical Outlook* 54 (March 1977):100–101.

*———, and Barber, E. J. W. "Greek Princes and Aegean Princesses: The Role of Women in the Homeric Poems."

*Auden, W. H. "The Shield of Achilles." In *Homer*, ed. George Steiner and Robert Fagles, 79–80. Englewood Cliffs, N.J., 1962.

Auerbach, Eric. "Odysseus' Scar." In *Mimesis*, translated by Willard Trask. Garden City, New York, 1957.

*Austin, Norman. *Archery at the Dark of the Moon: Poetic Problems in Homer's Odyssey*. Berkeley and Los Angeles, 1975.

Barnett, R. A. "Comparative Studies in the Homeric Epic and Other Heroic Narrative, Especially Sanskrit and Celtic with Special Reference to the Theory of Oral Improvisation by Means of Formulary Language." Ph.D. diss., University of Toronto, 1979. (Microfilm).

Basset, Samuel E. *The Poetry of Homer*. Berkeley, 1938. Discusses the symbiotic relation between Priam and Hektor, the cognitive relation between narrator and audience with respect to the characters, and Homer's character as simultaneously a realist and idealist.

Bell, Clive. *Art*. New York, 1914. Bell's statement applies to the shield of Achilles: "The contemplation of pure form leads to a state of extraordinary exaltation and complete detachment from the concerns of life . . . It is tempting to suppose that the emotion which exalts has been transmitted through the forms we contemplate, by the artist who created them" (68).

Benedetti, M. "Helen's Web: Time and Tableau in the *Iliad*." *Helios* 7, no. 1 (1979–1980):19–34. Study of the convention of suspended verisimilitude in the *Iliad*, approached through contemporary critical theory.

*Bespaloff, Rachel. *On the Iliad*. Translated by Mary McCarthy. New York, 1947.

Beye, Charles Rowan. *The Iliad, The Odyssey and the Epic Tradition*. Garden City, N.Y., 1966.

————. *Ancient Greek Literature and Society*. Garden City, N.Y., 1975. "One thing is clear: these are no inchoate, primitive attempts at poetry. They are sophisticated, fully developed narrative poems of unusual subtilty and control" (31).

Bolling, G. M. "Poikilos and Throna." *American Journal of Philology* (1958):275–82.

Bolter, J. D. "Achilles' Return to Battle: A Structural Study of Books 19–22 of the *Iliad*." Ph.D. diss., University of North Carolina, Chapel Hill, 1977. Summary in *Dissertation Abstracts* 38 (1978):7310A.

*Borges, Jorge Luis. "The Maker." In *Dreamtigers*, translated from *El Hacedor* by Mildred Boyer and Harold Morland. New York, 1970.

Bowra, Sir Maurice. *Tradition and Design in the Iliad*. Oxford, England, 1930. Bowra sees the fate of Troy as punishment for disorder: "Troy falls because the Trojans condone the guilt of Paris . . . His crime passed all the limits allowed to the heroic age; it violated not only wedlock but hospitality" (25).

————. *Heroic Poetry*. London, 1952. Bowra's commonsensical suggestion about the singer's anonymity agrees with Lord's: "the audience knows who the poet is" (405).

————. *Homer and His Forerunners*. Edinburgh, 1955. Most interesting is his argument that the scheme of generations in the *Iliad* is purely artistic (18).

————. "The Meaning of the Heroic Age." In *Language and Background of Homer*, edited by G. S. Kirk, 22–48. Cambridge, England, 1964. The special relationship between the king and the gods (28) and the anthropomorphism of Homer are discussed (47).

Broderson, K. "Zur ersten Rede des Zeus in der *Odyssee*: Erlangen und München Stift." In *Maximilianeum* (1977):32 ff.

Brooks, C. "The Heroic Impulse in the *Odyssey*." *Classical World* 70 (1977):455–56.

Bryce, T. R. "Pandaros, a Lycean at Troy." *American Journal of Philology* 98 (1977):213–18.

Budgen, Frank. "James Joyce: An Encounter with Homer." In *Homer*, edited by George Steiner and Robert Fagles, 156–57. Englewood Cliffs, N.J., 1962. Quotes Joyce's observation that we know more about a Homeric character, in terms of his social context, than we do about any other character in literature.

Calame, C. "Mythe grec et structures narratives: Le mythe des cyclopes dans l'*Odyssée*." *Ziva Antika* 26 (1976):311–28.

Calhoun, George M. "Homeric Repetitions." *Classical Philology* 12 (1933):112–14. Calhoun defines Homer as "a supremely great poet, working with the traditional material."

———. "The Art of Formula in Homer." *Classical Philology* 14 (1935):187–92.

———. "Polity and Society (i) the Homeric Picture." In *A Companion to Homer*, edited by Alan J. B. Wace and Frank H. Stubbings, 431–52. London, 1962.

Carp, T. "Teiresias, Samuel and the Way Home." *California Studies in Classical Antiquity* 12 (1979):65–76. The encounter with the dead in the *nekyia* of the *Odyssey* and in *I Samuel xxviii* serve as extended metaphors of mediation between mortal and god in the human quest for self knowledge.

Carpenter, Rhys. *Folk Tale, Fiction and Saga in the Homeric Epics*. Berkeley, 1946.

Carvalho, J. L. de. "Reflexoes sobre aspectos civilizaciones da *Odisseia*." *Euphrosyne* 8 (1977):7–42.

Chadwick, H. Munro. *The Heroic Age*. Cambridge, England, 1926. Chadwick analyzes the "break-up of normal relations as characteristic of an heroic age . . . a relaxation of the bonds of kinship, which shows itself especially in fatal strife between relatives" (359).

Clarke, W. M. "Achilles and Patroclus in Love." *Hermes* 106 (1978):381–96.

Cook, Arthur Bernard. *Zeus, A Study in Ancient Religion*. 1. New York, 1914.

Corno, D. Del. "Le avventure del falso mendico (*Odissea* 14.192–359)." *Rivista di Cultura classica e medioevale* 20 (1979):835–45.

Creed, Robert P. "The Singer Looks at His Sources." *Comparative Literature* 14 (Winter 1962):44–52. Creed argues for the authority of the epics from analogy: "If Demodocus had told inaccurately the story of the Trojan horse, the heroes who had performed the deeds recounted could themselves have corrected these first or early singers of their adventures . . . We are thus subtly assured that . . . Homer, who through Demodocus links himself with a singer contemporary with Odysseus, is telling us what really happened in those distant days."

Crossett, John. "The Art of Homer's Catalogue of Ships." *Classical Journal* 64 (March 1969):241–49. Crossett discusses the panning effects of progressing from genus to species to individual at the opening of the catalogue as a way of emphasizing the social impact of war (241).

Davies, M. "The Judgment of Paris and *Iliad* 24." *Journal of Hellenic Studies* 101 (1981):56–62.

Delcourt, M. *Hephaistos ou la légende du Magicien*. Paris, 1957.

Devereux, G. "Achilles' 'suicide' in the *Iliad*." *Helios* 6,2 (1978–1979):3–15. Achilles' slaying of Hector, who wore his old armor, can be interpreted as vicarious suicide.

Dietrich, B. C. *Death, Fate and the Gods: The Development of a Religious Idea in Greek Popular Belief and in Homer*. London, 1965. Dietrich discusses the twofold genealogy of Helen, her association with birds and with vegetation, her ambivalent attachment to Artemis and Aphrodite, and her generally chthonic affinities.

———. "Views of Homeric gods and religion." *Numen* 26 (1979):129–51.

*Dimock, George. "Review of Adam Parry, *The Collected Papers of Milman Parry*." *Yale Review* 60 (Summer 1971):585–90.

Dodds, E. R. *The Greeks and the Irrational.* Boston, 1951. Proposes the way in which intent is subordinate to act in the oral tradition (3); the gods are used to express the poet's sense of ultimate order, beyond the individual (18); that the Homeric poems reflect "stirrings of individualism in a society where family solidarity was still universally taken for granted" (47); and that the singer's mysterious relationship to the past, represented by the Muses, puts him in the same category as the seers (81).

Donlan, W. "The Structure of Authority in the *Iliad*." *Arethusa* 12 (1979):51–70.

Drews, R. "Argos and Argives in the *Iliad*." *Classical Philology* 74 (1979):111–35. The society of the *Iliad* has been variously placed in Mycenean Greece, the Dark Age, or Homer's 8th cent. B.C. None of these is entirely acceptable, and the old hypothesis that Thessaly is the origin should be reconsidered.

Duethorn, Gunther A. *Achilles' Shield and the Structure of the Iliad.* Amherst, 1962.

Dukat, Z. "The validity of the comparative method in Homeric studies." *Ziva Antika* 28 (1978):171–78. The difference in aesthetic quality between Homer and the epic song of the Yugoslav bards does not invalidate conclusions about oral poetry that can be reached by studying the latter.

Duysinx, F. "Homère et les instruments de musique." *Didaskalikon* 38 (1977):17–22.

Dyer, Louis. *Syllabus of Forty Lectures on Homer.* Oxford, England, 1898.

Erbse, H. "Ettore nell' *Iliade*." *Studi Classici e Orientali* 28 (1978):15–34. In contrast with the heroic warrior like Achilles, Hektor incarnates a civic ideal.

Falus, R. "Les invocations homériques." *Annalea Universitatia Budapestinensis* 2 (1974):17–38.

Finley, J. .H. *Homer's Odyssey.* Cambridge, Massachusetts: Harvard University Press, 1978.

Finley, M. I. *The World of Odysseus.* New York, 1965. Rev. ed. New York: Viking Press, 1978.

———. "Homer and Mycenae: Property and Tenure." In *The Language and Background of Homer*, 191–217. Cambridge, England, 1964. Provides a capsule statement of the social conflict reflected in the *Iliad*. "Alliance by kinship, marriage and guest friendship on the one hand, and allegiance to a king on the other, adequately explain a very large proportion of the obligations of Homeric society." Homer's visionary perspective is defined in its attempt to synthesize precisely these two systems of alliance.

Foley, H. P. " 'Reverse similes' and sex roles in the *Odyssey*." *Arethusa* 11 (1978):7–26. In similes of family or social relationships clustering around Odysseus's stay in Phaecia and the events following his return to Ithaca, Homer emphasizes the necessity for an interdependent relationship between male and female characteristics and spheres of action in the restoration of stability and normal social and economic conditions on Ithaca.

Frankel, Hermann. *Early Greek Poetry and Philosophy*. Oxford, England, 1973. Especially his chapter on "The New Mood of the *Odyssey* and the End of the Epic."

Friedrich, Paul. *The Meaning of Aphrodite*. Chicago: University of Chicago Press, 1978. A comprehensive structural analysis of the mysterious goddess.

———. "Sanity and the Myth of Honor. The Problem of Achilles." *Ethos* 5 (1977):281–305. Honor and value complexes linked with honor depended upon keeping women relatively deprived of honor and competing for women as symbolic of honor. The system is rooted in sexuality and its rationalization in non-sexual terms makes it appropriate to speak of a "myth" of honor which underlies subjugation by force.

Gardner, Ernest A. *A Handbook of Greek Sculpture*. Vol. 1. London, 1896. Gardner, in addition to providing general background on Hephaistos (66 ff.), notes that, in contrast with early Greek art in general, the scenes upon Achilles' shield are all from actual life—none from mythology (70).

Geddes, William D. *The Problem of the Homeric Poems*. London, 1878. Geddes notes Helen's connections with Hera (109) and the fact that Homer does not discuss Helen's guilt (100).

Glotz, G. *The Greek City and Its Institutions*. Translated by N. Mallinson. New York, 1929. Anthropological / sociological approach. Argues that "the 'polis' became a really 'political' institution without destroying the clans, the phratries or the tribes; indeed, it was only possible for it to become so by incorporating these groups" (12). He also underlines the significance of expatriate status.

Goold, G. P. "The Nature of Homeric Composition." *Illinois Classical Studies* 2 (1977):1–34. The *Iliad* and *Odyssey* were composed by a single poet using a process called "progressive fixation of a text." Neither inconsistencies within the epics nor the evidence of additions to them is evidence against a Homer who wrote the poems using traditional tales to fulfill his artistic vision.

Gordon, Cyrus H. *Homer and the Bible*. New York, 1955.

Gray, D. H. F. "Metal-working in Homer." *Journal of Hellenic Studies* 74 (1954):1–16.

Greene, Thomas. *The Descent from Heaven: A Study in Epic Continuity*. New Haven, 1963. Even though Greene concludes that Achilles' reentry is only a vendetta, "without purpose or hope, a ritual suicide" (42), many of his general statements ring true of the *Iliad*. He states that the epic "acquires an austerity that is peculiarly human" (14), that the hero "must be acting for the community . . . he may incarnate the City, but he must be nonetheless an individual with a name" (15); and that the epic "draws upon sexual springs to invigorate the imagination" (23).

Gresseth, G. K. "The *Odyssey* and the *Nalopākhyāna*." *Transactions and Proceedings of the American Philological Association* 109 (1979):63–85. The extensive similarities of theme and action between the *Odyssey* and the Sanskrit poem *Nalopākhyāna* show that the *Odyssey* presents the same basic story but has changed the use of the themes.

Griffin, J. "The divine audience and the religion of the *Iliad*." *Classical Quarterly* 28 (1978):1–22. The gods of the *Iliad* do play the role of omniscient watchers upholding justice, but, at times they more nearly resemble spectators at a sporting event or the audience of a tragedy.

Guthrie, W. C. *The Greeks and Their Gods*. Edited by Hammond, N. G. L., and H. H. Scullard. London, 1950. In *The Oxford Classical Dictionary*, 2d ed. Oxford, England, 1970. Includes a succinct and sensible discussion of the Homeric Question (524–25).

Hansen, W. F. "Odysseus' Last Journey." *Quaderni Urbinati di Cultura classica* 24 (1977):27–48. The story of Odysseus's last voyage (*Odyssey* 11.121–137) is witness to the ancient legend of the sailor who sails into the interior of the sea.

Harriott, Rosemary. *Poetry and Criticism Before Plato*. London, 1969. Harriott explains that, to the Homeric Greek, "Mnemosyne was both Memory, the accumulated story of inherited knowledge and the Reminder, who cause *klea andron* ('the glorious deeds of men') . . . to be recalled and kept fresh" (18). She emphasizes the oral process of education as a continuous one, by comparison with the literate process (107).

Havelock, Eric A. *Preface to Plato*. Cambridge, England, 1963. Havelock argues that the Homeric epic is a kind of "tribal encyclopedia" which records "public usage (nomos) and private habit (ethos)" (66). His insistence that critical attention must focus on the nature of the Homeric aesthetic effectively solves the problem of reconciling the poet's individuality with the collective tradition.

————. "Thoughtful Hesiod." *Yale Classical Studies* 20 (1966):61–72. Havelock argues that Homer, too, must have been aware of Hesiod's discrimination of Strife into two principles.

Hesiod. Translated by Richmond Lattimore. Ann Arbor, Mich., 1968.

Hillers, D. R. and McCall, M. H. "Homeric Dictated Texts: A Reexamination of Some Near Eastern Evidence." *Harvard Studies in Classical Philology* 80 (1976):20–23. The evidence from the catalogue of Ashurbanipal's library and from the Ugaritic texts, cited to support A. B. Lord's theory of Homeric dictated texts, does not withstand scrutiny and should not be so used.

Jaeger, Werner. *Paideia: The Ideals of Greek Culture*. Vol. 1, *Archaic Greece, the Mind of Athens*. 2d ed. New York, 1965. Corroborates the view of the Homeric epics as didactic poems; the definition of paradeigma, as "examples of imitation"; the integration of ethics and aesthetics in early Greek thought (35); the power of art "of converting the human soul" (36 ff); and the bond between poetry and myth.

Jebb, R. C. *Homer: An Introduction to the Iliad and the Odyssey*. Glasgow, 1887.

Kagan, Donald. *The Great Dialogue: History of Greek Political Thought from Homer to Polybus*. London, 1965. According to Kagan, "Agamemnon is more royal than Achilles less because he holds the scepter of Zeus than because he rules 'many hosts.' "

Kakridis, Johannes Th. *Homeric Researches*. London, 1949. In his discussion of Meleagros in Book 9, Kakridis isolates the "ascending scale of affection from wife to friends" (20) and points out many contrasting and comparable elements which relate the saga as Phoinix narrates it to the song itself (25 ff.). Kakridis sees the *Iliad* as embodying the conflict between two scales of affection: the older, in which the progression ascends from the conjugal to the filial; and the new order, from the conjugal to the fraternal to the filial (162).

————. "The Role of Women in the *Iliad*." *Eranos* 54 (1956):21–27.

Kalogeras, V. A. "A New Light on the *Odyssey*." *Platon* 29 (1977):3–25. Argues, based on archaeological evidence, that present-day Ithaki is indeed Odysseus's Ithaca.

Karp, A. J. "Homeric Origins of Ancient Rhetoric." *Arethusa* 10 (1977):237–58.

Keller, Albert G. *Homeric Society: A Sociological Study of the Iliad and the Odyssey*. London, 1902. The nature of Helen's crime can be judged in light of Keller's analysis: "Adultery proper was only possible in the case of the chief wife, the wife of status, from whom the line of succession took its origin; only in that case were the consequences far-reaching, demanding special vengeance, and was the succession endangered" (228). He explains that "the blame was one of social and economic import, for Paris violated the bond of guest-friendship and alienated his host's property" (229).

Kirk, G.S. "Dark Age and Oral Poet." *Proceedings of the Cambridge Philological Society* 187 (1961):34–48 (n.s. 7). Concludes that what are usually termed "heroic features" actually belong to "the centuries following a heroic age" (45).

————. *The Songs of Homer*. Cambridge, 1962. Argues that "the 'pattern of imagery' proves the unity of the epic tradition, not that there was one single originator of all the contexts in which such imagery occurs" (259). Nevertheless, Kirk feels that we must posit a single composer for the *Iliad* as we know it (255).

————, ed. *The Language and Background of Homer*. Cambridge, 1964.

Knight, W. F. Jackson. *Many-Minded Homer*. Edited by John D. Christie. New York, 1968. Discusses the combination of myth and allegory operating in Hera's seduction of Zeus in book 14.

Lang, Mabel L. "Homer and Oral Techniques." *Hesperia* 38 (April–June 1969):159–68.

Lawton, W. C. *The Successors of Homer*. New York, 1898.

Leaf, Walter. *Homer and History*. London, 1915. Still useful for its geographical delineations of Homeric Greece. Especially important is his discussion of the fourfold variation in the use of the term "Argos" (193 ff).

Lee, M. O. "Achilles and Hector as Hegelian Heroes." *Échos du Monde classique* 30 (1981):97–103. Both Achilles and Hector are heroes who bring about a new world. Achilles moves from a (polis)-oriented heroic code to a recognition of the worth of human relationships. Hector became the hero of chivalry in later times.

Leinieks, Valdis. "The *Iliad* and the Epic Cycle." *Classical Outlook* 52 (February 1975):62–64. A succinct summary of Swiss-German scholars' conclusions that the epic cycles dealing with the Trojan War "were not composed after the *Iliad* to fill in the events leading up to and following those narrated in the *Iliad*. Instead, these poems were already in existence before the *Iliad* was composed and the poet of the *Iliad* was thoroughly familiar with them" (63).

He dates the cycle as follows, in order of narrative chronology:

Cypria (Stasinus)	11 books	730
Iliad (Homer)	24 books	720
Aethiopis (Arctinus)	5 books	730
Little Iliad (Lesches)	4 books	710
Iliou Persis (Arctinus)	2 books	730

Lesky, Albin. *A History of Greek Literature.* Translated by James Willis and Cornelis de Heer. London, 1957. Lesky confirms the social role of Homeric song (14) and compares the singing on Achilles' shield to that of the bards in the *Odyssey* (15).

Lessing, Gotthold Ephraim. *Laocoon.* Translated by Ellen Frothingham. New York, 1968. Lessing notes the historical description of Agamemnon's scepter (96 ff.), the distinction between that scepter and the one cast down by Achilles as appropriate to the conflict of character (99), the description of Pandaros's bow in terms of its origins (99–100), and the general difference between poetic and artistic representation (109). He emphasizes that Homer describes the shield of Achilles in the making (116 ff.) and calls the shield "an epitome of all that was happening in the world" (232).

Levy, Gertrude F. *The Gate of Horn.* London, 1948. Levy states that the "frequent references to quarrels between kin in the preceding generations point to a transition from the old close blood union of the clan to dependence upon a chief's personal prestige" (265).

*Littleton, C. Scott. "Some Possible Indo-European Themes in The *Iliad*." In *Myth and Law Among the Indo-Europeans,* edited by Jaan Puhvel, 229–46. Berkeley: University of California Press, 1970.

Lidov, J. B. "The Anger of Poseidon." *Arethusa* 10 (1977):227–36. In the *Odyssey*, Poseidon speaks for giving each his due and proper place while Odysseus strives to become what his situation demands without respect for the principles of individual integrity and limitation which Poseidon upholds. In the course of his adventures Odysseus achieves the moral knowledge we see him exhibit first among the Phaiakians.

Lloyd, William Watkiss. *On the Homeric Design of the Shield of Achilles.* London, 1854. This dated analysis of Achilles' shield nevertheless holds much interest. Lloyd notes the connection between poetry and husbandry on the shield (19); the "almost undeviating use of the perfect tense" (20); the characteristics of the choreography (21–22), and the symmetry of the pictures of war and peace (31).

Longinus. *On the Sublime.* Translated by G. M. A. Grube. New York, 1957. "One might compare the Homer of the *Odyssey* to the setting sun: the grandeur remains but not the intensity" (15). "Homer's stories of wounds, factions, revenge tears, chains, and confused passions among the gods make the men of the Trojan War as far as possible into gods and the gods into men" (13).

Loomis, Julia W. "Homer, the First Psychologist." *Classical Outlook* 52 (February 1975): 64–67. Loomis argues that Homer's psychology, like Freud's, was a struggle "to differentiate between an instinct and controlling agency" and that Homer was fully conscious of instincts "such as the sex drive (*eros*), or the self-assertive drive (*menis*), or the societal instinct of right and wrong (*themis*). However, he never relegated them to the realm of forces in control (*theoi*). The ancient Greek mind could never accept the idea that instincts control human actions. They might be a motivating force, but hopefully, reason was in control. And reason was a gift from outside oneself. No man on his own determination could be reasonable; nor could he fall in love. Eros might bring two persons together, but unless Aphrodite (a *theos*, or force in control) passed by, there would be no love" (65).

Lord, Albert B. "Homer, Ithaca, and Huso." *Supplement to the American Journal of Archaeology* 52 (1948): 33–44.

————. *The Singer of Tales*. New York, 1965. Lord's conclusions about the analogical relationship between the Homeric and the Balkan songs are constantly thought-provoking. However, in implying that the oral tradition operative on Homer obviates entirely the serious influence of individual talent, Lord contradicts his own professional caution.

Lorimer, H. L. *Homer and the Monuments*. London, 1950.

Lowenstam, S. "Patroclus' Death in the *Iliad* and the Inheritance of an Indo-European Myth." *Archaeological News* 6 (1977): 72–76. Analysis of the account in *Iliad* 16 of Patroclus's return to battle and death in terms of elements inherited from an Indo-European archetype, which apparently demonstrated the ambivalent nature of martial prowess.

Lukacs, Georg. "To Narrate or Describe?" In *Homer*, edited by George Steiner and Robert Fagles 62–73. Englewood Cliffs, N.J., 1962. Characteristic of the *Iliad* is the observation that "objects have poetic life only through their relationship to human destiny . . . The epic poet . . . speaks of the tasks objects have in the nexus of human destinies, and he does so only when the objects share in those destinies, when they partake in the deeds and sufferings of men" (87).

Mackail, J. W. *Lectures on Greek Poetry*. London, 1910. Mackail calls Homer a "*deus absconditus*" (23) and says of Helen that she is "a thing enskied. Her words over the body of Hektor are the high-water marks of the *Iliad;* and it is not of Hektor they leave us thinking, but of her" (35–36).

MacKay, L. A. *The Wrath of Homer*. Toronto, 1948.

*Mariani, Alice. "The Forged Feature: Created Identity in Homer's *Odyssey*." Ph.D. diss., Yale University, 1967.

Martin, Roland. *Recherches sur L'Agora Grecque*. Paris, 1951. Martin shows that the Greek army in the *Iliad* was organized like the city, by clans, tribes, etc. Consequently, the war agora may be taken to be analogous to the peace agora on the shield (22).

Miller, D. A. "A note on Aegisthus as Hero." *Arethusa* 10 (1977): 259–265. The Aegisthus of Homer, analysed according to the comparativist theory of Dumézil, is found to be a complex heroic character as contrasted to the simple evil he represents in the tragic poets.

Motto, Anna L., and John R. Clark. "*Isê Dais:* The Honor of Achilles." *Arethusa* 2 (Fall 1969): 109–25. The authors see Achilles, "not as a scapegoat or a rebel, but as the avatar of society" (109). They argue against the interpretation that makes Achilles' alienation total.

Murray, A. S. *A History of Greek Sculpture*. Vol. 1. London, 1890. Murray argues that Homer meant "Helen's weaving to represent actual past scenes."

Murray, Gilbert. *The Rise of the Greek Epic.* 3d ed., revised and enlarged. Oxford, England, 1924. Murray has much to say about the pitiable state of the guest-stranger (84 ff.), especially in light of the "five deadly sins" of Hesiod (87). He also provides background data on Helen (205) and an excellent discussion on *arete* (59).

Myres, John L. *Who Were the Greeks?* Berkeley, 1930. Hephaistos's craft distinguishes him from the other gods (170); he is "insecurely married" to Aphrodite (172). Myres calls "the Homeric poems . . . a storehouse of coherent folk-memory about a real phase in the making of the Greek world" (31).

Nagler, Michael N. *Spontaneity and Tradition: A Study in the Oral Art of Homer.* Berkeley, 1974. Reopening the Homeric Question, Nagler regards the two epics "not as typical of the average performance by the average singer, but as typical of what a great singer could do with his tradition before a highly appreciative audience" (xviii).

―――. "Dread Goddess Endowed with Speech." *Archaeological News* 6 (1977): 77–85.

―――. "How Does An Oral Poem Mean?" *Arion*, n.s., 3, no. 3:365–77.

Niles, J. D. "Patterning in the Wanderings of Odysseus." *Ramus* 7 (1978): 46–60. The incidents of Odysseus's wanderings fall into a neat pattern of temptations, physical attacks, and taboos, all of which he survives, unlike his crewmen, by means of his self-control, his wits, and his obedience.

Nillson, Martin P. *The Mycenean Origins of Greek Mythology.* Berkeley, 1932. Identifies the heroic age which produced the epics with the Mycenaeans, associates the Tyndarean oath with Agamemnon's right to form an alliance (229); notes Helen's Minoan affinities (252 ff.): marks the exemplary function of mythical tales (294), and points out that only in the case of Achilles and Hephaistos does a mortal receive a gift from the gods (215).

―――. *Homer and Mycenae.* London, 1933.

North, Helen. *Sophrosyne: Self-Knowledge and Self-Restraint in Greek Literature.* Ithaca, N.Y., 1966. Although sophrosyne is not a "heroic" virtue, according to North, "since the two greatest fighting men . . . Achilles and Ajax, are the very ones who most notoriously lack this quality" (2), it does share with the Homeric *aidos* the "fear of overstepping boundaries" (6). Achilles perhaps approaches such a perspective toward the end of the *Iliad.*

Northrup, M. D. "Homer's Catalogue of Women." *Ramus* 9 (1980): 150–59. The catalogue of women in *Odyssey* 9.225–332 is not an awkward interpolation. The women correspond to the males described in 11.385–600. The women emphasize the possibilities of what Odysseus might encounter when he returns to Ithaca. The shades of the women suggest the interplay of past, present, and future.

Notopoulos, James A. "Mnemosyne in Oral Literature." *Transactions and Proceedings of the American Philological Association* 69 (1938): 465–93. Notopoulos terms Homer a "mnemo-technician," and stresses the didactic import of the poems: "It was the poet's task to conserve the living experiences and transmit them to posterity (468) . . . The poet is the incarnate book of oral peoples" (469). He talks about the "static" (i.e., retentive) and "creative" (thought synthesized with memory) functions of memory (469).

O'Nolan, K. "Doublets in the *Odyssey.*" *Classical Quarterly* 28 (1978): 23–27. The doublet, or combination of two essentially synonymous terms, functions similarly to the noun-epithet formula as an essential feature of Homeric style. Both present a single idea through a double image and tend to occur in the second half of the line, the location of the most traditional and preconceived elements.

Owen, E. T. *The Story of the Iliad.* Ann Arbor, 1946. A model of comprehensive exposition. Owen points out that we first see Achilles in a social role (5); that the *teikoskopia* is constructed with the audience in mind (34); and that the meeting between Glaukos and Diomedes provides a stark contrast with the brutality of battle (58–59). Owen's description of the way in which similar images evokes similar responses is highly apt: "As the scene necessarily comes back to mind, the poem responds to the recollection; it comes back in the words. The verbal repetitions do not make the recollection; they are the memory recording itself" (178).

Parodi de Lisi, M. C. "Algunas consideraciones acerca de la religión homérica." *Argos* 2 (1978): 47–69.

Parry, Adam. "The Language of Achilles." *Transactions and Proceedings of the American Philological Association* 87 (1956): 1–18. In Adam Parry's most important article, he proves that "Achilles is . . . the one Homeric hero who does not accept the common language, and feels that it does not correspond to reality." The hero's self-expression, of course, is limited by the traditional character of the Homeric speech. Therefore, "Achilles can only . . . ask questions that cannot be answered and make demands that cannot be met."

———. "Have We Homer's *Iliad?*" *Yale Classical Studies* 20 (1966): 177–216. Here Parry defines Homer as "the poet who composed the *Iliad* at the time when it was put into writing," noting that Milman Parry originally demonstrated the antithesis "not between the oral and lettered poet, but between the poet of a traditional and the poet of an individual style."

———. ed. Introduction to *The Making of Homeric Verse: The Collected Papers of Milman Parry.* Oxford, England, 1971. Adam Parry's judicious and succinct review of Homeric scholarship in this century makes another general review superfluous. His own critique of Milman Parry's work itself is a landmark, indicating that the deleterious effect of Parryism has given way to a saner perspective which combines its insights with more or less traditional critical appreciation of poetry.

Parry, Milman. "A Comparative Study of Diction as One of the Elements of Style in Early Greek Epic Poetry." 1923. In *The Making,* 421–36.

———. "The Traditional Epithet in Homer." 1928. In *The Making,* 1–190. Parry points out that Helen "is the only woman in Homer who clearly has distinctive epithets of her own" (97). Parry sets up the problem Dimock's analysis solves: "Here is a poet who marked his works with genius not because he was able to model the words on his own thought, but because he was able to make use of traditional words and expressions" (144). Dimock's argument is that the poet's own thought was likely to be metrical; Nagler's theory takes this a step further.

———. "Homeric Formulae and Homeric Metre." 1928. In *The Making,* 191–239. The difficulty of the memorization process outlined here (195) is also solved by Dimock's observation of the metrical patterns of thought. Parry's logic in this work is contradictory.

———. "Studies in the Epic Technique of Oral Verse-Making: I. Homer and Homeric Style." *Harvard Studies in Classical Philology* 41 (1930): 73–148. Parry here makes the assertion that "in treating of the oral nature of the Homeric style we shall see that the question of a remnant of individuality in Homeric style disappears altogether" (138).

———. "Cor Huso: A Study of Southslavic Song." 1933–35. In *The Making*, 439–64. Parry at this late stage in his thought argues that the *Iliad* and the *Odyssey* are each the work of a single singer.

———. "On Typical Scenes in Homer." 1936. In *The Making*, 404–7.

Peabody, Berkeley. *The Winged Word: A Study in the Technique of Ancient Greek Oral Composition as seen Principally in Hesiod's "Works and Days."* Albany, N.Y., 1970.

Perry, Walter Copland. *The Women of Homer.* New York, 1898. Perry reports the opinion of the scholia of Venice: "From the scenes embroidered on (Helen's) web . . . Homer took the greater part of his history of the . . . war."

Pound, Ezra. "Homer or Virgil?" In *Homer*, edited by George Steiner and Robert Fagles 17–18. Englewood Cliffs, N.J., 1962. Pound terms Homer "the imaginary spectator."

Powys, John Cowper. "Preface to Homer and the Aether." In *Homer*, ed. Steiner and Fagles, 140–47. Powys calls the *Iliad* greater than the *Odyssey* because it is more "realistic and natural" (140). He also observes: "The most significant and characteristic thing about his gathering, accumulating, enlarging, thickening, expanding, deepening story of human life . . . is his emphasis upon the family" (147).

Powell, B. B. "Word Patterns in the Catalogue of Ships (B494–709). A Structural Analysis of Homeric Language." *Hermes* 106 (1978): 255–64. Comprehensive study of the most conspicuously "formulaic" sequence in the corpus. It is possible to show that all entries in the catalogue, with one exception, follow one of three patterns, each truly striking for its structural rigidity.

Prendergast, Guy L. A. *A Complete Concordance to the Iliad of Homer.* Edited by Benedetto Marzullo. Hildesheim, West Germany, 1962.

*Redfield, J. M. *Nature and Culture in the Iliad: The Tragedy of Hector.* Chicago and London: University of Chicago Press, 1975.

———. "The Proem of the *Iliad:* Homer's art." *Classical Philology* 74 (1979): 95–110.

Reinhart, Karl. *Die Iliad und Ihr Dichter.* Gottingen, West Germany, 1961. Marks the anonymity of the great shield and calls it a "timeless, nameless glimpse of the continuity of life" (405).

Robert, Fernand. *Homère.* Paris, 1950. This work is useful for discussion of the background of Hephaistos (146 ff.); of Helen (210 ff.); of the marital conflict of the Olympians (92); and for emphasizing the hierarchical concern of the poem (216, 220 ff.).

Rose, G. P. "The Swineherd and the Beggar." *Phoenix* 34 (1980): 285–90. The long conversation of the disguised Odysseus with the swineherd Eumaeus plays an important part in Odysseus's recreation of the original order that had existed on Ithaca. Odysseus as swineherd gains Eumaeus's respect and affection on his own merit unaided by the automatic esteem afforded an aristocrat.

Rossignol, J.-P. *Les Artistes Homériques: Histoire critique de tous les artistes qui figurent dans l'Iliad et dans l'Odysée.* Paris, 1885.

Rouse, W. H. D. *Homer.* London, 1939.

Russo, Joseph A. "The Structural Formula in Homeric Verse." *Yale Classical Studies* 20 (1966): 219–40.

———. "Homer against His Tradition." *Arion* (Summer 1968); 275–95. Russo argues that Homer was capable of appropriate improvisation. Homer can break the "oral law," Russo argues. Four kinds of scenes are analyzed, "running from most traditional to least traditional or most inventive" (282).

———and Bennett Simon. "Homeric Psychology and the Oral Epic Tradition." *Journal of the History of Ideas* 29 (October–December 1968); 483–98. Charts the relationship between the psychology of the poet and that of his characters, underlining the communal emphasis in Homer, "the important social role played by the bard himself. His recitations serve as a cultural repository for the history, social ideals and general world-view of his society." The authors note the emotional involvement of the bard and his audience (p. 492) by which the boundaries of self are dissolved.

Sandstrom, Oscar R. *A Study of the Ethical Principles of Homeric Warfare.* Philadelphia, 1924.

Schrade, Hubert. *Götter und Menschen Homers.* Stuttgart, 1952. The connection between Hephaistos, the Egyptian Ptah and Chnum, and the Babylonian Ea is speculated upon (78); Hephaistos's gold robots and Pandora are related (87); and Hephaistos is seen as a stranger among the Greek gods (88), connected with Daidalos (91).

Scott, John A. *The Unity of Homer.* Berkeley, 1921.

Scully, S. P. "The Polis in Homer. A Definition and Interpretation." Ph.D. diss., Brown University, 1978. Cf. summary in *Dissertation Abstracts* 39 (1979).

———. "The Bard as the Custodian of Homeric Society, *Odyssey* 3, 263–272." *Quaderni Urbinati di Cultura classica* 37 (1981): 67–83. Identifies the "poet" with the principle of order.

Sealey, Raphael. "From Phemios to Ion." *Revue des Etudes Grecques* 70 (1957): 312–55.

Seymour, Thomas D. *Life in the Homeric Age.* New York, 1907. Discusses the adultery of Helen and of Klytaimnestra (149); Hephaistos's making jewelry for Thetis (171), the aegis for Zeus (291), armor for Diomedes (433), and a jar for Achilles' bones (433). Notes that Hephaistos is presented as the only married god besides Zeus (425).

Sheppard, J. T. *The Pattern of the Iliad.* London, 1922. Suggests that the shield-making process reflects the poet's rather than the blacksmith's art (6), emphasizes Achilles' peacemaking role in the games (201), and discusses the two kinds of strife (209). He calls "the central doctrine of Homer's . . . heroic faith — a recognition of the fact of our common humanity" (207).

Simon, Bennett, and Herbert Weiner. "Models of Mind and Mental Illness in Ancient Greece: I. The Homeric Model of Mind." *Journal of the History of the Behavioral Sciences* 2 (October 1966): 303–15. The authors details the "therapeutic role of the bard" (310), and the way in which "the audience quickly identifies itself with the characters" (311). They note the importance of contexts of creativity (312), especially "the poet within the poem" since "the 'mind' that is described in Homer is the 'mind' of the poets who created the Homeric poems" (312).

Simpson, R. Hope, and J. F. Lazenby. *The Catalogue of Ships in Homer's Iliad.* Oxford, 1970.

Snell, Bruno. *The Discovery of the Mind.* Translated by T. G. Rosenmeyer. New York, 1953. Snell's monumental work is indispensable to the student of the Homeric mind: it defines the role of memory in an oral culture (36); the ideal nature of the epic world (40); its metaphysical structure (41); and the way in which it reflects the replacement of chronic disorder with Olympian order (136).

Snyder, J. M. "The Web of Song. Weaving Imagery in Homer and the Lyric Poets." *Classical Journal* 76 (1981): 193–96. Weaving was linked in the Greek mind with singing, and this led naturally to the use of metaphors derived from weaving to describe the art of poetry as a web of song.

Solmsen, Friedrich. "The 'Gift' of Speech in Homer and Hesiod." *Transactions and Proceedings of the American Philological Association* 85 (1954): 1–15.

Sperduti, Alice. "The Divine Nature of Poetry in Antiquity." *Transactions and Proceedings of the American Philological Association* 81 (1950): 209–40. Sees singing on the shield of Achilles as being analogous to its role in Homeric society (266), underlines the importance of memorialization as a social motivation (266), and discusses the relationship among poetry, good government, and Zeus (231).

Stawell, F. Melian. *Homer and the Iliad.* London, 1909. The author notices the impression of simultaneity in the shield-forging process (197 ff.) and says of the shield's structure: "The arrangement of the scenes in concentric rings is not only the one most naturally suggested by the words of the poem: it is far the most effective as a symbol for the imaginative content."

Steiner, George, and Robert Fagles, eds. *Homer.* Englewood Cliffs, N.J., 1962. The authors, in their introduction, connect heroic deeds, aesthetic beauty, and glory (9), calling the similes "assurance of ultimate stability." They note that "myths . . . re-enact moments of signal truth or crisis in the human condition . . . The poet . . . is the historian of the unconscious. This gives to the great myths their haunting universality" (3). One of the greatest such human disasters is the fall of the city (3).

Stubbings, Frank H. "Crafts and Industries." In *A Companion to Homer*, edited by Alan J. B. Wace and Frank H. Stubbings, 504–22. London, 1962.

Svencickaja, I. S. "The Interpretation of Data on Landholding in the *Iliad* and the *Odyssey*" (in Russian). In *Vestnik Drevnej Istorii* 135 (1976): 52–63. The Homeric poems do not reflect a concept of communal property but, instead, a society of private estates transmuted to the male heirs of the property holders.

Swogger, J. H. "Odysseus the Magician." *Classical Bulletin* 58 (1981): 24–25. Odysseus's qualifications as a dream interpreter in *Odyssey* 19.535 ff. are due to his being a magician.

Symonds, John A. *Studies of the Greek Poets.* Vol. 1. London, 1893. Helen, according to Symonds, has "a mysterious virginity of soul. She is not touched by the passions she inspires . . . Like beauty, she belongs to all and to none" (109).

Tashiro, Tom T. "Three Passages in Homer, and the Homeric Legacy." *Antioch Review* 25 (Spring 1965): 63–92. Comments on the analogous relationship between Achilles' rejection of Agamemnon's offers and Agamemnon's of Chryses' (66); on the connection between the marriage and judicial scenes on the shield of Achilles (66); on the historical significance of the necropolis (75); and on the hierarchical significance of Zeus' golden chain.

Thomas, C. G. "The Roots of Homeric Kingship." *Historia* 15 (1966): 387–407.

Thomson, George. *Aeschylus and Athens: A Study in the Social Origins of the Drama.* London, 1941. Discusses endo- and exogamous relations among the various levels of social organization (40), and concludes that "even after its basis in kinship had crumbled away, the tribal system still seemed the necessary foundation for any form of ordered society" (40). Thomson also distinguishes between the character of the feudal-like "king-vassal" relationship and that of kinship.

Tolstoy, Leo. "Homer and Shakespeare." In *Homer,* ed. Steiner and Fagles, 15–16.

Tsagarakis, O. *Nature and Background of Major Concepts of Divine Power in Homer.* Amsterdam Gruner, 1977.

Turolla, Enrico. *Saggio su la poesía di Omero.* Bari, Italy, 1949.

Vanderlinden, E. "L'homme de *l'Odyssée." Les Études Classiques* 46 (1978): 293–316.

Vico, Giambattista. *The New Science of Giambattista Vico.* Translated by Thomas Goddard Bergin and Max Herold Fisch. 1948. Revised and abridged. Ithaca, N.Y., and London, 1961. Provocative for drawing attention to the shield of Achilles presentation of the creation story and of the relationship between social order and "the arts of humanity." Vico's "Search for the True Homer" (269–74) are seminal essays despite their obvious prejudices. He perceives the connection between memory and imagination (260); that "the nations should speak in verses so that their memories might be aided by meter and rhythm to preserve more easily the histories of their families and cities" (262), implying the direct connection between poetic and political action; and the equation of Homer with "the Greek peoples . . . themselves" (270–74).

Vivante, Paolo. "Homer and the Aesthetic Moment." In *Arion* 4 (Autumn 1965): 415–38. Proclaims the universality of Homer's art: "What we find here is an exhaustive nomenclature, a whole system of attributes and qualifications, as if poetry had set out to explore the universe and render its outlines" (417).

———. *The Homeric Imagination: A Study of Homer's Poetic Perception of Reality.* Bloomington, Indiana, 1970.

———. "Men's Epithets in Homer: An Essay in Poetic Syntax." *Glotta* 58 (1980): 157–72.

*———. "Rose-Fingered Dawn and the Idea of Time." *Ramus* 8 (1980): 125–36.

*Voegelin, Eric. *The World of Polis,* Vol. 2 of *Order and History.* Baton Rouge: Louisiana State University Press, 1957.

Vries, G. J. De. "Phaeacian Manners." *Mnemosyne* 30 (1977): 113–21.

Wace, Alan J. B. "Houses and Palaces." In *A Companion to Homer*, ed. A. J. B. Wace and F. H. Stubbings, 521–32.

——— and H. P. Wace. "Dress." In *A Companion to Homer*, Wace and Stubbings, 498–503.

Wace, Alan J. B., and Frank H. Stubbings, eds. *A Companion to Homer*, London, 1962.

Wade-Gery, H. T. *The Poet of the Iliad*. Cambridge, England, 1952. "Homer's achievement was . . . to reduce . . . oral technique to writing" (39).

Walcot, P. "Odysseus and the art of lying." *Ancient Society* 7 (1977): 1–19.

———. "The Judgement of Paris." *Greece and Rome* 24 (1977): 31–39.

Ward, Donald. "The Divine Twins: An Indo-European Myth in Germanic Tradition." *Folklore Studies* 19 (1968).

Webster, T. B. L. "Greek Theories of Art and Literature Down to 400 B.C." *Classical Quarterly* 33 (July–October 1939): 167–79. Webster, too, argues for the audience's expectations of veracity in epic poetry.

———. *From Mycenae to Homer*. 2d ed., enlarged. New York, 1964. Like Lorimer and Stubbings, Webster proves that while elements within the poem are historical, their contemporaneous existence with other elements indicates that the chronology of the Iliadic world is itself fictional.

———. "Polity and Society (ii) Historical Commentary." In *A Companion to Homer*, ed. Wace and Stubbings, 452–62.

Wender, D. "Homer, Avdo Mededovic, and The elephant's child." *American Journal of Philology* 98 (1977): 327–47. The Wedding of Smailagic Meho is nearly as long as the Odyssey and displays a unified plot, but is clearly inferior in narrative and dramatic skill to the Homeric poems.

*Whitman, Cedric H. *Homer and the Heroic Tradition*. New York, 1958.

Willcock, Malcolm M. *A Companion to the Iliad, Based on the Translation by Richmond Lattimore*. Chicago and London, 1976. The line-by-line commentary is a valuable aid to students reading the poem in English for the first time; includes useful appendixes on "Transmission of the Text of the *Iliad* and Commentaries on It," "Methods of Fighting in the *Iliad*," and "Mythology and the Gods."

Wilson, Pearl C. "The *Páthei Máthos* of Achilles," *Transactions and Proceedings of the American Philological Association* 69 (1938): 557–74. One of the few interpretations of Achilles' development which takes full cognizance of his changing social attitudes.

Yoshida, A. "La Structure de l'Illustration du Bouclier d' Achille." *Revue Belge de Philologie et d'Histoire* 42 (1964): 5–15. Yoshida sees the tripartite Indo-European pattern of social structure in Mycenaean civilization.

Young, Douglas. "Never Blotted a Line?: Formula and Premeditation in Homer and Hesiod." *Arion* 6 (Autumn 1967): 279–324. Argues against Lord's assertion that the epics were composed simultaneous with performance.

*Zarker, John W. "King Eëtion and Thebe as Symbols in the *Iliad*." *Classical Journal* 61 (December 1965): 110–14.

INDEX

Achaians, 1, 28–32
Achilles, 6–8, 112, 138–39; wrath of, 65–70; *See also cholos*; Shield of Achilles
Aegisthus, 31
Aeneas, 58, 98
Aeneid, 58–61, 158
Aeschylus, 3
Agamemnon, 10–11, 16–17, 24, 31–32, 141–42
Alkinoos, 181–86
Andromache, 9, 28–36, 127–32, 147–52; headdress of, 9, 159–65
Antigone, 15–36
Aphrodite, 134; *See also* Judgment of Paris
Apollo, 23, 24
Archery at the Dark of the Moon (Austin), 9–10, 61n, 169–80
Ares, 24
Aristotle, 4, 113–26; *Poetics*, 6
Atchity, Kenneth, 1–12, 15–36, 159–65
Athene, 2–3, 4, 10, 21, 24–36, 135
Auden, W.H., 6–7, 111–12
Auerbach, Eric, 11, 212
Austin, Norman, 9–10, 61n, 169–80

Barber, E.J.W., 15–36
Bespaloff, Rachel, 7–8, 127–32
Bible, the, 5–6
Borges, Jorges Luis, 4, 13–14
Boyer, Mildred, 4, 113
Briseis, 148–52, 161
Butterworth, E.A.S., 10, 181–86

Calypso, 10–11, 18, 31, 75–77, 200–211
Cassandra, 42–43, 165
Cavafy, Constantin, 11, 223–24
Charybdis, 169–70
cholos, 65–70, 74; *See also*, Achilles, wrath of

Chryseis, 31, 148–52, 161
Circe, 18–19, 27, 169–71, 198–200
Cyclops, 25, 26–27, 181–86, 199

Dante, 1, 106
Descent from Heaven: A Study in Epic Continuity, The (Greene), 8–9, 222n
Devereux, George, 4
Dido, 58–61
Dimock, George, 6, 11, 106–109
Divine Comedy, 1
Donne, John, 9, 167–68
Dumézil, Georges, 8, 22, 24, 34n, 132–45

Elektra, 15–36
eros, 70–75
ethics, 7
Eumenides (Aeschylus), 24, 192–93
Euripides, 29–31
Eurycleia, 11, 174, *211–23*; and the boar episode, 11

fiction, 7
Fitzgerald, Robert, 5, 37–50

Gilgamesh, 10, 187, 200
Gordon, Cyrus, 5
"Greek Princes and Aegean Princesses: The Role of Women in the Homeric Poems" (Atchity and Barber), 4–5, 15–36
Greene, Thomas, 8, 222n

Hector, 7–9, *127–32*, 136, 152–59, 160–69
Helen, 2, 15–36, 70–75
Hephaistos, 2, 112
Hera, 23, 135
Hermione, 17, 20–36
hexameter, 3
Homer: archeological discoveries about life

of, 28–36; instruments used by, 38; life, speculation about, 1, 3; place of women in works of, 15–36; poetic method, 10, 106–109, 119–26; *See also Iliad; Odyssey*

Homer and the Bible (Gordon), 5
Homer and the Heroic Tradition (Whitman), 6, 83n, 152n
Homeric Question, the, 2–3, 6
Homeric simile, 7
Homeric society, 15–36
Homer's Iliad: The Shield of Memory (Atchity), 9, 159n

Iliad: astrology in, 169–80; authorship of, 46–47, force in, 8–9, 152–59; helmets, importance of, 102; humor in, 40; imitation, as method of composition, 113–24; influence of, 1; leading characters, 8; metaphor in, 83–105, 106–109; order and disorder in, 62–83; relation to *Odyssey*, 81–83; simile in, 83–105; time, concept of, in, 51–61; translations of, 5, 37–50; *See also* Homer; *Odyssey*
"*Iliad* or the Poem of Force, The" (Weil), 8–9, 152–59
"Image, Symbol, and Formula" (Whitman), 6, 83–105
"Imitation" (Redfield), 7, 113–26
Indo-European heritage, 4, 8–9, 15–36, 132–45
Ion (Euripides), 29–30
Iphigeneia, 15–36
Ithaka, 3, 10–11, 20–21
"Ithaka" (Cavafy), 11, 223–24

"Judgment of Paris," 8, 135–36

"King Eëtion and Thebe as Symbols in the *Iliad*" (Zarker), 8, 146–52
Klytaimestra, 15–36

Laertes, 21, 193
Lattimore, Richmond, 151n, 179n
Leda, 16–36
Littleton, C. Scott, 8, 26, 35n, 132–45
Lord, Albert, 103n, 109

"Maker, The" (Borges), 4, 13–14
Making of Homeric Verse, The (Milman Parry), 2, 6, 106–109
Mariani, Alice, 11, 211–23
matrilineal society, 4–5, 15–36
Menelaos, 17, 20–21, 32, 70–75

Merwin, W.S., 37
Miller, Dean, 4
Mimesis (Auerbach), 11, 212, 221n
Minoan civilization, 16–36
Morland, Harold, 4, 13
muses, 113–26
myth, 1

Nature and Culture in the Iliad: The Tragedy of Hektor (Redfield), 7, 113n
Nausikaa, 18, 83–105
Nestor, 32
nomos, 23–36

Odysseus, 2–3, 9, 20–21, 24, 32, 83–105, 168–69, 169–73, 181–86, 211–23
"Odysseus's Scar" (Auerbach), 11
Odyssey: astrology in, 169–80; authorship of, 46–47, boar episode, 11, 211–23; fertility rites in, 196–97; humor in, 40; imitation, as method of composition, 113–26; influence of, 1; metaphor in, 83–105, 106–109; narrative, 8; order and disorder in, 62–83; relation to *Iliad*, 81–83; religion in, 187–211; ritual in, 187–211; simile in, 83–105; time, concept of in, 51–61; translations of, 5, 37–50; *See also* Homer; *Iliad*
Odyssey and Primitive Religion, The (Sommer), 10–11, 187–211
Oepidus, 4, 24
Oedipus at Colonus, 4
"On First Looking into Chapman's Homer" (Keats), 6–7
On the Iliad (Bespaloff), 7, 127–32
"On Translating Homer" (Fitzgerald), 5, 37–50
oral tradition, 3, 6, 32
Order and History (Voegelin), 5–6, 62n
Oresteia, 3
Orestes, 16
Ortega y Gasset, José, 4, 12n

Paris, 20–21, 70–75, 125–37
Parry, Adam, 2, 6, 106–109
"Parryism," 2, 6, 106–109
Parry, Milman, 2, 6, 51, 103n, 106–109
patrilineal society, 4–5, 15–36
Patroclus, 149–52
Pedasos, 148–52
Penelope, 2–3, 9, 10–11, 15–36, 95, 168–69, 172–74; *See also* weaving
Phaiakians, 18–19, 183–86
Poetics (Aristotle), 7, 113–26

Polyphemus; *See* Cyclops
Poseidon, 25–36
Priam, 127–32, 165
Pushkin, Alexander, 1

Redfield, James M., 7, 113–26
"Renaming of Odysseus, The" (Mariani), 11, 211–23
"Rose-Fingered Dawn and the Idea of Time" (Vivante), 5, 51–61

Sarpedon, 149–52
shield of Achilles, 2, 4, *111–12*, 133–45
"Shield of Achilles, The" (Auden), 6–7, 111–12
Sirenes, 40
Socrates, 23
"Some Possible Indo-European Themes in the Iliad" (Littleton), 8, 132–45
Sommer, Richard J., 10–11, 187–211
Sophocles, 4, 24
Sparta, 20–21
Stevens, Wallace, 9, 168–69
Stutynski, Udo, 4, 20, 35n

"Tales Odysseus Told Alkinoos, and an Akkadian Seal, The" (Butterworth), 10, 181–86
Teiresias, 4, 24, 27, 191
Telemachos, 10, 21, 32, 39

tekhne, 25–36; *See also* Athene
Thebe, 8, 146–52
themis, 23–36, 65–70, 81
Tree at the Navel of the Earth, The (Butterworth), 10, 181n
Trojan Wall, 31
Troy, 2, 8, 21
Tyndareus, 16–17, 21

uxorilocality, 16–36

"Valediction: Forbidding Mourning, A" (Donne), 9, 167–68
virilocality, 16–36
Vivante, Paolo, 5, 51–61
Voegelin, Eric, 5–6, 62–83

war, 7
weaving, 2, 27–36, 95, 159–69; *See also* Penelope
Weil, Simone, 8–9, 152–59
Whitman, Cedric, 6, 83–105, 152n, 205n
"World as Meditation, The" (Stevens), 9, 168–69

Yoshida, A., 133–45

Zarker, John, 8, 146–52
Zeus, 3, 4, 16–36, 137

Beecher and Woodhull were both social reformers who shared the premise that increasing some types of privacy—protecting intimacy, shielding relationships from public surveillance, leaving people alone—was a good idea, even the basis for a better world. Beecher seemed to have viewed his own adulterous affairs as the occasional by-product of his efforts to explore spirituality and morality in friendship and love. It is easy to see Beecher's philosophy merely as a smoke screen for his lust or as a rationale for his narcissism, but doing so misses half the story. However hypocritical and destructive some of his actions, he was grappling with a real problem. As was Victoria Woodhull.

In both their experience, traditional, authoritarian family life had been painful. Woodhull's father and alcoholic first husband had both abused her. Beecher, it seems, sorely felt his lack of maternal love. They were trying to define a way of living that would allow freer, fuller, and richer private relationships. This would include the freedom for a woman to control her sexuality or leave an abusive husband, for a child to renounce destructive parents, for a man to seek from a second the love a first wife didn't provide—the freedom to make private choices in search of intimacy and love that were not exclusively controlled by external codes. Much of what they sought has in fact become law or common practice.

A similar complex web of intimate friendships that thrived among the transcendentalists thirty years earlier is described by Joan Von Mehren in her biography of Margaret Fuller, *Minerva and the Muse*. Their experiments, though less overtly sexual and more cerebral, prefigure Beecher and Woodhull. Fascinated by the possibility of intimacy, by passionate friendships, by the development of their own ideas and psyches, men and women like Ralph Waldo Emerson, Bronson Alcott, Sarah Ripley, and Elizabeth Palmer Peabody held long conversations and wrote many letters to each other. Recounting a similar phenomenon even earlier (in a seventeenth-century London salon), Theodore Zeldin writes, "As the yearning for more intimate conversation grew, and the obsession with sincerity became more absolute, only letters seemed an adequate refuge for the pondered exchange of private thought."[17] One thinks of Vermeer's seventeenth-century woman, alone at the window, letter in hand.

Von Mehren describes how the transcendentalists read each other's diaries or circulated packets of their letters. For example, Margaret Fuller lent Ralph Waldo Emerson portfolios of letters she had exchanged with Sam Ward and Anna Barker.[18] Deeply interested in the individual, both Fuller and Emerson understood that people could use privacy in the form of intimate friendship to explore and expand each other and themselves. In a sense, they anticipated something that later would become codified within psychotherapy.

Emerson was drawn to Margaret Fuller. He loved her, at times intensely, but she made him nervous. When she drowned, shipwrecked tragically within sight of Fire Island returning from Italy with her husband and son, Emerson was grief stricken. He sent his friend Thoreau to look for traces of her or her manuscript that might have floated ashore. On July 19, 1850, Emerson wrote in his journal, "I have lost in her my audience." Emerson's comment is poignant, his loss devastating. Anne Sexton wrote, "You don't write for an *audience,* you write for some *one* who'll understand." Margaret understood.

A few paragraphs later, Emerson continues:

> She poured a stream of amber over the endless store of private anecdotes, of bosom histories which her wonderful persuasion drew out of all to her. When I heard that a trunk of her correspondence had

been found and opened, I felt what a panic would strike all her friends, for it was as if a clever reporter had got underneath a confessional and agreed to report all that transpired there in Wall Street.[19]

No doubt Emerson felt his share of panic remembering the private thoughts and feelings he had confessed to her. The translation of his fears into an image of a reporter under the confessional is vivid and prescient. It captures perfectly the dilemma of privacy that encourages intimacy and self-disclosure: Feeling more alone, I feel more urge to confide. By confiding in you, I am freed to become more myself because your love and interest confirms and emboldens me. But I also worry how you will hold what I have told you, how you will feel toward me, what you will say to others. What will happen to me if my private words are broadcast abroad, turned into headlines? How will I bear the shame of being seen and known in ways I did not intend? What is said in one moment, in one context, might be repeated and misconstrued in another.

Emerson's journal entry suggests that the turn inward toward the more private self made the development of the image of a nosy press (the reporter under the confessional) psychologically predictable. The press became the collective projection of the anxiety, guilt, and shame people felt not only about revealing their thoughts and feelings, but probably also about an upsurge of illicit wishes. Tempted by increased privacy to confessions or actions that could publicly shame them, people handled their anxiety in part by worrying that newspaper reporters were spying on them. For famous people like Emerson, this could have been true; for most, it had little basis in fact. But because people tend to read celebrity stories feeling unconsciously, "I wish this had been me" or "I fear this could have been me," there was a psychological identification that gave basis to their fears.

In the late nineteenth century, newspapers offered the diverse city dwellers stories they could hold in common. Collective stories create a shared culture, and their task was partly to replace the informal gossip of village life; it was impossible to whisper fast enough to pass important gossip to a whole city, and few were inclined to whisper to strangers.

During the era of the American Revolution, when newspapers first proliferated, it was not because they sent reporters to write up precise and evenhanded political stories. There were no reporters. Newspapers were produced by printers, and they made a place for themselves by printing gossip. They collected hearsay—often allegations against British soldiers—circulating on the street. In the years leading up to the Revolution, writes the newspaper historian Thomas Leonard, "printers were modest about claiming their news was true."[20]

Truth was secondary. What mattered was spreading a story that spoke to people. Since their earliest days, newspapers have had two main purposes. One has been to provide information—the departure schedules of boats, a merchant's list of wares, the time and place of public meetings, bits of domestic and foreign news. Their other function has been to address the collective psyche. In its barest outline, the psychological struggle of the revolutionary era was over the question of whether or not you owed obedience to your father, Great Britain. Was his authority legitimate, and therefore were you bad for defying him? Or was he corrupt, and therefore were you entitled to rebel? Stories were gathered and published, debating the psychological point. When the colonial newspapers spread stories about a grandfather who found a British soldier in bed with his granddaughter, they were declaring "father" corrupt.

The media serves a similar psychological function today. An astute friend observed during the 1991 Clarence Thomas/Anita Hill